AFRICA'S INTERNATIONAL RELATI

AFRICA'S INTERNATIONAL RELATIONS

The Diplomacy of Dependency and Change

ALI A. MAZRUI

Professor of Political Science, The University of Michigan, Ann Arbor

HEINEMANN
London Ibadan Nairobi

WESTVIEW PRESS
Boulder, Colorado

Heinemann Educational Books Ltd
22 Bedford Square, London WC1B 3HH
P.M.B. 5205 Ibadan. P.O. Box 45314 Nairobi
EDINBURGH MELBOURNE AUCKLAND
SINGAPORE HONG KONG KUALA LUMPUR
NEW DELHI KINGSTON PORT OF SPAIN EXETER (NH)

ISBN 0 435 96521 2

First published 1977
Reprinted 1979

Published in the United States of America 1977
by Westview Press, Inc.
1898 Flatiron Court
Boulder, Colorado 80301
Frederick A. Praeger, Publisher and Editorial Director

Library of Congress Cataloging in Publication Data
Mazrui, Ali Al'Amin.
Africa's international relations.

Includes bibliography.
1. Africa—Foreign relations.
2. Africa—Politics and government—1960.
I. Title
DT31.M375 327.6 77-595
ISBN 0-89158-671-1

Set in 'Compugraphic' Baskerville 10 on 11 point
Printed in Great Britain by Biddles Ltd, Guildford, Surrey

CONTENTS

PART THREE: THE GLOBAL ISSUES

ACKNOWLEDGEMENTS

Most of the first draft of this book was written when I was Visiting Fellow at the Hoover Institution on War, Revolution and Peace, Stanford University. But before the manuscript went to press in its final form two other institutions provided a base and support for the book. These were the Institute for Development Studies at the University of Nairobi and the Center for Afro-American and African Studies, University of Michigan, Ann Arbor. I am greatly indebted to all three institutions for their support and encouragement.

The book itself was started at the invitation of Robert C. Markham of Heinemann Educational Books, a long-standing friend from the days when we were next-door neighbours at Makerere University, Kampala. For part of the period when I was at the Institute for Development Studies, Nairobi, in 1974, I lived in Bob Markham's house and used his study to write certain chapters of this book.

James Currey and David Hill, also of Heinemann, were actively involved in prodding me (with both charm and offers of concrete help) to complete the manuscript. With such encouragement from friends the work gathered momentum.

In its preparation the book knew a number of different typists scattered across more than ten thousand miles. Specially involved in the work were Jeanne Nickerson of Palo Alto, California, Penny McMullen of Stanford, Vina Shah of Nairobi and Carol Katz of Ann Arbor, Michigan. I am indebted to them all.

Over the years, Molly, my wife, has been intimately involved in all my works in one way or another. But not until this book was she drafted to type a chapter. The final versions of chapters 4 and 9 sent to the publishers were a credit to her newly acquired skill. But even more fundamental has been her sustained interest and absorption in all my writings — an articulate companionship which has helped to shape the writer's intellect.

As for fellow political scientists who have given their time over the years to discussing African international relations with me, I am particularly indebted to Dr Yashpal Tandon of the University of Dar es Salaam, Dr A. G. G. Gingyera-Pinycwa of Makerere University, Kampala, and to Dr Donald Rothchild of the University of California, Davis. Chapter 12 in this book was co-authored with Dr Gingyera-Pinycwa. I appreciate his permission to use it in this way.

Ali A. Mazrui

PART ONE
THE GLOBAL CONTEXT

CHAPTER 1
Africa & the International Structure

This book approaches the study of Africa's international relations with a consciousness not only of past events but also of future prospects. Attempts will be made in the analysis to discover what trends in the world are significant for Africa, what their origins are, and what their future directions are likely to be. We define 'black diplomacy' as the international experience of black peoples, the rules and values which have conditioned that experience, and the emerging patterns of communication between black peoples and the rest of the world. Our focus will be on Africa south of the Sahara, but in many matters we will be concerned also with the African continent as a whole, recognizing the simple geo-historical fact that Africa is an Afro-Arab continent.

There will also be occasions when the emphasis will be on the black peoples everywhere, not merely those of the African continent, when the experience of Black America, the Caribbean, and other parts of the black world will be indispensable in the effort to understand the dynamics of black diplomacy.

To emphasize that we are concerned with the future, as well as the past and the present, this analysis of the international structure of the world will begin with a speculative leap into the immediate future, and then return to the present situation and its implications. This is a conscious departure from the type of approach which begins with the historical background before discussing the present, let alone the future. The main approach used attempts to link the three stages of temporal experience—yesterday, today, and tomorrow—partly in response to traditional African systems of knowledge, often based on an indissoluble bond between the living, the dead, and those yet to be born.

Plunging directly into political speculation, it is probable that a revolution in South Africa will come in the 1980s. If black Africans controlled the gold-mines of South Africa, and the Arabs in the Middle East controlled more than half the world's monetary reserves, a new alliance between Africa and the Middle East could at last bring the entire world monetary system crumbling to the ground. The world would then have to invent alternative arrangements. Gold would have become 'Black'; dollars would then be Arabized. And all the debates about which currency should be devalued and which revalued would sustain a rude interruption.

The exodus which will follow the collapse of white rule in South Africa will include yet another exodus of Jews. Most of the Jews of Southern Africa will probably choose to go to Israel in search of solace and reassurance for their future. If they succeed in leaving Southern Africa with a large proportion of their wealth, which is immense, the collapse of white rule in South Africa could inadvertently reinvigorate Israel. But the future of Israel itself will probably still be very much in doubt. And the politics of the Middle East will by then be even more interlinked with African politics.

Nigeria — helped by oil and the size of its population — is on its way to becoming the first major black power in modern international politics. Had the Biafran civil war succeeded in splitting Nigeria, such a black power in world politics would not have been possible. Nigeria's role in Africa will be similar to Brazil's role in Latin America — the first among equals. In another twenty years both countries will probably be more influential internationally than either Britain or France, but their influence will not necessarily be based on comparable technological development.

Political instability is likely to continue in Africa, but to be accompanied by new economic possibilities and considerable cultural and artistic vigour. The cultural leaders of Africa will probably be Zaire (formerly Congo-Kinshasa) and Nigeria, though the Arab world will remain important in terms of religious leadership among African Muslims.

The alliance between the Arabs and Black Africa — symbolized in 1973 by Africa's almost unanimous break with Israel — was fragile from the start and was bound to have setbacks. The Arabs should be particularly careful not to be paternalistic towards black Africans. But in the long run this alliance will probably be reinvigorated and endure on a new basis. In terms of population there are, after all, more Arabs within Africa than outside — though there are more Arab *states* outside Africa than within. New links will be forged between the Arab League and the Organization of African Unity.

From the point of view of millions of Asians and Africans, the Arab oil sanctions against select Western countries will probably rank in history alongside Japan's victory over Russia in 1905 — as milestones in the story of how Asians and Africans discovered their own potential power against Caucasian might. The only irony in the situation is that by 1973 Japan was among the principal casualties of the Arab oil boycott.

The Arab oil boycott had a meaning far beyond the state of Israel and the Middle Eastern crisis. The boycott's immediate political purpose of the reversal of the USA's policy on Israel might have been too ambitious, but the mere fact that small countries in the Persian Gulf and the Arabian Peninsula could cause so much anxiety among the mighty introduced a new dimension in relations between the industrialized north and the primary producers in the southern hemisphere.

Indeed, until the 1970s most Third World leaders believed that a country had to be economically developed in order to be economically powerful. Most Third World countries felt helpless in the face of the economic might of the West and the Soviet Union. But from 1973 a distinction has needed to be sharply drawn between *economic development* and *economic power*. Holland is more economically developed than Saudi Arabia, but Saudi Arabia is, in global terms, more economically powerful than Holland. Power after all includes real or potential control over the destinies of others. Saudi Arabia is so endowed; Holland is not.

We define the Third World as the world of the less developed countries in Africa, Asia, Latin America, and scattered islands across the world. The question which arises is whether the new power which the Third World is beginning to discover among some of its members can be used for development in the Third World, and not merely as a diplomatic weapon on a specific issue like Israel. It is too early to know the real impact of Third World power on Third World development. But as a leverage against the rich, certain Third World resources will become the equivalent of organized labour in the history of the industrialized countries. Labour became a resource which the industrial giants could not do without. The threat of withdrawing labour became a weapon which the underpaid and overworked poor learned to use to improve their lot. The question posed by Arab use of oil to exert pressure is whether the Third World is on the verge of learning the techniques of withholding a much needed resource (be it a mineral or the sweat of the brow) as a basis for collective bargaining.

The world is divided on the basis of wealth and power. Until now there has been an international class system and an international *caste* structure. Some of the least developed states seemed as doomed in their misery as an untouchable caste. Arab pressure over oil—even if it finally fizzles out—could signify the beginnings of a new international redistribution of wealth and power.

And yet such predictions should be handled cautiously. Much might depend on whether the oil producers will have the will and imagination to use their resources to facilitate not only their own development but also the development of their Third World allies. Oil prices for less developed countries might need also to be re-examined. The old international system dominated by the big powers may be more stubborn than we think. And some of our predictions may be premature.[1]

We propose to demonstrate in this chapter that the international system of economic ranking or economic stratification has the rigidity of a caste system. To that extent the white industrial nations are more like the privileged Brahmin caste of India than the middle classes of the West. But to the extent that the global concerns of these industrialized nations, and certainly in their relations with the Third World, are often capitalistic, the developed states also perform international bourgeois functions in the Western tradition. We might, therefore, look upon international ranking as a system which combines the rigidity of a caste system (like that of India) with the ethics of a capitalist system (like that of the West). We shall discuss more fully in the next chapter how Africa relates to some of these economic ideologies of the world.

The global system which confronts us today has more stability than might first appear – for better or for worse. By contrast, almost each country in the Third World is in the throes of either active, imminent, or latent instability within its own borders. We have then the paradox of a stable international system combined with acute internal dislocations in individual Third World countries.

Our illustrations in this analysis will, of course, come primarily from Africa, but the theoretical and analytical scope of the chapter is wider than that.

Caste and Class in International Relations

Within individual societies such as India a caste system has four major defining characteristics. The first is *heredity*, by which membership of a caste is determined by hereditary descent. The second is *separation*, a principle which keeps different castes exclusive from each other socially – contact between castes socially is minimized and intermarriage strongly discouraged if not prohibited. The third is *division of labour*, by which caste, either in reality or by historical definition, is associated with a particular profession or occupation. The fourth is the *principle of hierarchy*, determining rank and status within the society.[2]

What emerges strongly from these characteristics is the element of rigidity within caste systems. And a rigid system should be significantly more predictable than a flexible one. One would therefore have thought that in the whole science of forecasting, caste systems provide relatively happy areas for accuracy. But rigidity is not the same thing as stability. There are rigid systems which, because of their very inflexibility, are vulnerable to a sudden revolutionary upheaval. Edmund Burke was substantially right when he argued that a system entirely without means for its own reform is basically without means for its own preservation. Some responsiveness to urgent intimations for change is required if a social system is to be spared periodic ruptures.

What gives caste its stability is to some extent a tautology – it is the sanction of primordial custom over a substantial period of time. In other words, the survival of the system is partly strengthened by its prior survival, as well as by a certain degree of responsiveness to changing circumstances.

A. L. Kroeber has even seen caste as a special stage in the evolution and consolidation of classes. Kroeber enumerates the characteristics of endogamy, heredity, and relative rank, and then goes on to argue in the following terms:

> Castes, therefore are a special form of social classes, which in tendency at least are present in every society. Castes differ from social classes, however, in that they have emerged into social consciousness to the point that custom and law attempt their rigid and permanent separation from one another. Social classes are the generic soil from which caste-systems have at various times and places independently grown up . . .[3]

But clearly for a class system to rigidify into a caste system special circumstances have to emerge. Pre-eminent among the conditions would be a special motivation by the upper classes to move in the direction of stopping others rising to the same level. Entry to the ranks of the elite would thus be closed. Another condition is the readiness of the lower classes to accept their place in society as required by custom. The major difference between a class system and a caste system remains the difference in the capacity to move up in the world. Once a member of a low caste, always a member of that caste. A class system allows for the ambitious and the fortunate to rise to a new status.

But are the two concepts of caste and class applicable also to the international system? Certainly class analysis has already been applied to international relations. The division of the world between the 'haves' and the 'have-nots' has captured the attention of scholars and political practitioners alike. Many have portrayed that division as one of the most important issues in the last third of the twentieth century. The whole concept of a Third World is rooted in proletarian ideas. Asia, Africa, and Latin America have increasingly come to see themselves as proletarian or underprivileged continents, struggling against the power and influence of Europe and North America. The United Nations Conference on Trade and Development (UNCTAD) has increasingly become an arena reminiscent of collective bargaining between labour unions and management. The Third World is out to negotiate for better working conditions, and better returns for production, at the door of the global employment agency.

The non-alignment movement has also increasingly shifted its emphasis from cold war issues to issues of economic confrontation between the developing and developed world. The movement, in the days when it was dominated by Nehru of India, Nasser of Egypt, Nkrumah of Ghana, and Tito of Yugoslavia, was a movement eager to avoid entanglement in the ideological and military issues which divided the West from the Communist world. Non-alignment was, at the least, a refusal to be tied to a military alliance with one of the major powers. But gradually non-alignment developed into a broader concept of autonomy and the right to experiment, a reaffirmation by small powers that they were entitled to an independent say in world affairs. Issues of trade and the use of world resources were still substantially outside the non-alignment movement as such.

The first major economic factor to enter the movement was the issue of foreign aid. A doctrine of balanced benefaction emerged, by which it was assumed that relative independence for poor countries lay in diversifying their benefactors. A country which was heavily dependent on the USA was less autonomous than a country which managed to get foreign aid both from the USA and the Soviet Union. Non-alignment became an exercise in balanced dependency—an assumption that a client with more than one patron was freer than a uni-patronized dependant.

However, by the time the non-aligned countries were assembling in Algiers in the summer of 1973 a major shift had taken place. Non-alignment was now concerned with more than just keeping out of military alliances or getting the most in foreign aid from Western and Communist countries. The concerns of the non-aligned movement now encompassed not only issues which were previously handled only by UNCTAD but also a newly discovered capacity to use the natural resources of the poor countries as political and economic weapons against the affluent sectors of the world.

The British term 'trade unionism' began to make better sense in the international domain than in domestic arrangements. What was at stake in the international domain was indeed trade and the share of world trade, in the sense of exchanging goods on a commercial but also fairly balanced basis. The old meaning of 'trade', in the sense of an occupation or skill, had been overtaken by events. Unionism within individual countries was, as the Americans call it, a movement of *labour* unions. But the new unionism of the Third World, as it has sought to use its resources to extract economic and political concessions from the developed world, is more fittingly *trade* unionism. And yet the very fact that Third World countries are poor and underprivileged creates legitimate comparison with domestic labour movements. Class analysis becomes relevant, and class interests become internationalized.

But where lies the relevance of the concept of caste in the international system? If Kroeber is correct in saying caste is a special stage in the consolidation of social classes, and if the issue of comparative social mobility is what ultimately differentiates caste from class, we have to examine the international system from the point of view of relative rigidity.

A simple analysis in terms of per capita income would give at least the appearance that the international system is a class system. Where growth does occur, and per capita income rises, we might get the impression that the system permits substantial social mobility. Countries move up from much lower levels either of gross national product or of per capita income. The flexibility is reminiscent of a class system.

But the question arises whether the international system is indeed that flexible. Social mobility does not only mean more ability to improve the lot of the poorer sections of a particular society; it must also mean the possibility of narrowing the gap of affluence between the poorest and the richest. Even if the gap between the developed world and the developing countries were to remain constant, while each part of the world was at the same time improving the standards of living of its inhabitants, the situation would still not be one in which social mobility had taken place. What is at stake once again is comparative disadvantage. The poor must not only be earning a little more than they used to; they must also have reduced the gap in income between themselves and those who are wealthier. If the gap is maintained, the sense of deprivation continues. If the gap is widened, the sense of deprivation could be worsened. To the extent that the gap between the richer and poorer countries of the world is widening rather than narrowing, it can be argued that the international system lacks the kind of social mobility necessary to make it a class system rather than a caste structure. The rich are getting richer and, on the whole, the poor are getting less poor, but the rate of rising affluence in the USA, the Soviet Union, Western Europe and Japan is faster than the rate of diminishing poverty in the Third World. If the international system was, in the first half of the twentieth century, a class system, it is now moving in the direction of rigidity. We may be witnessing the consolidation and sanctification of a global caste structure. The only hope lies in the capacity of the Third World to use their natural resources more effectively as leverage for reform.

But just as there are hereditary factors in domestic castes, so there are hereditary elements in international castes. Pre-eminent among those factors is the issue of *race*. The most affluent societies in the world are overwhelmingly of European racial extraction. The poorest countries in the world are overwhelmingly black and African in racial extraction. Certainly those countries categorized as the poorest by the United Nations are disproportionately situated in the African continent. If people of European extraction are the brahmins of the international caste system, the black people belong disproportionately to the caste of the untouchables. Between the highest international caste and the lowest are other ranks and estates. There are non-white people that are honorary white men. So far these are limited to the Japanese, who enjoy the status of honorary Caucasians in the Republic of South Africa. There are also honorary coloured people. These include white sections of Latin America. The population of Latin America is indeed a mixture, consisting of European, Amerindian, African, and other strands. But on the whole the dominant elites of Latin America are of European extraction. To the extent that Latin America forms part of the Third World, and has shared the humiliation of being exploited and dominated by her northern neighbour, the United States of America, even white Latin Americans must be regarded as in some sense honorary coloured people. They have shared with coloured people the experience of indigence and indignity. The Latin Americans provide a foil to the Japanese. After all, the Japanese have shared with white people historically the arrogance of power, racism, and dominion of others. The ambiguous situation of Japan and Latin America makes the international caste system somewhat complex. But the main outlines are certainly there. There is an element of race in the global stratification system, and it provides a functional equivalent to heredity in domestic caste.

As for the characteristic of *separation* in the social domain which we attributed to domestic caste, the equivalent of this internationally is the imbalance in physical mobility or capacity to travel as between developed and developing societies. By far the most mobile people in the world in the sense of ability to travel are Americans, Europeans, and the Japanese. An unbalanced system of mobility creates a special kind of separation. The master can enter the hut of his slave at any time, if only to remind him of his obligation to work; but the slave has no automatic access to the house of the master. American soldiers may roam around South-east Asia; German tourists may descend on East Africa; Japanese businessmen may conclude deals in the Middle East and Brazil. But in relative terms the flow of traffic is one way. And even when Algerians are permitted into France, or West Indians into Britain and Canada, the roles they are to play in the developed societies are often those that would not be touched by Frenchmen, Englishmen, or Canadians. The Third World immigrants perform 'untouchable' functions.

The international system also betrays the caste characteristic of division of labour. Some aspects of specialization in production are rooted in geographical conditions, which are themselves basically inflexible. The sharpest factor in the global division of labour is that which separates countries heavily dependent on primary products from countries which are industrialized. For the time being, a country whose entire economy rests on one or two agricultural products confronts hazardous fluctuations. In spite of recent shortages in certain kinds of food products in the world market, Third World countries are still engaged in an uphill struggle. There has been some improvement in the prospects for primary products in the last few years, but in agriculture the improvement is not likely to be dramatic enough to transform the overall economic performance of the countries concerned. Some of these are already involved in serious attempts to diversify their economies, both by producing a greater variety of primary products and by inaugurating the process of serious industrialization. However, for the present the rigidity persists in this aspect of the international caste system.

Both domestically and internationally division of labour is also connected with *hierarchy*. In some ways this is the most serious thing in human terms about caste as a social phenomenon. But here a fundamental distinction needs to be made between a horizontal and a hierarchical division of labour. A horizontal division is one which is basically between equals. The equals may be either all underdeveloped or all developed. But the division of enterprise between them does not contain inherent disadvantage of a continuing kind to one party. Nor does it involve a relationship of submissiveness and inequity. A hierarchical division of labour, when it is rigid, is the kind which leads to a caste structure. Sentencing the countries of the tropics to a life of primary production indefinitely, while the Northern Hemisphere continues along the path of industrial and post-industrial development, would amount to a hierarchical division of labour. Certainly the old partnership of the imperial order, of producers of raw materials in the colonies and manufacturers in the metropolitan powers, amounted—in terms of real disparities between the two sides—to a hierarchical order.[4]

It is because the international system shares these characteristics of heredity, separation, division of labour and hierarchy, that the system is more like a caste structure with its rigidities than a class system with potential social mobility.

However, the energy crisis creates new possibilities. As the oil producers insist on exchanging their oil for Western technology, they are insisting on fundamental diversification of their economies. Countries with other types of primary products and minerals might not have the same leverage at the moment as the oil producers, but the activities of the Organization of Petroleum Exporting Countries (OPEC) have been followed closely by the producers of copper, bauxite and tin. The possibility of a demonstration effect is there, but the international system may be more rigid than the reformers believe.

While the global stratification system is thus rigid and relatively stable, the stratification systems in individual countries in the Third World, especially in Africa, are under pressure. Indeed, in a number of countries within the African continent, social classes are fluid. Domestic social mobility can be very rapid both upwards and downwards. Men rise fast to the commanding heights of the economy—and then come tumbling down with the latest political upheaval. While an individual country's prospects in the global system may be fairly accurately predictable, the precise fortunes of its leaders or of its domestic, social and economic system could be far from responsive to precise prior calculation. Domestic instability is thus combined with international rigidity. The next section looks more closely at the implications of this paradox for the African states and societies.

The Blacks and the Brahmins

Of the three continents of the Third World—Asia, Africa, and Latin America—it is pre-eminently Africa which has most often been treated as the equivalent of a lower caste. The racial factor is particularly important in this regard.

A number of writers have already drawn attention to similarities between caste systems such as that of India and systems of racial ranking such as those of South Africa and the old south in the United States of America. We mentioned Kroeber's idea linking caste with class on a continuum. On the other hand, Lloyd Warner, in a famous article in 1936, argued that while whites and blacks in the USA made up two castes, each group in turn was stratified internally into classes. The blacks of the upper class were thus superior from the point of view of class to the poor whites, while at the same time being inferior to them from the point of view of caste.[5] In that article and in subsequent work Lloyd Warner intimated a strong resemblance between the American system of race stratification and the caste system of India. In the southern states of America the disabilities under which the blacks laboured, the difficulty for them to 'pass', the strong disapproval of either marriage or commensality between whites and blacks, all provided legitimate grounds for equating race relations in the American south with caste relations in India. Therefore, for the comparative sociologist and social anthropologist these are forms of behaviour which must have the same term applied to them.[6] Gunnar Myrdal argues that 'caste may thus in a sense be viewed as an extreme form of absolutely rigid class' and in the USA caste therefore constituted 'a harsh deviation from the ordinary American social structure and the American Creed'. He also writes that 'the scientifically important difference between the terms "caste" and "class" as we are using them is, from this point of view, *a relatively large difference in freedom of movement between groups*'.[7]

The American caste system has in fact been disintegrating since Gunnar Myrdal wrote this classic, but the overall global position of the black people as a lower caste has not as yet fundamentally changed. Racial disabilities are bequeathed by heredity. Separation between racial castes continues by a residual distrust of racial mixture, the relative isolation of sub-Saharan Africa from the main stream of international affairs, and the drastic imbalance in popular mobility between the peoples of the Northern Hemisphere of the world and the black races south of the Sahara. Division of labour imposes on much of the African peoples a life as 'hewers of wood and drawers of water'. Most of the poorest nations of the world are within Africa, and many of the economies are based on monoculture. And the principle of hierarchy emerges from the economic and technological disabilities sustained by the black peoples under the cruel, marching boots of history. The unkindest cut of all are the white enclaves in Southern Africa. Within the very continent of the black races, a few hundred thousand whites in Rhodesia have so far reduced to military impotence millions of Africans not only in Rhodesia itself but also in the black states of the continent. Technological and organizational superiority, when enjoyed either by the Israelis in the Middle East or the white Rhodesians in Southern Africa, can keep millions of technologically less sophisticated races at bay in spite of all their anger and sense of injustice.

But such situations are characterized by a latent instability. One might usefully distinguish here between active, imminent and latent instability. Active instability is characterized by rapid changes and severe political uncertainty. Prediction in such a situation is particularly difficult. Institutions arise and collapse, men emerge and are then submerged, policies fluctuate. The Congo (Zaire) was engulfed in severe active instability in the first four years of its independence. Imminent instability is when change and turbulence are expected at any time, and yet no such change or disruption takes place. Many black African countries have an air of imminent instability even when the regime in power appears to be in full control. The instability is imminent when one is not surprised to hear of a military coup or a similar upheaval from one day to the next, and yet the air of stability continues. For the forecaster, such a situation is caught between the assurance of continuity and the imminence of sudden change. Sheikh Abeid Karume of Zanzibar certainly lasted in power much longer than most people expected in spite of the instability of Zanzibar, and yet to the extent that one was not particularly surprised when he was finally assassinated in 1970, Zanzibar under him had an air of imminent, though not active, instability.

At first glance latent instability looks very similar to imminent instability, and yet there are fundamental differences. While one would not have been surprised if the ruler of Zanzibar had been overthrown the week after he came to power, one would indeed be surprised if the apartheid system of South Africa crumbled next week. In Zanzibar under Karume instability was imminent in that it could have happened at almost any time, even if it did not happen for quite a long time. But in the South African racial system the instability is latent, and could be delayed for many years, and yet inherently within the system are the seeds of its own destruction.

Similarly in the Middle East, if no peace settlement is reached shortly, one could say that Israel's regional supremacy has a latent instability, while peace in the area is characterized by imminent instability. Without American help, Israeli military supremacy hinges on organizational and technological sophistication. But the sophistication of the Arabs in the skills of war may also increase in time and narrow the gap between them and the Israelis sufficiently to make Arab numerical preponderance at least relevant.

In South Africa change in instability may come partly out of a potentially widening demographic gap between whites and non-whites to the advantage of the latter; partly out of a growing political consciousness among important sectors of the black population; partly further out of the potentially enhanced organizational sophistication among the non-whites in the country; and finally out of the greater dependence by white industries on black labour at higher levels of skills than was previously the case. The convergence of these four factors could in time tip the scales in South Africa and convert latent instability at long last into active instability. If that were to happen, change in the direction of greater black power should indeed be well under way.

An ethnic caste system in which the oppressed are a minority, as in the USA, could change into a more flexible class system without extensive violence and disruption. But an ethnic caste system such as that of South Africa in which the white brahmin class is a minority, defensively protecting its privileges against an oppressed majority, could not easily transform the caste structure into a system of adequate social mobility without violence and destruction.

Again in this case the forecaster has to rely partly on precedent as a basis of predicting the future. Here it is worth distinguishing between colonial systems and racial systems within Africa. The British and the French had colonial systems, and later withdrew from at least some aspects of their relationship with their former dependencies. Decolonization in the sense of withdrawal of a distant colonial power has therefore been proved feasible in Africa without resort to violence. But deracialization in the sense of ending a white minority government in a situation where the white government does not rely on the metropolitan power for survival, has so far not been accomplished non-violently. There is for the time being no precedent of a beleaguered white community, isolated in power in a former colony, being willing to give up that power without violent struggle.

Even Algeria and Kenya are not illustrations of white settlers surrendering their power to Africans. They were both instances of the colonial government being no longer willing to support the white settlers in maintaining themselves in power. The Algerians won their independence when de Gaulle withdrew the French commitment to the status quo, and gradually recalled the French army back to France. The local white Algerians were furious and felt betrayed.

They would never have given Algeria to the Algerians if they had had the power to refuse. Similarly, the Kenya settlers would not themselves have granted independence to black Africans but for the fact that the British government in London was no longer prepared to maintain a white settler regime in Nairobi. On the basis of these precedents, the forecaster might feel confident enough to predict that the situation in South Africa and Rhodesia would not change without further violence. A final explosion in South Africa itself would end many decades of latent instability.

The Portuguese colonies are somewhat different. These are indeed part of the colonial system, rather than a racial system in the South African sense. Nevertheless while no racial system in the South African sense can ever be overthrown without violence, there are also colonial systems which can only be ended in a similar manner. Not all colonial systems are responsive to Gandhian techniques of non-violent resistance. Angola and Mozambique turned out to be more like Algeria than like either Nigeria or the Republic of South Africa.

Towards the end the Portuguese territories belonged to the category of imminent instability, rather than latent instability. Indeed, there was some active instability in at least certain parts of the Portuguese colonies, as areas changed hands back and forth between the Portuguese army and the African guerrilla fighters. On the basis of such trends, it was predictable that the first part of the white-dominated section of Africa to collapse would be the Portuguese colonies.

After the triumph of African liberation fighters in Angola and Mozambique, the only white brahmins left in Africa were the white regimes of South Africa and Rhodesia, each trying to keep the latent instability of its system from finally erupting into fatal activism.

Stability as a Middle-Class Value

But what about stratification within the black African states? Class structures in black nations at the present stage of their history are subject to substantial modifications imminently.

Africa approached independence with considerable evidence that it was evolving a power elite based on education. Some societies elsewhere may have evolved an oligarchy based on birth and ascription, as indeed some African societies have done. Other societies may have developed oligarchical systems based on wealth differentials, with the rich exercising power because they were rich. What seemed to be happening in Africa was the emergence of a class assuming critical areas of influence and prestige because it had acquired the skills of modern education. The elite started by being, in part, the bureaucratic elite – as major positions in the civil service were rapidly Africanized. Among the criteria for such Africanization was modern Western education. The emergence of an educated bureaucratic elite was accompanied by a slightly less educated political elite. The triumph of anti-colonial movements had thrust leaders into the forefront of affairs—leaders who would not have attained such pre-eminence but for at least some basic exposure to modern schooling. Indeed, many of the modern leaders, and certainly a high proportion of the politicians, were drawn from the schools where they had previously served as teachers. The modern educational system had served as a recruiting ground, and surrendered some of its own pioneer African teachers to politics as a new profession.[8]

Meanwhile Africa's new armed forces had been recruiting from the rural and less educated sections of the population. At the time the recruitments started no one had been astute enough to forecast the power of the military in African affairs. On the contrary, many political scientists, while claiming adherence to a discipline which aspires to predict future trends, nevertheless got Africa all wrong. One Western political scientist after another discussed the great potential of political parties in Africa, and almost totally ignored the armed forces as a factor in their calculations. Some political scientists even went as far as to dismiss the armed forces of Africa explicitly as being too small to cause a real challenge to the principle of civilian supremacy in politics. James S. Coleman asserted at the time that 'except for the Sudan, none of the [sub-Saharan] African states has an army capable of exerting a political role. . . .' Coleman allowed 'that the army could become a political force of increasing and perhaps decisive importance in certain countries', but the three countries he cited in this connection were South Africa, Rhodesia, and Ethiopia.[9] James Coleman was among the most perceptive of all academic writers about Africa at the time, and yet even someone like him could miscalculate. Coleman was also an illustration of those who saw in political parties major media of societal transformation in Africa. Events have proved both predictions wrong. Political parties almost everywhere in Africa have turned out to be paper tigers; while the armed forces have emerged as effective panthers.

But precisely because the military has become a major factor in politics, the domestic stratification system has become fluid. One army coup might favour one group; another might open doors to other ethnic communities previously peripheral. In some African countries the educated class has at last been cut down to size, and a lumpen militariat has assumed control.

For the international system new problems arise precisely because of these fluctuations. Stability, which is so often congenial to social forecasting, is at the same time profoundly bourgeois or middle class as a value. At any rate it is a value most favoured by those who have already arrived. Calls for unity in any individual society are at their most earnest when they come from those who are satisfied with the status quo. In the international system those who have already arrived might not mind a certain degree of instability among the less privileged, provided the global system as a whole is left relatively undisturbed. In fact, the world of international relations generally is dominated in its norms by the values of the middle classes and the international intelligentsia. Internationally law itself was a product of the thinking of European middle and upper classes on how diplomacy was to be conducted and relations between states organized and controlled. There are subtleties and refinements in embassies throughout the world, and in the corridors of international organizations, which are distant from some of the bluntness and relative spontaneity of truly rural societies.

Problems arise when individual countries find themselves with a peasant for head of government. The peasants in all countries of the world are among the least sensitized to international issues, and they are often the most obstinately parochial in their view of the universe. Because of this, the whole phenomenon of relations between states has remained something shaped, organized, and controlled by the values of the middle and upper classes and their respective intellectual wings.

Idi Amin, like Nikita Khrushchev before him, has brought to the refined diplomatic world of the middle and upper classes the rustic embarrassment of inadequate inhibition. Like Russia's Khrushchev in the 1950s and early 1960s, Idi Amin is today a peasant bull in the china shop of diplomatic history.

Among the middle classes one needs to have one's social arrangements fairly predictable. Appointments need to be made, and visits are often by invitation except among truly close friends or relatives. But in peasant areas one could visit even casual friends without being invited. The necessity of an invitation is a quest for stabilized social relations among middle and upper classes. Amin came into power, and proceeded to treat diplomatic visits not on the basis of bourgeois values of international diplomacy, but in relation to the more flexible and less predictable ways of rustic casualness. Israel, Britain, and France had claimed to be friends of his regime at the beginning. He visited each of these primarily at his own initiative. He also visited the German Federal Republic with the casualness of one peasant knocking on the door of his rural acquaintance. Of course in reality arrangements had to be made in advance to receive the President of Uganda, security had to be ensured, major diplomatic banquets had to be held. The refinements of European diplomacy, so dominant in the world as a whole today, had to be extended to this visiting rural dignitary from Uganda. But the spontaneity of going there without invitation had all the bearings of the cumulative rural socialization which Amin and his kind often manifest without thinking. To that extent their casualness disturbs the canons of predictability within the refined societies.

Then there are the other surprises that Amin is capable of flinging into the international arena, ranging from the expulsion of Uganda Asians at relatively short notice to the detention of American Peace Corps volunteers who stopped briefly at Entebbe on their way to Zaire.

Peasants do not normally send telegrams to each other. Amin has learned to use this particular medium, but with some rustic bluntness. And his messages have ranged from wishing Richard Nixon a quick recovery from the Watergate scandal to a reaffirmation of deep, and even dramatic affection, for Julius Nyerere, 'though your hair is grey'. Some of these tendencies are personal to Amin rather than to his social origins. But the very fact that he lets his personal tendencies have such free play while occupying the top office of his nation might have been influenced by the relative spontaneity of rural upbringing among the Kakwa.[10]

If Idi Amin has been a peasant ruler in charge of a relatively small developing country, Nikita Khrushchev was a peasant ruler in charge of a super power, the Soviet Union. Like Amin, Khrushchev offended the canons of refined predictability. Khrushchev basically held the initiative in international relations during most of his period in office, making surprise moves, exasperating the West, and giving the Soviet Union an image of revolutionary dynamism:

> The most striking feature of West-East relations during the Fifties and early Sixties is the fact that throughout the whole period the initiative remained with the Soviet Union. The Soviet leaders pursued a dynamic policy even in unfavourable conditions; they initiated new moves, unleashed crises, published ultimatums, if necessary made sudden concessions even when the situation on the domestic front or within the Communist camp was far from stable. Western statesmen by contrast, seemed lackadaisical, even lethargic; sometimes they reacted with vigour to Soviet moves, but seldom took any major initiative.[11]

The crises during this period ranged from Hungary and Suez in 1956 to the U2 incident in May 1960.

Khrushchev's style also offended the refined tastes of the West. He was capable of shouting loudly at another head of government or of taking off his shoe and banging it on the table at the United Nations. Like Amin, he was capable of threatening the firing squad against dissenting intellectuals and students. And like Amin, Khrushchev was despised by many intellectuals in his own society, as well as abroad. 'Among the intelligentsia there was a great deal of contempt for the leader who was regarded as little better than an uneducated, uncouth muzhik. . . .'[12]

And then came the Cuban missile crisis. Eyeball to eyeball, Khrushchev and Kennedy confronted each other in 1962. The world hovered on the brink of nuclear war. Yet that peasant in charge of a super power was capable of seeing when to withdraw from the brink. With astute statesmanship, Nikita Khrushchev capitulated to John

F. Kennedy's challenge, promised to remove the missiles from Cuba, moved towards establishing a hot line between Washington and Moscow, and began at last to respect the canon of refined predictability of international diplomacy.

In some respects, the Cuban missile crisis was the beginning of the embourgeoisement of the Soviet Union. Khrushchev was later replaced. His successors, though in some cases descended from origins as humble as Khrushchev's, were by now bureaucrats rather than rural folk in style and temperament. The Soviet Union relinquished some of the dynamic capacity for surprising initiatives which Khrushchev had brought into the role of the socialist super power. The Soviet Union became internationally more predictable, more stable – more congenial to the science of forecasting the country's own moves. The caste factor had once again intruded to influence issues of predictability.

Conclusion

We have sought to demonstrate in this chapter that the degree to which social and political events are capable of being predicted is partly the result of the distribution of wealth and privilege. A system of rigid stratification need not always be stable. Its very rigidity could at times spell out its own doom. But there are occasions when the caste structure appears to be assured of maintaining itself for a long time to come.

We have argued that the international system of stratification is for the time being more like a caste structure than a class structure. There is considerable rigidity in the factors which determine which countries are poor and which more affluent. The burden of relative deprivation is likely to weigh heavily on the human race for quite a while to come. The poor may get less poor, but the rich will also get considerably richer and the gap between the two could continue to widen. The international system of stratification therefore shows little sign of adequate improvement for the peoples of the Third World. A few of those who are now regarded among the more affluent may experience worse days, as their economic systems decay. But those who are at the bottom of the international hierarchy are unlikely to penetrate very far into the more elevated reaches of privilege unless a fundamental international change takes place.

Africa is clearly part of the lowest caste in the international hierarchy. It has a preponderance of the least developed and poorest countries. To the extent that sub-Saharan Africa is a black region, there is also caste in the racial sense, involving generations of degradation and the continuing insult of an apartheid system within the African continent itself.

Within South Africa itself we have argued that the system has latent instability. It may be secure for one, two or more decades, but the nature of the stratification system, and the prospects for demographic and economic change, spell out a sentence of long-term doom to the system.

Within the black states of Africa there is either active instability, in the sense of turbulent changes taking place already, or imminent instability in the sense that any political disruption in any particular week would not surprise anybody *if* it occurred.

The class system within individual African societies is at the moment in a state of fluidity, as institutions arise and collapse, and leaders ascend and then disappear in a cloud of gunsmoke. Peasants stand a chance of easing out of power established aristocracies overnight. And peasant styles of diplomacy could proceed to alarm or amuse the bourgeois of world leadership.

What needs to be ultimately grasped in the science of forecasting is that while domestic stratification in individual African societies is so fluid, Africa's place at the bottom of the international hierarchy threatens to be rigid. There are four signs of hope. First, there is hope in the discovery of more resources like oil, and Nigeria and Gabon have raised African hopes with their wealth of resources. Secondly, hope lies in a new capacity for organized joint-action by Third World countries to obtain better terms for their resources from the industrialized consumers. The policies of OPEC and the diplomatic alignments and experiments between Arab and African states may be signs of the future. Thirdly, African hopes may also lie in other areas of organized self-reliance, including ideological autonomy. We shall examine this more fully in the next chapter. Finally, there is the strategy of 'counter-penetration' into the developed world—the strategy of establishing a Third World presence in the Northern Hemisphere which is as significant as the economic and cultural presence of the big powers in the lives of the peoples of Africa, Asia, and Latin America. All these strategies of the future are perhaps on the verge of being born. We shall address ourselves to these more fully in the coming chapters.

References and notes

1. Although in other contexts I have distinguished between prediction and forecasting, in this chapter I shall use the two words almost interchangeably. An earlier paper of mine which drew a sharp distinction between the two was 'Political science and political futurology: problems of prediction', presented at the Annual Social Science Conference of the Universities of Eastern Africa, held at Makerere University, Kampala, in December 1968.
2. Consult Célestin Bouglé, *Essais sur le régime des castes*, p. 4; English translation of the introduction in *Contributions to Indian Sociology*, II (1958). (Célestin Bouglé, *Essays on the Caste System*, trans. D. F. Pocock. [Cambridge University Press, 1971].) See Louis Dumont, *Homo Hierarchicus: the Caste System and Its Implications* (Paladin, 1972), pp. 57-8.

3. A. L. Kroeber, 'Caste', *Encyclopedia of Social Sciences,* Vol. III (1930 edition), 254b-257a.
4. These issues are discussed in a related context in Ali A. Mazrui, *A World Federation of Cultures: an African Perspective* (New York: Free Press, 1976).
5. W. Lloyd Warner, 'American caste and class', *American Journal of Sociology,* **XLII** (1936), 234-7.
6. W. Lloyd Warner and Allison Davis, 'A comparative study of American caste', in Edgar T. Thompson, ed., *Race Relations and the Race Problem* (Durham, North Carolina: 1939), p. 233.
7. Gunnar Myrdal, with the assistance of Richard Sterner and Arnold Rose, *An American Dilemma, the Negro Problem and Modern Democracy* (New York: Harper & Row, 1944) pp. 675 and 688. The emphasis is in the original.
8. This issue is discussed in a related context in Ali A. Mazrui, 'The Lumpen proletariat and the Lumpen militariat: African soldiers as a new political class', *Political Studies* (United Kingdom), **XXI**, 1 (March 1973), 1-12.
9. Gabriel A. Almond and James S. Coleman, eds, *The Politics of the Developing Areas* (Princeton, N.J.: Princeton University Press, 1960), pp. 313-14.
10. This point is discussed in similar terms in Ali A. Mazrui, 'Ethnic stratification and the military-agrarian complex: the Uganda case', a paper written for presentation at the Ninth Meeting of the Social Science Conference of the Universities of East Africa, Dar es Salaam, December 1973, and at the Sixteenth Meeting of the Canadian-African Studies Association, Halifax, Nova Scotia, February-March 1974.
11. Walter Laqueur, *Europe Since Hitler* (Penguin Books, 1972) p. 406.
12. Ibid., p. 494.

CHAPTER 2
Africa & International Ideologies

At least since the beginning of this century Africa has been an intellectual melting pot. External influences have reached their most diverse intellectual form in the last seventy to eighty years. The penetration started earlier, but the momentum gathered more recently. In the African situation ideologies sometimes were profoundly conditioned by religion. Both Islam and Christianity as systems of ideas came to Africa from the earliest days of the religions. Ethiopia has been Christian longer than many parts of Europe, including England; and North Africa was substantially Islamized from the first century of Islam. Islam later spread to other parts of the continent; and when European penetration got under way in the nineteenth century Christianity conquered the souls of more Africans as it spread under the imperial banner.

But our concern here is not with the spread of religions as such but with the dissemination of ideas and values of direct political implications. We shall address ourselves first to the entry of liberal and capitalist ideas, with reference to their mutual interconnection. We shall then examine the rise of modern nationalism, and proceed to consider its initial alliance with socialism. Finally, we shall turn to the persistent and resilient phenomenon of traditionalism.

The Birth of Liberal Capitalism

Liberalism and capitalism have been intimately related historically. Though analytically they can be examined independently of each other, liberalism is that system of values which puts a special premium on the importance of the individual and his autonomy. To ensure the freedom and dignity of the individual, liberalism has sought to devise constraints on governments. Liberalism has been distrustful of concentrated power. The idea of periodic elections, and the very principle of constitutionalism, have been designed to draw outer boundaries of power beyond which governments are not to go. American liberalism has also gone to the extent of basing itself on a system of separation of powers, by which the executive, the legislative, and the judicial branches of government are deemed to be co-equal and mutually autonomous. Again behind the separation of powers in the USA was a fear of governments becoming too strong. It was therefore intended that the powers of the judge, the president, and the legislature, should not be concentrated in the same individual or group of individuals. These powers, by being kept separate, were intended to serve as 'checks and balances' against each other for the sake of maintaining a free society.

At its most extreme, liberalism was a creed of political bachelorhood, sometimes of confirmed bachelorhood. Freedom consisted in remaining an independent individual. In the history of American liberalism, the rugged individualism of the frontier was a form of fanatical political bachelorhood. The totally committed frontiersman moved further west whenever society caught up with him.

But on the whole the individual can never remain totally in isolation. The individual gets married to society. In such cases, liberalism used to insist that the individual must retain all his freedoms of bachelorhood and combine them with the advantages of married life. The social contract which formed a society was deemed to be a marriage contract, with the individual as clearly the senior partner. The freedom of the bachelor was to be deemed sacred even after marriage. Extreme liberalism sometimes came quite near to asking society to 'love, honour and obey' the individual, without asking the individual to reciprocate and assert: 'With all my worldly goods I thee endow'!

But the bachelor became domesticated, especially during this century. The nineteenth-century idea of laissez faire, permitting both economic man and political man to do substantially what he liked, has declined even as an ideal. It was always an ideal, and not really translated into reality. On the contrary, only the most privileged members of liberal societies in the nineteenth century really enjoyed those freedoms. The bulk of the population in some cases did not even enjoy the vote, and certainly many were too poor to be effective either economically or in politics.

With the expansion of franchise in one Western country after another, and with the emergence of the principle of welfare as a duty of government, a new form of welfare liberalism has come into being. Individualism is still fostered, but the power of government has increased considerably so as to ensure that the resources of the country are more justly shared among the population. Liberal systems of government are usually of a multi-party kind, in which the different parties compete periodically for power, and try to form governments. One aspect of liberalism is the relative independence of the judiciary, so that judges are not constantly under the pressure of politicians, bureaucrats, or political parties. Also fundamental to liberalism is the idea of a free press, able to criticize national leaders and discuss the more sensitive national issues with as few restrictions as possible.

Capitalism in western countries grew alongside liberalism, and the two reinforced each other. The liberal distrust of government resulted in the growth of private industry and the insistence that political authority should not interfere with the profit motive of individuals. In his speech on 'rugged individualism' on 22 October 1928, President Herbert Hoover said:

> Liberalism is a force . . . proceeding from the deep realization that economic freedom cannot be sacrificed if political freedom is to be preserved. . . . For a hundred and fifty years liberalism has found its true spirit in the American system, not in the European systems.[1]

How did Hoover arrive at this relationship between economic and political freedom? Theoretically, there was first the assumption that freedom was essentially an absence of government control—and economic freedom could therefore only exist where there was very little government control in the economy. But what was excessive control? The liberal at that time would argue that government should act only as an umpire or referee in the economic game. When the government went further than that, it became a player in the economic game, and such a role for the government was inadmissible. In Hoover's words:

> Commercial business requires a concentration of responsibility. Self-government requires decentralization and many checks and balances to safeguard liberty. Our government to succeed in business would need to become in effect a despotism. There at once begins the destruction of self-government. . . . Liberalism should be found not striving to spread bureaucracy but striving to set bounds to it.[2]

During the depression when Hoover was in office, he was opposed even to direct unemployment relief from the Federal Government. He himself had been elected in 1928 at the floodtide of prosperity which preceded the crash. His speech on rugged individualism was a campaign speech in 1928. The liberal optimism that an invisible hand would finally guide the economy back to prosperity made Hoover believe that the forces which had made the economic crisis come would follow a cycle and bring back prosperity without government intervention. Such were the excesses of liberalism even in this century. It took the interventionist policies of President Franklin D. Roosevelt to create the precedent of welfare liberalism in the USA, and soften some of the ruggedness of individualism.

Ideas connected with both western liberalism and western capitalism arrived together in Africa, through a variety of media. Christianity itself was an important factor in transmitting certain related values and ideas. The very Christian concept of personal accountability was clearly related to individualism. Although Christian denominations varied in their interpretation of how personal the accountability was to be, there was more of the individualistic factor in Christian approaches to morality than in indigenous African approaches.

The Protestant ethic, especially, came with its economic implications. While Catholicism continued to have ideas of weekly confessions in church, and intercession by the Virgin Mary and the saints to mitigate the personal element in accountability, Protestant denominations emphasized sharply the individual's own responsibility. Protestant individualism, as Max Weber, the German sociologist, brilliantly theorized, has had a historical interconnection with the rise of capitalism. The most successful capitalist countries in history so far have been disproportionately Protestant, and their Protestantism may have been connected with the success of free enterprise in their countries.

In Africa there are more Catholics than Protestants, but in British Africa there was a strong tendency for Protestants to have an edge in influence and sometimes in power. To the extent to which liberalism and capitalism came with Christianity, we ought to say that they were more directly transmitted by Protestant denominations than by Catholicism. Catholicism sometimes erred on the side of promoting deference towards authority, and reducing personal initiative among African converts. To that extent the Catholic Church did not make things easy for the growth of either liberalism or capitalism under African conditions.

A second factor sharpened by the imperial experience, and relevant to liberal capitalism, was the concept of private property. The idea was not by any means absent in indigenous economic systems before the white man came, but private property was considerably circumscribed by most indigenous customs. The principle of freehold ownership of land, capable of being sold at any time by the owner, regardless of any offence that might be caused to ancestors buried in that area, and regardless of obligations to kinsmen, was quite alien. In fact, Tanzania soon after independence abolished the principle of freehold land precisely on the argument that it was inconsistent with traditional African economic thought.

A third factor in imperialism which favoured liberal capitalism was the consolidation of the principle of exchange and the money economy. Many African societies when the white man arrived engaged at the most in barter, and the question of money as a medium of exchange was in some cases entirely unknown.

When white men began to settle in parts of Eastern and Southern Africa, one of their early problems was how to get Africans to work for them for wages. These white immigrants needed cheap labour, not only as domestic servants, but also for plantations and mines. How could you induce the native population to take up these jobs? Money was alien to many of them, and they were happy to till their own little plots of land in their own villages rather than trek to European plantations and mines.

Imperial and European authorities therefore devised ways of forcing Africans to work. In some cases it was literally forced labour, ranging from the use of convicts to direct conscription from the villages. In other cases taxation was devised as a way of getting Africans to work for money. If Africans annually had to pay tax in the form of newly introduced currency, and if they could only obtain that currency by working for it, a process of monetizing African economic habits would get under way.

The enterprise was successful, sometimes beyond the white originators' wildest dreams. The monetization of African economic habits began to lay the foundation of future African capitalism. The indigenous African arrangements were sometimes based on subsistence. A subsistence economy is perfectly compatible with socialism. Villagers can raise just enough food for their own needs, but raise it jointly, and share the food justly. But a subsistence economy is incompatible with capitalism by definition. Capitalism after all requires a system of exchange based in part on capital accumulation and investment profits. The very nature of capitalism implies a certain standard of minimum affluence and surplus. A total lack of surplus could be not only compatible with socialism but an aid to socialism. But a lack of surplus, which characterized many African societies until this century, was implicitly a negation of capitalism.

The fourth imperial factor which favoured the introduction of liberal capitalist ideas into Africa was in fact that part of colonialism which was a negation of liberalism. Intellectually, a colonial system was not a free market of ideas. The colonial rulers asserted a monopoly of intellectual control over their subject peoples. The imperial experience was bringing into Africa values and ambitions which the imperial experience itself made impossible to realize.

Capitalist ideas and values were finding free access, but anti-capitalist ideas, especially Marxism, were systematically kept out by regulations concerning the importation of books and by specific strategy in the educational system involving ideological censorship. Missionary schools in Africa especially were alert to any threat of communist ideas among their pupils, and radical publications were therefore ruthlessly kept out or suppressed. In the case of the Catholic Church, a system of declaring certain books as being on the Vatican's list also contributed to the trend towards censorship. The colonial administrators were also intellectually intolerant, and sought to ensure that the marketplace of ideas in their own colonies was *not* based on a system of intellectual free enterprise. Even liberal ideas which might make the colonized peoples feel that they had democratic rights against the very systems of values of the colonial powers were not always given free access into the colonies. But enough liberal and capitalist ideas entered African countries to give them an advantage against alternative schools of thought in Europe which were opposed to either capitalism or liberalism or both.

A fifth factor which favoured liberal capitalism in Africa was the prestige of the culture and values of the colonial power in Europe itself. The British system of government, therefore, enjoyed considerable prestige among Africans ruled by Britain. Everything British had that edge of prestige at that time in different parts of the British empire. Everything French enjoyed similar pre-eminence among peoples ruled or dominated by France. Because the British system of government was liberal and capitalist, that system of government therefore widely commanded admiration among politically conscious subject peoples.

The sixth and final factor favouring liberal capitalism was the extent to which certain liberal ideas could in fact become nationalistic values. Liberalism as a system of norms came to favour not only individual freedom but also the whole principle of collective self-determination. To some extent that was what the American Declaration of Independence from Britain was all about. The first country ever to be liberated from British colonial rule was to become the leading model of liberal capitalism. The assertion of national autonomy and respect for individual autonomy internally were historically related. By the end of the First World War, President Wilson of the USA had carried a liberal principle of self-determination for all peoples to the central stage of world politics.

In reality liberal countries, like most Christian countries, did not practise in their colonies what they preached at home. Nevertheless, the idea of self-determination provided a connecting link between the influence of liberal capitalism and the rise of modern nationalism in Africa.

Race and Nationalism

The emergence of the principle of self-determination helped to provide a whole new rhetoric for African nationalism. Increasingly, the members of the new educated elites of African countries formulated their aspirations in terms of the rights of all peoples to determine their own destinies. The liberal notion of the dignity of the individual had become collectivized into the dignity of the nation as well. The transition from individualism to nationalism was helped by the connecting liberal concept of majority rule. The system of values which permits elections to take place on the principle of the choice of the majority, and which bases parliamentary procedures on similar majoritarian decisions, was bound to provide the critical missing link between liberal individualism and national self-determination. Some Africans were educated in the USA, and acquired a rhetoric which

combined these different liberal postulates. But even Africans educated in the United Kingdom, such as Julius Nyerere, were known to refer to such American rhetorical currency as Lincoln's statement about 'government of the people, by the people, for the people'. Abraham Lincoln was a liberal in a profound sense, and his views concerning the emancipation of slaves combined both the concept of the dignity of the individual and the worth of the collective community.

The Africans in individual colonies began to use these liberal techniques in order to assert majoritarian supremacy. Africans began to insist on 'one man, one vote' as a basis of electing representatives to the colonial legislative councils. The notion of 'one man, one vote' was steeped in liberal assumptions of individualism; while the principle of 'undiluted democracy', as espoused by a number of African nationalists during the colonial period, sought to realize the effective triumph of numerically preponderant Africans and their capture of the colonial legislature. Africans in the colonies kept on demanding wider and wider franchise, hoping thereby to increase their own credentials for the supremacy of the black majority. In those countries which had sizeable populations of non-Africans, these for a while had representation in the local legislature out of all proportion to their numbers. Indeed, countries such as Kenya had a majority of Europeans in the colonial legislative council although in the country Europeans were outnumbered by a hundred to one. The strategy of the new anti-colonial agitators from the black population was therefore aimed towards increasing the proportion of Africans in the legislative council, leading finally in 1960 to an African majority and the arrival of internal self-government as a stage towards total independence.

But concepts of nationalism at this stage were inseparable from concepts of racial identity. Africans began to recognize themselves as a people being dominated in their own continent, and black Africans began to sense the relevance of their own colour through the treatment they were receiving from their white rulers. The emergence of African nationalism is inseparable from the emergence of race consciousness among Africans.

The growth of pan-Africanism as a movement was also deeply conditioned by an emerging race consciousness. Gradually, with improved communications, Africans in East Africa found out about black people in West Africa and what was happening to them. Africans in Central and Southern Africa in turn discovered the shared experiences of Africans in Eastern and later in Northern Africa. The bond which brought together black Africans was the bond of being all black; but the bond which linked black Africans with Arab Africans was in part based on the solidarity of being *non-white*. The link in sub-Saharan pan-Africanism was that of shared blackness; but in the continent as a whole the ultimate unifying principle was that of shared humiliation and colonization by the white races. We shall return later to the distinction between pan-Africanism and pan-Blackism. An alternative approach is to distinguish between four related phenomena. First, there is sub-Saharan pan-Africanism, an assertion of solidarity among black Africans south of the Sahara. Secondly, there is trans-Saharan pan-Africanism, emphasizing the links between Africa south and north of the Sahara (the Organization of African Unity is based on the principle of trans-Saharan pan-Africanism). Thirdly, there is trans-Atlantic pan-Blackism, constituting links between Africa south of the Sahara and the Black Diaspora—the solidarity of shared blackness is extended to black Americans, West Indians, black Brazilians, and other black people in the Western Hemisphere. Fourthly, there is trans-Atlantic pan-Africanism, bringing together the Black Diaspora in the Western Hemisphere with all Africans in the continent, both black and Arab. The several dimensions of pan-Africanism are discussed in detail in Chapter 4.

Behind it all continues the song of self-determination as the starting point of self-realization. The self-determination was sometimes applied to individual countries, sometimes to the black peoples at large, sometimes to the African continent both north and south of the Sahara, and sometimes to all those who had been denied the dignity of determining their own destinies. This is where we have to distinguish between self-determination as a universal ethic and self-determination as a nationalist assertion. When it is a universal ethic, self-determination claims the right of all peoples to enjoy opportunities for determining their own futures. When it is a nationalist assertion, the preoccupation is with the autonomy of a particular nation or group of nations.

It would be totally inaccurate to say that the principle of collective self-determination as a nationalist assertion was unknown in Africa before the Europeans came. On the contrary, the history of Africa is full of instances of resistance and rebellion against the European colonizer. Many Africans were inspired by a desire to maintain their autonomy, and were unwilling to capitulate without a struggle to the new European presence in Africa. The range of African resistance is from Sultan Attahiru Ahmadu of the Sokoto Caliphate in nineteenth-century Nigeria to the Maji-Maji rebellion in Tanzania, from the so-called mad mullah of Somalia to the Shona-Ndebele risings in Zimbabwe in the late nineteenth century. These were what have been called primary resistance movements against colonialism, to be distinguished from secondary resistance movements which came with modern political parties in Africa. Both forms of resistance can be seen as instances of self-determination in the form of nationalist assertion.

Some analysts have seen direct connections between primary

resistance and modern mass nationalism in Africa. The modern movements have at times been profoundly influenced by prior illustrations of patriotism. Addressing the Fourth Committee of the United Nations in December 1956 Julius Nyerere spoke in moving terms about the Maji-Maji rebellion against German rule in Tanganyika at the beginning of this century:

> The people fought because they did not believe in the white man's right to govern and civilize the black. They rose in a great rebellion, not through fear of a terrorist movement or a superstitious oath, but in response to a natural call, a call of the spirit, ringing in the hearts of all men, and of all times, educated and uneducated, to rebel against foreign domination. It is important to bear this in mind in order to understand the nature of a Nationalist movement like mine. Its sanction is not to create the spirit of rebellion but to articulate it and show it a new technique.[3]

The Embu resistance in Kenya was broken by the British in less than two weeks after they penetrated the area in 1906. The warriors, in humiliation, gave up their arms at a place called Ngoiri, and the Embu were from then on denied the right to bear arms like men. But memories of such events run deep. An Embu historian has told us:

> Ever since the tribe has been as law-abiding as its neighbours, although the memories of 1906 still remain fresh. . . . In fact, at the feeder road leading to Ngoiri Primary School, built on the scene of the surrender of the weapons, there is a signboard on which is written the words: 'RETURN OUR SHIELDS AND OUR SPEARS'. The signboard was planted there in 1963 on Kenya's Independence Day, and demanded the return by the Wazungu of the weapons burned at Ngoiri in 1906.[4]

There may indeed be connections between resistance by 'naked tribesmen with spears' and 'educated Africans citing Shakespeare' when both were demanding greater autonomy. But self-determination in this case was not an ethic which wanted all peoples to enjoy the right of determining their own destiny but an assertion of the right of the particular African communities to be left alone by foreign intruders.

The West was important not in inventing self-determination per se, but in formulating it as a universal ethic. Western thought thus put forth the principle of self-determination as something which all peoples were entitled to; whereas African nationalists before Western intellectual influence raised their spears in defence of self-determination for themselves.

Yet by a curious historical anomaly, the Western world evolved the ethic of self-determination by practising the nationalism of self-determination. Western nations granted themselves the right to liberty and freedom, and even fought Hitler in defence of that right. Yet at the same time they set out into the world and colonized millions of other human beings far away from their own homes. Indians and Filipinos, Africans and Arabs—all fell under the yoke of European powers which had themselves evolved the ethic of self-determination.

Africans, while formulating self-determination only as a principle of nationalist autonomy, nevertheless basically observed the ethic of self-determination as a universal entitlement. It is true that some African empires were indeed established, but imperialism in Africa was a much more modest phenomenon than imperialism in Europe from Alexander the Great to Cecil Rhodes. Of course, both formulations are to some extent a simplification of historical trends, but the simplification does not do too much violence to the essentials of European imperial history as against the more modest history of African societies engaged in blissful parochialism and self-sufficiency.

What European intellectual influence brought into Africa was not the idea of freedom and love of country, since these were deeply anchored in the traditional past of the Africans. What was new was the universality of certain moral principles, which had anyway been better respected by the Africans than by the Europeans who formulated them theoretically.

Black Militancy and White Marxism

Another international ideology to have played a significant part in Africa's modern history is European socialism, with special reference to the Marxist intellectual tradition.

While liberalism had included elements of nationalism, Marxism included a major theme of anti-imperialism. The difference between what constitutes nationalism and what constitutes anti-imperialism is itself significant. Anti-imperialism is a negative assertion. It is a declaration of opposition to international exploitation. Nationalism, on the other hand, is an affirmative declaration, defending the rights of the exploited nation rather than merely condemning the wrong-doings of the exploiter.

Nationalism and anti-imperialism could therefore go well together. And because Marxian socialism, especially as modified by Lenin, offers a brilliant language of indictment against imperialism, Marxism gradually began to be fascinating to Third World intellectuals. Marxists and other socialists in Europe were in the vanguard of their own countries' criticism of colonial policies and colonial annexation itself.

To some extent the most logical development might have been a new synthesis in Africa between liberalism, nationalism and socialism. The aspects of liberalism which favoured national self-determination and the aspects of socialism which opposed imperialism could both effectively serve the cause of African nationalism. For a while the trend in Africa seemed to be in that direction. The liberalism which had come with Christianity and capitalism was beginning to be tamed and domesticated in the African habitat.

On the other hand, Marxism and other schools of European socialism, after an initial struggle to overcome the effects of missionary propaganda against them inculcated in colonial schools, proceeded to acquire prestige and some support among sections of the new intellectuals of Africa. The distribution of Marxist ideas in the African continent was uneven. During the colonial period French Africa felt the influence of Marxist ideas sooner than British Africa did. A major reason was that the French Communist Party was much larger than the British Communist Party. French communists could therefore influence domestic politics in France and in the French colonies far more than British communists could ever influence events in Britain and the British Empire.

The French colonial policy of partial political integration between the colonies and France facilitated an early alliance between African intellectuals and the French Left. A number of African leaders, because of this partial political integration, were deputies in the French parliament in Paris. Houphouët-Boigny, who later became president of the Ivory Coast, was not only a member of the French parliament but also of several French cabinets under the Fourth Republic. Léopold Senghor was also pre-eminent in Paris, and took part in drafting the constitution of the Fifth Republic. This system was fundamentally different from that followed by Great Britain in her relations with British colonies. It would have been inconceivable under the British arrangements to have had Kwame Nkrumah of Ghana, Kenneth Kaunda of Zambia, or Jomo Kenyatta of Kenya, as members of the British parliament at Westminster, let alone as members of the cabinet.

Because a number of leading French-speaking African intellectuals took some part in the politics of metropolitan France itself, their links with the French Left were for a while much more immediate than they might otherwise have been. It is the nature of French educational policy, in the extent to which it was more philosophically-oriented than British educational policy, which helped to promote among French-speaking African intellectuals a fascination with ideas and abstract analysis. This created a potential intellectual constituency for such concepts as dialectical materialism, historical materialism, and class struggle. On balance, English-speaking African intellectuals took longer to acquire a taste for intellectual Marxism than French-speaking intellectuals.

What should be noted is that in the years after independence many African intellectuals apart from those who were in power, and sometimes including those in power, developed a new interest in Marxist vocabulary and symbolism as they sought to assert their intellectual and economic independence. It is true that the Marxist vocabulary could succeed in creating a mood of militant economic independence. But the use of Marxist ideas as a method of asserting African intellectual independence is basically a contradiction. Many Africans resent the great cultural dominance that European civilization has exerted over their lives. The range of this dominance is wide. Educational systems in Africa are heavily derived from European educational traditions. Universities are very often replicas of western universities. But there are the more basic factors that Africans cannot even begin to escape. These include the simple facts that each year is divided into months called January, February, March, onwards to December, with numbers of days chosen by civilizations external to Africa. Each hour of the day is divided on the basis of calculating units of time derived from alien civilizations. The choice of Greenwich Mean Time as the reference point for determining time in Africa is itself an outgrowth of alien civilizations. The technology which Africans need, the science which is to form the basis of both knowledge and its applications, the very clothes African rulers wear, are often a product of western civilization. The alien influence in Africa is omnipresent. It ranges from the European languages embraced by the elite to the adoption of the Gregorian calendar. In the face of this massive presence of alien civilizations, especially European civilization in the lives of Africans, it is more than understandable that many Africans should seek to rebel against this dependency and assert a militant autonomy.

Yet there is a basic contradiction between this desire and the use of Marxism as a strategy in rebelling against Europe. It cannot be emphasized too often that Marxism is simply one alternative European intellectual tradition, and Asians and Africans who capitulate to its fascination are often demonstrating once again the impact of European ideas on the rest of the world.

But here one must distinguish between two stages of intellectual and mental dependency. One stage might be called submissive dependency, signifying excessive deference towards metropolitan standards, a keenness to imitate the dominant culture, a compulsive subservience to the inner commandments of the conquering civilizations.

In Uganda there is a story about a humble African who went berserk, climbed a tree, and refused to come down. He spent hours there, refusing to accept food, and obstinately clinging to life among the branches. His wife came and begged him to come down, but he firmly declined. His relatives came begging. Persuasion which could be used by those who loved him failed to bring him down. And then a European came. He stood at the bottom of the tree, looked up at the man sternly, and commanded in the most imperious voice imaginable, 'Come down this minute!' Instinctively the man scrambled to some kind of attention up in the trees, and then hurried downwards to the bottom in compulsive obedience to the command of the white man. Obviously this pitiful individual was betraying a deep conditioning of deference and subservience to those who represented the dominant culture. When he responded instinctively to that voice from the ground, after declining all the loving persuasion from those much nearer to him in affection and loyalty, he was in fact betraying a deep submissive dependency.

Aggressive dependency comes at the moment of rebellion against the dominant culture, but in a form which falls short of genuine self-confidence. Aggressive dependency manifests itself in forms which range from refusing to talk to a white man because he is white to a readiness to kill a white child because the child is white. Aggressive dependency sometimes denotes a profound lack of adequate social direction, an experience of anomie or alienation, yet with a clear target for one's grievances, a clear villain to blame for one's self-hatred. When a white tourist asks an African, or an Indian, or a black American, or an Arab, for the way to the post office, and the native spits and walks away in a theatrical display of disgust, we have in this whole phenomenon an illustration of aggressive dependency deeply working itself out in the heart of the native.

European Christianity, as propagated in Africa, created for a while instances of submissive dependency. There were Africans so deferential to the white missionary that it was impossible to tell whether the deference was to the white man or to the missionary. The original approach of Christian missionaries was in any case based on the assumption that Africans were 'heathens', and the Christian duty was to rescue all Africans from the sins and evils of their own cultures. At that stage European Christianity was what could be described as a *monopolistic system of values*, asserting that one could only be a true Christian by giving up all values external to Christianity. A monopolistic system of values insists on 'all or none'—that one must be 'all Christian' or not a Christian at all. With this monopolistic approach African cultures were inevitably put firmly on the defensive. Some aspects of African culture succumbed and were either destroyed or transformed. For others a gallant fight was put up against the encroaching monopoly of European Christian standards. Female circumcision among the Kikuyu, for example, was an indigenous institution which had to be defended against the practical consequences of European and missionary hostility. Belief in less dramatic African rituals has often also proved more resilient than might at first have been thought possible. Even polygamy among otherwise Christianized Africans has far from completely disappeared. Some aspects of indigenous ways, no matter how horrifying to European and Christian standards, put up a grim fight for survival in spite of massive propaganda against them. Nevertheless, there were many Africans who were either genuinely totally Christianized or at any rate formally renounced all allegiance to values external to Christianity. Many of these Africans were sincere converts, and many retained a deep inner self-confidence in spite of the conversion. There were even more though who simply acquired the habit of obedience to a hierarchy of church policy-makers, ranging from the local priest, to the Pope in the Vatican or Lambeth Palace under the Archbishop of Canterbury. The structure of authority inevitably had its headquarters outside the African continent. For a while this very fact created a system of religious dependency which took many years to reduce. Of course it cannot be totally eliminated, by the very nature of the history of Christianity and its entrenchment in the Western world. But what we are referring to for the time being are the earlier excesses of Christian conversion, with their tendency to make of their converts true specimens of submissive dependency.

Then many Christianized Africans began to pay more attention to the liberal component of European civilization than to the strictly religious factor. Liberalism, in contrast to Christianity, is an ideology which values pluralism and diversity. Liberalism, by putting a special premium on the value of the individual and his autonomy, and by emphasizing the virtues of a free market of ideas, was part of the process by which the Western world itself became secularized. Liberalism in the West helped to reduce the influence of the church, and prepared the ground for the principle of secular democracy.

Within Africa liberalism and Christianity, though arriving within the same imperial vehicle, had in reality contrary tendencies. The Christian ethic, especially as expounded by the Catholic Church, put a special premium on conformity and obedience. Original sin itself was the sin of disobedience. The liberal ethic, however, put a special premium on individual autonomy, even if that autonomy went to the extent of moral disobedience. Liberalism as a system of values could not therefore be accused of monopolistic tendencies, although within a colonial situation liberalism was often distorted and at times totally negated by the very people who practised liberalism in their own societies in Western Europe.

The golden age of liberalism in Africa were the last years of colonial rule and the first years of independence. The idea of majority rule, electoral freedom, a free press, competitive parties, and open debate, found genuine realization in many African countries during those years. To the extent that the domestic forces of African societies were permitted to exert their influence, and local interests were permitted to formulate their own positions, these were the years when Africa briefly hovered over the line separating submissive dependency and genuine indigenous readjustment. During the last years of colonialism African liberalism was still basically a manifestation of submissive dependency, betraying an easy imitation of the precise liberal approaches to government of the western democracies, and using almost identical vocabularies. But in the first few years of independence in countries ranging from Uganda to Nigeria and Senegal, there was a real possibility of indigenous innovation arising out of the free interplay of indigenous political and cultural forces. Ethnicity, culture, religion, and class briefly utilized the political arena, and sought to acquire economic and political goods through the process of competition and bargaining. But then African governments themselves began to be politically monopolistic, intolerant of competitors for power, and inclined towards asserting their own pre-eminence against all rivals even if it involved total suppression.

Some members of the counter-elite in Africa, in indignation against both their own governments and the continuing economic dominance of the Northern Hemisphere, began to acquire a renewed interest in Marxism. Marxism as a collection of symbols suitable for protesting against domination, began to glitter in the eyes of many African and other Third World intellectuals. Marxism offered them a basis of explanation and a platform of rebellion against both their own regimes and the total international structure of power and privilege. Marxism, in an understandable way, became the opium of large numbers of Third World intellectuals. They fell under its spell, many becoming morally and intellectually intoxicated by its dialectic and hypnotic effects. Many African and Asian intellectuals forgot that this system of values was part of the cultural domination of European civilization. The range of those who forgot is from Mao Tse-tung and the eight hundred million Chinese who followed him, to the solitary black intellectual on a university campus in the USA or in a French-style café in Dakar, Senegal. Many of these Third World intellectuals have suspended their disbelief, engrossed in the drama of one more European tradition of ideas.

Like Christianity in Africa, Marxism also is a monopolistic system of values. One can only be a Marxist if one rejects alternative social directions and alternative explanations of society and its dynamics. Like Christianity as introduced in Africa, Marxism has a tendency to insist on 'all or none'. Either one is all Marxist, or one is not a Marxist at all. Such a system of ideas is basically a closed intellectual system. A section of the African intelligentsia has moved from the closed system of Christianity into the pluralistic system of liberalism and then onwards to the closed system of Marxism. This transition is from submissive dependency as exemplified in imitative Christianity, then onwards to the beginnings of individualism and open competition among rival values and interests, and then onwards again towards aggressive dependency under Marxism. For many African intellectuals the time has yet to come for an autonomous African mind. The risk in embracing Marxism lies precisely in the fact that it is a closed system, and might therefore discourage even internal domestic intellectual innovation. Marxists look for leadership almost inevitably to outside

Africa, many owing allegiance either to Moscow or to Peking, all owing allegiance to a nineteenth-century German called Karl Marx.

To the extent that liberalism at its most tolerant allows for diversity and experimentation, liberalism could serve Africa better as a laboratory for intellectual innovation. This laboratory, by refusing to be monopolistic or closed, could have permitted itself to be stimulated by aspects of Marxism, aspects of other intellectual traditions, as well as the domestic heritage of the African continent. In liberal societies which sincerely uphold their values, Marxist books and ideas compete in the open market, Marxist newspapers are freely published, communist parties are formed, and individual communists can attain national pre-eminence. By contrast, neither the Soviet Union nor Communist China, nor indeed the majority of communist countries, allow similar latitude to those of their nationals who might prefer the values of liberalism or capitalism, or indeed of some alternative Marxist tradition antagonistic to the official one in their own country. A continent like Africa which is still feeling the heavy burden of external intellectual dominance should permit itself the possibility of indigenous experimentation in diversity, rather than enslave itself to yet another foreign closed intellectual system.

But the liberalism which could serve Africa well must be only that part of the tradition which is concerned with the rules of the game, with permitting diversity and freedom of thought. The actual *institutions* of the liberal West need not be re-enacted in the African continent. Africa could grope for alternative institutions but might nevertheless permit its scientists, philosophers, artists, and traditional sages to contribute to a new cultural melting pot of their own. Liberalism in Africa has to be tamed and conditioned by African nationalism and Third World solidarity. We shall return to this theme in the concluding chapter.

The Resilience of Tradition

Although many African traditions have felt the stifling weight of foreign dominance, there is a theme of resilience and durability. Traditionalism as a system of values is almost by definition the most African, partly because traditionalism implies a continuity with the pre-colonial past, and asserts the primacy of roots. For the traditionalist, the future, if it has to change, should only change by responding fully to the intimations and lessons of the past. In the words of Edmund Burke, the Anglo-Irish philosopher, 'People will not look forward to posterity who never look backward to their ancestors.' This has been a theme in Africa too, and lies substantially behind such phenomena as ethnicity, tribal norms, and cultural nationalism.

Because African nations of today are relatively new, they often have multiple cultural traditions, and their competing claims at once constitute national richness and a hazard to national survival. Tribal confrontations sometimes bring out the tensions between the blessing of cultural diversity in Africa and the curse of deep ethnic cleavage. Traditionalism has also known the pains of both submissive and aggressive dependency. There are occasions when in fact it might even be impossible to disentangle what is truly traditional from what is an effect of external influence. Genuine cultural fusion has sometimes taken place in the space of a few decades.

The experience of Uganda is important in this regard. The most traditional institutions in Uganda until 1966 were the kings. The most important of the kings was the Kabaka or King of the Baganda. The last Kabaka, King Mutesa II, was a man of two countries: he was a man of Buganda and a man of England. His entire life-style was conditioned by this profound cultural ambivalence. He was educated by an English tutor in Uganda and went to Cambridge University in England for his degree, thus becoming an African king steeped both in the traditions of his country and many of the ways of his conquerors, the British. He even spoke English more fluently than he spoke Luganda. He was revered by his people, dressed at times like a traditional Muganda, and at times like an impeccable Englishman.

Mutesa's entire life was divided, as it were, between Buganda and England. Yet curiously enough he was twice forced to go to England for refuge at just the time when he was defending the rights of his people, the Baganda. In 1953 he defended what he regarded as Buganda's rights against the policies of the British governor, Sir Andrew Cohen. Sir Andrew exiled Mutesa to England. Mutesa lived in exile while his people agitated for him. British liberalism found yet another expression. An African king triumphed over a British governor during the colonial period. Mutesa returned in 1955, a great hero, a more popular figure than he ever was when Sir Andrew Cohen exiled him. Then, after independence, he confronted a black rival in independent Uganda. The King of Buganda, one part of the country, confronted Milton Obote as Prime Minister of Uganda as a whole. In the end the King had to flee in dramatic circumstances, and he turned up again in England. Mutesa died in England in November 1969. He was buried there, until Milton Obote was overthrown by Idi Amin in 1971. Amin then sent for Mutesa's body, which was reburied in Uganda. It was as if Mutesa had not only shared his life between Buganda and England, but also his death. He was pre-eminently a cultural half-caste, combining important Kiganda cultural traits and significant British traditions. Mutesa was clearly a case where traditionalism fused with cultural dependency, and yet the man was capable of defying the British in defence of his cultural kingdom.

Curiously enough, the man who finally brought about Mutesa's downfall was also a case of fusion between traditionalism and dependency, though in a different way. Milton Obote was opposed to kings. In 1966 and 1967 he finally succeeded in bringing the monarchical history of Uganda to an end. Obote himself came from a community which was much less centralized than that of the Baganda. His community, the Lango, did not have elaborate centralized indigenous institutions. Obote was republican and anti-monarchical partly because the indigenous culture from which he sprang was itself relatively egalitarian and distrustful of highly powerful hereditary institutions. Yet Obote in his republicanism was also influenced by John Milton, the author of *Paradise Lost*. When he was a child at school his headmaster read to the class both Plato's *Republic* and Milton's *Paradise Lost*. Obote became fascinated by both these works of literature. In the case of Milton, Obote paid the poet the ultimate compliment in such a situation—he adopted the name Milton as his own first name. John Milton was himself a republican in the Cromwellian era in England, and was perhaps the most respected intellectual voice of the republican sector of that period of English history. But in addition, Milton's republicanism influenced his portrayal of Satan in relation to God in *Paradise Lost*. Satan in the poem emerges in heroic dimensions, in spite of John Milton's intention to legitimize the ways of God to man by writing such a poem. Satan emerges heroic partly because Milton's God inadvertently emerges as vain and sometimes petty. The same Milton who was so opposed to royal pomp and civilian servility in England came to pour all his own grand imagination into a concept of God which was truly imperial. The Almighty sat there, listening to endless flattery from the devout, extolling his qualities of omnipotence, omniscience, and infinity. Given that conception of God, Satan does sound persuasive when he proclaims, 'Better to reign in Hell than serve in Heaven'. Out of all the lines in *Paradise Lost*, that perhaps more than any other captured the ambition of one African who was later destined to rule his country in the years of independence. The African, Apolo Obote, decided to wed a Miltonic vision to his own tribal system of values. Both were anti-monarchical and anti-pomp and splendour. By a curious destiny, a poem written in England touched the life of this young Langi boy so deeply that the boy merged his own identity with that of the poet, and became Milton Obote. Here once again was the fusion between indigenous culture and imported tradition which at the same time could be combined with Obote's capacity to rebel against both.

Conclusion

What the examples of King Mutesa and Dr Milton Obote illustrate are the potentialities of eclecticism in Africa's cultural experience. The question which arises is whether *creative eclecticism* is in fact the answer to Africa's future in the realm of ideas.

We have distinguished in this chapter four systems of thought which have profoundly influenced Africa in this century: the liberal-capitalist system, the complex of nationalism and race consciousness, socialism with special reference to the Marxist tradition, and the resilient forces of traditionalism and primordial values. In reality there is an interplay among these systems of thought, and yet each at the same time does have a dynamic of its own. In the African situation, Christianity itself also came as a part of the liberal-capitalist complex, as we indicated, and helped to prepare the way for a colonial responsiveness to the western impact.

An important distinction to bear in mind is one between a closed intellectual system and a pluralistic and open intellectual system. European Christianity for quite a while insisted that an African could not at the same time be a 'proper' Christian and a follower of some important indigenous religious traditions. Marxism, too, as we have indicated, is a monopolistic intellectual system in almost the same sense, and an African who wants to be a 'proper' Marxist will find it difficult to reconcile himself to alternative ideological convictions, be they also foreign or uniquely indigenous.

In reality, no foreign system of values succeeds in obliterating all other rival elements or in remaining pure. The experience of China illustrates that certain factors in Chinese history and culture could themselves reassert some relevance, and modify their imported Marxism-Leninism. Nevertheless, China could have conducted her revolution on a banner other than that of imported ideologies, and could have permitted Chinese culture a better chance in the struggle against alien ideas than was in fact conceded. For a while Mao's China suspended indigenous creativity. A rigid embrace of Marxism-Leninism implied a decision to opt out of indigenous innovativeness. But China is too large a country, with a tradition too rich and extensive, to permit itself eternal intellectual servitude. Another cultural revolution may be on the way in the future, to restore a better balance between the heritage of European Marxism and the heritage of China herself. An adequate emergence of a Chinese personality may be on its way in the remainder of this century.

African traditions are also old, but they are more vulnerable because they often belong to much smaller groups and smaller societies who had previously not experienced joint government, joint language, shared tastes and images, or adequate cultural integration.

What needs to happen is first a process of fusing the multiplicity of subcultures domestically into larger complexes of national and regional cultures. The other process which is needed is a new basis of interaction between indigenous cultures and the imported heritage from the outside world. The latter process might for the time being be called vertical cultural integration, implying a mobility of African values into world culture as well as an African receptivity to the influences of the global heritage. Vertical cultural integration implies not merely a relationship between Africa and Western civilization but a relationship between Africa and all major external civilizations—indigenous Chinese civilizations, Indian civilizations, Islamic civilizations, and others. As the dominant culture of the world becomes more diverse, and no longer purely European, Africa's relations with that world culture might be vertical without being any longer hierarchal.

Indigenous subcultures also need to be interacting and fusing. This becomes a process of horizontal cultural integration, as the Baganda begin to borrow culturally from the Acholi and Langi, the Kikuyu to borrow from the Luo, the Hausa from the Ibo, perhaps one day the Zanzibaris will borrow culturally across thousands of miles from the Yoruba in Nigeria.

If, then, vertical cultural integration is to be a new relationship between Africa and world culture, and horizontal cultural integration is to promote mutual interpenetration among African subsystems of values, we have to know what conditions would make this possible. That is why we distinguish between liberal institutions and liberal rules. The institutions of Western liberalism include in some cases a sovereign parliament, as in the United Kingdom, and in others separation of powers between the legislature, the executive, and the judiciary, as in the USA. Sovereignty of parliament and separation of powers are mutually exclusive as institutional principles.

The liberal rules of the game, however, are in both societies substantially similar. They include some degree of responsiveness to public opinion, some degree of accountability to the electorate, a relatively fair chance for those who are out of government to campaign to discredit the government and hopefully prepare the way for their own triumph, a toleration of diversity and pluralism in the society, a reduction of governmental arbitrariness, and a respect for intellectual non-conformity.

The liberal institutions as they have been evolved by the Western world are probably unsuitable for African conditions, and would have to be modified through a process of trial and error. For example, the institution of the political party might vary very drastically in conception and purposes when utilized in Africa as against its utilization in Western Europe, the Soviet Union, or North America. The question also of whether a multi-party or two-party system is necessary for democracy in the liberal sense is also something which Africans have debated. It is possible that the liberal rules of substantial governmental accountability to the public and toleration of diversity might be subsumed under a one-party system. That is being experimented in Tanzania, for example.

If Africa is to find a fair basis of horizontal cultural integration among its own subsystems of values, and a basis for vertical cultural integration between itself and external cultures which range from indigenous Chinese and Indian values to Marxism, the liberal rules concerning toleration of diversity are indispensable. Liberalism may have been discredited because it came with capitalism, and capitalism for Africans was discredited mainly because it came with imperialism. But we know it is possible to have capitalism without liberalism, as examples in places like Brazil and Spain would indicate. But is it possible to have liberalism without capitalism? Scandinavian countries are among the most liberal in the world in the freedoms they give to individuals, ranging from free speech to free love, and yet the Scandinavian countries have also achieved some substantial control over their capitalism. Capitalism to some extent has been tamed, socialized, and more deeply liberalized in those conditions.

The experience of the Scandinavian countries might not be relevant for African countries, in spite of sharing smallness of size. But there might well be aspects of Tanzanian experiments that ought to enter the process of vertical integration linking Africa to Scandinavia through the mediation of a world culture. Only a relatively pluralist approach to these problems in Africa, divorced from closed systems and monopolistic intellectual traditions, could permit the continent to move towards both genuine self-discovery and a just relationship with the human heritage as a whole. What the black poet Aimé Césaire said of the process of artistic creation might also be true of other areas of cultural development:

> Tradition? Evolution? The entire opposition becomes futile in and through artistic creation, for art is a truth that fuses and blends analytically disparate elements in a single impulse.[5]

Perhaps that is what creative eclecticism is all about.

References and notes

1. *New York Times*, 23 October 1928.
2. Ibid., 24 October 1928.
3. Speech by J. K. Nyerere, 20 December 1956 to the 578th Meeting of the Fourth Committee of the United Nations. The newspaper of the Tanganyika African National Union, once asserted, 'On the ashes of Maji-Maji our new nation was founded', editorial comment in *The Nationalist*, 18 September 1967.
4. D. Namu, 'Primary resistance among the Embu' and 'Background to Mau Mau amongst the Embu', Research Seminar Paper [University of Dar es Salaam], October 1965 and November 1966. I am grateful for these references and citations to Dr T. O. Ranger, 'Connections between "primary resistance" movements and modern nationalism in East and Central Africa', Parts I and II, *Journal of African History*, **IX**, 3 (1968), 437-53, and **IX**, 4 (1968), 631-41.
5. Aimé Césaire, 'The responsibility of the artist', *Présence Africaine* (February-March 1959).

CHAPTER 3

Early Struggles against Dependency: Nkrumah versus de Gaulle

Perhaps the most basic dialectic in Africa's history since the Second World War has been that between the quest for continental autonomy and the pull of a continuing relationship with Europe. The quest for continental autonomy came to be symbolized by Nkrumah's version of African nationalism and its commitment to pan-African solidarity. The continuing pull of Europe is best illustrated by French-speaking Africa, and was facilitated by the personality of Charles de Gaulle and its impact on Francophone Africans.

To a certain extent the conflict between the ambition of a self-reliant Africa and the cosmopolitan ideal of 'Eurafrica' is part of a wider dialectic between nationalism and internationalism in the post-war world.[1] In this chapter we shall, therefore, first touch upon this wider dialectic of nationalism versus internationalism and relate it to the genesis of African self-assertion.[2] We shall then focus our attention more specifically on the interaction between the age of Nkrumah and the last years of de Gaulle in relation to Africa's political evolution.

There are times in the history of nations when focusing on personalities is one effective way of capturing the dominant moods of the age. In times characterized by high ideals and great emotions, the focus on symbolic leaders becomes a particularly fruitful approach towards understanding the basic areas of political interaction. The age of Nkrumah in Africa was an age characterized by nationalist ambitions and self-conscious assertion. To examine the role of Nkrumah is thus to examine more than one fundamental aspect of Africa in his time: it is to choose one broad perspective in the study of political Africa as a whole during the period. Similarly, to study de Gaulle from 1958 to 1969 as a presence behind Francophone Africa is to capture the centrality of his influence as the architect of France's role in the post-imperial age.

The interaction between the forces symbolized by these two historical figures has to be placed in the wider context of the dialectic between nationalism and internationalism at large. For Africa especially the twentieth century is a century of that dialectic, and Nkrumah personified it eloquently. The age of Nkrumah might well be said to have begun in 1945 when he assumed an important organizational role in that historic Pan-African Congress held in Manchester, England.[3] We shall return to this Fifth Pan-African Congress later. Meanwhile it should also be noted that 1945 was a vital year, too, for de Gaulle. It was in that year that Charles de Gaulle left England to return to a France newly liberated from Nazi occupation.[4] We might best capture the dreams of both personalities for their homelands by tracing them back to their respective periods of 'exile' in foreign lands.

Exile and Return

To study Kwame Nkrumah and Charles de Gaulle together is to study the nature of nationalism itself in a grand manner. It has often been said that de Gaulle had a love for France which was almost mystical; Nkrumah had a love for Africa which was equally profound. In de Gaulle we saw the nationalism of a big power trying to reassert itself after a period of internal decay and external decline. In Nkrumah we saw the nationalism of weaker countries, seeking to build an air of dignity in spite of their weakness, and seeking to rise from the depths of insignificance. In de Gaulle we saw the sense of history in proud austerity; in Nkrumah we had a sense of the future in impatient dynamism.

Both had a love for their own country and for the continent in which it was situated. In other words, there was in de Gaulle both French nationalism and European nationalism; just as there was in Nkrumah both Ghanaian and African nationalism. But the balance of these forms of nationalism within the two personalities was different. It is true that de Gaulle aspired to eliminate or mitigate against the American hegemony in Europe, and had a vision of Europe which sought to ignore the ideological gulf between East and West. De Gaulle dreamt of a Europe in a form of solidarity extending from the Urals to the Pyrenees. But de Gaulle was first and foremost a Frenchman—a French nationalist first and a European nationalist second. Indeed, even his concept of a united Europe postulated sovereign components retaining their independent existence. He could not see France merged into a big entity which included Germany, Czechoslovakia and Italy, and in which France would lose its historic distinctiveness altogether. De Gaulle's vision of a united Europe was, in his own words 'a Europe of the fatherlands'.

But, if de Gaulle was French first and European second, Nkrumah was African first and Ghanaian second. This combination was both Nkrumah's strength and weakness. His dreams about the continent and its place in world affairs captured one of the fundamental urges of modern Africans in diferent parts of the continent. Nkrumah became the ultimate spokesman of the most ambitious school of pan-Africanism. He also became the ultimate symbol of the defiant assertion of African dignity in a hostile neo-imperial world. But his commitment to Africa was not matched by a similar consideration for Ghanaians. Within Ghana he drifted towards policies of bungling through, and left Ghanaians much poorer and, as individuals, less free than he found them. It would be foolish to say that Nkrumah did not love Ghana. A man of such political sensitivities in a nationalist sense could not escape the more immediate patriotic ties. But it is true that he put greater emphasis on African dreams than on Ghana's realities.

Both Nkrumah and de Gaulle knew about plotting for their country's independence in the 1940s in England. For de Gaulle, it was the earlier 1940s when France was under German occupation, and the French name was humiliated by the rapidity of the country's defeat by the Germans. De Gaulle, without a power base, became the voice of free France outside France, settling in London in an atmosphere of cool diplomacy. De Gaulle was stubborn and proud, and became profoundly unpopular with President Franklin Roosevelt of the USA. Churchill too had strong reservations about this Frenchman, who was enjoying the hospitality of Britain in a difficult period, and was being given a say in the affairs of allied strategy against the Germans, but who, in fact, had no power of his own, nothing except the dignity of France, to contribute to the allied effort. De Gaulle himself had reciprocal reservations about Churchill and his policies—reservations captured in an immortal reply he made to Anthony Eden in 1943 when Eden asked de Gaulle what he thought of the British. De Gaulle answered: 'I think your people are admirable. But I cannot say the same of your politics.' Much later Churchill was to confess that he both admired and resented de Gaulle. In Churchill's own words: 'I understood and admired, while I resented, his arrogant demeanour.'[5]

De Gaulle, then, schemed in wartime Britain for the liberation of France from Nazi rule, and tried to work with allies who were on the whole rather cool in their attitudes towards him. In 1944 France was liberated and in 1945 the war came to an end. De Gaulle returned to his country, to a heroic welcome. In 1945, also, Nkrumah was scheming in a different direction. He was helping to organize the Fifth Pan-African Congress in Manchester, as part of the movement for the liberation of Africa. And yet, even at that time, there was an issue which later came to lie at the heart of Nkrumah's relations with de Gaulle's France. This was the issue of the participation of French-speaking Africans in the pan-African movement. Virtually the nearest thing to the representation of French-speaking Africa at the meeting in Manchester was the presence of Dr Raphael Armattoe from Togoland. Armattoe was not really committed to the cause. He was very much a detached guest among African militants. As a measure of his aloofness we might recall the story that Nkrumah, as Secretary of the Organizing Committee of the Manchester conference, told about him:

> I remember one evening Makonnen came to see me behind the scenes in a state of great agitation. Could I possibly see a Dr Raphael Armattoe, he said. Dr Armattoe, a native of Togoland, who had been invited to speak at the conference, came in and declared that he had lost his portmanteau in which he had several things of value. He felt that since we had been responsible for his attendance at the conference, we should make good the loss he had sustained. He proceeded there and then to list the items and assess their value and presented me with the account. The Congress was already very much in debt but I decided it was better to pay the man and get over it the best way we could.[6]

Nkrumah was learning about some of the more profound differences between English-speaking Africans and French-speaking Africans and their attitudes to their former imperial powers. Were the French-speaking Africans simply not capable of nationalist assertion against France? Nkrumah was agitated by this question in 1945, and was still agitated in 1965 – his last complete calendar year as President of an independent Ghana.

At the Congress in Manchester in 1945 the issue of Francophone involvement in the pan-African .movement came up. Raphael Armattoe had something to say to his fellow black people at the Congress: 'It is sometimes questioned whether French West Africans have any feeling of national consciousness, but I can say that French West Africans would be happier if they were governing themselves.' Nevertheless, Armattoe went on to add that French West Africans 'sometimes envy the British Africans their intense national feeling'.[7]

Nkrumah was puzzled by this Francophone aloofness from nationalist fervour, but he resolved, even at that early stage, to play his part in trying to involve French-speaking Africans in the great movement for dignity among black peoples. De Gaulle had just returned to France, to the enthusiasm of a liberated nation. Nkrumah followed soon after. His mission in France was different. He was keen on trying to reawaken in French-speaking Africans a commitment to African liberation.

Nkrumah had by then become the Secretary of the West African National Secretariat. His activities included organizing meetings, working for the Coloured Workers' Association of Great Britain and trying to start a nationalist newspaper, *The New African*. It was in an attempt to involve French-speaking Africans in the pan-African activities then gathering momentum that Nkrumah crossed the English Channel for the first time, and went to see African members of the French National Assembly. Perhaps the fact that Africans were able to become members of the National Assembly in Paris and be involved in metropolitan politics partly explained why French-speaking Africans were less rebellious against their metropolitan power than English-speaking Africans were already beginning to be. Nkrumah wanted to find out about all this. He wanted to see these people who were members of the French National Assembly. He wanted to talk to them, and to remind them of a bigger cause affecting their continent and their race. In France he was successful in seeing Sourous Apithy, Léopold Senghor, Lamine Gueye and Houphouët-Boigny. Nkrumah seems to have received sympathetic hearing from some of his French-speaking colleagues. Unlike him, they were not firebrand nationalists; at any rate, they did not see African liberation in quite the same terms. But at that stage of the game they were capable of respecting the Nkrumah version of African nationalism. As a result of Nkrumah's visit Apithy and Senghor later went to London to represent French West Africans at the West African conference which Nkrumah organized.[8]

Both Nkrumah and de Gaulle had become national symbols while in exile in England. In the case of Nkrumah, it was his organizational skills and the beginnings of his journalistic attempts which finally came to the attention of political figures in the Gold Coast. It was not long before Nkrumah received letters from Ako Adjei and J. B. Danquah urging him to go back to the Gold Coast and become General-secretary of the new United Gold Coast Convention. After some heart-searching, Nkrumah accepted. On 14 November 1947, Nkrumah left London on the first stage of his journey back home to the colonial Gold Coast.

Both de Gaulle and Nkrumah soon became disenchanted with the politicians they were dealing with. In the case of de Gaulle, he developed a contempt for the squabbling tribe of French politicians always jockeying for positions and always effectively preventing a dignified assertion of authority within the nation. Almost in disgust, de Gaulle left politics. On a Sunday morning in Paris, on 20 January 1946, de Gaulle summoned the members of the government to the War Ministry. Here since the liberation of France he had, as President of the Provisional Government, laboured to restore the fortunes of the nation. The members of the government sat in this vast room, reportedly hung with tapestries and stocked with medieval armour. With characteristic abruptness, and with hardly any preamble, de Gaulle declared that he had had enough. He was withdrawing forthwith, and handing his resignation to the President of the National Assembly. His decision was not negotiable. It was final and irrevocable. He made his exit from the French scene, firmly convinced that the politicians would lead the country to another disaster. But somehow he also believed that one day the nation would once again look to him for salvation after the chaos which the parliamentarians were likely to leave. In this latter prophecy he was once again to be proved right.

In the case of Nkrumah, the disenchantment with the politicians who had invited him was for different reasons. It was not so much that they were too flippant and unaware of their responsibility to their nation. It was more that as distinguished lawyers of the Gold Coast, they seemed to have the wrong priorities and were not populist enough or radical enough for the next phase of Ghana's struggle for independence.

The pressures from the younger and more proletarian parts of Nkrumah's following began to be felt. One day Nkrumah was confronted by an excited crowd which wanted him to resign as General-Secretary of the United Gold Coast Convention, dominated by lawyers, and form a more radical party of his own. 'Resign,' the crowd shouted – 'Resign and lead us!' Nkrumah suddenly felt that they meant it. He made up his mind to resign not only the General-Secretaryship but also his membership of the United Gold Coast Convention. Standing on the platform, surrounded by an expectant crowd, he asked for a pen and a piece of paper. And then, using somebody's back as support, he wrote out his official resignation and read it out to the people. The enthusiasm of the crowd was deafening. Then, one of the women supporters jumped up on to the platform and led the singing of the hymn, 'Lead, kindly light'. Nkrumah relates:

> What with the strain of it all and the excitement, the singing of this hymn was more than I could take. I covered my eyes with my handkerchief, a gesture which was followed by many others . . . the impact of all this made me suddenly humble and lonely, and the tears that came were shed not from sorrow but from a deep sense of gladness and dedication.[9]

The sense of disenchantment with the prominent politicians of their countries led de Gaulle, on the one hand, and Nkrumah, on the other, towards different courses of action. For de Gaulle it led to his withdrawal from active politics soon after his return to France following the Second World War. It led to his splendid isolation, until recalled from obscurity by the events of 1958. In the case of Nkrumah, however, disenchantment with the politicians of the United Gold Coast Convention led not to a withdrawal from active politics but to a greater democratization of his political base. He stopped being secretary to a middle-class nationalism and engaged himself in a movement of verandah boys.

Colonialism by Consent

The end of the Second World War initiated two processes which have left their impact on the second half of the twentieth century. One was the process of decolonization on a grand scale following the fatigue and impoverishment of Britain after the war. The other event was the inauguration of the nuclear age, dramatically ushered into fiery existence by the dropping of atomic bombs on Hiroshima and Nagasaki.

Nkrumah and de Gaulle came to clash in their policies in these two areas characteristic of the post-war era. They clashed on the limits of decolonization, and over the issue of nuclear status in international politics. We shall address ourselves to both these themes in the interaction between de Gaulle and Nkrumah.

The impending clash between them on the issue of decolonization was foreshadowed by the relative Francophilia of French-speaking Africa in the 1940s and its excessive attachment to metropolitan France. Nkrumah's first trip to France was in pursuit of the greater involvement of Francophone Africans in African nationalist movements. The confrontation between Nkrumah and de Gaulle came fairly soon after de Gaulle's return to power. Little more than a year separated Nkrumah's achievement of independence for Ghana and his emergence as an international figure, and de Gaulle's return to a position of authority in France. Nkrumah assumed power as the head of an independent government in 1957. In 1958 de Gaulle resumed authority and glory in France. It is reported that on 11 May 1958 de Gaulle went on his usual Sunday stroll through the village of Colombey—a village of 350 inhabitants, each of whom he knew. The story goes that one of these villagers, commenting on the latest events in France and Algeria, said: 'Things are looking bad. You don't suppose they'll recall you, General?' De Gaulle's answer was: 'I do not believe things are bad enough yet for that'.

Within a few days rumours started to spread about an impending military coup. France was anxious, the Western world was anxious, the Eastern bloc waited. The Algerians wondered, engaged as they were in a bitter war for independence. Soldiers were getting impatient with the politicians in Paris. Or at any rate they were blaming the politicians in Paris for their own frustrations in Algeria, and the degree to which they still failed to subdue the National Liberation Movement there. A military coup was a tempting solution to their frustrations. Only one man could save France from either civil war or a military take-over. That man was Charles de Gaulle. The nation started clamouring for him. De Gaulle declared his readiness to serve, and left his village for Paris. But the politicians, true to form, tried to bargain with him about his terms. He refused to consider any more negotiating tactics, and returned to his village. The government hesitated and then it fell. By the end of May 1958, President Coty had extended the invitation to de Gaulle just in time to save the country from the army's planned seizure of power. De Gaulle formed the last administration of the Fourth Republic as it tottered on the brink of disintegration. On 1 June 1958, the politicians in the National

Assembly gave him a comfortable majority in his task of restoring the nation to stability.[10]

De Gaulle's return to power had been through a military insurrection; but he was determined to restructure the nation and achieve constitutional legitimation. He was going to create a new republic, and he was going to ask all Frenchmen, and all subjects of France in the colonies, to vote 'Yes' or 'No' in a massive referendum. Internally in France he was going to reduce the power of the National Assembly, and strengthen the Executive: he was going to restore order and authority at the centre of governmental affairs.

It was in regard to his policies for the colonies that his mission clashed with that of Kwame Nkrumah. De Gaulle visited the colonies, explaining what was at stake, offering them the choice of pulling out altogether from the French embrace, or joining with France in the creation of a new French community. France's subjects in the West Indies and in Africa, excluding Algeria, were going to be offered independence if they wanted it. But if they chose independence, de Gaulle made it quite clear that it would have to be total independence—the severance of every tie with France, political, financial, economic and educational.

The terms were somewhat forbidding for many French-speaking Africans. Did they dare to declare such a total severance of ties? Would they be able to stand on their feet in view of the degree of integration with France which had taken place in their economies? Would the educational system be able to support itself if French teachers departed? Would their welfare services, then subsidized, be able to withstand the withdrawal of French support? Would their products, accorded easy and protected access in France, be able to get adequate alternative markets? Would their nations be viable at all? The stark choice with which French-speaking African countries were faced was forbidding. The dilemmas of the situation could not have been more agonizing. How many French colonies would dare vote in favour of independence?

Nkrumah watched on the sidelines. He had already declared that the independence of Ghana was meaningless if it was not accompanied by the independence of the rest of Africa. In 1958 Ghana was still the only black country south of the Sahara to have won independence from either Britain or France. Nkrumah needed companions in the great movement for Africa's liberation. Here, in the de Gaulle referendum, lay the possibility of having several additional black African states emerging into independence. Nkrumah sent out feelers to different African political leaders, offering certain kinds of support to help the cause of voting in favour of independence.

Nkrumah perceived what was at stake in the de Gaulle referendum. Quite a while ago African chiefs had sometimes been given the impression by colonial powers that they had a right to decide for themselves what was going to happen to their territory. In fact, as a rule, the sovereignty accorded to African chiefs by the imperial powers was the right of self-alienation. The African had the right to surrender all his rights to someone else. This sort of reasoning led to the myth of negotiation between the colonial power and the African chief who was just about to be dispossessed. Solemn treaties were sometimes drawn up between Queen Victoria and tribal potentates. Thus the doctrine of colonialism by consent was born. In some ways this exercise in negotiation in the British imperial tradition lasted a long time. In the beginning the British negotiated with chiefs and African kings in their own compounds in Africa in order to prepare the way for colonization. Fifty years later Britain was negotiating with politicians, sometimes at Lancaster House in London, in order to prepare the way for decolonization.

In French-speaking Africa, the doctrine of colonialism by consent assumed concrete, if brief, realization with that de Gaulle referendum of 1958. The African colonies were being asked to decide in a popular referendum whether or not they were prepared to be independent of France. Nkrumah was very keen to ensure that as many as possible said 'Oui'.

Nkrumah's contacts differed from one country to another. In Niger, for example, he seems to have sought the support of Djibo Bakary, a Marxist-oriented politician and journalist, and one of the main organizers of the communist-oriented trade union movement. Earlier in 1958 Djibo was already among the most vociferous and militant advocates both of a new French West African federation and of immediate independence from France. When the referendum came he announced that he would campaign for an anti-imperial vote. He seems to have announced this decision even before Sékou Touré of Guinea reached a similar decision. How implicated was Nkrumah in Djibo's campaigning? Djibo was certainly connected with an inter-territorial movement in French West Africa, and his influence was, therefore, not limited to his immediate base in Niger. But, even at that time, there were already rumours circulating in Niamey, Niger, speculating about Nkrumah's involvement. In the words of Virginia Thompson, a specialist on French-speaking Africa:

> Unverified rumours circulated in Niamey to the effect that Djibo had received financial support from Prime Minister Kwame Nkrumah of Ghana, who was eager at this time to encourage all elements seeking independence from France.[11]

But everywhere, except in Guinea, Nkrumah came to be disappointed in that momentous referendum of September 1958. Colony after colony voted in favour of retaining the imperial link with France. In Niger itself the voting in favour of the French community was by no means overwhelming. The poll was relatively low, and there was a significant percentage of negative votes.[12]

But Sékou Touré in Guinea rose to the occasion. He managed to mobilize the masses of the Guinean electors to vote in favour of independence. Nkrumah was reportedly ecstatic. Amittedly those who had fallen short of this courageous 'Yes' disappointed him deeply. But that there was one African country in the French-speaking[13] zone which had stood up to General de Gaulle and said, 'We are not French'—this was enough to atone for much of the disappointment.

And yet Guinea paid heavily for it. De Gaulle was a man who, above all else, was inclined to take his own words seriously. He had said that a vote for independence was a vote for total severance. He proceeded to implement this in the case of Guinea. French facilities, French personnel, French equipment, were pulled out of Guinea, lock, stock and barrel. It is reported that even telephones were pulled out of the walls and taken away to France. There was no doubt that de Gaulle intended to leave Guinea in the manner he had threatened.

Nkrumah realized that what Sékou Touré needed above all else in that initial shock was, at least, a morale booster. He needed to know he had friends. Nkrumah not only promptly congratulated Sékou Touré and the people of Guinea for their vote in the de Gaulle referendum; he also promptly made a grant of financial support to Guinea to tide her over during that initial period of independence. It was a move worthy of the head of government of the first black African country south of the Sahara to win independence from colonialism. It was a move worthy of a true son of Africa. Nkrumah made available to Guinea a loan of *ten million pounds*, and the two countries planned closer association. Two months later Ghana and the Republic of Guinea took another step forward, by making formal moves to unite. They described their union as a nucleus for a Union of African States. They also envisaged it, in effect, as an alternative to de Gaulle's vision of a French community. This would be an African association to rival the ties that France was forging with her former colonies. Nkrumah plotted to rescue more and more of the French colonies from the French orbit, into the mainstream of pan-Africanism and African unification.

In fact, formal independence for the French colonies came sooner than many people expected. After the referendum and the vote to remain under France, some people assumed that the colonies would, therefore, remain colonies indefinitely. But de Gaulle's vision soon allowed for the granting of formal sovereignty to the colonies, though with the retention of close economic and cultural ties with France. Nkrumah was not satisfied with these concessions to African political status. But at that time he was more interested in promoting African unity than in ending French neo-colonialism in West Africa.

The next convert after Guinea to this vision of pan-Africanism was Mali. And the Ghana-Guinea-Mali Union came into being, again more ambitious in intent than in implementation. The Union of African States, as it was called, envisaged a common currency which never materialized. There was a proposal that each country should have a resident minister serving in each other's capitals, but this was never fully worked out. There was a proposal to co-ordinate internal economic and social policies, but no concrete implementation was achieved. The residual solidarity was the solidarity of periodic consultation on African and international affairs by the three Presidents—Nkrumah, Sékou Touré, and Modibo Kéita.

Then Nkrumah turned his attention to Upper Volta, seeking to woo the Voltaic nation away from the domination of Houphouët-Boigny and de Gaulle. There was even a ceremony of 'knocking down the wall' when Nkrumah and the Voltaic President, Maurice Yameogo, declared their determination 'by concrete measures quickly to achieve the total independence and effective unity of Africa'—and as a first step they agreed to knock down a wall, specially erected for the purpose. This was to symbolize the agreement that 'freedom of movement for persons and groups shall be the rule'. More concretely, there was an agreement for the equitable refund of customs dues collected on re-exports from Ghana to be paid into the Upper Volta Treasury. Nkrumah's economic agreement with Upper Volta cost Ghana three-and-a-half million pounds. Nkrumah saw it as a stage towards the imminent inclusion of Upper Volta in the Ghana-Guinea-Mali Union. But his co-Presidents in the Union, Sékou Touré and Modibo Kéita were less optimistic about Voltaic participation. Indeed, the Presidents of Guinea and Mali pointedly stayed away from the ceremony of 'knocking down the wall'.[13] On the whole Touré and Kéita were right in their pessimism about the seriousness of Upper Volta's intentions; Nkrumah was wrong in his optimism.

The Drift towards Subversion

Meanwhile new issues intruded to divide Ghana from the majority of French-speaking countries. Some of them were issues on which de Gaulle had firm opinions. Pre-eminent among these was the future of Algeria. De Gaulle had come into power, partly in response to the dislocation and disintegration which seemed to have been unleashed by the Algerian crisis. France was unequal to the years of war in Algeria, and needed new leadership, either to assert ultimate French supremacy or to disentangle France from the mess with honour.

When the soldiers clamoured for the change in Paris, and hailed de Gaulle's assumption of power, they thought de Gaulle would establish for them victory in Algeria, and retain Algeria as part of France. De Gaulle did regard that as one major possibility for him to consider— a vigorous attempt to heal the wounds of the war and retain Algeria as a province of France.

In the Arab world the Algerians had a lot of support, including support among those countries of North Africa which had been under French rule. But in Africa south of the Sahara the cause of the Algerians was, as yet, inadequately understood. Nkrumah was among the first voices to be unequivocal in support of Algeria's separation from France. As he put it in an address to the United Nations in 1960:

> The flower of French youth is being wasted in an attempt to maintain an impossible fiction that Algeria is part of France, while at the same time the youth of Algeria are forced to give up their lives in a conflict which could be settled tomorrow by the application of the principles of the United Nations. . . . France cannot win a military victory in Algeria. If she hopes to do so, then her hopes are false and unrelated to the realities of the situation. . . . From whatever angle you view this problem you cannot escape from the fact that Algeria is African and will always remain so, in the same manner that France is French. No accident of history, such as has occurred in Algeria can ever succeed in turning an inch of African soil into an extension of any other continent. Colonialism and imperialism cannot change this basic geographical fact. . . . Let France and the other colonial powers face this fact and be guided accordingly.[14]

De Gaulle was supremely contemptuous of the United Nations, especially of the world organization's capacity to deal with the situation in Algeria. A major difference between de Gaulle's nationalism and Nkrumah's nationalism might be related precisely to their attitudes to the world organization. Nkrumah had bitter feelings about Big Power control of the United Nations, especially in relation to the problem of the Congo at a time when Lumumba, Kasavubu and Tshombe were struggling for political survival and power. In some ways de Gaulle had been right in his estimation of the UN's incapacity to deal with situations of acute instability. It was certainly unlikely that the United Nations would have been very effective in resolving the issue of Algeria. Perhaps the United Nations as a body was a symbol of bigger things than it could accomplish. It was an aspiration. Nkrumah's vision of the world had room for such an organization, and envisaged more effective African participation in the world body. But de Gaulle's vision of the world did not include such global supranationality. He was against the UN involvement in the Congo, let alone any United Nations participation in the solution of the Algerian problem.

Most French-speaking African states were solidly behind de Gaulle, and strongly critical of the Nkrumah school of African nationalism and what it stood for. The solution of the Algerian problem was, in the eyes of the French-speaking black states, to be left for ultimate negotiation between Algeria and France. The rest of Africa was, of necessity, to remain a bystander. The rest of the world should keep out.

Meanwhile, the concept of 'Eurafrica' was consolidating itself in the economic field as well as in diplomacy. The Treaty of Rome of 1957 had been concluded before de Gaulle's resumption of power. That Treaty had associated French colonial territories with the European Economic Community. But by 1960 most of French-speaking Africa had become formally independent. The concept of 'Eurafrica' received a new boost when the association was now envisaged as between a sovereign Africa and a sovereign Europe. And yet de Gaulle at first felt he had to impose outer limits to this association. When Harold Macmillan initated British moves to enter the European Economic Community, de Gaulle had reservations not only about British entry, but also about the extension of associate status to English-speaking Africa. De Gaulle was later to relent in these latter reservations, enough to permit the association of Nigeria, and later the East African Community, with the EEC. But in the initial stages of bargaining, the French Government under de Gaulle was militantly protective of the interests within the EEC of former French Africa.

In the face of these developments, and especially after his experience with Upper Volta, Nkrumah became even more disenchanted with the policy of wanting to convert those who were already in power in the former French colonies. He became increasingly convinced that many of them were no more than, to use his own words, 'client states, independent in name'. Their lukewarm attitude towards the FLN in Algeria was only one manifestation of their continued dependence on France. This view of France's relations with her former colonies influenced Nkrumah's judgement on the issue of African Association with the European Economic Community. He even viewed the Treaty of Berlin of 1885 as a kind of precursor of the Treaty of Rome of 1957 which set up the European Economic Community. Nkrumah said:

> The former Treaty established the undisputed sway of colonialism in Africa; the latter marks the advent of neo-colonialism in Africa . . . [and] bears unquestionably the marks of French neo-colonialism.[15]

As Nkrumah became disillusioned with the policy of trying to convert the actual office-holders and presidents in French-speaking African countries, he adopted the alternative policy of supporting dissidents from French-speaking countries. Ghana became a sanctuary and a haven for rebels from Francophone Africa. In part, this arose out of Nkrumah's conviction that most of his neighbours were, in any case, under 'puppet regimes'. It was therefore proper for Ghana to harbour and even sympathize with the indigenous opponents of those regimes. This factor, perhaps more than any other, aroused the anger of the French-speaking African states at their meeting in Nouakchott in February 1965. And it was this which made them threaten to boycott the meeting of the Organization of African Unity, scheduled to take place in Accra later in the year. The price which they momentarily exacted for their attendance in Accra was a new 'Good Neighbour' policy to be followed by Ghana, especially in regard to the rebels from French-speaking Africa. Ghana would still give political asylum, but she was no longer to afford the rebels a public platform for their grievances, or a training ground for their resistance.[16] There were occasions when Nkrumah was blamed for assassination attempts on his colleagues. In 1965 he had to write a special letter to President Hamani Diori of Niger denying any links with the attempt that year to assassinate the President.[17]

Although Ghana made gestures to her neighbours along these lines, and was particularly keen to ensure that the OAU Conference in Accra was successful, all indications remained that Ghana would find it hard to maintain good neighbourliness. On the contrary, the general evidence suggested that Ghana under Nkrumah was prepared to alienate herself from most of the current regimes of Francophone Africa, in the hope of a more militant pan-African partnership in the future. Nkrumah seemed to be of the opinion that time was on the side of the more radical French-speaking Africans who were in opposition to the current regimes.[18]

In assessing Nkrumah's impact on relations between African states, we might divide the African continent itself into three categories—Arab Africa, English-speaking black Africa, and French-speaking black Africa. Nkrumah tried to establish closer ties with each of these categories. Within twelve months of each other he contracted two marriages with symbolic significance. One was his own personal marriage to an Egyptian girl, a quiet trans-Saharan marriage of pan-African significance. The other was the token territorial union between Ghana and Guinea on 23 November 1958, a loudly and proudly proclaimed marriage between the first black colony to achieve independence from Britain and the first to free itself from France. But in the years which followed, Nkrumah's role in relations between different sections of Africa varied. In relations between Arab Africa and black Africa, his influence was on the whole unifying; but in relations between English- and French-speaking black Africa he was, on balance, a divisive factor.[19]

If France had continued on her downward trend following the Second World War, it is conceivable that the mystique that France held for many Francophone Africans might have been tarnished enough for the bonds to loosen. There was no doubt that part of the neo-colonial relationship between France and the majority of Francophone African states was due, not simply to economic factors or special concessions to products from those countries, but also in a fundamental sense to an apparently mystical spell which France could still cast on many of those who had grown up under her tutelage. If economics had been all that mattered, Guinea and Mali would not have attempted to assert themselves; Upper Volta would not have come so near to pursuing an autonomous foreign policy. But while French aid to her former colonies, and French concessions in trade remained paramount, there was, in addition, simple attachment and awe.

It is especially with regard to this last factor that de Gaulle was so important. His success in reawakening the pride of France, and in establishing a towering French presence in international affairs, helped to consolidate the mystical bonds between France and those she had ruled. Following decolonization it was quite clear that Britain blundered her way into a dramatic decline. Prime Minister Harold Macmillan did something to lend an air of Edwardian anachronism, and his era as prime minister ended with personal scandal in high places and general economic chaos in the country. English-speaking Africans in the colonies had also once felt the spell of imperial splendour, and bowed in respect to the image of England. When independence came it was inevitable that some of this romantic spell should evaporate. And yet much of it could have been saved if post-imperial Britain had succeeded in symbolizing in one man the new dignity suitable for the post-imperial era. But Britain did not produce a de Gaulle. England's spell on those who had grown up under her tutelage was well and truly broken after the bonds of the Empire were severed. But France's spell on her former colonies retained its hold partly because de Gaulle had assumed power at that critical moment in the period of decolonization. The very act of disengaging from Empire was made to appear by de Gaulle as a grand design of French magnanimity. De Gaulle succeeded in creating the impression that France in imperial decline was, at the same time, France in international ascendancy. French-speaking Africans continued to follow him with awe.[20] Nkrumah's rival design to liberate French-speaking Africans and to bring them into the mainstream of pan-Africanism was, therefore, doomed to failure for the time being. The personality of de Gaulle was an important factor behind Nkrumah's failure.

In their different ways these two historic figures had plotted in London in the 1940s for the liberation of their respective fatherlands. Nkrumah continued to recall his first trip to France to see Senghor and Houphouët-Boigny. He remembered the early attempts to involve Francophone Africans in the great movement of self-assertion among black peoples. He recalled their relative aloofness from it all. Nearly two decades later, Nkrumah found, to his bitterness, that the situation was not much different. And that fellow exile of his in London, General Charles de Gaulle, had a lot to do with the perpetuation of Francophone neo-dependence.

Two Nuclear Visions

We have discussed the clash between Nkrumah and de Gaulle within the process of imperial disengagement. In what way did they clash within that other arena of the second half of the twentieth century—nuclear status in world politics?

Again much of the divergence was connected with their different conceptions of nationalism. For de Gaulle, the leader of a big power, the acquisition of nuclear status was inseparable from a resurgence of France as a world power. He ordered the entire technocratic and scientific resources of the country to address themselves to the great ambition of enabling France to enter the nuclear age. He looked forward to a Europe self-reliant in defence. But for the time being he wanted to ensure that France was not a mere puppet in American nuclear strategy. To the dismay of his Western allies de Gaulle started demanding a reform of the NATO Command. He also refused to allow American nuclear weapons to be stock-piled in France except on condition that they should be under French control. Concurrently he pushed forward the policy of developing a separate nuclear capability for France.

By contrast, Nkrumah's vision of the world included a commitment to the elimination of nuclear weaponry. Nkrumah was consistent in this, going back to some of the positions taken on the eve of independence with regard to the general implications of the Bandung Conference of Afro-Asian countries in 1955. Kwame Nkrumah was capable of censuring both the West and the East on matters connected with nuclear power. In September 1961 the first world conference of non-aligned powers was held in Belgrade. It was quite clear that one of the commitments of the non-aligned countries was to the goal of reducing tension in the world: mitigating the dangers of warfare and, if possible, eliminating the hazards of nuclear confrontation. There was also considerable unease about the implications of nuclear tests, particularly in view of the dangers of fall-out and the spread of radiation. And yet, in spite of the fact that the non-aligned countries were meeting in Belgrade, the Soviet Union decided to resume nuclear tests on 1 September 1961. In some ways, it was almost like a calculated insult to the cause of the non-aligned powers.

The nature of international politics at the time was such that the non-aligned countries could not risk open censure of the Soviet Union without risking a big cleavage among themselves. The communiqué of the conference did not therefore specifically condemn the Soviet Union. It said:

> The participants in the conference consider it essential that an agreement on the prohibition of all nuclear and thermo-nuclear tests should be urgently concluded. With this aim in view, it is necessary that negotiations be immediately resumed, separately or

> as part of the negotiations on general disarmament. Meanwhile, the moratorium on the testing of all nuclear weapons should be resumed and observed by all countries.[21]

But some of the leading figures attending the Belgrade conference expressed their reservations about the Soviet resumption of nuclear tests. India's Pandit Nehru asserted, 'I regret it deeply'. Egypt's Nasser called the tests 'another cause for deep regret'. And Nkrumah declared emphatically that the Soviet tests had been 'a shock to me'.[22]

Nkrumah's position was that disarmament was necessary not only because of the destructiveness and madness of the armaments race, but also because it reduced the world's capability to deal with the problems of poverty and under-development. In Nkrumah's own words:

> It has been estimated that one-tenth of the expenditure involved in armaments would be enough to raise the whole of the less developed world to the level of a self-sustaining economy. The influence of the uncommitted nations must be exerted to the full to restore a proper sense of values to the world.[23]

In pursuit of this aim Nkrumah's government set aside £50 000 for an assembly to be held in Accra, in June 1962, to which would be invited representatives of all organizations throughout the world whose aim was the ending of the threat of nuclear war and the establishment of world peace. In March 1962, in the town of Zagreb in Yugoslavia, the Preparatory Committee for this Anti-nuclear Assembly in Accra agreed that the subjects to be discussed would include means of reducing international tensions, methods of effective inspection and control of disarmament, the transformation of existing military nuclear materials to peaceful uses, the economics of disarmament and 'the examination of such fundamental problems as hunger, disease, ignorance, poverty and servitude, with a view to utilizing for social purposes resources now misused as a result of the armaments race'.[24]

The most direct clash between Nkrumah's vision and de Gaulle's came over the issue of French nuclear tests in the Sahara. De Gaulle had pushed on with his ambition to create a French nuclear capability, and 1960 was the year when France's entry into the nuclear age could at last be tested by the explosion of a nuclear device in the Sahara. Ghana became the platform from which not only African protests but also protests from other liberal organizations throughout the world could be launched against the French experiment. In December 1959 and January 1960 an international team of representatives from Africa, as well as from Britain, the USA, and even from France itself, attempted to enter the testing site at Reggan in the Sahara. Their starting point was Ghana, under the leadership of the Reverend Michael Scott. But the team was prevented from proceeding beyond the borders of Upper Volta. They were confronted by armed guards under the direction and control of French authorities. The guards did not only ensure that the team could not get past them. They also ensured that no attempts could be made to reach the testing centre from any other direction. They confiscated the vehicles and equipment.

Nkrumah was indignant about this series of events. Somehow even the idea of nuclear fall-out seemed to vindicate his notion that the borders of colonialism in Africa were meaningless. Just as he believed that Ghana's freedom was incomplete as long as any part of Africa was still under foreign rule; so he believed that Ghana's safety was not secure as long as any part of Africa was used for nuclear purposes. Nuclear fall-out was no respecter of boundaries. Neither was Nkrumah's plan for pan-Africanism. These two tenets caused an outcry of protest as de Gaulle pursued his plan to take France into the nuclear age. Nkrumah called for positive action against French nuclear tests—a mass non-violent protest movement crowding into the testing area.

> It would not matter if not a single person ever reached the site, for the effect of hundreds of people from every corner of Africa and from outside it crossing the artificial barriers that divide Africa, risking imprisonment and arrest would be a protest that the people of France, with the exception of the de Gaulle government . . . could not ignore. Let us remember that the poisonous fall-out need not and never will respect the arbitrary and artificial divisions forged by colonialism across our beloved continent.[25]

As soon as the French tests took place, Nkrumah froze French economic assets within Ghana 'until the extent of the damage to the life and health of her people becomes known'. And when France exploded a second bomb, Nkrumah recalled her Ambassador to France. In April 1960 he called a special conference in Accra to discuss 'positive action and security in Africa'. He called the conference in consultation with other African states. Many of the French-speaking ones were dubious, if not hostile. But for once Nigeria and Ghana saw eye to eye on the gravity of de Gaulle's nuclear experiments in the Sahara. Nkrumah hoped to urge greater exertion by African peoples themselves to proclaim their indignation at this nuclear rape of their continent. His attempts to mobilize large-scale protest movements were not successful. But in trying to mobilize such a protest Nkrumah managed to attract the kind of publicity which focused attention even more firmly on de Gaulle's games on African soil.

De Gaulle was trying to pull a major power back into a position of influence and prestige. In some important sense nuclear status for de Gaulle became a functional alternative to imperial status in the world.

France was losing an empire. Algeria was in the final stages of a struggle for autonomy. De Gaulle, who had come into power partly with the purpose of consolidating France's control over Algeria, was moving in the direction of recognizing the inevitability of decolonization. The part of the Sahara which he used for his nuclear test was, in fact, in Algeria, the use of whose land was one of the last services rendered by that colonized country in the grand design of French power. De Gaulle played it well. He gradually disengaged from the notion that Algeria was French, and began enigmatically to sing the song that Algeria was Algerian.

But he could not wait until the mission of decolonization was complete before embarking on an alternative path to France's grandeur. France would remain great, not by clinging on to an empire, but by making use of her scientific capability and by looking at the world once again as a new arena for independent diplomatic initiatives. In an important sense, de Gaulle's France became the first major power to opt for non-alignment. Of course, he did not join the ranks of the smaller non-aligned nations; but his desire to disengage from too close a military entanglement with the USA, his abrupt and unilateral withdrawal of the French fleet from NATO's Mediterranean Command, his attempt to forge new links with the Soviet Union and explore the possibilities of European co-operation from the Urals to the Pyrenees, his independent foreign policy with regard to Vietnam and to the Middle East—all were part of the profound diplomatic revolution which he contrived for France. One of the Big Five was, to all intents and purposes, becoming a non-aligned major power in effect if not by name.

Nkrumah saw the utilization of the Sahara for nuclear tests as a violation of the sanctity of Africa's soil. He also saw it as a manifestation of the arrogance of a big power which evolved methods of mass destruction in a spirit of supreme indifference as to who might be harmed by its poisonous game. As Nkrumah put it:

> General de Gaulle is reported to have said recently that while other countries have enough nuclear weapons to destroy the whole world France must also have nuclear weapons with which to defend herself. I would say here . . . that Africa is not interested in such 'defence' which means no more than the ability to share in the honour of destroying mankind. We in Africa wish to live and develop. We are not freeing ourselves from centuries of imperialism and colonialism only to be maimed and destroyed by nuclear weapons.[26]

But in the few years which followed, Nkrumah began to think more deeply about the meaning of nuclear science for the age in which he and de Gaulle lived. De Gaulle had decided already that the honour of France could not be safeguarded without French entry into the nuclear age. Could Africa's honour be safeguarded without a similar nuclear initiation? Nkrumah began to dream about pan-African participation in nuclear science. His conception of involvement in the nuclear age was still different from that of de Gaulle. Nkrumah did not dream of building an African nuclear capability to rival that of the big powers. He did not dream of nuclear militarization. But he did dream of developing a competence in nuclear technology in Africa effective enough to give Africa a significant status in the world.

While de Gaulle linked nuclear science to French patriotism itself, Nkrumah preferred to link nuclear science to socialism:

> We must ourselves take part in the pursuit of scientific and technological research as a means of providing the basis of our socialist society. Socialism without science is void. . . . We have therefore been compelled to enter the field of atomic energy because this already promises to yield the greatest economic source of power since the beginning of Man.

Nkrumah was speaking at the ceremony at which he laid the foundation stone of Ghana's Atomic Reactor Centre at Kwabenya, near Accra.[27]

The reactor was an extravagance which Ghana could ill afford. Nkrumah related it to socialism, but in effect, as with de Gaulle, nuclear status was related to nationalism. African dignity began to be associated in his mind with African participation at the highest levels of science.

On 24 February 1966, Nkrumah was overthrown by a military coup. Three years later de Gaulle stepped down from power after a defeat in a referendum. The contrasts between their entries and their exits are themselves symbolic. It was a military insurrection in 1958 which brought de Gaulle into power, and a constitutional judgement in a referendum which led to his fall from power. In the case of Nkrumah the means were reversed. It was a military act which threw him out of power and it was a constitutional judgement which brought him into power in an election in Ghana more than a decade earlier. The very interplay between the military and politics captured the central area of interaction between these two historical figures: nuclear power and its dimensions for security; imperialism and neo-colonialism and their implications for freedom. These were the areas within whose bounds two figures in history—one an African, the other a Frenchman—had moments of contact and conflict.

Towards the Future

What is the legacy that these two figures have left behind in connection with the interaction between Africa and Europe? Nkrumah's views about the nature of neo-colonialism and external manipulation have gained wider acceptance among intellectuals in Africa since his day, though they may not necessarily have transformed the policies of governments on the continent. An important area of discussion in the whole notion of Eurafrica has hinged on the question of its development and need for external assistance. The French record of massive aid to her former colonies, making her the largest contributor among the donors of aid in relation to gross national product, has been part of the historical picture which unfolded under de Gaulle's leadership. Sometimes Nkrumah shared the belief held by other African nationalists that the very act of receiving aid—be it from the East or the West—was fundamentally an acceptance of a neo-colonialist relationship. How then could Africans accept aid without being overcome by neo-colonialism? For an answer, Nkrumah sometimes enunciated the doctrine which we might call the doctrine of balanced benefaction—the idea that the great defence against neo-colonialism lay in the diversification of one's benefactors. In this case both the East and the West are deemed to be neo-colonialist in intention, but one could prevent them from being neo-colonialist in practice by balancing the aid from one side with aid from the other. Nkrumah could himself obtain from the World Bank and the Western powers assistance to build the Volta River Project, and obtain from the Soviet Union money for the generation of power in some sectors of the project. This was viewed by Nkrumah as non-alignment in action. And yet Nkrumah himself underestimated the liberating potential of the European Economic Community for Francophone Africa. Reliance on a community of six countries could mean greater economic sovereignty for French-speaking Africans than reliance on France alone.

Since Nkrumah's fall, the torch of African self-reliance has been passed to Mwalimu Julius K. Nyerere, President of Tanzania. Tanzania has taken on a decisive load in trying to live up to the doctrine of balanced benefaction. Over the years the country's benefactors have included the USA, the Soviet Union, the Communist Chinese, the West Germans, the East Germans, Israelis, Egyptians, and others. Even on specific projects Tanzania has sometimes, either by accident or design, ended up dividing one project between two ideological camps. The preliminary survey for the Tanzania-Zambia railway was to be paid by the West (Britain and Canada) whereas the actual railway was scheduled to be financed by mainland China.[28]

In many ways we might say that the person nearest to being a successor to Nkrumah in the views he represents is indeed Julius Nyerere. Domestically he has represented a radical school of social transformation; and continentally he has captured the role of being the most militant voice of pan-Africanism. The two roles overlapped over the issue of Rhodesia in 1965. The foreign ministers of the African countries had given Britain an ultimatum—to bring down the regime of Ian Smith or face a break of diplomatic relations with African states. When the time came for African states to implement their resolution, the great majority backed down. Among the countries within the Commonwealth only Nyerere's Tanzania and Nkrumah's Ghana carried out the ultimatum, and broke off diplomatic relations on the deadline given. Nyerere announced his severance of relations with Britain first. He became ecstatic when news reached him that Nkrumah had followed suit. The two leaders' roles as the most militant voices of pan-Africanism overlapped on that issue. That was in December 1965. Within less than three months Nkrumah was no longer in power. He was overthrown in February 1966, and the torch clearly passed to Julius Nyerere as the protagonist of African radicalism.

History may not repeat itself, but there are occasions when events are strikingly reminiscent of the past. It was Nkrumah who rose to the occasion and went to the aid of Sékou Touré of Guinea in 1958 when de Gaulle ruthlessly cut Guinea off and left her destitute. In November 1970 a different kind of threat seemed to be poised against Guinea. This time a contingent of mercenaries, the bulk of whom were seemingly Portuguese, threatened the independence of Conakry, the capital of Guinea. Africa vibrated with the news of the attempted invasion by foreign mercenaries of independent Guinea. The first African country to rise materially to the occasion was Nyerere's Tanzania. In 1958 Kwame Nkrumah had provided ten million pounds to help Guinea when French imperialism abruptly moved *out* of Guinea. By 1970 Julius Nyerere provided ten million shillings to Guinea when a new form of imperial threat was attempting to come *into* the country. Both Nkrumah and Nyerere were trying to strengthen Guinea's capability for autonomy and sovereign dignity.

But has there been a successor to Charles de Gaulle as well? This is less clear. In some ways different aspects of de Gaulle's policies have been inherited by different figures after his departure from power. But within Africa the nearest successor to de Gaulle's influence has in fact been the President of the Ivory Coast, Félix Houphouët-Boigny. Again there was a period of overlap in orientation between de Gaulle's influence and the influence of the Ivory Coast under Houphouët-Boigny on the rest of French-speaking Africa. Sometimes the overlapping, curiously enough, included areas of shared policy with Tanzania. Pre-eminent among these was the issue of Biafra while the war in Nigeria still raged. De Gaulle's sympathy for Biafra was well known, though he did not go as far as extending French recognition. But Houphouët-Boigny of the Ivory Coast did extend that recognition to Biafra, in the hope of strengthening the secessionist province's capability to maintain a separate identity. Before the Ivory Coast, Nyerere's Tanzania had set the grand precedent of recognizing Biafra. On the issue of Biafra, de Gaulle himself, de Gaulle's prospective successor in Africa, and Nkrumah's ideological successor did, for different motives, share a policy orientation.

There were other areas of overlap between de Gaulle's own influence and the neo-Gaullist influence exercised by Houphouët-Boigny. Even that great test of strength over the allegiance of Upper Volta, and Nkrumah's attempts to break the boundaries separating Ghana's economic life from the economic life of Upper Volta, was in the end a contest for influence between Nkrumah and Houphouët-Boigny. And Houphouët-Boigny's influence on Upper Volta finally prevailed.

An issue of even broader international implications concerned the Republic of South Africa. De Gaulle had not shared either the vision of totally isolating South Africa or the belief that United Nations resolutions on such issues were to be taken seriously. On the contrary, many of the United Nations' moves to isolate South Africa encountered French opposition within the world body itself. De Gaulle's legacy to France had therefore been in part a legacy of accepting the reality of a racialist South Africa, and ensuring that French interests did not suffer in response to any pan-African pressures against the Republic. The record of French sales of planes, submarines and military equipment to South Africa was part of the diplomatic bequest left by de Gaulle to his successors. And South Africa could be at the heart of Europe's relations with Africa already.

In 1970 the Conservatives returned to power in Britain, and the issue of British resumption of the sale of arms to South Africa began to bedevil Anglo-African relations. The question arose as to why such pressure was being put on Britain when France was conducting a very profitable trade with South Africa in critical areas of military significance. At a meeting of the Organization of African Unity in Addis Ababa in September 1970, there was an attempt to frame a denunciation of France in terms which were comparable to those levelled against Britain. But again the old identification between French-speaking Africa and metropolitan France asserted its political efficacy. The resistance of French-speaking Africans to any public denunciation of France over this issue was impressive by its frankness and vigour. There was no doubt that French-speaking Africans were more protective of the reputation of France, and less willing to denounce or humiliate France publicly, than English-speaking Africans were in relation to Britain. The whole history of assimilation and integration which France had once pursued in relation to her colonies seemed to continue to haunt the diplomatic postures of independent Francophone states within the African continent.

Again, before very long it appeared as if the Ivory Coast's President, Monsieur Houphouët-Boigny, was among the leading Gaullist influences on this issue. By October 1970 he had mobilized the continent into attention by suggesting a possible dialogue between South Africa and the African states. Houphouët-Boigny became the first black African state leader to suggest an actual meeting of heads of African states to discuss a re-evaluation of Africa's approach to South Africa, and a possible initiation of a dialogue with the white-dominated regime. A debate started vibrating all over the continent on the issue. French-speaking Africans were among the first to rally to the support of this suggestion. Niger's President at the time, Hamani Diori, joined the debate by asserting that a policy of negotiation was not inconsistent with the continuation of the war against apartheid. After all, there were discussions going on round a table in Paris about the ending of the Vietnam War, while the war itself continued to rage far away on the Asian continent.

Again there were echoes of the Nkrumahist past worth bearing in mind. Nkrumah sometimes suggested that the two most serious problems in Africa were the consequences of French nationalism on the one hand, and the survival of the South African regime on the other. The implications of French nationalism had included a continuing French presence in Africa and its consolidation in those parts of it which were once under its formal colonial rule. The task of asserting an African autonomy, and forging a continental solidarity of the kind Nkrumah dreamed about, seemed profoundly bedevilled by de Gaulle's notion of France's grandeur and its impact on the fortunes of former French Africa. Nkrumah in addition saw the French Sahara tests as being both harmful in themselves as a violation of Africa's 'sacred soil', and symbolic of the deep implications of French nationalism itself. As Nkrumah said to the meeting held in Accra in April 1960 to discuss positive action and security in Africa:

> Fellow Africans and friends: there are two threatening swords of Damocles hanging over our continent, and we must remove them. These are nuclear tests in the Sahara by the French Government and the apartheid policy of the Government of the Union of South Africa. It would be a great mistake to imagine that the achievement of political independence by certain areas in Africa will automatically mean the end of the struggle. It is merely the beginning of the struggle.[29]

But the issue of South Africa remains part of the larger question of Europe's relations with Africa. And even after de Gaulle we continue to have a convergence of issues involving South Africa, relations between French-speaking and English-speaking Africa, and the role of France in Afro-European relations. The conclusion of a commercial treaty between South Africa and the Malagasy Republic in November 1970, which encompassed the promotion of Madagascar's tourist industry by South Africa, was symbolic of the Gaullist legacy of pragmatic self-interest in relations with the white-dominated Republic.

Conclusion

We have attempted to outline some of the basic areas of interaction between the quest for continental autonomy within Africa and the pull of a lingering connection with Europe. We started from the premise that one important dimension in politics is the interaction between politically significant *persons*. Some of the main tensions and ambitions, some of the main elements of the mood of a particular period, can best be captured by focusing analysis on the most representative exponents of that mood.

Our decision to focus on de Gaulle and Nkrumah had additional, and in some cases more compelling, reasons. It just so happens that French-speaking Africa has remained the clearest illustration of continuing pulls of relationship between Africa and Europe. French-speaking Africa attained formal independence while France was under the rule of Charles de Gaulle; and the very architect of the Fifth Republic and of the nature of its relationship with the former colonies was, in the ultimate analysis, de Gaulle himself. Kwame Nkrumah was an important symbolic figure in a nationalist sense. He was profoundly representative of the African aspiration for continental autonomy. His commitment to the cause of loosening the ties which Francophone Africa retained with France was symptomatic of this deeply felt ambition. Behind both historical giants was the massive fact of the nuclear age, and the belief by both, ultimately, that some kind of participation in the science of the age was an important precondition of dignified status within the age. The nationalism of Nkrumah and the nationalism of de Gaulle both clashed and converged in the fields of science and imperial relations.

When de Gaulle died a French literary figure said of his dead compatriot: 'He was a man of the day before yesterday, and a man of the day after tomorrow.' De Gaulle had combined grand anachronisms with inspired visions of the future. Nkrumah's sense of history was not as developed as de Gaulle's. Nor was Nkrumah's nationalism so stimulated by a deep mystical nostalgia for an ancient glory. Few would describe Nkrumah as 'a man of the day before yesterday' in that sense. But in his vision of a united Africa, in his ambition to loosen the apron-strings which tied Africa to her imperial past, in his commitment to the dream of placing Africa at the heart of world affairs, and in his growing conviction that Africa must marry her culture to the new science, it may well be movingly true that Kwame Nkrumah, like Charles de Gaulle, was indeed 'a man of the day after tomorrow'.

References and notes

1. Consult speech of the Rt Hon. Oliver Stanley to the American Outpost, London, 19 March 1945. See *British Speeches of the Day* (British Information Services, 1945), pp. 318-20.
2. Some issues related to those discussed here are analysed more extensively in Ali A. Mazrui, 'The United Nations and some African political attitudes', *International Organization*, **XVIII**, 3 (Summer 1964); reprinted as chapter 12 in Mazrui, *On Heroes and Uhuru Worship* (Longman, 1968), pp. 183-208.
3. Consult, for example, George Padmore, ed., *History of the Pan-African Congress* (1947; William Morris House, 1963, 2nd ed.) pp. 19-20. See also Ali A. Mazrui, *The Anglo-African Commonwealth: Political Friction and Cultural Fusion* (Pergamon Press, 1967), pp. 53-5.
4. The year 1945 also saw the birth and reaffirmation of the United Nations' Charter.
5. Winston Churchill, *Second World War* (Cassell, 1948-54), Vol. 4, *Hinge of Fate* p. 611.
6. See *Ghana: the Autobiography of Kwame Nkrumah* (Nelson, 1957), p. 54.
7. See George Padmore, ed., *History of the Pan-African Congress,* op. cit., p. 36.
8. See Nkrumah, *Ghana,* op. cit., p. 47.
9. Ibid., pp. 107-108.
10. For a colourful and sometimes moving account of these events consult Duncan Grinnel-Milne, *The Triumph of Integrity: a Portrait of Charles de Gaulle* (New York: Macmillan, 1962), especially pp. 297-316.
11. Virginia Thompson, 'Niger', in *National Unity and Regionalism in Eight African States,* ed. Gwendolen M. Carter (Ithaca, New York: Cornell University Press, 1966), chapter III, pp. 162-3.
12. 'Of the country's 1,300,000 or so registered electors, only some 500,000 went to the polls: of these 102,000 cast negative votes.' Cited by Thompson, op. cit., p. 162. La Documentation Française, *La République du Niger* (Paris) 26 February 1960, p. 9.
13. For the declaration of the Ghana-Guinea Union, as worked out by 1 May 1959, see Appendix 6, and for the declaration by Ghana, Guinea and Mali of 24 December 1960, see Appendix 12 of Colin Legum's book *Pan-Africanism: a Short Political Guide* (Pall Mall Press, 1965). For a report on the agreement between Ghana and Upper Volta and the ceremony which accompanied it see *Ghana Today* (London), 5 July 1961. I am indebted to Colin Legum's book for information about some of the moves which surrounded these events.
14. Kwame Nkrumah, *I Speak of Freedom: a Statement of African Ideology* (Mercury Books, 1962), p. 272.
15. Address to the Ghana National Assembly 30 May 1961. The Treaty of Rome was, of course, concluded before de Gaulle's resumption of power, but the concept of associating independent French-speaking African countries—as contrasted with the old French colonies—emerged under de Gaulle's regime.
16. See Victor Le Vine, 'New directions for French-speaking Africa?' *Africa Report*, **10** (March 1965).
17. See *Ghanaian Times*, 27 April 1965.
18. Among such radicals was the group which Wallerstein called 'the ultramodernists, the opponents of the internal class struggle'. See Immanuel Wallerstein, 'Elites in French-speaking West Africa', *Journal of Modern African Studies*, **III** (May 1965), especially pp. 31-2.
19. This point is discussed more fully in Ali A. Mazrui, *Towards a Pax-Africana: a Study of Ideology and Ambition* (Weidenfeld & Nicolson and the University of Chicago Press, 1967), chapter IV, pp. 59-73.
20. There were of course other causes behind the special attachment of Francophone Africans to France. They included France's policy of 'assimilation' in education and cultural socialization in the colonies.

21. *The Conference of Heads of State or Government of Non-Aligned Countries, September 1-6, 1961* (a collection of documents) (Belgrade: Publicistico-Izdavacki Iavod, 'Jugoslavia', 1961).
22. A useful early analysis of the interrelationship between non-alignment and nuclear disarmament is Homer A. Jack's article 'Non-alignment and a test-ban agreement: the role of the non-aligned states', *Journal of Arms Control,* I (October 1963), pp. 636-46.
23. See Nkrumah, *Africa Must Unite* (Heinemann, 1963), p. 199.
24. Ibid.
25. Nkrumah, *I Speak of Freedom,* op. cit., p. 215.
26. Ibid., pp. 215-16.
27. See *Ghana Today* (London) No. 21, 16 December 1964.
28. See *East African Standard,* 27 March 1968. The preliminary Anglo-Canadian *feasibility* survey is not to be confused with the subsequent *operational* survey by the Chinese in readiness for construction. The former survey produced the Maxwell Stamp Report which found the project viable. But the West was still not keen on participating in the actual construction. The doctrine of balanced benefaction in relation to Tanzania is also discussed in Ali A. Mazrui, 'Socialism as a model of international protest: the case of Tanzania', in *Protest and Power in Black Africa,* ed. Robert I. Rotberg and Ali A. Mazrui (New York: Oxford University Press, 1970), pp. 1139-52.
29. Nkrumah, *I Speak of Freedom,* op. cit., p. 213.

PART TWO

INTER-REGIONAL RELATIONS

CHAPTER 4

Africa & the Black Diaspora

One out of every five black men lives outside Africa. The great majority of those who are outside are in the Western Hemisphere. Some are now native-speakers of Spanish, like the black Cubans. Some have grown up with the Portuguese language in the ghettos of Brazil. Still others are part of the French-speaking world, scattered from Haiti to Martinique. There are also a few Arabic-speakers in parts of the Middle East. But the largest single group outside Africa are Afro-Saxons, black people whose mother tongue is the English language.[1] They include black Americans, Jamaicans, Trinidadians and, increasingly, black Britons and black Canadians.

The slave trade played the most critical role in dispersing Africans to other parts of the world. But it was not until late in the nineteenth century and in the course of the twentieth century that pan-Africanism as a movement of black solidarity got under way.

Five Dimensions of Pan-Africanism

Here we must distinguish five levels of pan-Africanism—sub-Saharan, trans-Saharan, trans-Atlantic, West Hemispheric and global. Sub-Saharan pan-Africanism limits itself to the unity of black people or black countries south of the Sahara. It could take the form of sub-regional unification, like the East African Community or the experimental Economic Community of West African States. Or it could be a commitment to limit solidarity to black African countries, excluding both the Arab states and the black people of the Americas. Trans-Saharan pan-Africanism extends solidarity to those who share the African continent across the Sahara desert—the Arabs and Berbers of the North. Trans-Saharan pan-Africanism insists on regarding the great desert as a symbolic bridge rather than a divide, a route for caravans rather than a death-trap. Trans-Atlantic pan-Africanism is the third level of solidarity, encompassing the peoples of the Black Diaspora in the Americas as well as of the African continent. One form of trans-Atlantic pan-Africanism limits itself to black people and excludes the Arabs of North Africa. Under this version Afro-Canadians, Jamaicans, black Americans, black Brazilians and others find common cause with Nigerians, Zimbabweans, Namibians and Ugandans, but find little in common with Egyptians, Libyans and Algerians. However, there is another version of trans-Atlantic pan-Africanism, under which Stokely Carmichael of the Black Diaspora was a hero in Algiers, and Colonel Gaddafy of Libya extends financial support to black Americans. West Hemispheric pan-Africanism encompasses West Indians, black Americans, black Brazilians and other black people of the Western Hemisphere. Within this version of pan-Africanism the strongest links so far have been between black Americans and English-speaking West Indians. This has included movements of population. In the first thirty years of this century alone, 300 000 people from the Caribbean moved to the USA, taking humble jobs in coastal towns and gradually becoming part of the racial mosaic of the United States. At the outside, one out of every twenty black Americans today is descended from a West Indian male who moved into the United States some time since emancipation. One important bond of West Hemispheric pan-Africanism lies in the fact that almost all black people in the Western Hemisphere are descended from slaves. This contrasts with trans-Atlantic pan-Africanism which includes descendants of slave dealers both north and south of the Sahara. Trans-Saharan pan-Africanism emphasizes the quality of having been jointly *colonized*; West Hemispheric pan-Africanism finds solidarity in having been jointly *enslaved*; while the trans-Atlantic idea encompasses the broader concepts of having been jointly exploited by the Western world.

As for global pan-Africanism, this brings together all these centres of black presence in the world, and adds the new black enclaves in Britain, France and other European countries, which have come partly from the Caribbean and partly from the African continent itself. Potentially these black enclaves in Europe are the most radicalizable of them all because of a combination of their demographic smallness and economic weakness, and the fluctuations of the European economies themselves.

Black Australasia

Finally, there is the potential 'Africanization' of parts of the black world which previously had no known connection with Africa. The inhabitants of those parts of the world are now beginning to raise questions which may later make them at least honorary members of the pan-African movement.

For example, should aborigines be renamed 'black Australians'? With that question the very concept of the black world undergoes a change. Until recently the idea of the black world referred almost exclusively to Africans and people of African descent. These included black Americans, West Indians in the Caribbean, black Brazilians, as well as the indigenous inhabitants of Africa south of the Sahara. That is why black political movements were at one time indistinguishable from pan-African movements. Men like George Padmore and Marcus Garvey, two West Indians, and W. E. B. Du Bois, a black American, were among the founding fathers of pan-African movements. In their day the dignity of the black man meant the dignity of those who were of African descent. But in recent times conferences of black people have begun to include Papuans, Niuginians, Australian aborigines, as well as people more clearly descended from black Africans. In Australia one does meet a distinguished aboriginal here and there who attended a major black conference in places ranging from Atlanta, Georgia, to Dar es Salaam. And when I lectured at the University of Papua New Guinea in 1970 I came across students there who identified themselves with the Black Power movement in the USA and Britain.

Niuginians and aborigines may not be biologically descended from Africans, but the first symptoms of mutual identification may have just started. At least in a political sense, we may shortly witness a partial Africanization of Niuginians, to be followed in due course by the partial Africanization of the aborigines of Australia. Such a process would imply a groping by Niuginians and aborigines for new bonds of identification with black Africa, black America and the Caribbean. I have reason to believe such a trend has started, though it will take a while before it matures politically.

As Papua New Guinea approached independence, it paid particular attention to Africa's constitutional experience, as well as to the experience of more geographically close countries. Two Kenyans were invited by the Chief Minister to serve as constitutional advisers. One of the Kenyans, Professor Yash Ghai, had served as Dean of the Faculty of Law at the University of Dar es Salaam. The government of Papua New Guinea showed considerable interest in Tanzania's political and constitutional experiments since independence. Educational policy-makers in Papua New Guinea also showed great interest in tribal societies in Africa and how they have responded to Western education. The University of Papua New Guinea has also shown some preference in its recruitment of staff for people with African experience. As for the politicians of Papua New Guinea, those with international interests have tended to be intrigued by Africa's ethnic, cultural, linguistic and political experience. Some of the parliamentarians have toured Africa with such concerns in mind.

As for Australia, it is purely by a convergence of two historical accidents that Australia does not have former slaves of African descent, similar to those in America today. The first historical accident was that Australia was discovered fifty years too late for that to happen, and the second was that Britain was the foremost opponent of the slave trade in the second half of the eighteenth and the first half of the nineteenth centuries, and it was to British sovereignty that Australia fell. It seems fairly certain that had Australia been settled fifty years sooner, the demands for labour would have led to the importation not only of white convicts from England but also of black slaves from Africa.

To some extent the Australian situation resembled that of Central America at the time of the Spanish conquest. The local Indians in Central America did not make good workers for the white conquerors. On the contrary, there was a serious danger of genocide both through direct killing of Indians, and through forcing them to work. The Indians developed a high mortality rate working on the plantations and in the mines, as well as from sheer white brutality. In response to the presumed genetic indolence of the Amerindians—notwithstanding the evidence of their previous civilizations—the Spaniards turned gradually to Africa for labour. Even such a distinguished humanitarian as Las Casas, who appealed to King Ferdinand and Queen Isabella for justice on behalf of the Indians of Mexico and Peru, was happy to encourage at the same time the importation of African slaves into Spanish America in a bid to reduce the brutalization of the Indians.

The response of the aborigines in Australia to conquest and new forms of labour resembled that of the Indians of the Americas. The aborigines, like the Indians, retreated into a fortress of psychological withdrawal, displaying signs which were interpreted as genetic indolence, and for a while they appeared to be on their way to extinction as a people. It seems virtually certain that had Australia been settled at the beginning of the eighteenth century, instead of within the second half of that century, the settlers would have thought of Africa as an alternative source of labour as inevitably as those in the Western Hemisphere had done before them. After a while two sets of black people would have shared the status of underprivilege in that new continent—the Africans and the aborigines. Intermarriage might in time have fused those two groups, and Africanized the aborigines biologically well before their probable political Africanization in the remaining quarter of our own century.

We have in this whole speculation the simple argument that Australia escaped by a bare half century a big policy debate between convict labour and slave labour as the initial economic base of the new continent. What we know for certain is that Australia became a major convict colony partly because Africa turned out to be unsuitable for that purpose. Following the end of the American War of Independence, England began to worry about alternative dumping grounds for her domestic convicts. The English jails were getting overcrowded again, and even humanitarians sometimes argued that the transportation of these criminals to new social settings gave them new challenges and responsibilities, and opened the way for rehabilitation. Some convict shipments from England to West Africa had been tried on a small scale during the American War of Independence itself. But out of 350 men exported to the Gold Coast in 1782, only seven were still at their allotted settlement in 1785. The rest had deserted to the Dutch, or escaped and become pirates, or died from malaria and other diseases. In 1776 Governor MacNamara of Senegambia in West Africa had recommended Bintang on the River Gambia as a suitable place for an experimental convict colony. And when the American war ended other influential British voices worked out schemes for using convict labour from England for the economic development of West Africa in the interest of British trade. It was in 1784 that the government in London sought the authority of Parliament to select a place overseas for convict settlements. The most popular territorial candidate at this time was the Gambia in West Africa. Among those who opposed the whole idea was none other than Edmund Burke, the British Parliamentarian and political philosopher. In 1785 Burke denounced transportation of convicts to the Gambia as a disguised death penalty, 'after a mock display of mercy'. In May 1785 a committee of the House of Commons began to hear evidence. There were a number of competing proposals. South West Africa now appeared as a strong rival candidate to the Gambia. At last Australia featured as a prospective alternative. Sir Joseph Banks, Cook's colleague on the trip to Australia, came with a startling new possibility—Botany Bay in New South Wales. But it was not Botany Bay that won the first round in London. The committee of the House of Commons rejected both the Gambia and New South Wales, and chose South West Africa instead. A feasibility study was then undertaken, but the survey team from South West Africa came back with a negative report. If the mosquito helped to save the Gambia from British convict settlements, the Namib Desert saved South West Africa from a similar fate. The Home Office abandoned Africa as a viable proposition for this enterprise, and ordered a fleet to get ready for Botany Bay instead. In the words of the American historian Philip D. Curtin, 'the effort to develop West Africa [after the American War of Independence] ended in the foundation of Australia.'[2]

Curiously enough, just as Africa was part of the background to the founding of Australia as a convict colony, so later Africa featured in the events which led to the termination of convict transportation to Australia. Earl Grey became Secretary of State in charge of the colonies in 1846, having been Parliamentary Under-secretary in the Colonial Office in the 1830s when he was Lord Howick.

Earl Grey as Secretary of State had two important obsessions on migration. One concerned the black world of the Southern Atlantic, with special reference to West Africa and the Caribbean; the other concerned Australia. He was in favour of encouraging voluntary migration of West Africans to go and work or settle in the British Caribbean islands. He even devised special inducements. One purpose behind this kind of exercise was to undermine the prosperity of Cuba and Brazil as countries which continued to use slave labour. It was thought that a demonstration of effective and industrious free black labour in the British Caribbean could help to reduce the economic competitiveness of slave labour on Cuban and Brazilian plantations. But although Earl Grey was in favour of promoting free labour in the black world, he was also curiously keen on reviving and expanding convict labour for Australia. In 1848 he revoked the Order-in-Council which had ended transportation to New South Wales. Two vessels of convicts arrived in 1849. The passengers were refused permission to land in Melbourne, and were diverted to Sydney where they were allowed to disembark under protest. Feelings ran high, and in 1851 Earl Grey's revocation of the 1840 Order-in-Council was itself revoked.

Both Tasmania and South Africa were still regarded by Grey as fair ground for British convicts. Grey dispatched a shipload of Irish convicts to the Cape colony in South Africa; and when the white colonists of the Cape indignantly refused to let the passengers land, the vessel turned towards Hobart in Van Diemen's Land. The uproar which broke out was a contributory factor towards the termination of convict transportation to Australia. In the words of the historian Charles Bateson in his book on the convict ships to Australia:

> The storm evoked by this vessel's arrival (from Cape Town) was an important factor in the formation of the Anti-Transportation League in the following year. Van Diemen's Land was now aligned with the mainland in opposition to transportation. The British Government had no option but to bow to the will of the colonists, and in 1853 (the year following Grey's retirement) the abolition of transportation to Van Diemen's Land was formally announced.[3]

History had once again chosen to link the history of convicts in Australia with the history of settlements in Africa. The end of transportation to Australia did not come until 1868, but the affair of that vessel of convicts rejected by the Cape colonists was an additional precipitating factor behind the final closure of this chapter of Afro-Australian history.

Later on Australia, which had escaped the fate of having to accommodate black slaves, itself became the colonizer of a small black population—the population of Papua New Guinea. In 1970 I entertained in my home in Uganda a group of parliamentarians from Papua New Guinea. They were touring a number of African countries, seeking clues to their own constitutional problems. Some of those parliamentarians are now ministers. Earlier that year I had been lecturing in Port Moresby on how far Africa was relevant for Papua New Guinea. I looked at those black people, and wondered whether the assertion that they had no biological link with Africa might not be a little premature. Such thoughts were themselves an indication of a desire to transcend the immediate evidence of racial distance between those islanders and the black people of my own continent. There in Port Moresby an African speculated and mused about the possibility of a shared genesis with his black hosts of Papua New Guinea. It is of such primordial racial mysteries that great political myths are made.

How Real is Black Interdependence?

Although the non-African black world is fascinating because of its uniqueness, and deserves to be studied further in the years to come, African ancestry remains the fundamental core of black solidarity outside Australasia. Yet how meaningful is this solidarity? How real are its rewards?

For the time being the rewards of sub-Saharan pan-Africanism are to be assessed partly in relation to the struggling experiments in regional integration such as the East African Community. This particular community is in trouble, but for a while it survived military border clashes between Tanzania and Uganda from 1972 to 1974 and also survived the first skirmishes of potential economic war between Tanzania and Kenya. The clouds of economic warfare gathered over the region when Tanzania banned some Kenyan commercial lorries from passing through Tanzania in their trade with Zambia, and Kenya retaliated with the closure of her economically vital border with Tanzania. A community which survived both military and economic confrontations between its members must have been stronger than it seemed. Sub-Saharan pan-Africanism also shows results in connection with support for liberation movements in Southern Africa. The Portuguese empire has collapsed, and the future of Zimbabwe remains inconclusive.

Trans-Saharan pan-Africanism, by linking black Africa with the Arabs, may be laying the foundations of an Afro-Arab economic and industrial partnership in the future. Three organizations of potentially critical significance for Africa happen to have overlapping membership. These are the Organization of African Unity, the Organization of Petroleum Exporting Countries and the Arab League. The strongest voices for African needs in OPEC are Nigeria, Algeria and, on some issues, Libya. The strongest champions of African interests on the Arab League are Somalia, Algeria, the Sudan and, to some extent, Libya. Egypt under Sadat is less involved in African questions than it was under Nasser, but Egyptian understanding of African sensibilities is still more sophisticated than, say, Libya's. This understanding plays a part in the deliberations of the Arab League.

Through the Organization of African Unity, Arab states have sought to extend their political influence in black Africa as a whole.

The OAU's commitment to the Palestinian cause is one tangible success. The black states of the OAU have in turn sought to use the organization as a mechanism for getting a better economic and energy deal from the Arab world. The Arabs have for the time being committed themselves to providing more than $1,500 million for African development, but their black colleagues are pressing for greater development aid and better terms than the Arabs have so far been willing to extend. Potentially, the economic rewards of trans-Saharan pan-Africanism are great, but considerable mutual education is needed between the Arabs and Africans before tangible results materialize.

But while trans-Saharan pan-Africanism may be primarily economic in its potential rewards, trans-Atlantic pan-Africanism is at best a political promise. How meaningful is that promise?

It is sometimes easier to see why Africa is important for the Black Diaspora than to recognize the future significance of the Diaspora for Africa. Black men abroad may have problems of identity which can only be adequately resolved by a reconciliation between their new nationalities and their ancestral continent. Black minorities in white lands may in the future look to independent African states for diplomatic pressure on the white governments in pursuit of a fairer deal for blacks in exile. What can be so easily overlooked is the considerable potential value of the Diaspora for Africa. Particularly significant in this regard may be black Brazil and black America, the two largest concentrations of people of African descent outside Africa itself.

The question of what constitutes a black man in Brazil is a complex one. In the USA any person who is racially mixed is regarded as black or Negro, regardless of the shade of skin-colour the person may have acquired, and regardless of whether it was the mother or the father that was white. In Brazil racial categories are diverse, encompassing intermediate categories like mulatto and mestizo as well as the racial poles of black and white. Had Brazil inherited a system of racial classification similar to that of the USA, black Brazil would have been larger than black America. As matters now stand black Brazil is probably two-thirds of the size of black America. Four questions are important for the future of black Brazil. First, will all Brazilians with African blood in time decide to identify with the African part of their ancestry, regardless of whether they are categorized as mulatto or Negro? Second, will black Brazilians be recruited in sufficiently large numbers into their country's armed forces to be an influential lobby when their country is under military rule? Thirdly, will their economic status also improve at a rate adequate for greater articulation of their interests and wider expansion of their social and political horizons? Fourthly, will Brazil's relations with the newly liberated Portuguese-speaking African countries (Angola, Mozambique and Guinea-Bissau) help to enhance the status of black Brazilians, as well as increase their influence on their country's foreign policy towards Africa as a whole?

As the second largest country in the Americas, and economically one with the fastest growth rate, Brazil may be standing on the threshold of world power status, Its population is extending beyond a hundred million; its industrial capacity shows signs of doubling within a decade. Brazil, Nigeria and India should be members of 'the Big Ten' in world politics before the end of the twentieth century. The large black and mixed population in Brazil could become an important factor behind Brazil's interaction with the rest of the Third World, and one of the credentials Brazil may use for her inevitable bid for leadership in that world.

But when all is said and done, the most important pocket of the Third World within the heartland of the Northern Hemisphere is in fact the black American population. Given the system of racial classification in their country, black Americans can be regarded as the second largest black nation in the world, but a black nation which is at the same time part of the most powerful country in the world. The political consciousness of black Americans has increasingly included a sensitivity to Third World status, and an expanding empathy with the peoples of Africa, Asia and Latin America. The impact of black Americans on the foreign policy of the United States is still very modest, but the potentialities emerge as considerable once we contrast that modest influence of American blacks with the immense influence of American Jews.

In October 1973 the government of the USA ordered a nuclear alert in connection with the Middle Eastern crisis. The alert was world-wide, and carried the logic of readiness to initiate a nuclear war rather than risk the defeat of Israel. At the moment it is inconceivable that any United States administration would order a nuclear alert in defence of the rights of black people in Southern Africa. What is being pointed out here is the enormous difference between an American readiness to commit great economic and military resources in defence of the rights of Israelis as against a conspicuous lack of similar commitment in defence of black South Africans or black Rhodesians.

The United States Senate continued to link the issue of Jewish emigration from the Soviet Union with the issue of what type of economic relationship America should have with Russia. The proposal to extend the most favoured nation treatment to the Soviet Union floundered repeatedly in the United States Senate against the rock of Jewish emigration from Russia. American senators were correctly asserting that the Jews in Russia were denied the right to emigrate without paying a tax. But these were not American citizens being victimized by the Soviet Union, nor were they Israelis endangered by the Arabs, they were citizens of Russia by birth and descent. There was no obligation that the American Senate had to take into account.

The blacks of South Africa have often been denied not only the right to emigrate to other lands, but even the right of movement from one part of the same country to another, or one section of the same city to another. Elaborate pass laws within South Africa have been in operation for generations. Visits among relatives and friends have been drastically curtailed within South Africa, and marriage across racial boundaries has been prohibited. But it is as yet inconceivable for an American Senate to threaten strong economic sanctions against South Africa on the issue of the right of black people to move around within their own country, let alone to emigrate to a distant land. The rights denied to many blacks in South Africa are far greater in number and in substance than the simple right to emigrate withheld from Russian Jews. Yet the American Senate has not as yet produced the equivalent of Senator Henry Jackson, to be totally dedicated to the freedom of movement of black people within South Africa, and immensely influential among fellow senators on an issue of this kind.

As it happens, the Soviet Union has for the time being refused to accept the terms of the Trade Act that Jackson and his colleagues had sought to impose on them. Revisions would need to be made, especially if Jackson's strategy has harmed rather than helped the cause of Jewish emigration. But the significant thing in this analysis is the continuing power of the Jewish lobby in the USA, in spite of the US President's frustrations with the Israelis in recent times. One cannot blame American Jews for doing their best to influence their government through constitutional channels. But one can blame the system which denies comparable influence to other citizens.

Although black Americans outnumber Jewish Americans by more than four to one, their impact on American foreign policy is less than one per cent of that so far exerted by Jewish Americans. When four black Americans begin to count for as much as one single Jewish American of the present period, it might at last be conceivable for an American president to order a nuclear alert in defence of bewildered Zimbabwe or South African freedom fighters, and conceivable at last for an American Senate to threaten economic sanctions against the government of South Africa if freedom of mobility from one part of Johannesburg to another is not fully conceded. The American Revolution was born on the slogan of 'no taxation without representation'. Soviet policy concerning citizens who wanted to go elsewhere and change their national status was based on the doctrine of 'no emigration without taxation'. The Russian rationale was that every citizen had received substantial benefits from the country which had educated him, and a decision to change citizenship and establish new loyalties entailed the payment of a tax. American Jews have been influential enough to arouse powerful disapproval of such a doctrine within the government structure of the United States. American blacks have yet to attain a similar level of political leverage to influence the policies of their own mighty country in the direction of a better deal for their racial kinsmen in other parts of the world.

When American blacks do finally attain a level of influence such as that enjoyed today by American Jews, the value of the black American enclave for the Third World would rise dramatically. This black enclave in the mightiest nation in the world would indeed become a powerful lobby and instrument of counter-penetration, valuable not only for black Africa but for the Third World at large. By that time there should also be greater contact between black Americans and Latin Americans generally, including Brazilians both white and black. Until now West Hemispheric pan-Africanism has been mainly a phenomenon involving Caribbean adventurism and mobility. There are links between Caribbean blacks and blacks in North America, as well as between Caribbean blacks and blacks in Latin America. Labour migration from the Caribbean has been a major factor in this. But, as we have indicated, there is little interaction so far between blacks in North America and blacks in Latin America. The question for the remaining quarter of the twentieth century is whether West Hemispheric pan-Africanism will at last become complete across the hemisphere as a whole, and not be left entirely to the heroic and adventurous mobility of such islanders as Jamaicans and Trinidadians.

Towards a Black Commonwealth of Nations?

Against the background of such possibilities, important questions arise concerning the future of the black world. Among the most important is the precise nature of black solidarity in the years ahead. Is there a chance of creating a black commonwealth of nations, embracing the sub-Saharan members of the Organization of African Unity, the black States of the Caribbean, representatives of such large sub-national black enclaves as black Americans and black Brazilians, and conceivably even non-African blacks like Papuans, Niuginians and Australian aborigines?

Here we must distinguish between pan-Africanism as a movement of liberation and pan-Africanism as a movement of integration. Would the proposed black commonwealth of nations be a temporary mechanism of liberation? Or would it aspire to create a truly organic solidarity among black nations and sub-nations, ranging from purposeful increase in mutual trade to the promotion of technical assistance, from joint educational programmes to the creation of a joint development fund?

On this issue sub-Saharan Africa on its own becomes an important laboratory for the black world as a whole. Until now pan-Africanism has had greater success as a liberating force than as an integrative quest. The liberation movement has concerned itself with exerting pressure in favour of decolonization, giving support for the black man's dignity everywhere, and lobbying for the isolation of the white minority regimes of Southern Africa. Joint action at the United Nations in pursuit of African independence was remarkably successful from the moment of Ghana's independence in 1957 until Ian Smith's unilateral declaration of independence for Rhodesia in November 1965. The eight years separating Ghana's independence and Rhodesia's UDI were momentous for African decolonization. African states, though sometimes divided bitterly on tactics and even strategies, were able nevertheless to maintain a viable spirit of solidarity in pursuit of decolonization. From 1965 onwards the frustrations of the remaining areas under white control began to mount as African states felt relatively helpless in determining the fates of Rhodesia, Namibia, South Africa, and the countries under Portuguese rule. Nevertheless, even in this period of mounting frustrations, there was also an undercurrent of achievement for pan-Africanism. The solidarity of African states made it difficult for Britain to ease sanctions against Rhodesia, contributed to the emergence of Guinea-Bissau as a partially independent country, strengthened the activities of liberation movements in Rhodesia and the Portuguese territories, and increased the trend towards the diplomatic isolation of South Africa in world politics. In addition, the rise of independent African states has helped to give greater determination to Diaspora blacks in the Caribbean and the USA to fight for their own rights.

Pan-Africanism as a movement for greater political and economic integration has had a much less impressive record even just south of the Sahara. Those countries which started with a substantial level of regional integration later experienced acute tensions, and the level of integration declined. The East African Community, consisting of Kenya, Uganda and Tanzania, is one case in point. In June 1963 hopes were high that these three countries would soon evolve into a full federation, under one government. But that mood of political optimism, even of euphoria, did not last long. Tensions began to be felt, and one after another the services and links between the three countries were either lessened or ended altogether. Movement of goods among them ceased to be free, movement of people among them became more strictly controlled, a shared currency came to an end, a shared system of internal revenue was dismantled, a joint university existing parallel to but not within the East African Community broke up into three separate universities, the shared airline collapsed, and moments of actual military confrontation were experienced.

French-speaking Africa also witnessed fluctuating fortunes in its quest for greater integration. Organizational and functional experiments had their ups and downs. Countries would join an economic community, only to withdraw two years later; services would be made subject to regional control only to be dismantled into national units not long afterwards.

Nigeria in 1964 began to move with a greater determination towards creating a more viable West African Economic Community, independent of the linguistic barriers inherited from the colonial past. But the struggle to get West Africans to transcend the cultural and linguistic differences inherited from Britain and France was an undertaking too big to be accomplished very rapidly. Nigeria's efforts in this direction were in conflict with attempts within French-speaking Africa. Most of the French-speaking African states seemed for a while to be in favour of creating a community of their own, to which English-speaking states could later accede. Nigeria argued that there was a fundamental difference between joining a community which had already been formed by others, and participating in defining what the community should be from the outset. Nigeria was pleading for joint participation in the very founding of such a community on a basis which disregarded the Anglophone-Francophone divide.

The tensions continued within integrative movements of this kind all over the continent, both north and south of the Sahara. That spirit of solidarity which could be mobilized into relative effectiveness in the domain of African liberation often proved inadequate in the domain of African integration. The struggle for greater cohesiveness threatened to be hard and long.

If the integrative process has been so tough even within sub-Saharan Africa on its own, how much tougher would it be in any endeavour to create a black commonwealth of nations? It might have to start as a movement for cultural liberation and general diplomatic consultations. Black cultural liberation at the global level would have to include changes in the educational systems of countries ranging from Ghana to Trinidad, and Kenya to black America.

In October 1974 a meeting was held at the University of the West Indies, on the Jamaican campus, to discuss the introduction of African material into the curriculum of Jamaican schools. The meeting was organized by the African Studies Association of the West Indies, funded in part by the Jamaican government, and opened by the best-informed Cabinet Minister on African affairs in the Jamaican government, the Hon. Dudley Thompson. Minister Thompson, having practised law in East Africa for a while, spoke Swahili. He urged the conference and his own government to forge greater cultural and diplomatic links with Africa. The conference at the Mona campus made a number of recommendations concerning the introduction of African literature, history and social studies in Jamaican secondary schools. Other voices urged the use of African educational material from the kindergarten. Underlying all the deliberations was a quest for greater cultural balance in the Jamaican educational system as an approach to cultural liberation. There was a plea to learn about

Soyinka as well as about Shakespeare, to study the impact of Chaka as well as the work of Churchill. The educational working committees of the proposed black commonwealth of nations could co-ordinate such efforts, exchange teachers and teaching materials, and ensure a more systematic use of Caribbean and other diasporic material in African schools, as well as the other way round.

Consultations on diplomatic issues could also take place under the umbrella of the black commonwealth, including such questions as the best strategies for persuading oil producers to extend better terms to less developed economies. In October 1974 Guyana negotiated special development assistance from Kuwait. A few months earlier black African states at Mogadishu in Somalia were using the Organization of African Unity as a mechanism for putting pressure on the Arabs to grant more economic and financial concessions to black Africa. Greater co-ordination among black states of the world could enhance their effectiveness as negotiators for a more just economic order.

Conclusion

Historically one would have expected pan-Africanism to start from the smaller units of the sub-continent south of the Sahara, and then move outwards to encompass north Africa, and then ultimately re-establish contact with the Black Diaspora. But it is arguable that, in the twentieth century at any rate, pan-Africanism started with the trans-Atlantic version before it focused more narrowly on the African continent itself. And in the birth of trans-Atlantic pan-Africanism the Black Diaspora was critical. It might even be argued that the movement started with alienated black nationalists in the Caribbean and North America, sometimes eager to start the process of a black return to the African continent, while at other times merely emphasizing the need for black liberation both in Africa and the Americas. We know that the founding fathers of trans-Atlantic pan-Africanism include black Americans like W. E. B. Du Bois and West Indians like George Padmore and Marcus Garvey.

Partly as a result of initiatives by black nationalists in the Diaspora, sub-Saharan pan-Africanism also began to gather momentum. Black Africans in West Africa began to feel a greater bond with each other, and to discover more fully the shared predicament of black Africans elsewhere within the continent. As the twentieth century unfolded, East Africans gradually learnt that there were countries called Nigeria and the Gold Coast with black people in situations similar to their own. West Africans in turn discovered the existence of Kenya, Uganda, or Nyasaland. Trans-Atlantic pan-Africanism developed as a movement of ideas and emotions, with little institutionalization apart from periodic conferences without a standing secretariat. Trans-Atlantic pan-Africanism has so far found greater articulation in the cultural domain than in the political. The festivals of black pan-African art, held in places ranging from Paris to Lagos, and Dakar to Algiers, have provided greater demonstration of transatlantic fervour than some of the political congresses within the same movement. Sub-Saharan pan-Africanism was even less institutionalized on the scale of the sub-continent, though it did influence the formation of smaller sub-regional economic and functional communities like the East African Community and OCAM.

Although race-consciousness was the original fountain of pan-Africanism, it was neither the trans-Atlantic movement nor the sub-Saharan movement which found institutional fulfilment first. It was in fact trans-Saharan pan-Africanism, in spite of the significant racial differences separating parts of north Africa from parts of Africa south of the Sahara. The beginnings of pan-African solidarity at the institutional level provided a foundation for joint action in some spheres between Arabs and black Africans. The Organization of African Unity was finally formed in 1963, encompassing states across both sides of the great continental desert, and providing a framework for periodic meetings of African heads of state and government.

For a number of generations black nationalists both within the continent and in the Diaspora have taken pride in old civilizations of Africa—the ancient civilizations of Egypt and the historic civilization of Ethiopia. Cultural nationalism among otherwise humiliated African intellectuals found a moment of pride in contemplating the achievements of pharaonic Egypt and the uninterrupted history of Ethiopia as a sovereign African nation. But for quite a while neither modern Egypt nor Ethiopia reciprocated this identification with black nationalists. The black nationalists moved forward to embrace the memories of Egyptian and Ethiopian achievements, but modern Egyptians and Ethiopians maintained their political and cultural distance from the rest of Africa. And then, in the second half of the twentieth century, two individuals began the process of restoring the balance of identification. One was an Egyptian soldier, who reminded his countrymen that they were Africans, as well as Arabs and Muslims. The other was an Ethiopian Emperor, who reminded his countrymen that they were part of an African reality as well as of an Ethiopian history. Gamal Abdul Nasser began the process of re-Africanizing Egypt while Haile Selassie I inaugurated the re-Africanization of Ethiopia.

Yet for a while it was Kwame Nkrumah of Ghana who became the most eloquent voice of both trans-Saharan and trans-Atlantic pan-Africanism. Nkrumah captured important longings and emotions prevalent at a given moment in history across much of the African continent and the Black Diaspora, and gave these emotions and aspirations persuasive articulation. Before long Accra became the capital of the *principle* of pan-Africanism, at least until May 1963 when Addis Ababa became the capital of the *practice* of pan-Africanism.

Meanwhile other levels of pan-Africanism had been operating. The West Hemispheric version continued to affect relations between black Americans and English-speaking West Indians, but links between these and black Brazilians have remained minimal for the time being. However, interaction between Brazil and Portuguese-speaking Africans has been increasing. Indeed, Brazil may in time become a more important external power than Portugal for countries like Angola and Mozambique. Brasilia's influence will almost certainly supplant or outweigh Lisbon's before the end of the century. And the black population in Brazil should serve as an important lobby in favour of more enlightened African policies from Brasilia.

The search for a black commonwealth of nations may continue. Some of the initial steps included the Sixth Pan-African Congress in Dar es Salaam, in June 1974, in spite of all its weaknesses. Once again black people from all over the world had assembled to reaffirm a commitment to global transformation.

In 1974 discussions also began about giving some of the Caribbean nations observer status at the Organization of African Unity. The Jamaican government was also exploring ways of extending greater support to African liberation movements, including the possibility of allowing Jamaican volunteers to join the ranks of the liberation fighters in Zimbabwe and South Africa when the time comes.

There have been occasions in the past when black people engaged in profound self-examination, and stood on the threshold of history. These occasions included the Fifth Pan-African Congress in Manchester in 1945. It was an obscure meeting in a northern English town, attended by earnest but obscure black people. Among the relatively unknown participants was a West African called Kwame Nkrumah, and an East African called Jomo Kenyatta. Better known in some circles but still relatively uncelebrated were two blacks from the Diaspora—W. E. B. Du Bois and George Padmore. The British press almost unanimously ignored this conference. Yet the event was, in retrospect, historical. The unknown figures attending the meeting became some of the makers of twentieth-century history. A small meeting of black people in a Lancashire town in 1945 was pregnant with destiny. Perhaps another moment of destiny for black people is at hand, subsuming the promise of broader amity, higher ambition, and more complete fulfilment for black men and women everywhere.

References and notes

1. Consult Ali A. Mazrui, *The Political Sociology of the English Language: An African Perspective* (The Hague: Mouton Publishers, 1975).

2. I am greatly indebted to Philip D. Curtin's book, *The Image of Africa: British Ideas and Action, 1780-1850* (Macmillan, 1965) for general stimulation on this subject and for bibliographical guidance.
3. Charles Bateson *The Convict Ships, 1787-1868* (Glasgow: Brown, Son & Ferguson, 1959), p. 8.

CHAPTER 5
Africa & Western Europe

Of all the regions of the world, two have been fundamental in influencing the course of Africa's history and conditioning the internal life-styles of Africans—Europe and the Middle East. The influence of Europe has had both positive and negative consequences. We shall examine both in the course of this chapter.

Africa's relations with Europe may usefully be examined within four broad categories: culture, politics, economics and science. The oldest relationship between Western Europe and black Africa was motivated by economics; but the most fundamental relationship from the point of view of long-term consequences might well be cultural. The domain of culture in this regard includes the infiltration of European values and tastes into Africa, the penetration of European educational systems, the triumph of European languages, and the growth of European versions of Christianity.

The economic domain goes back to the voyages of exploration by sea and the motives behind those voyages. The economic domain also includes the painful interlude of the slave trade as beads and guns came from Europe to Western Africa, slaves were exported from Western Africa to the Americas, and gold and sugar were exported from the Americas back to Europe. This was the 'Triangle of Shame' in Europe's relations with Africa, and was ultimately economic both in its motivation and in its long-term consequences. As we shall see in a later chapter, the ocean explorers helped to establish in due course a sea route to India and the Orient. European trading and refuelling posts and forts grew up along that route, from north-western Africa to the eastern seaboard of the continent.

But the subsequent land explorers from Europe were not motivated by pure economics, any more than space exploration in our age has been primarily economic. On the contrary, in both cases considerable economic resources were contributed by people who got very little by way of economic returns. It is true that Europe itself later on benefited considerably from exploration of the African continent, and the degree to which that exploration facilitated imperial annexation later on. But the actual individuals who contributed money to make exploration possible were seldom the economic beneficiaries of colonialism. Many of the contributors to European exploration in the eighteenth and nineteenth centuries were excited more by scientific and moral considerations than economic ones. The moral considerations would fall into our category of culture, while the enthusiasm of the Royal Geographic Society for the 'discovery' of African mountains and rivers would often fall within our category of science.

The Western Europeans who have had the most direct impact on Africa in the modern period have been the British, the French, and the Portuguese. All these incorporated large sections of the African continent into their own empires.

What ought not to be overlooked is the indirect impact of Germany and Holland on Africa's destiny. It was a German city, Berlin, which provided the diplomatic setting for the partition of the African continent among European powers. It was a German-initiated war, the Second World War, which more than half a century later came to provide the background to Europe's political withdrawal from large parts of Africa.

The Conference of Berlin was a meeting of representatives of fifteen nations called by Otto von Bismarck partly in order to reduce the danger of war between European powers over the partition of Central Africa. The clouds of war were indeed hanging over Europe in connection with this expansionist fever. The immediate cause of the tension lay in the British and Portuguese distrust of Belgian and French ambitions in the Congo, as well as the distrust of German expansionist aims in East Africa and the Cameroons. The Conference of Berlin gave recognition to the 'Congo Free State' as a personal possession of King Leopold of the Belgians. The conference also afforded access to the sea to this new entity, agreed on methods of suppressing slavery and the slave trade, and guaranteed freedom of navigation on the Congo River and the Niger River. At least as important were the decisions of the conference concerning spheres of influence for the European powers within Africa, designed to prevent the scramble for colonies from leading to a major war. The co-operation between the Germans and the French at the Conference of Berlin was also one of the major attributes of this European diplomatic venture. Here then was a German statesman, Bismarck, anxious to help avert war among European powers, partly because by that time he had a vested interest in maintaining the international order in Europe which he himself had helped to establish.

In the following century it was Hitler's Germany that created conditions for the Second World War. And by a strange destiny, this war helped to weaken European powers so seriously, and to arouse political consciousness among colonized peoples so effectively, that the end of the war inaugurated the beginning of decolonization. If

Bismarck, in his attempt to prevent a European war, facilitated a smoother colonization of Africa, Hitler created conditions for its eventual decolonization.

The Germans had for a while also possessed colonies in Africa, which included the Cameroons, Tanganyika, and South West Africa. But after the First World War, these were administered as mandates of the League of Nations. All but South West Africa later became trusteeships under the United Nations, but South Africa refused to recognize the United Nations as the legal successor to the League of Nations, and therefore declined to recognize the jurisdiction of the United Nations over South West Africa. This pretext helped South Africa to retain control over South West Africa which the League of Nations had originally entrusted to South Africa for administration. Both the United Nations and the International Court of Justice were later to make formal pronouncements disqualifying South Africa from administering South West Africa without the United Nations' authority. By this time a national liberation struggle had started, and the name of the territory for the nationalists and for the United Nations became Namibia.

Behind the power of South Africa was the indirect historic influence of Holland. This influence took the form of Dutchmen moving to South Africa, becoming hardened settlers, adopting the new name of Afrikaners, and disproportionately wielding power within the republic of South Africa. These former sons of Holland also evolved a whole system of racial stratification and discrimination known as apartheid or separate development. Afrikaners control all South Africa, have considerable influence in Rhodesia, and continue to be one of the immense political facts about Africa in the second half of the twentieth century.

The case of the Belgians in Africa is a little more complicated. Should they be included among the British, the French and the Portuguese, as sources of direct long-term impact on Africa in the modern period? Or does the lack of a distinct language of their own, combined with their cautious colonial policy, reduce the claims of the Belgians to be a distinct influence in Africa's destiny? If the cultural domain in Africa's relations with Europe is indeed the most fundamental, is there indeed a Belgian culture which penetrated Africa as a distinctive element? And was such a Belgian culture in any case promoted and inculcated in the educational systems of Belgian Africa with a vigour which made the penetration deep and durable? Or was the very fact that independence came to the Congo with such a dramatic absence of graduates to take charge of the country itself an indication of the relatively meaningless impact that Belgium will turn out to have had on the peoples she has ruled? In short, the Belgian significance in Africa's history amounts to no more than having served as a medium of transmitting the *French* language to Zaire, Rwanda and Burundi. Was the very scale of violence between ethnic groups in these countries, almost as soon as the Belgians left, a measure of the minimum role which Belgium played in forging these countries into nations?

Answers to these questions may still be in the process of formulation in the history of the peoples concerned. For the time being there is a suspicion that the most incidental of all the European influences we have mentioned might well turn out to be that of the Belgians. The Germans might have lost their colonies, but their impact on European history resulted in major consequences for the African continent. The Dutch might simply have contributed sons and daughters to the southern part of the continent, but the importance of the Afrikaners for the history of Africa might turn out to be considerable, especially if they succeed in holding on to power for so long that great devastation becomes inevitable as a method of ending apartheid. The British and the French contributed two world languages to the African continent, and penetrated the cultures of African countries deeply.

The Portuguese could conceivably be as incidental as the Belgians, partly because their attempt to change the colonized peoples in their own image was so lukewarm. On the other hand, the Portuguese do have a language and a distinct culture, and did have an empire in Africa for more than five hundred years—certainly longer than any of the other European powers involved. Finally, there was the question of Portugal's stubbornness combined with a readiness for a while to be part of a grand white alliance in Southern Africa against the forces of African nationalism. Portugal's participation in that alliance until 1974 could, in a negative sense, increase the significance of Portugal's position in the history of Southern Africa. The Belgians did not put up a fight when faced with African nationalism. It is to their credit that they recognized that their time was up, and proceeded to scramble out. But the very pragmatism of the Belgians from 1958 to 1960 helped to make them incidental in African history. The Portuguese, by fighting back for much longer, earned their place as greater villains in Africa's history than the Belgians.

In the ultimate analysis, Europe's penetration of the African continent was at its most comprehensive when we look at the British and French contributions. The overwhelming majority of both the peoples and the states of Africa were previously ruled in one way or another by either Britain or France. When we examine the domains of culture, politics, economics and science, we have to pay special attention to their manifestations in Afro-British relations and Afro-French relations.

Let us now examine more fully the four domains of interaction beginning with culture.

Captives of Culture

The beginnings of imperialism lie in the universe of values; and values are ultimately what culture is about. In reality, culture is an all-inclusive category, within which we might just as easily absorb the political, economic, and even scientific categories. But here we use culture in a narrower sense, primarily to denote values and the means by which they are articulated. We shall pay special attention to moral and religious values, and focus also on language as a means of communicating values.

The religious factor in modern African history assumed a particularly significant role. This is partly because the missionaries became important allies of colonizers and administrators; but also because missionaries became educators. Christianity in Africa played the dual and paradoxical role of being part of the vanguard of a new religion, on the one hand, and the vanguard of a secular Western civilization, on the other. The missionary schools in the African continent proclaimed the word of God, but they also came with the skills and normative orientations of a Europe which had already witnessed the industrial revolution. A related paradoxical role played by the missionary was that of being at once part of a new cultural conditioning in Africa based on European interpretations of Christianity, and part also of a new intellectual ferment which could generate potential innovative leaps. One therefore has to see the role of Christianity in Africa, not only in relation to the whole experience of colonialism but also in relation to the history of science in Africa. We shall return to the scientific factor later on.

For the time being, a critical point to grasp is that colonialism was based on both a structure of domination and a structure of damnation. The structure of domination included the whole machinery of colonial control, ranging from the Colonial Office in London to the governor in the main city of the colony, and from investors in London to the local company in an African township or African mine. The structure of domination was one of direct control.

The structure of damnation used the sanctions of religious experience as part of the process of obtaining obedience and submission. The fear of God and the wrath of God could be used in the task of 'pacifying the natives'. The missionaries could be recruited to promote the ethic of submission and obedience in the colonies. Indeed, if the original sin was the sin of disobedience, the structure of damnation could be used to encourage greater compliance among newly converted Africans. Even the doctrine of 'turn the other cheek' could be abused by imperially motivated Europeans to inculcate a spirit of subservience among African peoples. At his trial at Kapenguria on charges of managing Mau Mau, the following statement was attributed to Kenyatta: 'The Europeans told us to shut our eyes and pray and to say Amen . . . and while our eyes were shut, they took our land.'[1] Kenyatta's political opponent after independence, Mr Oginga Odinga expressed similar views: 'One of the reasons why Africa was poor was because the white man used the Bible to soften our hearts, telling Africans not to worry about earthly worth as there would be plenty in Heaven.'[2] For a while Christianity created a structure of damnation to support the colonial structure of domination.

But it would be a mistake to regard the missionaries as being primarily motivated by a desire to consolidate colonialism. On the contrary, many missionaries were active in trying to get European governments to intervene partly out of a desire to create good conditions for the spread of the gospel in Africa. In the words of the American political scientist, James S. Coleman: 'Tropical Africa held a special attraction for the missionary. The heathen was his target, and of all human groups the Africans were believed to be the most heathen.'[3]

By the time of independence the missionaries had succeeded so well that Christianity itself may now be described primarily as an Afro-Western religion. Christian nations in the world, in the sense in which Christians are in control or at least are preponderant numerically, are either black or white. More than half of Black Africa consists of Christian nations in that sense. Then there are the Christian nations of the Caribbean, also preponderantly black, and the Christian nations of Western Europe, North America, and Latin America, all preponderantly white. Although Asia has millions of Christians, it is not a continent primarily controlled by Christians. Only in isolated cases are Christians politically dominant. The Philippines as a country stands out in this regard. On the whole it is Black Africa and the Western world that have been overwhelmingly influenced by Christianity to the extent of determining effective political power.

But while Christianity is an Afro-Western religion, Islam is an Afro-Asian religion. Virtually all Muslim nations are either in Africa or Asia. There are indeed Muslims in some parts of Europe, especially Eastern Europe; there are Muslims elsewhere as well. But the distribution of this religion is primarily bicontinental. The Islamic Summit Conference held in Lahore in Pakistan in February 1974 was, to all intents and purposes, an Afro-Asian affair, though its repercussions were potentially significant beyond those two continents.

If Christianity, then, had by the second half of the twentieth century become an Afro-Western religion, while Islam was an Afro-Asian religion, what the two religions had in common geographically was the African continent itself. Africa then became the connecting link in distribution between these two universal creeds. Africa itself has thus become a kind of religious melting pot. Christian, Islamic, and indigenous beliefs and values have sometimes competed and sometimes merged with each other to create a new African synthesis.

But because Christianity has been specially close to the civilizations of imperial Europe, its impact on the values and styles of Africans, even those who are not Christian by religion, has been considerable. Many men in Africa have acquired scruples that neither they nor their parents thought of in the past. And the scruples themselves are often conditioned either by Christian inhibitions or at any rate by Western preferences. A relative standardization of morality has taken place in the Afro-Western world, partly as a result of the impact of the West. New ways of looking at things have entered Africa, new perspectives, new intellectual horizons, new prejudices, new virtues, and new vices.

John Plamenatz, the Oxford political philosopher and historian, once observed that 'the vices of the strong acquire some of the prestige of strength'.[4] Political colonialism may in a sense be a thing of the past, but the moral and cultural consequences of colonialism are still very much part of the present.

But it was not simply the religion and morality of the West which helped to transform Africa culturally; it was also the languages of the West. The role of the English and French languages has been especially important in their transformation of Africa.

Just as almost all Christian nations are either white or black, almost all English-speaking nations are also either white or black. We do not mean countries where English is used for some purposes but not as the main official language for the nation's business, but countries such as Great Britain, the USA, Nigeria, Ghana, Jamaica, New Zealand, Australia, and Zambia where English is the dominant language politically, and where there does not seem to be any prospect of a change in the foreseeable future.

This is fundamentally different from situations like that of Tanzania and India, where an indigenous language is on the way to becoming potentially the senior partner in the business of communication at the highest political level. Hindi in India, while facing considerable difficulties in asserting itself as intended by the Indian Constitution in 1947, has nevertheless been growing in influence partly at the expense of English. Similarly, Swahili in Tanzania has also been growing in influence at the highest level of politics partly at the expense of English. But in the majority of the former British colonies in Africa and the Caribbean, the future of the English language is well and truly safe. In fact, many of those countries are on their way towards producing a sizeable section of the population which speaks English at least as fluently as any indigenous language. The world is on the verge of witnessing the growth of Afro-Saxons, a population of people who are black but who speak English as their native tongue, to stand alongside the traditional Anglo-Saxon.[5] This categorization of the English language as being primarily a language of white and black native speakers is to some extent an exaggeration, but there is enough truth in it to make it a meaningful generalization.

As for the French language, the majority of individuals who speak it are in Europe; but the majority of states that have adopted it as their official language are in Africa. It is true that there are many speakers of French in the Americas, especially Quebec, and in parts of Asia, especially Indo-China. But Africa has more than fifteen countries that have adopted the French language as their official language. That means that within the United Nations most of the states that have adopted French as their own language are black states. But most speakers of the language as individuals are still in the European continent itself, concentrated in France, but also in Switzerland and Belgium. French is also spoken as a secondary language all over the rest of the European continent.

Within Africa, French-speaking states are either former French colonies or former Belgian colonies. English-speaking states are almost entirely former British colonies. But Liberia on the west coast and, in a partial sense, Ethiopia, are English-speaking states that do not have a prior British affiliation. Liberia was colonized by imported black Americans; Ethiopia has been promoting the study of English alongside Amharic as a result of a special relationship with the USA, rather than Britain. The emergence of Ethiopia as the capital of pan-Africanism, as a result of being the headquarters of the Organization of African Unity and the United Nations Economic Commission for Africa, also helped to tilt the balance in favour of one of the major European languages of Africa since it was necessary for pan-Africanism. Ethiopia moved towards the English language.

European languages became so important to the Africans that they defined their own identities partly by reference to those languages. Africans began to describe each other in terms of being either Francophone or English-speaking Africans. The continent itself was thought of in terms of French-speaking states, English-speaking states, and Arabic-speaking states. None of the three languages was indigenous, but at least Arabic was the language of the majority of the people who lived in the countries that were called Arabic-speaking states. But English and French were languages of a minority of westernized Africans, in power in those states, and accepted widely by the general population as being in some sense *special* simply as a result of their competence in the European languages concerned. In other words, the prestige of English and French even among peasant Africans who did not speak those languages had become so great that those who acquired the relevant linguistic skills also acquired special political and economic privileges. The whole structure of power in many black African countries has been based on those who had learned either the literary skills or the military technology of the West.

Under civilian rule in African countries it is usually those who have excelled in, or at any rate been initiated in, the verbal and literary skills of European civilization that have acquired power and influence. These have been the Nkrumahs, the Mboyas, the Nyereres, the Senghors, the Obotes of the first wave of African leadership after independence.

The military rulers, on the other hand, acquired their power not through Western linguistic and literary skills but through the control of Western military technology in their own societies. Some facilitated their military coups by being in command of special battalions, well equipped with Western weapons and with the necessary skills for using those weapons. In this kind of situation, the choice of rulers in post-colonial Africa is directly dependent on competence in either Europe's heritage of words or Europe's heritage of weapons. These factors make the cultural domain omnipresent in Africa's political experience this century.

Science and Control

The very link which later established itself between political power and military technology among African soldiers was present at the very beginning when imperialism established control in the African continent. How did Europe manage to subjugate so much of the rest of the world? What difference had occurred between Europeans and other peoples to give Europeans the capacity to subject so much of the rest of the planet to European power? A fundamental factor was Europe's technological breakthrough.

Two branches of technology were particularly important in giving Europe the necessary superiority. One was the technology of mobility; the other, the technology of violence. The technology of mobility gave Europeans the type of expertise which enabled them to establish relative naval supremacy, a capacity to traverse the oceans, and later a capacity to make precise calculations about overland travel and exploration. Both the ocean explorers and the land explorers within Africa coming from Europe were substantially aided by a technology of mobility. This technology ranged from superior ships to superior maps and compasses. The wheel, the sail, the compass, and the map provided the foundations, soon to be improved and made more sophisticated by European ingenuity and innovation. By the beginning of the twentieth century Europeans were laying down railway lines, and bringing the steam engine into the hinterland of the African continent. By the second half of the twentieth century they had not only perfected the technology of flying airplanes, but were about to engage in space exploration itself. The technology of European mobility, later carried further by Europe's extensions in the Americas, was a critical variable in the establishment of Western hegemony in the world.

The other relevant technology was the technology of violence. Basically this concerned the invention and improvement of weapons of destruction, from the handgun to the machine gun, from the cannon ball to tanks and B-52s.

In the earlier days of annexation, Europe's technology of violence was not as sophisticated as it was later to become under American and Russian military capabilities. But European technology in this domain in the eighteenth and nineteenth centuries was already way ahead of anything in the African continent. The brave African warriors with their bows and arrows, or with their spears, soon discovered the massively conclusive argument of gunfire.

We discussed earlier the mutual reinforcement between a structure of domination and a structure of damnation. What we should also note here is the accompanying system of terror—the terror of gunfire and the terror of hell-fire. The terror of gunfire lay in the superior military technology which Western man brought with him as an argument in the quest for allegiance and annexation in the African continent. Gunfire was demonstrated to those as yet unconvinced of their own vulnerability. Some bought guns of their own, especially in West Africa, and attempted to confront the European invader with his own weapons. Other groups elsewhere relied on an antiquated military technology of spears against the devastation of the Maxim gun. Still others capitulated not because they themselves had suffered the humiliating destructive power of Europe's technology of violence, but because they had heard enough from neighbouring communities about this power to give up in despair beforehand.

The history of European colonization is full of instances of resistance on the part of Africans. It is not correct, as many have assumed, that Africa capitulated without struggle. On the contrary, all over the continent there were instances of brave resistance. But in the end the difference in this technology of violence, coupled with the difference in the technology of mobility, sealed the fate of African societies—and assured the triumphant power of European imperialism in the continent.[6]

In time the fear of hell-fire accompanied this dread of gunfire. The fear of hell-fire was in part a ritualization of terror. The use of supernatural symbols under European Christianity consolidated the readiness to submit which had been exacted by the new military technology. The God of Christianity was not really the God of the Old Testament full of revenge and capacity to use power. Nevertheless the control of the church in many African countries used the incentives of salvation and the disincentives of damnation. In the case of the Catholic Church—and African Catholics outnumbered African Protestants south of the Sahara—the threat of excommunication was an additional invocation of hell-fire as an accompaniment to gunfire. Many radical publications, especially those that were directly Marxist, were banned in missionary schools. The *Communist Manifesto* and *Das Kapital* were on the list of prohibited books, and the use of such literature in the colonial period was dangerous not only from a political point of view but also from a religious one. Once again the fear of religious damnation facilitated the process of political domination; once again the fear of hell-fire, as it was subtly fostered by religion, reinforced the fear of gunfire as induced by Europe's superior technology of violence.

The difference in technological capability between Europe and Africa in the modern period was due to a prior difference in scientific achievement. Technology after all is the application of the socially relevant aspects of science. There is surely no debate concerning Europe's scientific lead from the seventeenth century to the early decades of the twentieth century. And even in the twentieth century it has been Europe's prodigal son, the USA, that has kept the ultimate lead, though with some competition from European Russia and also from Japan.

The question of differing scientific capability has had intimate links with many of the myths of racism. There is little doubt that in the modern period the black man has been scientifically marginal, in the sense of being left in the outer periphery of the scientific and technological achievement. And racists in Africa and elsewhere had pointed to the black man's scientific marginality as evidence that the black man was genetically less well endowed with mental and intellectual capabilities.

One day when I was still at Makerere University in Uganda my secretary buzzed my telephone to announce a long-distance call from Durban in South Africa. 'Durban?' I asked in surprise, as I had no special connections there. When the call was put through it turned out to be an editor of a South African magazine. The editor wanted me to review a particular book. Considering the trouble he took to make a rather expensive long-distance call, I became curious about the whole assignment. The book was by a man called Barnett. The title of the book was *The Fault Black Man . . .*, derived from Shakespeare's *Julius Caesar*: 'The fault, dear Brutus, is not in our stars but in ourselves that we are underlings.' The South African editor said that the book had created a stir in Southern Africa, and he wanted me to write a rebuttal. The central assertion of the book was: 'The fault, black man, is not in your stars but in yourself that you are an underling.' The argument was that the black man had been ruled and dominated by others not because of bad luck but because of something inherent in himself. I agreed to write the rebutting review of the book.

The book itself did not pretend to be scholarly or even sophisticated, but the white man who had written it used the evidence of greater scholars than he could pretend to be. In part he used Arthur Jensen's article in the *Harvard Educational Review*, asserting that research among white and black American schoolchildren had indicated that blacks performed less well than whites intellectually for reasons which were partly genetic. Jensen's article had reactivated a long standing debate concerning the question of whether races differed genetically in intellectual competence.[7]

Barnett Potter linked the findings of Jensen's research to the tribute paid to the Jewish community by C. P. Snow, the British physicist and novelist. C. P. Snow had drawn attention to the remarkable achievements of the Jews in the sciences and the arts. A crude measure such as examining the names of the Nobel Prize winners would indicate that up to a quarter of those winners bore Jewish names. Why should a population of little more than fifty million Jewish people in the world produce one-quarter of the best scientific and scholarly performance in a world of approximately three thousand million people?

> Or is there something in the Jewish gene-pool which produces talent on quite a different scale from, say, the Anglo-Saxon gene-pool? I am prepared to believe that may be so. . . . One would like to know more about the Jewish gene-pools. In various places—certainly in Eastern Europe—it must have stayed pretty undiluted, or unaltered for hundreds of years.[8]

Lord Snow did not seem aware of the partial contradiction in his statement. The Jews who performed particularly impressively in recent times, and won Nobel Prizes, were not in fact primarily from Eastern Europe where Snow regarded the Jewish gene-pool to be particularly pure and 'unaltered for hundreds of years'. On the contrary, the best Jewish intellectual achievements in recent times have been overwhelmingly from Western Jews, in many ways the least pure in 'gene-pool' among all the Jews of the world. But whatever the partial contradiction in C. P. Snow's analysis, there is indeed a phenomenon to be explained in the Jewish intellectual achievement in Western history. Barnett Potter, as a white Gentile, used the Jewish intellectual edge as proof that blacks were genetically inferior. But he too fell short of the logic of his own position. If Jewish intellects in the Western world itself have performed disproportionately in relation to white Gentiles, are we also to conclude that white Gentiles are genetically inferior intellectually to their Jewish neighbours? Certainly Barnett Potter would regard that conclusion as too high a price to pay for the comfort of proving that the fate of the black man was not in his stars but in his genes.

But what could be the explanation both for the Jewish intellectual edge and for the black scientific marginality? Let us take the Jewish question first. A number of factors could be invoked to add up to an explanation. There is first the observation that some scholars have made concerning the composition of the original Jews who fled from Palestine two millennia ago. It has been argued that these were disproportionately intellectual as a class. Those who ended up in the Persian Empire became especially valued for their intellectual skills in the same manner in which many German Jews in the twentieth century became valued in top American universities.

This issue is also connected with the whole question of the relationship between professional specialization and intellectual performance. Partly because many alternative avenues of professional life were closed to Jews in Europe, the community began to specialize in commerce and later the liberal professions. The cumulative effect of specialization provided not a Darwinian natural selection, but a specialized cultural selection. Succeeding generations of Jewish intellectuals produced in turn children who were intellectually oriented. Specialization could provide the opportunity for the discovery of brilliance.

A related factor is the whole tradition of Jewish prophets and of rules which are not only observed but continually enunciated and often intellectualized. Jewish children grew up under the intellectual stimulation of the Talmudic tradition.

It might also be fortunate that Judaism does not demand celibacy of its rabbis. Had Jewish rabbis been expected to be celibate like Catholic priests, the Jewish intellectual contribution to world civilization might well have been significantly reduced. It has been estimated that many of the most impressive Jewish scholars have been sons or grandsons of rabbis. The tradition of the prophets has again helped to consolidate prior intellectual specialization. In each case cultural and environmental variables are enough to explain the Jewish intellectual edge without invoking the Jewish gene-pool.

With regard to black scientific marginality, there have been a number of different responses to the phenomenon. Among some black people, one response has been to *deny* that they have been scientifically marginal. Those who react in this way among black people then proceed to mention a number of famous black names in the intellectual history of the world. These would range from Alexander Pushkin, 'the father of Russian literature', to Alexandre Dumas, the French literary romantic. Both these had the blood of black people in their ancestry, and many black men elsewhere have taken pride in that.

The tendency to deny that there has been a black scientific marginality has been specially manifest among black Americans. It might well be that the precise nature of their humiliation from the slave days has created a resolve among their cultural nationalists to affirm black greatness in history.[9] This kind of response is not unknown among black Africans either. In Ghana while it was still under the presidency of Kwame Nkrumah a number of postcards were issued with paintings depicting major achievements that had taken place in Africa. These included a painting with figures in the attire of ancient Egypt, showing the first paper about to be manufactured. The caption was 'Ancient African History: Paper Was Originated in Africa'. Then there was a painting of 'Tyro, African Secretary to Cicero, [who] Originated Shorthand Writing in 63 B.C.'. There were also cards asserting how the science of chemistry originated in Africa, and how Africans taught the Greeks mathematics, and the alphabet. The Ghanaian postcards under Nkrumah were, in a way, in the tradition of black American cultural assertiveness, but transposed to the African continent.[10]

An alternative response to black scientific marginality is not only to affirm it but also to take pride in it. Black countries ruled by France produced a whole movement called Negritude, which revelled in the virtues of a non-technical civilization. In the words of the poet, Aimé Césaire:

> Hooray for those who never invented anything
> Who never explored anything
> Who never discovered anything!
> Hooray for joy, hooray for love
> Hooray for the pain of incarnate tears.
> My Negritude is no tower and no cathedral . . .[11]

Clearly this is a response to scientific marginality which is fundamentally different from the tendency to trace a black ancestry in the geneology of Robert Browning, and of Pushkin and Alexandre Dumas.[12]

Léopold Senghor, President of Senegal, is the leading exponent of Negritude in the African continent. He too has affirmed the non-technical nature of indigenous African civilizations, emphasizing intuition and emotive sensibilities as the main epistemological characteristic of that civilization. In the words of Senghor: 'Emotion is black . . . reason is Greek.'

The third type of response is neither to deny black scientific marginality nor to affirm it with romantic pride, but to explain it as rationally as possible. In this there is an acceptance that black people have been on the periphery of scientific advancements in the modern period, but this acceptance carries with it no special inferiority complex. It simply demands in turn a rational explanation of the phenomenon.

We noted that a number of factors together could go some way towards explaining the Jewish intellectual edge, but each of those factors taken on its own would be inadequate. Similarly, in attempting to understand black scientific marginality, a number of factors have to be examined together.

One factor is *spatial isolation*. Africa is at once the most central of the ancient continents physically and the most peripheral in terms of cultural interaction. We are in this case referring to the ancient continents of Europe, Asia, and Africa. But even if we included the New World, Africa still remains the most central continent in the physical sense. The equator divides Africa almost in half. Africa is also the only continent which is traversed evenly by both the Tropic of Cancer and the Tropic of Capricorn. In a physical sense, the continent is in the middle of the global scheme of things. But apart from the coastal areas, the interior of Africa had less interaction with external cultures than Europe and Asia experienced. Even interaction among African cultures themselves was considerably hampered by the absence in many societies of adequate means of travelling long distances. Many African societies lacked the wheel with which to make travelling wagons. Still others lacked the horse or comparable beast for long-distance travelling. The tsetse fly in large parts of the continent made the rearing of such animals difficult and sometimes impossible. The absence of both the wheel and the mobile beast of burden sentenced many African societies to spatial isolation.

A related consequence is *cultural autarchy*. Many African cultures found themselves, either by conviction or necessity, self-sufficient. There was inadequate stimulation from any but the most contiguous cultures. It is true that some African peoples travelled far. Both the Bantu and the Nilotes covered long distances in impressive migrations. These migrations did result in cultural interaction and important innovations. But migrations must be distinguished from the capacity to travel and trade with a distant country and still be able to return to an ancestral home. They are fundamentally different from situations where at least the ruling elite of countries travelled widely, and conducted diplomatic and trade relations, and sometimes scientific exchanges, across huge distances. Africa's limited capability for mobility continues to be a problem to the present day, but that is substantially because there was little prior development in the direction of increasing effective trade and cultural interaction among African peoples themselves. If science depends in part upon a readiness to question past assumptions, and upon the related capacity to innovate as well as to criticize, a people whose belief systems are too protected from competing values are a people partially isolated from scientific possibilities.

We have so far discussed spatial isolation and cultural isolation. The third factor to bear in mind is *temporal isolation*—the sense of being seriously cut off from important aspects of one's own past. In the absence of the written word in many African cultures, many tentative innovations or experiments of a previous era were not transmitted to the next generation. The trouble with an oral tradition is that it transmits mainly what is accepted and respected. It does not normally transmit heresies of the previous age. A single African individual in the nineteenth century who might have put across important new ideas among the Nuer of the Sudan, but whose ideas were rejected by the consensus of his own age, is unlikely to be remembered today. Oral tradition is a tradition of conformity, rather than heresy; a transmission of consensus rather than dissidence.

Imagine what would have happened to the ideas of Karl Marx if in the nineteenth century Europe was without the alphabet. If Karl Marx was simply propounding his ideas orally, from one platform to another, European oral tradition would have been insensitive to this revolutionary. After all, Karl Marx was not a particularly well-known figure in polite society in his own age. John Stuart Mill makes no reference to Marx in his own writings, betraying perhaps a total ignorance of Marx's contributions to the political economy of the nineteenth century. Marx had many revolutionary followers, especially in continental Europe, and he wrote interesting newspaper features for an American readership. In spite of that his fame for much of his own life was relatively modest. His fame by the second half of the twentieth century was greater than that of any other single figure in the nineteenth century. The fame that Karl Marx enjoys in the second half of the twentieth century, and the influence he has exerted on political, sociological, and economic thought in the twentieth century, would have been impossible had his ideas not been conserved by the written word and translated to a more receptive generation than his own.

The absence of the written word in large numbers of African societies was therefore bound to create a sense of isolation to some extent in a temporal sense, keeping one African century from another in terms of stimulation and interaction, suppressing innovative heresies, burying genius under the oblivion of the dominant consensus of a particular age.

In addition to the absence of literacy was the absence of numeracy. It was not simply the lack of the written word that delayed scientific flowering in Africa; it was also the lack of the written numeral. Jack Goody has drawn attention to the relationship between writing and mathematics, and the implications of the absence of both in some African societies. He notes that the development of Babylonian mathematics depended upon the prior development of a graphic system, though not necessarily an alphabetic one. And he refers to the short time he spent in 1970 revisiting the Lo-Dagaa of Northern Ghana, 'whose main contact with illiteracy began with the opening of a primary school in Birifu in 1949'. Goody proceeded to investigate their mathematical operations. He discovered that while boys who had no special school background were efficient in counting a large number of cowries (shell money), and often did this faster and more accurately than Goody could, they were ineffective at multiplication:

> The concept of multiplication was not entirely lacking; they did think of four piles of five cowries as equalling twenty. But they had no ready-made table in their minds (the 'table' being essentially a written aid to 'oral' arithmetic) by which they could calculate more complex sums. The contrast was even more true of subtraction and division; the former can be worked by oral means (though the literate would certainly take to pencil and paper for the more complex sums), the latter is basically a literate technique. The difference is not so much one of thought or mind as of the mechanics of communicative acts.[13]

The absence of mathematics at the more elaborate level was bound to hamper considerably black Africa's scientific development.

Another factor in black scientific marginality has been the kindness of nature in Africa. If necessity is the mother of invention, abundance is the mother of inertia. In much of tropical Africa nature, though sometimes cruel, was not so cruel as to deny the immediate necessities. Some communities lived quite easily from gathering fruit and other natural products, or from hunting. Others engaged in agriculture, sometimes doing damage to the soil in the absence of adequate safeguards against soil erosion. But since land itself was abundant, even this did not create crises of immediate day-to-day survival. In tropical Africa at any rate there were no equivalents of long seasons when almost nothing grows; there are few equivalents of prolonged land hunger. There were parts of West Africa where this was less true. The margin between the forests, the savannah, and the desert was not always smooth. But it is arguable that the tropics afforded sufficient natural abundance to delay at least that kind of innovation which comes from an immediate crisis of survival.

Then there was the impact of the slave trade, and later of imperialism, on Africa's capacity to innovate. The slave trade drained Africa of large numbers of its population. Those that reached the Americas and survived to be effective slaves, were often a fraction of those who were captured in the first instance for enslavement. The drastic depopulation of important parts of Africa was bound to have significant consequences on the continent's capacity to achieve important breakthroughs in the different branches of knowledge. Imperialism later, when Africa fell more directly under alien domination, once again delayed in at least some respects the capacity of Africa to attain new levels of scientific and technological initiatives.

But here the picture gets a little more complicated. It is possible to argue that while slavery did harm Africa's potential for scientific innovation, imperialism later on helped to create a new infrastructure for potential inventiveness. After all imperialism, while it was indeed a form of humiliating political bondage, nevertheless proceeded to reduce the spatial, cultural, and temporal isolation which had previously been part of Africa's scientific marginality. European imperialism, almost by definition, ended for some societies that isolation in space and culture which had previously been an element of their very being. New values, as well as new modes of travel and mobility, created new intellectual possibilities. The arrival of the written word and the numeral, again began to establish a foundation for a new African entry into the mainstream of scientific civilization. Imperialism could be interpreted to be in part a mitigation of the consequences of the slave trade, imperialism, by introducing new intellectual horizons, was inadvertently, and in spite of itself, laying the groundwork for a future intellectual liberation of the black man.

The final factor to be borne in mind in evaluating black scientific marginality is an exercise in humility – that is to say, that we might not know enough of the causes of intellectual flowering and maturation among human beings generally. It was Lévi-Strauss who reminded us about how recent in absolute terms was the history of manifest human genius. The history of mankind is much older than the history of the revelation of major human intellects. Lévi-Strauss argued:

> I see no reason why mankind should have waited until recent times to produce minds of the calibre of a Plato or an Einstein. Already over two or three hundred thousand years ago, there were probably men of a similar capacity, who were of course not applying their intelligence to the solution of the same problems as these more recent thinkers; instead they were probably more interested in kinship![14]

Even if we reduce the life of mankind from Lévi-Strauss's three hundred thousand to fifty thousand, the question he raises is still significant. Why out of the fifty thousand years of the existence of the human race do we have to look to the last four thousand years for major indications of intellectual and scientific genius?

The black man might also refer to the anomaly of masculine preponderance in intellectual and scientific genius. Why have the main giants in this field of human excellence been so overwhelmingly men? It is not true that women are intellectually inferior to men, yet the list of female inventors, female composers, female discoverers, female literary and cultural giants, is very modest against masculine achievement. If we are indeed convinced that the female of the species is not less intellectually endowed than the male, why has her manifest achievement been more limited? Perhaps Barnett Potter would once again assert: 'The fault, dear Eve, is not in your stars but in yourself that you are an underling!' Once again prejudice would disguise itself by claiming prior genetic superiority. Both the white racist and the male chauvinist could use as evidence the relatively modest scientific performance of both the black man and the white woman as evidence that they are genetically inferior. The conclusion is indeed a prejudice.

Power and Political Control

Given economic skills, the technology of mobility, and military capability, the white man was able to take advantage of the scientific marginality of the black man, and subjugate him. In its most immediate form, colonialism was political control. Economic, military, and mobile power was invoked to establish hegemony in Africa. The motives for the colonization of Africa were mixed. They included the pursuit of economic profit, the quest for political advantage against other European powers, the arrogance of commitment to 'civilize' the natives, the missionary zeal to Christianize black Africa, and the humanitarian resolution to end the Arab slave trade and African domestic slavery within the continent. The different European powers adopted different strategies of political control once colonization had taken place. At least theoretically, British colonial policies came to be profoundly influenced by the doctrine of indirect rule, while French colonial policies fluctuated under the inspiration of doctrines of assimilation and integration.

The doctrine of indirect rule was defined by its greatest exponent, Lord Lugard, in the following terms:

> . . . rule through the Native Chiefs, who are regarded as an integral part of the machinery of Government, with well-defined powers and functions recognized by Government and by law, and not dependent on the caprice of an Executive Officer . . . there are not two sets of rulers—British and Native—working either separately or in cooperation, but a single Government in which the Native Chiefs have well-defined duties and an acknowledged status equally with the British officials. Their duties should never conflict, and should overlap as little as possible; . . . the Chief himself must understand that he has no right to his place and power unless he renders his proper services to the State.[15]

This doctrine had wider implications than merely the utilization of 'Native Chiefs'. The doctrine appealed to the British partly because they are themselves a pragmatic nation, often suspicious of doctrinaire attitudes, and prepared to make allowances for cultural differences among peoples. British colonial policy was to some extent Burkean, often based on the supposition that people should be ruled according to principles they understood. This had consequences for colonial policies beyond the political institutions. It concerned also language policies pursued in the colonies, media of instruction for children in schools, and the range of customs to be respected. In reality British toleration of African cultures was far from complete. Major areas of Africa's cultural experience were deliberately suppressed. And when the missionaries were given a free hand in some sectors of African education, even certain African dances were rigidly discouraged.

Nevertheless, the British were on balance more tolerant of African culture than the French. French assimilationist policy, in those instances where it was genuinely applied, started not only from the premise of the absolute superiority of French culture, but also from the premise that very little in African cultures deserved to be preserved. The French paid far less attention than the British to the study and systematization of African languages. Their use of African languages as media of instruction in African schools, at least in the lower grades, was far less than the British. French policies on chiefs were more mixed. It is arguable that in some French colonies indigenous administrative institutions survived more effectively than in some British colonies. This would even be true of that paradigm of French assimilation, Senegal, where some administrative and religious institutions retained a life at least as real as any indigenous institutions surviving in a country such as Kenya.

But in spite of the narrowness of differences between the realities of French assimilation and the realities of British indirect rule, a residual significant difference remained. The British were more racially arrogant than the French; the French were more culturally arrogant than the British. The British organized elaborate ways of keeping black and white separate as far as possible in the colonies, with segregated hotels, parliamentary representation, schools, residential areas, and public lavatories. In addition the British disapproved of mixed marriages more strongly than the French, and treated the children of mixed marriages with some distaste. The French were not entirely innocent on the racial front. On the contrary, French racism in the colonies has often been underestimated. Residential segregation was far from unusual, and contemptuous treatment of black people was common. Nevertheless, it would be true to say that a black man who became assimilated into French culture had easier access to white French circles in the colonies than an Anglicized African had to the circles of white settlers in places such as Kenya, colonial Zambia, and Rhodesia. The French were more culturally arrogant than the British in their entire approach to colonial education, in their militant promotion of the French language, and in their persistent conviction that not much in the indigenous cultures of their subject peoples deserved to be protected, let alone developed and enhanced.

The two most successful cases of British indirect rule in Africa were Nigeria and Uganda. The doctrine was not uniformly applied to all the different sub-regions of these two countries. The minimalist concept of indirect rule was the utilization of traditional *political* institutions as specific instruments of administration. Lugard exercised power in both Uganda and Nigeria, and developed the theory of indirect rule in relation to both countries. The Buganda Kingdom lent itself particularly well to this administrative strategy. At that time the Buganda Kingdom was often equated with Uganda as a whole. In regard to political control, Lugard said: 'The object to be aimed at in the administration of this country is rule through its own executive government.'[16] And in the case of Northern Nigeria it was, in Lugard's estimation, 'desirable to retain the native authority and work through and by the native emirs'.[17]

In both instances Lugard was making recommendations about the nature of the administrative machinery. But could an administrative machinery remain traditional while the rest of the society's culture was changing? This was the dilemma of indirect rule. And Lugard responded with a deep suspicion of trends to 'Westernize the natives'. A major instrument of acculturation were the European languages themselves. Lugard was worried about the implications of the English language for Africa and for his ideal of indirect rule. He felt that 'the premature teaching of English . . . inevitably leads to utter disrespect for . . . native ideals . . . and to a denationalized and disorganized population.'[18]

The newly educated Africans were in turn profoundly suspicious of indirect rule. They disagreed with the idea of preserving and strengthening indigenous chieftaincies. To this grievance against his principles of indirect rule, Lugard retorted:

> It is inevitable that, in spite of much high-sounding talk in the local press, they could not be popular with the semi-educated portion of the population, for the man who has but a partial education considers himself superior to the illiterate chief and resents his authority.[19]

It is true that for a while many educated Africans were more contemptuous of African culture than many British administrators in the colonies. The consequences of cultural and intellectual dependency had created in the newly Westernized African a sense of self-hate. Defenders of some local customs and rituals were often among British administrators rather than the new African intellectuals. In some cases it was not until the later days of African cultural nationalism that indigenous institutions and customs attained a new respectability. A distinguished product of the French assimilationist policy, President Leopold Senghor of Senegal, once congratulated Britain on her refusal to pursue the same policy of assimilation as the French had attempted. In a lecture delivered at the University of Oxford, Senghor said:

> Great Britain recognized the *Negro-African personality,* and considered it *digna amari*, worthy of fostering—a fact to which the United Kingdom had for a long time given expression through its policy of *indirect government*.[20]

But there is no doubt that the policy had difficult consequences after independence. The survival of effective traditional authorities in both Uganda and Nigeria were contributory factors towards severe political tension. By the time of independence each of these two countries had not only a dual economy but also a dual polity. A dual economy is the coexistence of subsistence agriculture with a money economy—to some extent, the parallel existence of traditional and modern sectors. We shall return to this later in the chapter. Dual polity is the coexistence of a traditional system of government with a modern or alien system superimposed.

The Kingdom of Buganda was to some extent a traditional polity. The King of Buganda, the Kabaka, occupied a legitimate and vigorous institution within the newly independent Uganda. He had his own ministers, and his own little parliament, the Lukiiko. Some of the structure of his government owed a good deal to ideas which came with the British, but the structure was certainly infused by what David E. Apter called 'neo-traditionalism'. According to Apter, the ideology of neo-traditionalism 'needs to embody the moral prescriptions of the past and apply them to modern conditions. The ideology is normally highly symbolic yet sufficiently adaptable to allow innovation to be traditionalized and thereby sanctified.'[21] The independence constitution of 1962 gave Buganda a neo-federal status within Uganda, with even a special police force for the Kabaka's government, and some powers of taxation. Concurrently with this neo-traditional kingdom was the whole paraphernalia of a modern state, with a parliament based on British Westminster procedures, a modern judicial system, a modern bureaucracy. The country had indeed inherited a dual polity.

But the relationship between the traditional and the modern was uneasy in Uganda. Although the Kabaka of Buganda also became the President of Uganda, the tensions between the traditional ruler and his more radical prime minister finally resulted in the crisis of 1966 when Prime Minister Obote's troops attacked the Kabaka's palace, the Kabaka himself fled the country and went to England, and before long the traditional institutions were abolished in Uganda.

In Nigeria, the dual polity was at its most vigorous in the North, with the Islamic institutions of the Hausa-Fulani. These institutions were not directly responsible for the events which led to the Nigerian civil war, but they did provide some of the background to the ethnic tensions which culminated in the civil war.

British indirect rule was, of course, the central factor behind the emergence of the dual polity in both independent Uganda and independent Nigeria. The dual polity in Nigeria, though drastically modified, is still part of the total political reality. But in Uganda it did come truly to an end, at least for a while, in the last years of the rule of Milton Obote. What is not clear is whether some of the consequences of military government in Uganda, in so far as they might result in giving new vigour to old traditions, might not resurrect certain elements of dualism in Uganda's political system.

But although some of the consequences of British rule were more divisive internally in Africa after independence than the consequences of French rule, the British tried harder to maintain larger African nations on attainment of independence than the French did. While the French let their old colonial federations of West Africa and Central Africa disintegrate on the eve of independence, the British resisted Buganda's bid to secede in 1960, and supported the federal government of Nigeria to prevent Biafra's secession from 1967 to 1970.

With the French, it was not during the colonial period that they divided in order to rule. For as long as they exercised colonial hegemony, they maintained large administrative units and sought to integrate this with a broader imperial political system. It was as they were about to withdraw from direct colonial control in Africa that the French permitted the forces of division within Africa to prevail, and allowed the emergence of a multiplicity of relatively small African countries. The French were guilty of helping to divide in order to continue neo-colonial control after independence, though they consolidated large sizes before independence.

The British record was more evenly unifying. The British tried hard to save Nigeria, just as they had once tried hard to save the Central African Federation of Rhodesia and Nyasaland. And in East Africa on the eve of independence the British tried to encourage discreetly greater unification between Kenya, Uganda, and Tanzania. Also, during the colonial period the British, like the French, brought together diverse traditional communities into new national entities.

But indirect control of both former French and former British Africa after independence has become increasingly difficult. The old strategy of de Gaulle to exercise hegemony in black Africa is beginning to crumble. The British Commonwealth has weakened. The big question in 1970 in Africa was less and less the direct political manipulation by Europe, and more and more concerned with the quest for new economic relationships between European powers and their former colonies. It is to this economic dimension that we turn now.

The Political Economy of Dependency

The economic dimension in Africa's relations with Western Europe is in many respects the oldest. Certainly the slave trade itself was a major economic adventure, with considerable consequences for Africa, Europe, and the Americas. Millions of Africans were exported, and many of them died on the way to the New World. At about the same time firearms came into Africa from the Western world, and played a paradoxical part. Firearms were used in the ominous enterprise of obtaining human merchandise, and then sending these men and women to the foreign slave-traders. Firearms also played a part in creating larger political entities in West Africa, and started the process of nation building and state-formation before European colonialism. An interaction between economics and politics was already under way during the gloomy period of trade in implements of destruction and human merchandise.

As we shall indicate later, in the chapter on Africa and the Middle East, important changes in the technology of production in the Western world led eventually to the redundancy of slave labour. Technological change in the Western world gradually facilitated and strengthened humane objections to slavery and the slave trade.

But technological change also made other raw materials of Africa more attractive to Western consumers. On the one hand, the modernization of economic techniques rescued Black Africa from slave raiders, as these lost their markets in the newly developing Europe and later the Americas. On the other hand, the industrial revolution itself which was under way in Europe made Europeans more conscious than ever of the importance of sources of raw materials for their new industries, and of potential markets for their new products. While technology helped to end slavery and the slave trade, it also helped to prepare the ground for European imperialism as an alternative strategy.

Here we must distinguish between economic imperialism and the economics of imperialism. Economic imperialism is the exercise of power through economic means, and usually for economic ends. For quite a while China before the Communist revolution was a victim of economic imperialism, as major Western powers imposed on China a variety of conditions to safeguard Western economic interests, and yet no Western power actually annexed China in the political sense of making it part of its territorial dominion. Iran in the nineteenth century was also a victim of European economic imperialism, as major European powers, including Czarist Russia, competed for control and for the imposition of special conditions to safeguard external economic interests. The principle of extra-territoriality, virtually making European traders exempt from Iranian laws, was in turn also imperialistic in this sense.

The economics of imperialism include the costs and benefits of territorial annexation itself, and the economic motives of building empires. Both the economic causes and consequences of territorial annexation have to be included in any comprehensive survey of the economics of the phenomenon at large. It was Cecil Rhodes, the arch imperialist from Britain operating in Africa, who said in 1895:

> In order to save the forty million inhabitants of the United Kingdom from bloody civil war, we colonial statesmen must acquire new lands to settle surplus population, to provide new markets for the goods produced by them in the factories and mines. The Empire, as I have always said, is a bread and butter question. If you want to avoid civil war, you must become imperialists.[22]

In the ideas of Lenin, and in Marxist thought generally since Lenin, 'imperialism' has had a special meaning which to some extent blurs the distinction between economic imperialism and the economics of colonial annexation. Imperialism in Leninist terms does not mean merely annexation of territory, or the use of economic means of control. The term includes monopolies in the metropolitan countries, the domination of financiers, as well as more narrowly defined colonial strategies. Lenin himself said: 'If it were necessary to give the briefest possible definition of imperialism, we should have to say that imperialism is the monopoly stage of capitalism.'[23] In Leninist terms an essential feature of imperialism is the 'scramble' – rivalry between a number of great powers in the striving for hegemony. This competition is such a vital part of capitalism that when monopoly characterizes the domestic economy of a major capitalist power, finance capital goes out to compete with other nations in lands beyond the sea. So keen was Lenin on retaining competition in his theory of capitalism that he took Kautsky to task for suggesting the possibility of an 'ultra-imperialism' – a *monopoly* of colonial possessions and overseas areas for investment.

Meanwhile within African domestic societies themselves, prior to European annexation, certain economic activity was of course taking place. Land was cultivated, and in some cases markets were growing, and forms of economic exchange were beginning to mature. In West Africa especially the experience of economic exchange came early, and moved rapidly towards a significant scale of operation. Kingdoms grew up, and trade across the Sahara operated down the centuries.

Women were economic agents quite early in a number of African societies. Certainly the role of women in agriculture as they cultivated the land has been ancestral, and women later developed marketing capabilities, and in some societies moved decisively into some of the central areas of entrepreneurship. It is arguable that in these societies women have been effective economic agents and activists for much longer than women in Western societies. The participation of African women in important areas of production made them further ahead in this domain as compared with their European and Arab sisters.

Even after the suffragette movement in Europe and North America, it continued to be true that in the economic domain African women were more productive than Western women. What the suffragette movement in the West inaugurated was greater *political* participation by Western women. Certainly in the twentieth century Western women have been more active in politics than African women, but still less active in their respective economies. The proportion of agricultural and industrial work carried out by Western women in relation to their men has been much smaller than the proportion of agricultural and marketing work done by African women in relation to their own men.

Following the introduction of colonialism, and the rise of urban economies, a new division of labour sometimes occurred in black Africa as between men and women. In a number of African societies, especially in Eastern and Southern Africa, there developed a partnership between female peasants and male proletarians. The women in the kinship groups remained on the land, cultivating either for subsistence or for marketing, while their men went to look for wage labour in the mines or the cities. Large numbers of men migrated hundreds of miles seeking jobs as wage-earners, often leaving their women behind as rural producers for the family. European pass laws in Southern Africa accentuated the trend towards creating a peasant class and a male proletariat. South Africa and Rhodesia had regulations which discouraged men from bringing their wives to the cities. And in any case since wage labour for women was more difficult to find, except in domestic jobs, women who did follow their husbands to the cities often ceased to be economically productive. They had to rely on their husbands' earnings for the upkeep of the family, while the plot of land at home passed on to other kinsmen. Considerations such as these have in many cases served as disincentives in the migration of women to the cities in large numbers. And the rural-urban continuum, in the sense of a residual link between migrant labourers in the cities and their rural origins, is to some extent a continuum between an emerging male proletarian class and a traditional female peasant class.

European class categories such as peasant and proletariat have so often been used without regard to the differences between patterns of division of labour between African and European societies. Although women were sometimes exploited as factory labour during the earlier years of the industrial revolution in Europe, this was regarded as enough of an anomaly that before long the women's share of that revolution was reduced drastically except in some specialized factories with 'softer' work. And on the land women more often dealt with milking cows and tending the fowls, than handling the plough or the hoe. On balance, the economization of women in the West has been slower than their politicization; while in Africa it has been the politicization of women which has lagged behind their economic activism.

As for broad national economies after independence, the domestic tensions for a while were between greater state intervention in the economy, sometimes described as socialism, and the promotion of private enterprise as an alternative strategy. Countries such as Kenya and the Ivory Coast embarked on policies to foster private enterprise and create indigenous entrepreneurship; while countries such as Tanzania and Guinea preferred to discourage individual private initiative and the profit motive and to promote public enterprise instead.

Even within these ideological categories there are important variations. Kenya is not only committed to maintaining a private enterprise system but also to a policy of rapid Africanization. For the Kenyan authorities it is not enough that there should be investment; it is also fundamental that the role of local African entrepreneurs should rapidly expand in the economy. For the Ivory Coast, on the other hand, the maintenance of a private enterprise system seems more important than its Africanization. Links with France in the economic domain continue to be substantially more intimate than Kenya's economic links with Britain. And the power of French business enterprises and businessmen in Abidjan seems clearer and more blunt than the power of British commercial interests and personnel in Nairobi. There seems to be more economic nationalism in the ruling African circles of Kenya than has been evident within the ruling Ivorian élite. As for regional economic co-operation, both Kenya and the Ivory Coast have so far been pivotal, but some changes are under way. Kenya has been in many senses the heartland of the East African community. The country was economically the most developed, and tended to attract further development. The processes of industrialization and commercialization in East Africa felt the pull of Kenya as the heartland. Nairobi became not only the political capital of Kenya but also the commercial, industrial, and financial capital of East Africa as a whole. But this pivotal role played by Kenya inevitably caused tensions among the partner states, Tanzania and Uganda. These tensions are still there, nor has full parity been established among the partner states, although some progress has been made towards enhancing the roles of Uganda and Tanzania in the economic and administrative processes of the East African community.

In West Africa the Ivory Coast has also often played a leading role in movements of regional integration, as indicated in Chapter 3. But French-speaking Africa is also experiencing the tensions of economic inequality within the region, and there is a certain groping for alternative arrangements. In the course of 1972 the Organization of African and Malagasy States (OCAM) underwent its crisis of malintegration. Zaire dramatically withdrew just before the eighth summit meeting of the organization scheduled at Lomé in April 1972. Later the People's Republic of the Congo also withdrew, and the whole organization went into a deep reappraisal of the reason for its existence.

In the course of 1973 two parallel movements seeking to create a West African Common Market got under way. The French-speaking countries wanted to create a West African community limited for the time being to those countries that spoke French, but with the possibility of encouraging English-speaking African countries to join. Nigeria wanted both linguistic groups of countries to start together and discuss what kind of community they were going to create, instead of initiating a community of French speakers and then encouraging others to join a club whose rules had already been determined. The Nigerian approach was to give as many states as possible the opportunity to work out the rules of the community jointly. Under the Francophone proposal Nigeria would not be involved in determining the constitution of the new West African Common Market, but would be eligible to apply for admission once that Common Market was consolidated. In March 1974 the French-speaking countries met in Ouagadougou to discuss the next moves. Nigeria meanwhile had established a special understanding with Togo to recommend the alternative approach of jointly negotiating the constitution of the West African Common Market from the start. The tensions between these two approaches illustrated the consequences of the traditions of different colonial powers, continuing to divide African states from each other, while at the same time uniting many African tribes.

Conclusion

Although Africa's relations with the Middle East are in many respects of longer standing than her relations with Western Europe, the massive impact of the transatlantic slave trade, and later of European colonialism generally, exerted on Africa's destiny a disproportionate influence. Western Europe became, at least politically and economically, closer than the Middle East to much of Africa in spite of the more recent association. European science and technology, combined with European political control, also resulted in the hegemonic power of European civilization in Africa. Black scientific marginality in the modern period made the black peoples particularly vulnerable to Europe's pre-eminence in technological capability, and prepared the ground for the subjugation of millions of Africans.

European hegemony since political independence was granted to Africa has persisted, especially in the fields of technology, economic arrangements, and cultural sway. The dialectic between African dependency and Africa's new assertive ambitions is at its most intimate in Africa's relations with Western Europe. The French concept of 'Eurafrica', implying the conversion of Africa and Europe as one intimately related bi-continental system, continues to cast a subtle but powerful spell on the imaginations of millions of formerly colonized black peoples.

References and notes

1. See Montague Slater, *The Trial of Jomo Kenyatta* (Mercury Books, 1955), 1965 edn., p. 76.
2. See *Uganda Argus* (Kampala), 5 September 1966, p. 3.

3. James S. Coleman, 'The Politics of sub-Saharan Africa', in Almond and Coleman, *The Politics of the Developing Areas* (Princeton, N.J.: Princeton University Press, 1960), p. 278.
4. John Plamenatz, *On Alien Rule and Self-Government* (Longman, 1960).
5. Consult Ali A. Mazrui, *The Political Sociology of the English Language: An African Perspective* (The Hague: Mouton Publishers, 1975).
6. For some of the literature on African primary resistance to colonial rule, consult T. O. Ranger, 'African reactions to the imposition of colonial rule in East and Central Africa', in L. H. Gann and Peter Duignan, *The History and Politics of Colonialism, 1870-1914,* Vol. 1 (Cambridge University Press, 1969), pp. 293-324; Michael Crowder, *West African Resistance: Military Response to Colonial Occupation* (Hutchinson, 1971); Robert I. Rotberg and Ali A. Mazrui, eds, *Protest and Power in Black Africa* (New York: Oxford University Press, 1970); and T. O. Ranger, 'Connection between "primary resistance" movements and modern mass nationalism in East and Central Africa', Parts I and II, *Journal of African History,* **IX**, 3 (1968), 437-53, 631-41.
7. Arthur R. Jensen, 'How much can we boost I.Q. and scholastic achievement?', *Harvard Educational Review,* 39 (winter 1969), pp. 1-123. See also the subsequent debate with J. S. Kagan, M. Hunt, J. F. Crow, Carl Bereiter, D. Elkind, Lee J. Cronback, W. F. Brazziel, and others, *Harvard Educational Review,* 39 (spring 1969) pp. 273-355 and 39 (summer 1969) pp. 449-631. Similar debates have since occurred in the USA in response to the racist views of Nobel Prize winner, W. Shockley of Stanford University in California.
8. *New York Times,* 1 April 1969.
9. Consult, for example, J. A. Rogers, *World's Great Men of Color,* Vols. 1 and 2 (1946; New York: Collier Books, 1972).
10. For information about the postcards produced in Nkrumah's Ghana, I am indebted to Mrs Simon Ottenberg, who later entrusted to my care her only set of those cards.
11. Aimé Césaire, *Return to My Native Land* (1939).
12. These issues are discussed in a related context in Ali A. Mazrui, *World Culture and the Black Experience* (Washington, Seattle: University of Washington Press, 1974).
13. Jack Goody, 'Evolution and communication: the domestication of the savage mind', *British Journal of Sociology* **XXIV** (March 1973), 7.
14. C. Lévi-Strauss, 'The concept of primitiveness', in R. B. Lee and I. de Vore, eds, *Man the Hunter* (Chicago: Aldine, 1968), p. 351.
15. Marjorie Perham, *Lugard,* Vol. II, *The Years of Authority* (Collins, 1960), p. 141.
16. Lugard, Lord, *The Rise of Our East African Empire: Early Efforts in Nyasaland and Uganda,* Vol. II (F. Cass, 1968), p. 649.
17. Marjorie Perham, op. cit., p. 140.
18. Lugard, Lord, *Annual Reports,* p. 646.
19. This quotation from Lugard's *Political Memoranda* is cited by A. H. M. Kirk-Green in *The Principles of Native Administration in Nigeria* (Oxford University Press, 1965), p. 89.
20. Léopold Senghor, 'Negritude and African socialism', lecture delivered at St Antony's College, Oxford, 26 October 1961, and published in St Antony's papers, *African Affairs,* No. II, ed. Kenneth Kirkwood (Chatto & Windus, 1963), p. 10.
21. David E. Apter, *The Political Kingdom in Uganda* (Princeton, N.J.: Princeton University Press, 1960), pp. 26-7.
22. Cited with relish by V. I. Lenin, *Imperialism: the Highest Stage of Capitalism* (New York: International Publishers, 1939).
23. Ibid.

CHAPTER 6
Africa & Asia

Although our focus in this chapter is on the modern period, Africa's relations with Asia go back many centuries. There is evidence of interaction with lands as distant as China and Indonesia. In many ways Africa's relations with the Middle East have been particularly intimate even if we exclude North Africa. The interaction between these two areas has been in a variety of fields, ranging from religion to architecture, from language to food. The Persians, the Turks, as well as the Arabs, have featured in this historical intercourse. We shall return to the Middle East more fully in the next chapter. Here we focus more on Africa's relations with the three giants of Asia—India, China and Japan—and trace these within the wider context of Afro-Asianism generally.

Until this century, India's relations with Africa were mainly cultural and economic. There was very little political interaction. The economic and cultural contacts antedated the establishment of European rule either in Africa or in India. There was trade from very early times between India and the eastern seaboard of Africa, some of it through intermediaries from the Persian or Arabian Gulf. Spices, crockery, hides and skins, dress material, bangles and beads, pots, and animals, were among the commodities which featured in the early trade between Africa, India and the Gulf.

India's cultural influence on the eastern seaboard of Africa also extended to food and music. To the present day the food culture of places like Zanzibar, Lamu, Dodoma, and even Dar es Salaam and Mombasa, in spite of their broader cultural mix, still betrays some significant Indian influence. Some of the spices used, and even occasionally the names of particular dishes, indicate a cultural convergence between Eastern Africa and other shores of the Indian Ocean. No doubt on those other shores in turn there are important cultural influences coming from Eastern Africa. Perhaps what we have on these coastlines is something which might be called the civilization of the Indian Ocean, manifesting points of historical and cultural contact in music, food, architecture, language, and the realm of ideas.

But it is in the twentieth century that we have seen, at least for a while, the full flowering of *political interaction* between India and Africa as a whole. In the modern period political interaction is not necessarily determined by geographical nearness. In the past, the nearer the different cultures were in physical distance the more likely they were to influence each other. But by the 1920s, and even earlier, it was possible for West Africans to be inspired by the Indian Nationalist Movement decades before East Africans were fully aware of the broader international significance of anti-colonialism in India. In East Africa it was more the white settlers than the black nationalists who sensed the wider imperial importance of figures like Gandhi and Nehru. But on the west coast of the continent the example of the Indian Congress Party had already inspired a number of educated West Africans to establish in 1920 the West African Congress, following a conference in Accra called by Caseley Hayford, the distinguished Gold Coast barrister and a founding father of Ghanaian nationalism.

For a while the most admired aspect of the Indian Nationalist Movement was its apparent success in unifying diverse groups. In 1920 the *Lagos Weekly Record*, a pioneer nationalist paper in Nigeria, made the following observations:

> West Africans have discovered today what the Indians . . . discovered 35 years ago, that placed as they were under the controlling influence of the foreign power, it was essential to their well-being that they should make a common cause and develop national unity.[1]

Other nationalist organs and leaders in West Africa, from Chief H. O. Davies and Chief Obafemi Awolowo of Nigeria to Dr Kwame Nkrumah of the Gold Coast, affirmed their admiration of the anti-colonial movement in India and drew inspiration from that example.

Two men in India acquired special significance in time. The first one was Mahatma Gandhi, who greatly influenced Africa's political strategies before independence. The other Indian figure was Pandit Jawaharlal Nehru, who came to influence African diplomatic strategies after independence. Gandhi inspired a number of Africans to adopt certain tactics as a method of disengaging from colonial rule; while Nehru came to inspire a strategy for disengaging from the cold war after independence.

Gandhi and Africa

Gandhi's impact came as a result of his ideas of non-violence and passive resistance. Quite early Gandhi himself had seen non-violence as a method which could be as well suited to the black man as to the Indian. He regarded it as promising for both black Americans and Africans. In 1924 Gandhi said that if the black people 'caught the spirit of the Indian movement, their progress must be rapid'.[2] By 1936

Gandhi was wondering whether black people, since they were in some ways the most humiliated of all peoples, might not be the best bearers of the banner of passive resistance. To use Gandhi's own words: 'It may be through the Negroes that the unadulterated message of non-violence will be delivered to the world.'[3]

Although this belief was not entirely vindicated by history, it was partially fulfilled. A significant number of black people both in Africa and the USA were inspired by Gandhian methods of fighting for racial dignity. In the late 1940s Kwame Nkrumah was already recommending to his people in the Gold Coast (now Ghana) a policy of 'positive action'—'the weapons were legitimate political agitation, newspaper and educational campaigns, and, as a last resort, the constitutional application of strikes, boycotts, and non-co-operation based on the principle of absolute non-violence, as used by Gandhi in India'.[4] Gandhi himself had first tried some of his tactics in South Africa while he lived there, and Nkrumah paid tribute to Gandhi for helping to initiate resistance to racism in South Africa through his method of non-violence and non-co-operation. Kenneth Kaunda in what was then called Northern Rhodesia (now Zambia) was almost fanatical in his attachment to Gandhism during the colonial period. Kaunda opposed absolutely the idea of violence as a method of attaining racial justice. Leaders like Kenya's Tom Mboya and Tanganyika's Julius Nyerere, though recognizing early the limitations of Gandhian methods in African conditions, nevertheless remained inspired by Gandhian ideals for quite a while.

A number of factors helped Gandhism to win converts in Africa. One factor was Christian education, which had made a number of leaders in black Africa already favourably disposed towards strategies of non-violence. Gandhians like Kenneth Kaunda, Chief Albert Luthuli of South Africa, and Martin Luther King of black America, were all deeply devout Christians. At least in their case Christian education was a good preparation for receptivity to Gandhian ideals. Another factor was the apparent success of Gandhism in India itself, as concessions began to be made to the Indian Nationalist Movement in the wake of the passive resistance. It was also clear to many African leaders that a violent challenge to British rule was hazardous. Kenyans later came to change their minds, and to initiate the movement which came to be called 'Mau Mau', against white settler domination and the disproportionate share of the best land reserved for white settlers. But across the board in Tanganyika (now mainland Tanzania) Nyerere's commitment was to a non-violent strategy of liberation. Many Tanganyikans remembered the Hehe and Maji-Maji wars, when the superior military technology of the German colonialists had inflicted devastating casualties on the African resistance movement of that time. Nyerere was all too conscious of that lesson in history, and wanted to make sure that the Tanganyika African National Union

(TANU) became a mechanism for peaceful agitation and finally peaceful liberation. To quote Nyerere:

> It was therefore necessary for TANU to start by making the people understand that peaceful methods of struggle for independence were possible and could succeed. This does not mean that the people of this country were cowardly, or particularly fond of non-violence; no, they knew fighting; they had been badly defeated and ruthlessly suppressed.[5]

The three factors then of Christian education, the success of the Indian struggle, and an African sense of realism as to what was possible under colonial conditions, prepared the way for African receptivity to Gandhian influence. After independence Gandhi's influence declined rapidly, and before long the limitations of his methods for purposes of liberation in Southern Africa were recognized. Nevertheless Mahatma Gandhi remains a significant point of ideological contact between India and Africa in the last few decades of colonial rule in West and East Africa.

While Gandhi was an inspiration before independence, Nehru was an inspiration after independence. Let us now turn to this second Indian giant and assess his meaning for Africa.

Nehru and Africa

When Jawaharlal Nehru died in 1964, Prime Minister Milton Obote of Uganda went on the radio to address his nation, and paid solemn tribute to Nehru as 'the founder of non-alignment'. Obote's tribute was no exaggeration. As Prime Minister of the newly independent India, Nehru had worked out a strategy of diplomacy for his country. The world was entering the period of the cold war between the Western powers and the Communist countries. A newly independent giant in Asia had to make up its mind how best to handle this bi-polar world.

For all those countries which were previously ruled by Britain, Nehru's India invented two principles which seemingly pulled in different directions. One was indeed the principle of non-alignment, implying at that time a refusal to be tied to any military alliance with either bloc in the cold war. To that extent the principle of non-alignment implied, on attainment of independence, a conscious attempt to widen the distance between a former colony and the former metropolitan power. Non-alignment created some tension at times between Britain and India, and between India and the USA.

But it was also Nehru who helped to hammer out the new multi-racial Commonwealth of Nations. India was sympathetic to the idea of continuing to be associated with Britain, but India was not prepared to owe allegiance to the British Queen as head of state after independence. And yet the British monarch until then had been regarded as a fundamental principle of Commonwealth membership, and was automatically head of state for all the member countries. These were the old Dominions of Canada, Australia, New Zealand and South Africa under white rule. Until India's independence, the Commonwealth was in that sense a white man's club. India was prepared to accede to membership provided she could also be a republic, and provided further that her foreign policy was not necessarily responsive to leadership from London. It was substantially India's political innovativeness which came up with the idea that the Queen could be head of the Commonwealth without being head of state of each member of the Commonwealth. This principle of membership, once invented, later also determined the direction of all African members of the Commonwealth when their turn of independent membership came. Nehru at once invented a method of maintaining association with Britain through Commonwealth membership and a method of increasing the distance between former colonies and Britain by inventing the principle of non-alignment.

Ideologically there were some links between Nehru's non-alignment and Gandhi's non-violence. The idea of refusing to be entangled in military alliances, which was central to non-alignment at that time, was in part a moral judgment on those who sought security in such alliances. But in spite of this link, Nehru himself was not a Gandhian. On the contrary, he set the grand precedent of fighting Portuguese colonialism through armed force. In 1962 he sent Indian tanks and artillery into Goa, and forcefully ejected the Portuguese presence from the Indian subcontinent once and for all. The Western world was indignant, condemning India's action. But much of Africa, from Kwame Nkrumah to Tom Mboya, went on record as fully supporting Nehru's action against Portuguese colonialism. If Gandhi had helped to arouse Africa's interest in non-violent passive resistance against colonialism in the first half of the twentieth century, Nehru helped to arouse Africa's interest in military solutions to the remaining colonial problems in the second half of the twentieth century. Non-alignment in the cold war could thus be combined with military solutions to colonialism. Again this was a combination which most African states came to accept, as they supported African liberation movements in Angola, Mozambique, Guinea-Bissau, South Africa and Rhodesia (Zimbabwe).

Nehru's commitment to African liberation went back to the days before the independence of India itself. Nehru was in touch with a number of Africans, including such anti-colonial old-timers as Kenya's Jomo Kenyatta. On the eve of his election as President of the Kenya African Union in June 1947, Kenyatta had sent a letter to Nehru with a member of a Kenya-African delegation to India. Nehru sent back a message not only of support in their struggle, but also one which reminded Indians in Kenya of the need to identify with the Africans.

> After India's independence in 1947, Nehru support grew more telling. With the appointment of A. B. Pant as High Commissioner in Nairobi in 1948, it was given in practical as well as moral terms. Through Pant the Indian community were led to subscribe money and scholarships in India [for Africans], while other Pant official contacts supplied legal advice and, in some cases, weapons and ammunition.[6]

Nehru was already helping to forge the new movement of Afro-Asian solidarity. India's voice became important in the United Nations on all issues connected with colonialism and racism. For as long as Communist China was not represented at the United Nations, India was in fact clearly the leader of Afro-Asian solidarity. Considerable pressure was exerted on the different bodies of the United Nations, ranging from the Trusteeship Council, in charge of countries like Tanganyika and Italian Somaliland, to the full General Assembly of the United Nations itself.

Even domestically in India certain decisions were taken by Nehru's government for the sake of maintaining good relations with Africa even at a time when not a single black African state had as yet been liberated from British or French colonialism. For example, the government of India announced in 1956 that the Central Board of Film Censors had decided not to license films which 'failed to portray the people of Africa in proper perspective', by presenting 'particular aspects of life in the interior'. The board felt that in the interests of maintaining good relations with the African peoples, films concentrating on 'primitive aspects' purely from the point of view of providing spectacular entertainment should not be shown. The films which were banned included *The African Queen, West of Zanzibar, Snows of Kilimanjaro, Below the Sahara, Mogambo, Tanganyika, African Adventure*, and *Untamed*. This was clearly a policy which involved denying one's own citizens certain entertainment out of consideration for the sensibilities of the African peoples. The use of film censorship for reasons of foreign policy has fluctuated in India from time to time, but this particular instance at a time when most African states were not yet independent clearly showed the commitment of Nehru's India to the principle of Afro-Asian solidarity.[7]

Uganda under Milton Obote was later to invoke film censorship at times for reasons of non-alignment. Not long after independence the film, *The Manchurian Candidate*, was banned from the screen in Uganda because its theme concerned techniques of brain washing in Communist countries, with special reference to China. Later a film about John F. Kennedy in West Berlin, denouncing the great wall which had been erected between West and East Berlin was also banned from public showings in Uganda to try to keep out of the cold war. Nehru's strategy of non-alignment had now been extended to the task of saving African audiences from certain kinds of one-sided propaganda on the cinema screens. Just as Nehru's censorship board had once spared the sensibilities of the African peoples at some cost to the domestic cinema audiences in India, so now Obote's censorship board was sparing the sensibilities of Communist countries at some cost to his own domestic cinema audiences.

In the course of the 1960s India's influence in the Third World began to decline fairly rapidly. Among the reasons for the decline were the increasing self-confidence of African states as their numbers in the United Nations expanded and their own experience was enhanced, the serious border dispute between India and China along with India's partial humiliation by China, the reduced diplomatic vigour of Jawaharlal Nehru in the last three years before he died, the end of bipolarity in the cold war as new centres of power emerged in China, and in the European Economic Community under the influence of Charles de Gaulle, and the beginnings of détente between the USA and the Soviet Union following the Cuban missile crisis in 1962. But India continues to be a major actor in the politics of the Third World. Perhaps it has not been so much a case of the decline of India in absolute terms, but simply a restoration of balance in her stature in the Third World. It is true that a country of five hundred million people should be conspicuous diplomatically by any standards; but the first fifteen years of India's independence gave India under Nehru an exceptional level of diplomatic and political influence. The decline which came in the 1960s was in part a decline towards a more realistic level of international influence. And yet, partly because of its size and partly because of its industrial and cultural potential, India's chances of becoming one of the major powers of the world remain excellent. When one day India enters the ranks of the super powers, two individuals in history would still remain important far beyond India's borders. Men in distant lands who study the origins of Afro-Asianism will remember the 'naked fakir', Mahatma Gandhi, who helped to shape the doctrine of passive resistance as a strategy of liberation in colonial days; and the Brahmin aristocrat, Jawaharlal Nehru, who helped to shape the doctrine of non-alignment as a strategy of liberation after colonial rule.

The doctrine of non-alignment has itself undergone some changes since the death of Nehru. While the emphasis in the earlier days was on military disengagement, non-alignment by the 1970s was becoming in part a doctrine of economic liberation. The old days of wanting to keep out of western or eastern military alliances have now been supplanted by a wave of new economic nationalism in the Third World. Africa, Asia and Latin America are now interested not merely in the negative ambition of wanting to keep out of things, but also in the positive ambition of wanting to be economically assertive.

By the time the non-aligned countries met in Algiers in August 1973, economic issues had become much more important than they were at the meeting in Belgrade way back in 1961. By the 1970s the term 'disengagement' in the Third World had come to mean *economic disengagement*, rather than military and the implications of the doctrine of economic disengagement were in the direction of loosening the ties which bound small poor countries to the international capitalist system. The fight against multi-national corporations, and other forms of external control of domestic resources in the Third World, had by that time got under way. The Third World itself consisted of Africa, Asia, and Latin America – linked together by the bonds of shared underdevelopment. The non-aligned conference of 1973 in Algiers had fewer Latin American countries represented than one would have expected if the links were those purely of economic underprivilege. But many governments in Latin America were not yet in rebellion against the ties which bound them to the international capitalist system. The clarion call of economic disengagement had therefore more enthusiastic applause among countries in Asia and Africa than among those in Latin America.

Nevertheless, the Algiers event aroused greater interest among Latin American countries than the previous Belgrade conference in 1961. The doctrine of non-alignment was undergoing important changes in direction not fully conceived even by the architect of the doctrine, Pandit Jawaharlal Nehru. Africa's links with Asia were extending beyond the two continents in the wake of a new Third World trans-nationalism.

The Yellow Paradigms

Although India's diplomatic decline was in part due to the challenge posed by Communist China, both Asian giants have been major figures in the entire Afro-Asian movement. Communist China is not of course a non-aligned country, but it has enjoyed considerable influence behind the scenes even within the non-aligned movement. There is a feeling in much of the Third World that China is a kindred spirit that has suffered humiliation in a world which was for a time dominated by the white races. The idea of a 'world community of coloured peoples' inspired many in both Africa and Asia, and encompassed within it the Chinese. The worst days of white racial arrogance are captured in the following rhetoric of the late black American giant, W. E. B. Du Bois, with all its evocative power:

> Immediately in Africa a black back runs red with the blood of the lash; in India a brown girl is raped; in China a coolie starves; in Alabama seven darkies are more than lynched; while in London the white limbs of a prostitute are hung with jewels and silk.[8]

The Japanese too were coloured people in that sense, and their technological achievements at first inspired many people in Asia and Africa. In the modern period the yellow peoples have been the first to challenge the technological and military supremacy of the white races. It started when Japan stood up to the Russian Empire, fought a war with Russia at the beginning of the century, and unexpectedly won. A number of historians have seen this event as a significant milestone in the evolution of national consciousness, especially in Asia. The war with Russia established Japan as a major power, and the balance of forces in the Far East was changed significantly.

> But much more significant is the fact that for the first time an Asian state defeated a European state, and a great empire at that. This had an electrifying effect on all Asia. It demonstrated to millions of colonial peoples that European domination was not devinely ordained. For the first time since the days of the conquistadors the white man had been beaten, and a thrill of hope ran through the non-white races of the globe. In this sense the Russo-Japanese War stands out as a landmark in modern history; it represents the prelude to the great awakening of the non-European peoples that today is convulsing the entire world.[9]

The author of this passage, L. S. Stavrianos, was carrying the argument further than was supported by contemporary history. The Japanese victory over Russia was not the first case of the white man being defeated since the days of the conquistadors. After all the Ethiopian emperor, Menelik II, succeeded in repulsing the Italian invasion of his country ten years before Japan's victory over Russia. The battle of Adowa between Italy's General Baratieri and Emperor Menelik's forces opened in the early morning of 1 March 1895. The outcome was complete defeat for the invaders. Official Italian figures put the casualties for the Italians as over forty per cent of the original fighting force. The Italians also abandoned all their cannons on the battlefield and most of their rifles. Menelik became a major international figure almost overnight.

> On October 26 the Italians agreed to the Peace Treaty of Addis Ababa, whereby they . . . recognized the absolute and complete independence of Ethiopia. . . . In the months which followed, the French and British governments sent diplomatic missions to sign treaties of friendship with Menelik; other missions came from the Sudanese Mahdists, the Sultan of the Ottoman Empire, and the Tsar of Russia. Addis Ababa thus emerged as a regular diplomatic centre where several important foreign powers had legations.[10]

The Adowa victory by Menelik II needs to be mentioned whenever we are evaluating the significance of Japan's victory over Russia in 1905. And yet there is no doubt that the Japanese victory did not merely defend the country's borders as Menelik's victory had done, but significantly altered the balance of power in that part of Asia, and served as a prelude to Japan's rapid rise in the world as a whole. The Japanese victory was indeed a challenge not simply to the Russians, but to all major powers. It was a claim for parity of esteem. In the very bid to become an equal of the European power, Japan was claiming the right to be as imperialistic as the European powers. Even the confrontation with Russia was basically caused by competitive expansionism between the two countries. By the treaty of Portsmouth (September 1905) Japan acquired the southern half of Sakhalin Island, and obtained recognition of her 'special interests in Korea'. Japan was not only defending her own autonomy but increasingly came to demand a bigger share of the spoils of global imperialism.

In spite of this, much of Asia was profoundly ambivalent about Japan, and so was intellectual opinion in black America, and increasingly in Africa also, The newly politically conscious black peoples saw in the Japanese achievements the beginnings of the end of white supremacy. In the course of the Second World War African soldiers were used by their imperial powers to fight Japan in places such as Burma, but the racial ambivalence was acute. In India Sobhas Surendra Bose defected to join the Japanese, to assert the principle of 'Asia for the Asians', and therefore demand British withdrawal from India. When Bose was killed in an air crash many Indian nationalists regarded him as a hero and even a martyr.

In 1945 the Americans dropped the atomic bomb on Hiroshima. Japan surrendered. The image of Japan changed from that of 'yellow man triumphant' to that of 'yellow man humiliated'. The big debate on whether the USA would have used such a weapon against fellow white people, the Germans, in Europe, was activated. Did Truman hesitate from threatening Germany with the bomb because the victims were part of a shared Western civilization and ancestry? Or did he hesitate because Europe was a continent, while Japan was an island where effects of radiation could be more localized? Or was Truman afraid that if the bomb did not explode, the Germans would be better able to break the secret of atomic weapons and manufacture them themselves than the Japanese were likely to do? Or was the bomb not ready yet for use in Germany at a time when the Germans were on the verge of surrendering under a different kind of pressure? And yet, could the Japanese have surrendered under such alternative pressures too, had the Americans not been keen on 'trying out the bomb on human material'?[11] All these questions have featured in the debates which have raged since the Americans dropped bombs on Hiroshima and Nagasaki. The Japanese themselves were among those who wondered whether these bombs would have been dropped on a European enemy. In the words of a former member of the British Mission to Japan which went out in November 1945, partly to assess the implications of the nuclear holocaust:

> Many Japanese feel they were singled out as no white enemy would have been, as something less than human; some of them may have seen pictures of Japanese looking like vermin [like the Nazi pictures of the Jews] that were current in America during the war. There was a rumor in Nagasaki when I was there that the atomic bomb burnt only dark-skinned people; it was not true, but it put the right pinch of scientific fact in the racial stew.[12]

The course of the war in Vietnam much later raised again the issue of whether Americans were prepared to do to non-white people what they would not consider doing in a war with a white country. When the USA used gas in Vietnam in 1965, many fellow white people in Europe wondered whether the Americans would have invoked such weapons had the war been in Europe. In a broadcast panel discussion in Britain on 24 March 1965, involving Sir Alec Douglas Home of the Conservative party, Gordon Walker of the Labour party, and Jo Grimond, then leader of the Liberal party, the issue was thrashed out at a high level of political debate. Prime Minister Harold Wilson was himself expected to take part in the discussion but did not turn up because of an impending debate on Vietnam in the House of Commons. He thought that he should not discuss the issue publicly before that debate. In the discussion it was Jo Grimond who argued explicitly that many Africans and Asians would see the use of gas in Vietnam as another instance of the West using weapons on coloured people that they would not use in Europe. Other weapons were used later in the course of the war, with similar lack of global or human sensitivity on the part of the military establishment of the USA. In 1972 Prime Minister Indira Gandhi of India similarly remarked on the war in Vietnam in terms which questioned whether the USA would have used all the devices they had used, or whether American soldiers in action would have perpetrated some of the atrocities, if the victims had been Europeans. The controversy concerning racial selection in the use of military weapons certainly went back to the fate of the inhabitants of Hiroshima in 1945.

Curiously enough, while the first victims of a nuclear weapon were indeed a yellow people, the Japanese, the first non-white nuclear power was also a yellow nation, the Chinese. The successful explosion of a nuclear device by the Chinese took place almost exactly twenty years after the nuclear ravaging of Nagasaki; and ten years after the famous Bandung Conference of 1955 which gave the Afro-Asian movement a new lease of life. On 18 April 1965, there was a celebration commemorating that first Afro-Asian conference in Indonesia in April 1955. In commemorating that event ten years later, President Sukarno of Indonesia was all too aware that China had just become a nuclear power. He said that at the time of the conference in the West Java town of Bandung ten years previously, Afro-Asianism was strong in spirit but weak in technology. 'But now one of us, the People's Republic of China, has an atomic bomb.'[13]

The Chinese themselves insisted that they were developing a nuclear capability in order to break the nuclear monopoly of the super powers, and in order to neutralize 'nuclear blackmail'. Ultimately, the Chinese argued, the future of the world would not be decided by nuclear weapons but by the will of the peoples of the world.

> Comrade Mao Tse-tung hit the nail on the head when he pointed out: 'The atom bomb is a paper tiger which the US reactionaries use to scare people. It looks terrible, but in fact it isn't. Of course, the atom bomb is a weapon of mass slaughter, but the outcome of a war is decided by the people, not by one or two new types of weapon.' Our country has successfully conducted its first nuclear test. This is a tremendous encouragement to the revolutionary people of all countries engaged in struggle.[14]

In the same month in which the *Peking Review* published this article, the President of Tanzania, Mwalimu Julius Nyerere, visited China. The theme of military self-reliance was referred to from the beginning by the Chinese. On the eve of independence Julius Nyerere had, in fact, wondered whether a country like Tanganyika, as it then was, needed an army of its own at all. Nyerere had been concerned that African armies would just be turned against other Africans. Ideally, he would have preferred a continental African high command, or even an arrangement under the United Nations, for any external military defence for Tanzania, but Nyerere was confronted with the realities of a divided Africa unable to create such a high command, and a divided United Nations without the capacity to undertake many Congo-type operations. In the end Tanzania did give herself an army, only to be landed with a mutiny in 1964, which nearly led to the fall of Nyerere's government. Yet, there was Nyerere in China, being reminded by his hosts that self-reliance had to include military self-reliance. In his speech welcoming President Nyerere, Chairman Liu Shao Chi referred to the founding of a national army of Tanzania as 'a matter of high significance'. Comrade Liu Shao Chi went on to note, 'The Tanzanian people know that without their own armed forces, a newly independent country can not be assured of independence.'[15]

By this time relations between Tanzania and China were getting closer. They became more comprehensive later with Chinese participation in some infant industries in Tanzania, and the impressive Chinese financial commitment to the railway line between Zambia and Tanzania. On 5 September 1967, an agreement concluded between China, Tanzania, and Zambia was signed in Peking. The railway was estimated to cost up to something like $400 million, and China granted a loan which was interest free for twenty-five years. Construction was scheduled to begin in March 1970, and was expected to take five years. Later, when Zambia was denied access to Rhodesia for her goods, their schedule for the construction of the railway linking Zambia to Tanzania was brought forward. There is little doubt that the Tanzania-Zambia railway line is the most important single project in foreign aid undertaken by the People's Republic of China. The project did indeed imply a significant sacrifice by the Chinese. As George T. Yu has put it:

> The estimated cost of 3,402,400 million [for the Tanzanian-Zambian railway] will double China's aid commitments to Africa. In view of China's own development needs, this cost is not negligible. China's own railway development, for example, has been poorly served. It has been estimated that China has added only 10,000 miles of railway since 1949 to the mere 12,500 miles which the regime inherited. It could be said that China will be deprived of the 1,060 miles of railway being contributed to Tanzania's and Zambia's development.[16]

The railway line has by no means been the only form of aid China has extended to Tanzania. The extent of her loans was second only to that of Britain for a number of years. Projects handled by the Chinese range from the Friendship Textile Mill to the multi-purpose Ruvu State Farm as a contribution to improved methods of agricultural production. Chinese instructors also play a part in activities such as physical training in village schools in Tanzania.

Until China became more systematically involved in Tanzania, her role in Africa was much more political than economic. On the other hand, the newly prosperous Japan conducted a strategy of diplomacy in Africa that was more economic than political. The Chinese political activities had a wide range. The Chinese were very significant in the liberation movements in Southern Africa, providing financial and sometimes technical assistance to liberation fighters against Portuguese, South African, and other white regimes. Over the years Chinese guerrilla instructors worked in countries such as Congo [Brazzaville]' Ghana and Tanzania. Explosives techniques and the uses of mines were given special emphasis. The skills of sabotage featured more prominently than those of positional warfare with submachine guns and rifles.[17] The Chinese also supported other types of opposition groups within African countries for a while. In Kenya relations between the government and the local Chinese Embassy cooled considerably because of the apparent Chinese financial and moral support for the opposition party and Oginga Odinga, until the opposition party was banned in 1968. In West Africa the Chinese used Nkrumah's Ghana as a base to give support to some opposition groups in neighbouring countries.

It was in these years that the Chinese presence in Africa was overwhelmingly political, while the Japanese entry into Africa was almost exclusively economic. The Japanese fostered trade with African countries, and included investment in South Africa. Politically, the Japanese maintained a low profile, taking hardly any major political stands in international affairs and concentrating almost entirely on constructing and consolidating economic relations of different kinds with African countries. For a substantial part of the 1960s Africa was a market place for Japanese goods and for Chinese ideas. The Japanese goods ranged from transistor radios to farming equipment; the Chinese ideas were from guerrilla tactics to the ideological sayings of Mao Tse-tung. But China was later to engage in a considerable re-evaluation of her African diplomacy. Although the political component remained quite strong, the Chinese became more selective in their choice of friends in Africa, looking for like-minded 'progressive' countries and consolidating friendships partly on the basis of a shared world view. Chinese support for liberation movements was maintained, but the era of the Tanzania-Zambia railway line was also an era of Chinese economic and functional participation in the development of Africa. The Japanese, however, continued to limit themselves exclusively to economic issues until the energy crisis hit them in 1973. With that crisis Japan began to be forced to take up political positions in the Middle East. The question arose whether Japan would also be compelled to take account of apartheid as a political issue. Until then South Africa was to Japan only one more trading partner.

Japan continues to enjoy a special status in South Africa—the only Asians to be given the honorary status of 'whites'. Japanese businessmen can stay in white hotels, while local South African Chinese are kept out. Frantz Fanon once wrote, 'You are rich because you are white; you are white because you are rich.'[18] The second part of the epigram found new vindication when the Japanese were regarded as white because they were rich.

The attempt to 'Aryanize' the Japanese goes back to the earliest days of their technological triumphs. Writing way back in 1915, the black American nationalist, W. E. B. Du Bois drew attention to the difficulties that the white establishment was having in trying to cope with Japan as a 'deviant case' in race relations:

> Yellow Japan has apparently escaped the cordon of this colour bar. This is disconcerting and dangerous to white hegemony. If, of course, Japan would join heart and soul with the whites against the rest of the yellows, browns, and blacks, well and good. There are even good-natured attempts to prove the Japanese 'Aryan', provided they act 'white'. But blood is thick, and there are signs that Japan does not dream of a world governed mainly by white men.[19]

It is indeed true that Japanese nationalism from the 1860s had become sensitively aware of issues of colour in world politics. In their rebellion against European and American imperialism, they sensed the bonds of partial solidarity which gave the white nations a shared perspective on Asia and Africa as fair domains for exploitation. When the atomic bomb was dropped on Hiroshima, as mentioned earlier, the Japanese themselves were among those who wondered whether this nuclear experiment could conceivably have been tried out on a European enemy.

The arrogance of white nations increased and strengthened Japanese nationalism, but that nationalism did not become pan-Asianism. The Japanese never entered into either the excitement of pan-Asian militancy or the stream of Afro-Asianism. And by the time the non-aligned movement came into being, and the concept of the Third World matured into world diplomacy, Japan was too powerful, technologically and economically, to belong to the ranks of the under-privileged. It was in these circumstances that leadership in Asia and Africa came to pass to the other two giants of that continent—India and China.

Conclusion

This chapter has sought to define the political meaning of India, China, and Japan for Africa in the modern period. To the extent that India, like much of Africa, actually formed part of the British Empire, the bonds of anti-colonialism between Africa and India were more immediate. Two personalities especially acquired immense stature in Africa. These were Mahatma Gandhi, who helped to shape the strategy of anti-colonialism in much of Africa through his ideas on passive resistance, and Pandit Nehru, who bequeathed to the Third World the policy and principle of non-alignment as a foundation of diplomatic autonomy and assertiveness.

In addition, we should note that in some countries in East, Central, and Southern Africa, India also exported her sons and daughters. These later became a major issue of contention and controversy, as newly independent African governments attempted to Africanize commercial and industrial enterprises in their own countries.

Indian minorities resident in Africa were, like the Japanese, much more important for Africa in the economic domain than in the political. By contrast, India herself as a country was, like China, significantly more important for Africa in political terms than in economic.

The Japanese influenced certain directions of African economic change after independence through international trade; the Indian minorities resident in Africa influenced certain directions of Africa's economic change through domestic trading patterns. India herself, along with China, had a stature in Africa's history more in the realm of dissemination of ideas and the bonds of Afro-Asianism than in the annals of economic interaction. The major economic adventure by the Chinese has so far been their participation in linking Tanzania and Zambia by a railway line.

The stream of history, as well as the waters of the Indian Ocean, continue to link the shores of Africa and her Asian neighbours.

References and notes

1. *Lagos Weekly Record,* 20 April 1920.
2. *Young Indian,* 21 August 1924.
3. *Harijan,* 4 March 1936.
4. See Kwame Nkrumah, *Ghana: the Autobiography of Kwame Nkrumah* (Nelson, 1957). p. 92.
5. Julius K. Nyerere, *Freedom and Unity* (Dar es Salaam: Oxford University Press, 1969), pp. 2-3.
6. Jeremy Murray-Brown, *Kenyatta* (Allen & Unwin, 1972), p. 233.
7. See *East African Standard* (Nairobi), 11 May 1956.
8. W. E. B. Du Bois, *Black Reconstruction in America, 1860-1880* (1935; New York: The World Publishing Company, 1964), p. 728.
9. L. S. Stavrianos, *Man's Past and Present: a Global History* (Englewood Cliffs, N.J.: Prentice-Hall,1971),p. 374.
10. See Richard Pankhurst, 'Emperor Menelik II of Ethiopia' *Tarikh,* No. 1 (1965). Cited in *Africa Reader: Colonial Africa,* ed. Wilfred Cartey and Martin Kilson (New York: Vintage Books, 1970), pp. 33-9.
11. One useful summary of the debate is the anthology *Hiroshima: The Decision to Use the Bomb*, ed. Edwin Fogelman, 'Scribner Research Anthologies'(New York: Charles Scribner's Sons,1964).
12. Consult J. Bronowski, 'The psychological wreckage of Hiroshima and Nagasaki', *Scientific American* (June 1968), 131-5.
13. One variant of President Sukarno's speech is reported in the *New York Times,* 19 April 1965.
14. Liu Yun-Cheng, 'People's militia in China', *Peking Review,* **VIII** (5 February 1965). Reproduced in *Survival,* **VII** (May-June 1965), 138-41, 144.
15. *Peking Review,* **XIII** (26 February 1965), 5-6.
16. See George T. Yu, *China and Tanzania: a Study in Cooperative Interaction*, China Research Monographs, No. 5 (Berkeley: University of California Center for Chinese Studies, 1970), p. 58. The relations between China and Japan are discussed in a similar context in Ali A. Mazrui, *A World Federation of Cultures: an African Perspective* (New York: Free Press,1976),chapter 7.
17. Kenneth W. Grundy, *Guerrilla Struggle in Africa: an Analysis and Preview* (New York: Grossman, 1971), pp. 51-2.
18. Frantz Fanon, *The Wretched of the Earth*, translated from the French by Constance Farrington (New York: Grove Press, 1963 edn.).
19. W. E. B. Du Bois, 'The African roots of war', *Atlantic Monthly,* **VII** (May 1915), 7-14.

CHAPTER 7
Africa & the Middle East

The history of the Arabs in Africa has included a number of contradictions. The Arabs have been both conquerors and liberators, both traders in slaves and purveyors of new ideas. With the Arabs came both Islam and commerce. Indeed, trade and Islam have been companions throughout much of the modern history of Africa north of the Zambezi. In Northern and West Africa caravans of Muslim traders go back for centuries. In East Africa others have come for a millenium from the Gulf of Oman and Southern Arabia, consciously engaged in trade and unconsciously in cultural dissemination. The spread of Islam in Africa has been due far less to consciously organized missionary activity than to trade and conquest. To the present day in West Africa the crescent has often followed the commercial caravan. The muezzin has called believers to prayer from the market-place. That is what the phenomenon of Hausa traders in contemporary West African societies is all about.

On the whole Islam in West Africa is older than in most parts of East Africa. It is odd that West African Islam should be older than Islam in places such as Tanzania and Kenya, considering the much closer proximity of the latter to the birthplace of Islam in the Arabian peninsula. Moreover, European colonialism arrested the spread of Islam in East Africa more effectively than in the West. West African Islam has continued to expand in spite of the impressive countervailing efforts of Christian missionaries and of the technological prestige of European civilization. In places such as Kenya, Uganda and Malawi, on the other hand, Islamization came to an almost abrupt halt in the face of the Euro-Christian challenge.

But the cultural impact of the Arabs on Africa is not merely in the religious field. It is also in the linguistic field. The most important non-European languages in the African continent are Arabic, Swahili and Hausa. All three languages have been deeply influenced by Islam. Swahili is the most international of all the indigenous languages of Africa. It belongs to the Bantu family of languages and, in terms of distribution and functional potential, it has become the most important of the Bantu languages. It has already been adopted as a national language by Tanzania, Kenya and Uganda, and is taken seriously in Zaire, Rwanda and Burundi. Swahili has also posed the most serious indigenous challenge to the role of the English language in Africa. The first experiment by black Africans to make an African language capable of serving modern and scientific needs will probably be based on the use of Swahili. Perhaps up to twenty per cent of the basic vocabulary of Swahili comes from Arabic—including the name of the language itself and much of its political vocabulary. The words for president (*raisi*), minister (*waziri*), law (*sharia*), department (*idara*) and politics (*siasa*) are all derived from Arabic.

The growth of both Hausa and Swahili is a good model for the future. Though partly stimulated by the Arabs, these languages remain African languages. Should the Arabs in the future become true partners in African development they should help in a way which permits Africans to remain themselves, after stimulating creative growth and change. Any other policy carries the danger of appearing as a new form of Arab imperialism. Arab economic aid to Africa in the future should follow the model of the history of Hausa and Swahili—enriching African culture without enslaving it! What needs to be grasped from the outset is the cultural foundation which history laid centuries ago for future political interaction between the Arab world and black Africa.

The Arabs were once *accomplices in Africa's enslavement,* and then became *allies in Africa's liberation.* The critical question for the future is whether the Arabs will also become true *partners in Africa's development*. Our analysis in this chapter will relate itself to these three fundamental roles.

From the Slave Trade to Apartheid

From the point of view of the role of the Arabs in the slave trade, the history of Eastern Africa has to be treated differently from the history of Western Africa. The transatlantic slave trade on the West Coast of Africa was oriented towards meeting the slave needs of Christendom. The Christian states of Europe and their colonies in the New World determined the extent of the market for the slave trade, provided the financing for the raids, offered advice on techniques of enslavement, and took risks with millions of black lives on overcrowded ships crossing to their plantations in the New World. The transatlantic slave trade was by far and away larger and more important than the Arab slave trade on the eastern seaboard. And just as Islam was compromised on the eastern seaboard because many who professed it were enslaving others, Christianity was compromised when Christian churches themselves, right into the nineteenth century, ranging from Roman Catholics to Dutch Calvinists, approved and sanctioned slavery as an institution and the slave trade as a commercial activity.

By the second half of the nineteenth century European and Western civilization had developed industrially beyond the primitive techniques of slave labour. Movements for the abolition first of the slave trade and later of slavery itself had been gathering momentum in Europe and in the New World, and these movements were helped in their aims precisely by the momentum of the industrial revolution and the extent to which it transformed both methods of production and the scale of international trade. Slavery became obsolete. And although the Americans had to fight a civil war before they could abolish it in 1865, the signs on the wall of history in the West indicated that this particular form of economic arrangement was by then anachronistic.

As between Westerners, Arabs, and black Africans, industrialization was setting the stage for one of those ironies of history. Until then, slavery was a form of energy—human energy to facilitate primitive modes of production, especially in North and South America, the Caribbean, and parts of the Middle East. As Europe and the New World of the Americas industrialized first, they discovered the obsolescence of slavery sooner than some Middle Eastern countries. Europe and the Western world therefore abolished slavery sooner than Arabia and parts of the Ottoman Empire.

The Western countries then began to require new sources of energy. The slaves on their plantations had constituted human coal; now they began to utilize mineral coal. The transition was from the black energy of African slaves to the black energy from coalmines, and later still the black energy of crude oil. It was not until the twentieth century that the Middle East's disproportionate endowment of the third black energy of oil was discovered. By the beginning of the 1970s it was estimated that the Middle East had more than half of the total oil reserves of the world. The Middle East was already the largest oil-exporting region of the world. Western Europe and Japan, on the other hand, were two of the largest oil importing areas of the world. The USA imported a much smaller proportion of its needs in oil than either Europe or Japan, but that proportion was large enough to cause significant discomfort, and some degree of economic dislocation in the United States as a result in part of the Arab oil embargo on sales to America. The Arabs and Westerners, who had once dealt in the black energy of African slaves, were now confronting each other on the issue of the black energy of petroleum.

In the modern period it was neither the Arabs nor the black Africans that first awoke to the realization that politically the Middle East and Africa were interconnected. It was the white settlers within Africa and the European imperial powers themselves. The Cape of Good Hope as an alternative to Suez featured early in the history of European imperialism and even earlier in European voyages of exploration. In her bid to get to the Orient, Western Europe discovered that the choice was either through the Middle East or around the African continent. The Cape of Good Hope was itself named because of the promise of such a route to India and the Orient. An important part of Africa was thus named because of its potential usefulness as a route to Asia. The Cape thus relinquished its older name of the Cape of Storms and assumed instead this new garb of optimism.

When the Suez Canal was at last created in the second half of the nineteenth century, the Cape of Good Hope lost some of its importance as a route to places such as India, but retained its significance for traffic going to places such as Australia and the more distant parts of Asia.

In the twentieth century the Cape route and the Suez route became in some respects complementary, and in others alternative, waterways. Strictly from a narrow point of view the South African government learned to welcome silently the closure of the Suez Canal in times of turbulence in the Middle East, both because this boosted the importance of South African ports and also because Western embarrassment with Arab nationalism would hopefully bring the West closer to South Africa in their joint evaluation of the risks of African nationalism as well.

Another waterway which linked the politics of the Near and Middle East was the River Nile, as the British Foreign Office and the British Colonial Office subscribed for decades to the doctrine of the unity of the Nile Valley. Two British historians, Robinson and Gallagher, remind us that 'the idea that the security of Egypt depended upon the defence of the Upper Nile was as old as the Pyramids'. They point out the effect of this doctrine of the unity of the Nile Valley on Lord Salisbury who, in 1889-90, decided that if Britain was to hold on to Egypt, she could not afford to let any other European power obtain a hold over any other part of the Nile Valley. Robinson and Gallagher go on to assert that, in so doing, Salisbury took what was perhaps the critical decision for the partition of Africa. 'Henceforward, almost everything in Africa north of the Zambezi River was to hinge upon it.'[1] Under Salisbury's successors the doctrine of the unity of the Nile Valley helped to seal the fate of Uganda. As Robinson and Gallagher put it with reference to Rosebury's vision, 'The Cabinet quarrels over Uganda were really quarrels over Egypt.'[2]

In some form or another this doctrine persisted in the British official mind until well after the Second World War. Indeed, when the Egyptian revolution took place in 1952, the British colonial government in the Sudan, ostensibly sharing power with Egypt in a condominium, was deeply disturbed. The British governor in Uganda was in touch with British authorities in the Sudan, as well as with fellow governors in Kenya, and Tanganyika, and the British resident in Zanzibar. Concern about the consequences of the Egyptian revolution was sensed by white settlers and white governments in black Africa well beyond the Nile Valley as well.

The radicalization of Gamal Abdul Nasser, the Egyptian leader, increased apprehension among white settlers in Kenya, the Rhodesias, South Africa, and the Portuguese colonies. Nasser's support for African nationalists south of the Sahara, as well as his increasing 'flirtation' with the Soviet Union, Czechoslovakia and other Communist countries, deepened the anxieties of the white settlers south of the Sahara and the colonial governments there.

The attitudes of most black Africans towards the Middle East were either indifferent or hostile. In Eastern African schools especially, the Arab record in the slave trade featured prominently in history books, and the British liked to justify their colonial presence in Eastern and Central Africa by arguing that the original motivation was to suppress the Arab slave trade. With one stroke colonial policy-makers could both discredit the Arabs and Islam as a religion, and at the same time give their own presence a high moral justification.

The white settlers in Eastern and Southern Africa continued to sense a potential radical alliance between Arab and African nationalism. And after the creation of Israel in 1948 many white settlers in Southern Africa began to identify with the Israeli predicament. Israël has emerged as a courageous and industrious immigrant community which has managed to defy a hostile environment and survive with honour. This hero-image of Israel has been important both for white South Africans and more recently for white Rhodesians. A minister for defence in South Africa once extolled Israel in the following terms: 'They stand alone in the world, but they are full of courage.'

Die Burger draws similar inspiration from Israel's example of victorious loneliness:

> We in South Africa would be foolish if we did not at least take account of the possibility that we are destined to become a sort of Israel in a preponderantly hostile Africa, and that fact might become part of our national way of life. . . .[3]

In June 1967 the response of white Rhodesians to Israeli successes was also enthusiastic. There was clear evidence of empathetic identification with Israel among the white Rhodesians. Israel was small; the Arab countries and their populations were large; and yet the Arabs had proved to be militarily impotent in the face of Israel. By the same token, Rhodesia was small; the African continent was large and its population impressive; and yet Africans were militarily impotent in the face of Ian Smith's government. Indeed, Rhodesia should be internally even weaker than Israel, for Smith represented a minority government imposed upon a potentially 'treacherous' black population, whereas the Israeli government had majority support in its own country for its anti-Arab policies. And yet both Israel and

Rhodesia had reduced to impotent frustration populations vastly bigger than their own. The white Rhodesians identified themselves as 'the Israelis of Africa', surrounded by hostile and less distinguished neighbours.

Many white Gentiles in Southern Africa were, paradoxically, both anti-Semitic and pro-Israel. They were anti-Semitic in their attitudes to their own Jewish citizens. Afrikaner nationalism shares characteristics with Hitler's National Socialism, including some distrust of the Jews. This distrust of local Jews among white South African Gentiles was aggravated by Jewish liberalism. The Jews in South Africa are among the least racialistic and the most liberal of the whites of that part of the world. Both because of their liberalism and because of their relative economic success even by the standards of white people in South Africa, the domestic Jews have sometimes had to confront strong social prejudice among fellow white people in the region. Yet those same anti-Semitic whites were capable of strong sympathetic identification with Israel. In their own way these white people were once again bearing witness to the interrelationship between politics in the Middle East and politics in Africa.

Towards Re-Africanizing North Africa

After the white settlers and the old imperialist powers, the next group to recognize this interrelationship between the Middle East and Africa were in fact the Arabs. This was the beginning of the Arab role as allies in Africa's liberation. It has been pointed out often enough that Gamal Abdul Nasser, in his *Philosophy of the Revolution*, envisaged Egypt as the centre of three concentric circles—that of the Arab world, the Muslim world, and Africa. Nasser committed himself and Egypt to participation in matters connected with all three. According to his *Philosophy*:

> We cannot, in any way, stand aside, even if we wish to, from the sanguinary and dreadful struggle now raging in the heart of the continent between five million whites and two hundred million Africans. We cannot do so for one principal and clear reason—we ourselves are in Africa.[4]

Nasser proceeded to give material and propaganda support to a variety of nationalist and dissident groups from African colonies south of the Sahara. Egypt opened her educational doors to African students, providing scholarships in subjects ranging from engineering to theology. Some scholarships were for children to complete secondary school in Egypt. Others were for militant insurrectionists from places such as Cameroun, Kenya and South Africa.

Within four years of his assumption of power, some sections of British opinion were already regarding Nasser as one of Britain's worst enemies. In the words of one British newspaper at the time:

> Who today is Britain's most immediate enemy? Who in the whole world does most to obstruct and damage the interests of this country? There can be no doubt about the answer. Colonel Gamal Abdul Nasser, Prime Minister of Egypt.[5]

Many white settlers in colonies such as Kenya and the Rhodesias were in agreement.

As the Arabs began to rediscover their links with the black people south of the Sahara and beyond, the Israelis were making a comparable bid for black African support. The Israelis used with some brilliance their financial and skilled manpower resources. Even before Ghana attained independence, Israel was providing considerable technical assistance and opportunities for the training of Ghanaians. The technique of concluding special agreements of co-operation between Israel and an African state was formulated and improved upon. In 1960 agreements were concluded with Mali, Upper Volta, and Madagascar (now the Malagasy Republic); in 1961, with Dahomey; in 1962, with the Ivory Coast, Uganda, Gabon, Sierra Leone, Rwanda, Cameroon, Gambia, and Burundi; in 1963, with Nigeria and Tanzania; in 1964, with Togo and Chad; and in 1965, with Kenya.

But the Israelis began to be hampered by their bedfellows. On the one hand, Israel was virtually the fifty-first state of the USA, with a massive American commitment to its preservation, and massive American contributions to its maintenance and upkeep. In that respect Israel was a piece of the Western world deposited deep in the heart of the Third World. On the other hand, there were the Israeli connections with white dominated Southern Africa. South Africa was the second largest non-governmental external financial contributor to Israel's funds. The money came from the white Jewish community in South Africa, itself part of the richest sector of South Africa's society.

Israel, sometimes genuinely interested in identifying with the liberation forces in Africa, nevertheless found herself supporting those against whom African fighters were waging a struggle. The voting pattern of Israel in the United Nations has shown how much a part of the Western world Israel is, and how influenced by its connections with Southern Africa Israel's policies have been. When nationalist opinion in much of Africa was aroused against Moise Tshombe's bid to pull Katanga out of the Congo, and protect Western mineral interests in Katanga, Israel sided with Tshombe in a large number of votes in the United Nations connected with the issue. The Arabs were not slow in pouncing on this Israeli ambivalence. In the words of one Arab publication at the time:

> If the Israeli Chiefs really supported the Africans, why did they not announce their support for the legal power in the Congo

[Lumumba's government then], the body on whom depends the victory of the Congo over her imperialist enemies? Instead, the Israeli Chiefs supported Moise Tshombe, Prime Minister of Katanga.[6]

When the first decade of African independence was coming to an end, there must have been some serious rethinking in Israel about its African policies. Things were not moving as smoothly as the Israelis would have liked, African votes in the United Nations were often hostile to the Israelis, and the record of Israel's own voting on issues of white supremacy in Southern Africa could have been much more liberal. A decision was made in Israel to offer financial support to African liberation movements with resources for education and medical facilities.

But as soon as Israel made that offer, Israel's vulnerability to pressures from the authorities in South Africa was revealed. The South African government intimated in no uncertain terms that if Israel provided financial support to African liberation movements, the money which Israel annually received from South African Jews would no longer be permitted to leave South Africa. The financial cost seemed heavy from Israel's point of view. Although the Israelis had not hesitated to aid Africans struggling against their own governments in places like Biafra and Southern Sudan, it was much more difficult for Israel to give assistance to Africans fighting against the white regimes of South Africa, Rhodesia, and the Portuguese colonies. When at last the gesture was made, and the South African government opposed it, the Israelis hovered on the brink of indecision. To their apparent relief, their dilemma was resolved by a firm rejection of the offer by the African Liberation Movement and the Organization of African Unity.

Until the coup in Lisbon in April 1974 Israeli links even with Portugal continued to be embarrassing from an African point of view. For when Guinea-Bissau declared its independence from Portugal in 1973, and sought recognition from the United Nations, the Israelis were not in a position to vote in favour of Guinea-Bissau and against Portugal's pretensions to continuing sovereignty.

Israel's need in turn for Portugal was revealed in October 1973 in the course of the war with Egypt and Syria. Western European countries such as West Germany and Greece had asked the USA not to use its bases in those countries as stopping stages for planes carrying war equipment to Israel. The Portuguese provided the necessary services for the American military air-lift to the Israeli forces fighting in Egypt, by permitting the use of the Azores for that purpose. Israel once again sensed her own links not only with the USA but also with those Europeans who were still controlling and ruling Southern Africa.

The interlocking experience between the politics of the Middle East and the politics of Southern Africa was now forging a link between the wars of the Middle East and the wars of Southern Africa.

The Political Shrinking of the Sahara

By this time it was not only white settlers and imperial powers who recognized that interconnection; nor was it the Arabs alone among the non-white masses of Africa. Increasingly black Africans also were moving in the direction of partial solidarity with the Arabs. But here one must distinguish between black Africans who are ideologically radical or at least left of centre, and the more conservative black Africans. In general, black radicals from quite early on had recognized the Arabs as Third World compatriots and identified with them.

Kwame Nkrumah of Ghana showed some awareness of these bonds even in his more conservative days of the first two years of independence. From the start he was already somewhat left of centre in his ideological orientation, but as he became more radical, he was even less inclined to recognize the Sahara as a legitimate political divide. Symbolically, Nkrumah even married an Egyptian girl which emphasized the solidarity of the African continent, north and south of the Sahara. Yet for a while Nkrumah's support for the Arabs was circumscribed, especially in view of his economic relationship with Israel. As late as 1960, in a speech to the General Assembly of the United Nations, Nkrumah called upon the Arabs to recognize realities—implying that since Israel was a reality, the Arabs might as well recognize its existence in spite of any presumed injustice which might have been committed at the time it was created. Arab diplomats retorted that white power in Southern Africa was also a reality, but that was no reason for recognizing it. An injustice did not acquire legitimacy simply by enduring for a long time, the Arabs argued. But even then Nkrumah's foreign policy was on the verge of moving further to the left. By 1962 Nkrumah was prepared to sign a communiqué, after a conference in Casablanca of radical African states, describing Israel as a 'tool of neo-colonialism'. He denied he had been pressured to sign a communiqué with such a denunciation of Israel. Nkrumah's economic relations with Israel remained unchanged for a little while, but the relationship was getting less warm.

Arab spokesmen, in their enthusiasm, prematurely asserted that after the Casablanca conference Israel had become an African problem as well as an Arab one. Such an assertion would have made better sense ten years later in 1972 and more especially in 1973. Nevertheless, Nkrumah's commitment to the Casablanca denunciation of Israel was in its own way an important milestone on a journey across the Sahara. The Sahara Desert might be expanding geographically, but would it shrink politically? Could black Africa evolve a relationship with North Africa which would amount to a political shrinkage of this sandy divide? The question remained open for the time being, but the behaviour of black African radicals indicated that such a shrinkage might well be on the horizon. Radical leaders such as Nkrumah of Ghana, Nyerere of Tanzania, Sékou Touré of Guinea, and Modibo Kéita of Mali, were already showing a responsiveness to the Arab cause, though still with some ambivalence.

But why were radical Africans already moving in the direction of a greater sympathy for the Arab cause? A number of factors are relevant here. We have already alluded to two of them. Israel was too much a part of the Western world. The existence of the country was capable of being interpreted as a form of colonization which was not fundamentally different from the settling of white people in Southern Africa. The related factor which made Israel look suspect to black radicals was the link which the Israelis had with regimes in Southern Africa, and the diplomatic record of Israel on issues connected with Southern Africa.

Paradoxically, the internal political system of Israel was one of the most genuinely socialist in both the Middle East and Africa. A high degree of compassion and egalitarianism characterized the Israeli polity. Welfare socialism interacted with welfare liberalism, with, of course, a deep attachment to Jewish nationalism. It is true that many Oriental Jews suffered handicaps socially and economically as compared with the European Jews in Israel. The degree of social and economic integration in the country was still seriously inadequate. Injustices which seemed to favour European Jews, even when they were newly arrived, appeared to create a stratified society in Israel. Even Jewish movements like the Black Panthers of Israel were a manifestation of a nation deeply disturbed and losing some of the high moral fervour and basic egalitarianism which had characterized Zionism at its best in the earlier years. But even after we have taken account of these internal cleavages in Israel, the record of domestic rule within the country compares very well with what has been achieved anywhere else in Africa and the Middle East. While diplomatically Israel seemed to have links with some of the least tolerant regimes in the world, her domestic arrangements were exceptionally democratic by comparison.

And yet that old commitment to create a Jewish state had produced unintended similarities with certain aspects of the official ideology of white-dominated South Africa. Israelis by the early 1970s had become terrified of the prospect of becoming a bi-national state. The population of the country was already ten per cent Arab, and their conquered territories since the 1967 war had given the country additional Arab labour, though not necessarily additional Arab citizens.

In South Africa the ideology of apartheid is also based on a profound distrust of a bi-national state. The dominant whites in South Africa would like to ensure that there are no blacks in white areas. The whole policy of Bantu homelands or Bantustans, has its roots in a form of ethnic or racial exclusivity similar to that which caused Israel to fear the mixing of Jews and Arabs into one country.

Israel's immigration policies are much more like those of South Africa and Rhodesia than they are like the policies of the USA. South Africa and Rhodesia try hard to attract as many whites as possible to settle in their countries; Israel tries hard to encourage Jews to immigrate into Israel. If the USA were to adopt a policy of immigration which discriminated on the basis of either religion or ethnicity, the same passionate debates which were previously activated by the old quota system into America would erupt once again. The United States has moved from a policy of discrimination on the basis of national origins to a more democratic policy of immigration. Yet Israel, by the very logic of Zionism, could never treat a Gentile the same as a Jew in terms of immigration. On the contrary, Israel has even rejected black American Jews when they applied for entry. The racial element implicit in such immigration policies could not escape the notice of the more radical black nationalists both in Africa and the USA.

Australia, until recently, had a white Australia policy, fundamentally similar to that of Israel, once you replace the word 'white' by the word 'Jewish'. Just as Australia went all out to bring in white people almost exclusively, so has Israel gone all out to bring in Jewish people almost exclusively.

With regard to repression, the bulk of the Palestinian refugees should morally be eligible to benefit by Israel's 'law of return'. The Arab Palestinians belong to Palestine at least as fundamentally as millions of American and Russian Jews are supposed to do. The great majority of these Russian and American Jews are presumed to be descended from folk long cut off from the Middle East, assuming their ancestors were ever there. Yet Israel argues that a Jew who left two thousand years ago has a greater right to return to Palestine than an Arab Palestinian peasant who ran for his life in 1948 when external Arabs were fighting with the Jews. This kind of ethnic exclusivity, tied directly to the political logic of establishing a *Jewish* state, is the moral problem which many Western intellectuals have been psychologically unable to recognize.

The consequences of Israel's racial or ethno-cultural exclusivity have resulted in forms of repression against Palestinians living outside Israel which sometimes bear comparison in their immorality with what has happened in South Africa. Between 1967 and 1973 the government of Israel gave orders for, or approval of, the killing of hundreds of Palestinians, most of whom were civilians. These were men, women, and children. Following the killing of the Israeli athletes in the Olympic Games, Israeli planes killed more than three hundred Palestinians living in Lebanon. These casualty figures were British figures at the time. They indicate the human cost inflicted on Palestinian refugees by the Israeli revenge following the death of nine Israeli athletes. The bulk of the world was more shocked by the death of the eleven people in Munich than by the scale of revenge which the Israeli government itself seems to have ordered in the air-raid bombing of Syria and Lebanon after the Munich tragedy in September 1972.[7]

The government of South Africa in that same period ordered the deliberate killing of far fewer people than did the government of Israel. Of course, the Israelis saw themselves as being in a state of war and, therefore, considered it fair game to bomb tents of refugees if Palestinian fighters were recruited from those tents. What was often overlooked was that the Israelis were in a state of war partly because Zionism had this logic of ethno-cultural exclusivity profoundly similar to the logic of apartheid. To the present day the Israelis show no sign of entertaining any serious proposal which would make Palestinian Arabs who ran away from Israel less than thirty years ago have the same right of returning to their homeland as European and American Jews descended from people who ostensibly left that area many centuries ago.

Sometimes Israelis ask why the Palestinian refugees were not instead absorbed into neighbouring Arab countries. This argument would be similar to a situation in which South Africa helped the departure of thousands of black South Africans, and then argued that these should be absorbed into the populations of Zambia, Kenya or Nigeria. Black South Africans are not only black, they are also South Africans. It is racialist to argue that they should be absorbed by other people abroad, rather than mixed with other races on their home ground. Similarly, it borders on racialism to suggest that Palestinians should be absorbed into Lebanon, Jordan or Syria. Palestinians are not only Arab, they are also Palestinian.

It is partly because of these basic similarities between the logic of apartheid and the logic of Zionism that many black radicals started quite early on to identify with the Arab cause. But there were two additional factors behind black radical identification with the Arabs. One is simply the fact that radicals in black Africa were trans-Saharan in their pan-Africanism. Their mystique was the mystique of the African continent as a whole, and not of the black sub-continent. People like Nkrumah and Nyerere genuinely regarded Algerians, for example, as fellow Africans. The other factor was that the Arabs have been part of the vanguard of anti-imperialism in the Third World. Countries such as Egypt, Syria and Algeria have been major participants in movements for Third World liberation. It is true that there are many Arab countries that are less radical, but even these seem to be constantly on the verge of being radicalized by internal forces. And figures such as King Feisal of Saudi Arabia, though feudal in their domestic rule, proved to be also nationalists.

Some Arab countries are radical socialistically, some nationalistically, some both. A country such as Libya is radical in terms of its passionate nationalist commitment to the Arab cause, to Arab culture, and to a lesser extent, to the cause of the Third World in general. But Libya and Gaddafi are animated more by Islamic fundamentalism than by modern revolutionary ideology. Nevertheless, Libya is one more Arab country which has to be placed in the mainstream of Third World militancy, displaying an impatience with the world as it is now constituted, and desiring to restructure the world in the direction of greater autonomy for the Third World peoples. Saudi Arabia and Kuwait are far from radical either nationalistically or socialistically, and yet enough concern has been shown by the rulers of these countries for the Arab cause, and for the welfare of Palestinian revolutionaries, to make even these relatively sedate and highly affluent Arab countries show signs of at least potential militancy in their foreign policies, even if their domestic feudalism continues. The ability of the Arabs to be in the mainstream of Third World militancy has been an important contributory factor to their status among radicals in the world as a whole.

Although a substantial part of the Arab world was ruled by either Britain or France, the Arabs showed none of the tendencies which made many other Africans and Asians choose to belong either to the British Commonwealth or to the French Community. Most Third World nationalists, ranging from Nkrumah to Nehru, succumbed to the temptation of maintaining formal links with the former metropolitan power. But the Arabs ruled by Britain and France were too self-consciously Arab to apply for admission either to the British Commonwealth or to the French Community. It was a measure of Arab rebellion against the global stratification system that most of them severed links with their former European rulers more completely than other Africans and Asians, although informal links with the ex-European imperialists were often maintained.

All these factors are relevant in explaining why many black African radicals, who themselves would have severed the links of their own countries with Britain or France had there not been certain difficult historical constraints, were drawn sympathetically towards the Arab cause.

But from 1972 onwards the picture began to change fundamentally. President Idi Amin set a new trend when he broke off Uganda's relations with Israel on 30 March 1972, without necessarily being radical in his orientation. The case of Uganda introduced a distinct issue—the political hazards which Israel incurred by her involvement in military training in an African country. At the invitation of Idi

Amin's predecessor, Milton Obote, the Israelis established themselves in Uganda as consultants and advisers on military affairs. Inevitably they cultivated friendships among both the politicians and the soldiers. Pre-eminent among the friends Israel made in Uganda was Idi Amin, who was second-in-command in the armed forces when the Israelis first came in 1964, and who later took full military command in 1966. In January 1971, Idi Amin captured supreme authority in the country itself when he overthrew Milton Obote in a military coup.

Circumstantial evidence supports Obote's claim that Amin's success in the coup, in spite of having only a minority of Ugandan soldiers on his side, was partly attributable to brilliant advice from some of his Israeli friends. There was probably an important difference of opinion on the eve of the coup between the Israeli embassy in Kampala and the Israeli military advisers close to Amin. The embassy was probably on the side of normal orthodox diplomatic inhibitions, opposed to intervention in changing the government of Uganda. But the Israeli military advisers, in the face of President Obote's increasing pro-Arab orientation in his last year in office, were inclined more towards *realpolitik*. If Amin was going to carry out a military coup anyhow, there was a case for helping him to succeed. The tactics which enabled him to control the mechanized battalion in Uganda, and tilted the balance of effectiveness between his minority of supporters and the majority of pro-Obote soldiers, probably owed a good deal to the advice of sophisticated Israeli tacticians.

Later Amin developed a fear of the Israelis—'Those who helped to make me can help to break me,' and yet he could not get rid of the Israelis as long as the Sudanese civil war was still being fought. Amin had relatives and allies among the Anyanya who were fighting the government in Khartoum.

In February 1972 a peace settlement for the Sudan was at last reached between contending Sudanese parties at the meeting in Addis Ababa, Ethiopia. Reports from Southern Sudanese sources at that time indicated that the Israelis were almost the only ones of their major advisers who were opposed to the peace settlement. Be that as it may, the very fact that a settlement had been reached provided a potential new basis for Amin's relations with the Israelis.

It has been suggested by Israeli officials in Tel Aviv and by observers elsewhere that Amin became anti-Israeli as a result of visiting Libya. The sequence and causation were probably in the reverse order. Amin visited Libya because he was already planning to expel the Israelis. But if he was going to expel the Israelis, it made good economic and diplomatic sense to extract advantages from Israel's enemies. The causes of Amin's rejection of the Israelis did not lie in the Arab world. They lay in the history of Southern Sudan, the personality of Idi Amin, and the fear that the Israelis might help to overthrow him. Amin owed the Israelis considerable amounts of money, but this was a subsidiary factor which the Israelis later decided to exploit in their own face-saving operation after their expulsion from Uganda. By the end of April 1972, there was not a single Israeli left in Uganda. It was not merely military advisers or airport builders who were required to leave. Also included were other personnel, some of them doing superb developmental work in rural areas and overcrowded schools.

Also in 1972 Chad and the People's Republic of the Congo broke off diplomatic relations with Israel. On 28 November 1972, Chad broke off relations with Israel, partly to reduce Arab involvement in Chad's own civil war involving a Christian government (then under President Tombalbaye who has since been assassinated in a military coup) against a Muslim separatist movement. On 31 December 1972, the People's Republic of the Congo added a new radical African state to those who had opted for severance. In 1973, before the October war, other African countries had become disenchanted with Israel for a number of reasons, ranging from a growing belief that Israel had become a mini-bully in the Middle East to strained relations between Israeli technical assistance personnel in individual countries and the people or authorities of those countries. Niger broke off relations in January 1973, followed closely by Mali. In May, Burundi, a country with a radical foreign policy, followed in the same direction. Togo joined these ranks in September 1973. And then in October 1973, while addressing the United Nations, President Mobutu Sese Seko surprised the world by doing the same. He told the General Assembly that he had been forced to choose between a friend, Israel, and a brother, Egypt. President Mobutu criticized Israeli territorial expansion. Explaining his break with Israel, the President said:

> We have taken this decision at a great risk, because many of our officers—and I myself—have received military training at the hands of Israeli officers who came to our country at our expense. By declaring this decision to the world from the largest Jewish city in the world [New York City], I mean to stress the fact that Zaire will never back down and will carry out the duties of African cooperation.[8]

Some commentators who should know better (including African journalists) have suggested that Africa broke off relations with Israel for the sake of cheaper oil from the Arabs. Such an analysis distorts the sequence of events. By the time the Organization of Petroleum Exporting Countries dramatically raised the price of oil, much of Africa had already sided with the Arabs on the Palestine question. If the trend against Israel in black Africa started in 1972, and had converted even Mobutu Sese Seko of Zaire to its side before the outbreak of the October War, that trend could not be attributed to the energy crisis since this did not hit the world until about the last ten weeks of 1973.

Countries such as Guinea and the Congo broke off relations essentially for reasons of ideological radicalism; Niger did it partly because of religious identification with the Arabs; Uganda under Amin feared the subversive potentialities of an Israeli presence in their midst; Tanzania believed in the Arab cause on its own merits; and countries such as Kenya, the Ivory Coast, and Ethiopia (under Haile Selassie), broke with Israel towards the end, partly because they did not want to be isolated from continental African diplomatic trends or break ranks with other members of the Organization of African Unity.

Within the United Nations new forms of alignments were emerging between African and Arab states. These were dramatized in two controversial decisions of the General Assembly in 1974—the decision to invite Yassir Arafat of the Palestine Liberation Organization to the Assembly, and the suspension of South Africa from the General Assembly for the rest of that session. A quid pro quo approach had already been emerging between Arab and African members of the UN. Acclaim for Arafat was acclaim for liberation movements everywhere. Into the Assembly came the PLO; out went South Africa. And significantly, in the chair of that session of the Assembly was Algeria, a strong activist in both pan-African and pan-Arab politics.

Nevetheless, it would be surprising if a few black African states did not resume diplomatic relations with Israel before long. Many, however, may continue to be put off by what appears to be a strengthening of ties between Israel and South Africa.

By a curious destiny black Africans were identifying with North Africa at precisely the time of some of the worst droughts in countries bordering the Sahara. Climate and politics seemed to be collaborating to make the simple point that while the Sahara was spreading physically, it was indeed shrinking politically. Never in modern history did there seem to be as much solidarity between Arab Africans and black Africans as there emerged, however inconclusively, in the course of 1972 and 1973.

Towards Economic Partnership

Solidarity was not without its tensions. Some black Africans expected special rewards from the Arabs following their break with Israel. When oil prices for black Africa failed to fall, there were frustrations. In Nairobi in June 1974, there were even suggestions made in the East African Legislative Assembly urging that the River Nile be diverted by the East African states so that they could then sell its water to the Arabs, in exchange for barrels of oil. Not every speaker in the Assembly seemed to realize that any attempt to divert the River Nile would be a declaration of war on the Sudan and Egypt. Neither country could be expected to stand aside and let its population be literally killed by thirst and starvation. There would, of course, have been little rationality for East Africa to declare such military hostilities against, say, the Sudan when the Sudan had no oil to sell to anybody. Why was the Nile Valley to be put on fire from Lake Victoria to the Mediterranean when Africa could not even overthrow Ian Smith's regime in Rhodesia without South Africa's help? Moreover the Arab countries that are on the Nile Valley are *not* the Arab countries which have oil to sell. If Uganda, for example, diverted the River Nile, Uganda would be declaring military hostilities against the *wrong* Arabs! Fortunately, all this kind of talk in East Africa was no more than a symptom of frustration. East African *governments* remained cool, collected and rational, while unofficial political commentators argued with passion.

The frustration had deeper causes in history. The central problem was the lack of symmetry in the inter-penetration between the Middle East and black Africa. The Middle East was more 'the giver'; black Africa more 'the receiver'. Black Africa had been penetrated culturally and economically, but had not managed to accomplish adequate counter-penetration. Black dependency was bound to result in black frustration. That is not a healthy relationship between two parts of the Third World.

But do the Arabs owe African states a debt of gratitude for the joint severance of relations with Israel in 1973? A major distinction which has to be drawn in Afro-Arab relations is between a political alliance and an economic partnership. When African states broke off relations with Israel, they were consolidating a political alliance with the Arabs. At the very minimum a political alliance involves sharing enemies. Black Africans, in asserting solidarity with the Arabs, treated Israel as a common enemy for the time being. What many critics of the Arabs forget is that the Arabs have already paid back this particular political debt well in advance. Just as most black African states have no diplomatic relations with Israel, most of the Arab world has had no diplomatic relations with South Africa and Rhodesia.

Black Africa has decided to treat Israel as a common enemy only recently, while most of the Arab world has treated South Africa as a common enemy for many years. Arab countries such as Algeria, Egypt and Libya were supporting black liberation movements in Southern Africa years before black Africa recognized Palestinians as a people with a grievance at all. But in October 1973 the political alliance between black Africa and the Arab world ceased to be one-sided. Both sides decided to share enemies.

Yet when Africans ask for cheaper oil and development aid from the Arabs, they are trying to move beyond the solidarity of a political alliance. They are demanding the establishment of an economic partnership. They are saying to the Arabs: 'Let us not merely share enemies; let us also share energy. To some extent, let us merge economies.'

This is not a bad argument, but the case for such a proposal does not rest on Africa's break with Israel. As indicated, the Arabs have already reciprocated by breaking with Smith and Vorster. The case for an economic alliance between the Arab world and black Africa rests on the proposition that a political alliance can best be consolidated by an economic partnership. We should remember that the USA and Western Europe have been engaged in a similar debate. The Atlantic Alliance was intended to be a military and political alliance; it was *not* designed to be an economic partnership. France has argued that the question of security should not be mixed up with questions of trade and monetary stability. The Atlantic Alliance was an exercise in *sharing enemies* rather than *merging economies*. But Henry Kissinger, when US Secretary of State, took the position that a political or military alliance could best be consolidated by an underlying economic partnership. Kissinger urged Europe to bear in mind the health of the American economy when Europe formulates trade and fiscal policies to serve purely European interests. An alliance based merely on common enemies could be very unstable. The Kissinger argument is similar to our own African position in our relations with the Arabs. We are asking the Arabs to strengthen the Afro-Arab political alliance by a decision to explore the possibilities of an inter-regional economic partnership between the Arab world and black Africa.

Should the Arab world agree immediately under the threat of an African resumption of ties with Israel? It is to be hoped that both black Africans and Arabs will be more mature than that. The North Atlantic Treaty Organization has been in existence for over twenty years, and yet it is only now that an attempt is being made to make it an economic partnership to some extent. The Ottawa meeting of NATO in June 1974 showed at least some recognition of the relevance of economic issues for such a political and military alliance. And the new NATO Declaration of Principles narrowed the gap between the French position and the Kissinger position regarding the relationship between shared security and shared prosperity. Disagreements among the political partners in NATO did not result in the immediate break-up of the alliance. On the contrary, twenty years of patience are now just beginning to bear economic fruit.

I happen to believe that the Arabs and other oil producers should indeed agree on a two-tier pricing system. The developed world should be charged one price, the developing a lower price. But I think these privileges should be open to countries such as India and Bangladesh, as well as to African countries. It is not always remembered that India supported the Arabs in the Middle East for twenty years before the majority of black African states were converted to the Arab side. Why then should Kenya or the Ivory Coast receive better treatment from the Arabs than India? The two-tier pricing system should apply to the Third World as a whole, and not merely to Africa south of the Sahara. The developing countries generally have a good case against the oil-producers.

There are people in both Africa and the USA who are not sure of the difference between a Muslim and an Arab. That seems to be part of the problem implicit in the recent outcry against Arab oil-producers. For example, more than two-thirds of the oil consumed by Kenya has been coming from Iran. Iran (or what some people still refer to as Persia) is of course a Muslim country without being an Arab country. What is more, Iran is the most militant of those oil-producers who want oil prices to go even higher. At the meeting of the Organization of Oil Exporting Countries held in Ecuador in June 1974 there was a strong lobby by Iran to raise the price of oil even higher, and equally strong demands by Saudi Arabia to lower oil prices. In other words, at that meeting the only country which stood strongly for lowering prices was an Arab country. Nigeria stood for at least the status quo level of prices, while Iran demanded an escalation. Yet some passionate voices in Kenya against oil-producers kept on referring to the Arabs, when in fact Kenya's oil came overwhelmingly from a non-Arab country, Iran, which in turn was the strongest advocate of ever-rising oil prices. Many Africans elsewhere also denounced the Arabs, when Iran was the main supplier of oil to South Africa as well as to others. The Arab states, on the other hand, had imposed at least a formal oil embargo on South Africa, Rhodesia and Portugal, when she was still a colonial power in Africa.

There seems little doubt that a few black African states will resume diplomatic relations with Israel in due course. When this happens, will the Arabs retaliate by establishing relations with South Africa?

Following the October war and black Africa's break with her, Israel strengthened relations with South Africa. Israel appointed a new chargé d'affaires, Michael Michael. But Michael had the personal rank of ambassador, and his appointment was designed to be an upgrading of the Israeli mission in Pretoria. The Israeli government was quoted by the American Press as saying: 'Our rejection of apartheid is unchanged, but we feel that Israel should have normal diplomatic relations with all countries, including South Africa.'[9] Full diplomatic relations have since been restored. While black African states were protesting against the tour of a British rugby team in South Africa in 1974, the Israel Philharmonic Orchestra accepted an invitation to tour South Africa. The South African government sees its relationship with Israel as both a modest political alliance and a modest economic partnership. The South African Consul-General in Tel Aviv, Charles Fincham, asserted earlier in 1974 that 'the Soviet push into this part of the world, which also affects South Africa' was one of the reasons for improved relations between South Africa and Israel. In the field of economic partnership, the South African Iron and Steel Corporation signed an agreement with Israel's Koor enterprise for the construction of joint steel works in Israel. Trade between Israel and South Africa expanded further in 1973. South Africa's exports to Israel tripled (from $11.6 million in 1972 to $32.4 million in 1973). Israel's sales to South Africa went up from $8 million to $11.8 million in the same period. All this adds up to a combination of political alliance and economic partnership between Israel and South Africa on a modest scale. In the words of the *Christian Science Monitor*:

> There is no doubt among veteran observers that the improvement in Israel's relations with South Africa—even though Israelis prefer to call it merely 'normalization'—has been spurred by the disappointing conduct of the black African states towards Israel in the October war.[10]

In their own relations with black Africa, will the Arabs be able in their turn to add economic performance to political cordiality? Now the world has entered the final quarter of the twentieth century, that might well be a basic issue to be resolved between these two contiguous regions.

Meanwhile, religious and cultural factors in Afro-Arab relations have been entering a new phase. The spread of Islam has been both unifying and divisive. Islam in Nigeria in the last decade before independence—fearful of the political militancy of Christian southerners—helped to reinforce the separatist tendencies of the North. The word 'Pakistanism' entered the vocabulary of West African politics. Slogans such as 'Down with Pakistanism' began to be heard. Nnamdi Azikiwe, who later became Nigeria's first president, formulated this fear in terms of an aspiration:

> It is essential that ill-will be not created in order to encourage a Pakistan in this country. The North and the South are one, whether we wish it or not. The forces of history have made it so.[11]

Ironically, separatism after independence moved southwards, with special reference to Azikiwe's community. It was Ibo Christians rather than Hausa Muslims who sought to break up Nigeria. And many Christian missionary organizations moved to the support of Biafra. Even the Vatican hovered dangerously on the brink of regarding the Nigerian civil war as a re-enactment of the crusade—a religious war rather than an ethnic confrontation. In reality the religious factor in the Nigeria civil war was at the most subsidiary and certainly not fundamental.

Southern Sudan and Eritrea provide two contrasting models of separatism. The Southern Sudanese secessionists were primarily non-Muslims, often led by Christian compatriots, and strongly supported morally and materially by Christian organizations all over the world. They fought for seventeen years. Eritrea, on the other hand, is primarily Muslim, in rebellion against a long-standing Christian theocracy which has now been taken over by its military establishment. The non-Muslim bid to secede from the Sudan has failed, but autonomy has been obtained for the South. The Muslim bid to pull out Eritrea from Ethiopia is still raging. Will a 'Sudanese solution' be found for Eritrea – a restoration of autonomy for Eritrea? Or will the war rage to the bitter end and result in tensions between black and Arabs, Muslims and non-Muslims all over Africa? It seems more likely that the religious factor would be played down by the propaganda machines of both sides in the contest. But the danger of large-scale continental cleavages is certainly there.

Secessionism in Chad is more like Eritrea than Southern Sudan – a rebellion by defensive Muslims against a perceived Christian threat, rather than the other way round. The death of Tombalbaye and the military take-over of April 1975 have left the main problems of Chad unresolved.

In Africa as a whole it would be misleading to emphasize only those cases where Muslim and Christians have not made comfortable bed-fellows. We should not forget that while the USA was trying to make up its mind in 1960 about whether to elect its first Catholic president, the Muslim voters of Senegal had already affirmed their support for their Catholic leader, Léopold Senghor. And the preponderant Muslims of Tanzania have continued to re-elect their own Roman Catholic *Mwalimu* or mentor, President Julius Nyerere, every five years since independence in 1961. Islam in Africa has sometimes shown levels of magnanimity higher than those it has attained in its ancestral home in the Middle East.

With the rising power of the Arab world in international diplomacy, the prestige of Islam in Africa may be on the way up. The prestige of a religion is often positively correlated with the political or economic power of those who profess it. The Organization of Petroleum Exporting Countries is about two-thirds Muslim in composition. The most influential of its members, Saudi Arabia and Iran, are not only Muslim but traditionalist. Saudi Arabia is the heartland of Sunni Islam; Iran the heartland of Shi'a Islam. A majority of the remaining members of OPEC are also Muslim. The influence of Islam in world politics is entering a new phase, and this will have consequences for Africa.

The Arab League and the OAU

There is a strong temptation among oil-rich Muslim countries to cultivate the rich industrialized countries and to invest either in white Christian countries or in black Muslim countries. Will black

Christendom be left out? In the long run that is not likely to happen, but for the time being shared profits in the Western world and a shared Prophet in the Muslim world are persuasive factors behind Arab economic behaviour. Libya, Kuwait and Saudi Arabia have probably spent more on Muslim Africa than the official figures show. In addition, Kuwait and Saudi Arabia are beginning to invest in projects ranging from Daimler-Benz in Germany to real estate in the USA.

Algeria among the Arab oil producers is perhaps more pan-African than pan-Islamic. Its relatively radical orientation has made it more responsive than the other oil-producing Arab states to Third World solidarity regardless of religion. In terms of material support for Southern African liberation movements, Algeria is more pan-African than the great majority of African states, both black and Arab.

Within the Arab League the strongest voices for black African interests are Algeria, Somalia and the Sudan. Somalia is the first non-Arab country to become a member of the Arab League. It is conceivable that before long there will be a black African sitting at sessions of the Arab League, as a representative of the Organization of African Unity. Nigeria and Algeria are the strongest voices for African interests within the Organization of Petroleum Exporting Countries. For the time being there is de facto reverse representation of the Arab League within the Organization of African Unity. After all nearly half the members of the League are also members of the OAU.

In 1974 two major potential functions of the OAU in Afro-Arab relations were revealed. The Organization is, on the one hand, becoming a mechanism by which the Arabs can *politically* influence black Africans. On the other hand, the OAU is also evolving into a mechanism through which black Africans might seek *economic* concessions from the Arabs.

The issues were dramatized at the summit conference of the Organization of African Unity in June 1974 in Mogadishu. The newly elected president of the Organization was the president of Somalia. But in addition the foreign minister of Somalia was also encouraged by the Arabs and other friends to stand for election as the next secretary-general of the OAU. It would have been the first time that both offices were held by citizens of the same country. The foreign minister of Zambia stood as a rival candidate for the secretary-generalship. One ballot after another was taken, but all were inconclusive. All the Arab states voted for the Somali candidate. Virtually all the English-speaking black states voted for the Zambian candidate. Had it not been for the French-speaking black states, this issue could have split the African continent neatly between black and Arab. But fortunately for the Organization, the Francophone countries were themselves divided on whether to support the Somali (Muslim) candidate or the Zambian (Christian) candidate. There was some positive correlation between voting behaviour and religious affiliation. In the end a third candidate was chosen to break the deadlock.

There was some bitterness among the English-speaking black states. The behaviour of the Arab states in their lobbying for the Somali candidate was interpreted as an attempt to put the Organization under either Arab or Muslim control, especially as it came after the election of the Somali president as the year's head of the Organization.

There is little doubt that the Arabs did attempt in 1974 to create conditions by which they could exercise greater political influence in the Organization. What many outside observers seemed to have overlooked was that the black states were in turn attempting to use the Organization as a mechanism for putting pressure on the Arabs for economic ends.

The bulk of Arab oil comes from outside Africa—from Saudi Arabia and the Gulf states. The bulk of Arab surplus petro-dollars are also in the hands of these non-African states. But could the Arab states *within* the continent be converted into a lobby for black African interests in the Arab world as a whole? If so, could the OAU in turn become a mechanism for pressuring Africa's own Arabs in that direction?

Arab publications have begun to recognize these trends as important developments in Afro-Arab history. Soon after the October war *An-Nahar* drew attention to the significance of President Léopold Senghor's decision to break off relations with Israel on 28 October 1973. It was President Senghor who, in 1971, had headed the ten African heads of state commissioned by the Organization of African Unity to study the prospects of peace in the Middle East. A committee of four men talked to leaders of Egypt and Syria, were partially rebuffed by Israel, and finally recommended the implementation of Resolution 242 of the United Nations in a manner which would not involve any Egyptian loss of land.

> Most important of all the diplomatic ruptures was that ordered by Ethiopia. Israel had always attached special value to its Ethiopian ties in view of that country's strategic position on the Red Sea and there had been strong rumours of an Israeli base on the Ethiopian Coast. One Israeli journal described Ethiopia as the most crucial state in maintaining Israeli security. A great deal of economic aid was accordingly sent to Emperor Haile Selassi [but now] Israel's friends in the African continent are fast greatly diminished, and this can only contribute to its growing sense of isolation in the world at large.[12]

Meanwhile the Arabs soon attempted to reciprocate with other gestures. An oil embargo was at last imposed by Arab oil producers on all exports of oil to South Africa, Rhodesia, and Portugal. A committee of the Organization of African Unity was set up to assess the unintended consequences of the Arab oil boycott and the new oil prices on the fragile economies of African states. Members of this committee met representatives of Arab oil producers in 1974. They were assured unlimited supplies of oil, but the Africans could not obtain special concessions on prices. Instead the Arabs planned to open a special Arab bank for African development, initially with the recommended capital of $200 million (later multiplied eightfold). The fund could be used for types of development which could partially offset some of the consequences of the high Arab oil prices. On the organizational front, it was proposed to establish special links between the Arab League and the Organization of African Unity.

The consequences of the oil prices seemed potentially severe for black African economies. And relations between black Africa and the Arab world had by no means as yet attained a platform of established and long-standing solidarity. Setbacks were predictable. Periodic moments of tension between individual African and Arab states do not necessarily mean that the sense of solidarity has crumbled forever, any more than occasional tensions between Egypt and Libya, or Jordan and Egypt, were an indication that Arab nationalism was not a reality.

There are hazards in the relations between Africa and the Middle East. These include the serious risk of Arab paternalism towards black Africa. It also raises the possibility of Arab neo-colonialism. A good deal will depend upon the Arab world's capacity to transcend the temptations of power and influence, and maintain instead a sound foundation for an Afro-Arab diplomatic and economic front. Further meetings between Arabs and Africans on issues of oil production and oil prices are to be held periodically. The United Nations Economic Commission for Africa also organized a meeting in Tripoli which focused on the energy needs of Africa.

What has been developing are the beginnings of *institutions* for diplomatic interaction between the Arab world and independent Africa. Black Africa could seek to influence the oil policies of, say, Saudi Arabia and Kuwait, through the Organization of African Unity—in spite of the fact that neither Saudi Arabia nor Kuwait were members of the Organization. Similarly, the Palestinians succeeded in influencing the policies of black Africa partly through the OAU—in spite of the fact that the Palestine Liberation Front had no direct representation on the African body. The politics of the Arab League were indeed interacting with the economics of the Organization of African Unity.

Conclusion

Much of the diplomatic discussion between Africa and the Arab world in 1974 was on multilateral aid—money from Arab sources, channelled through special banking institutions, for developing projects in Africa. Performance at this multilateral level has been slow and haphazard. There is still a residual deadlock as to whether Arab aid should come through a new Arab Bank for African Development or should be channelled through the existing African Development Bank.

But while the debates about multilateral aid and two-tier oil pricing have continued, performance in the field of bilateral aid from OPEC members to Third World countries has been improving. By April 1975 Western aid officials—who had been so sceptical about OPEC efforts in aid—were revising their estimates. In the words of Maurice J. Williams, Chairman of the Development Assistance Committee of the Organization for Economic Co-operation and Development (OECD), 'in speed and effectiveness the aid record [of OPEC countries] has been impressive'. By early 1975 that aid already accounted for a sixth of official development aid from rich to poor countries. In 1974 the oil-exporting countries gave away $2.5 billion in official programmes. The Western industrial states distributed $11.3 billion; the Communist countries' contribution was $1.1 billion. The total of official aid was $14.9 billion.

According to these figures of the OECD Committee, the oil states gave 1.8 per cent of their gross national product in 1974, compared with 0.33 per cent in the Western industrial states. Aid given by the USA had in fact fallen from 0.57 per cent of its total output of goods and services in 1963 to 0.21 per cent in the latest figures analysed by the committee.[13]

The main aid donors among the OPEC group were Iran, Saudi Arabia, Kuwait, the United Arab Emirates and Venezuela. Partly because OPEC is so Islamic in composition, and partly because the 'Fourth World' or poorest countries are disproportionately Muslim, about 80 per cent of aid from oil-exporting countries has gone to Muslim countries. Outside Africa this has included Bangladesh, Afghanistan and Pakistan. Within Africa, Muslim recipients of Arab aid have included Mali, Somalia, Senegal, Guinea and Sudan. Uganda is not a Muslim country but has had a Muslim head of state since the army took over power in 1971. Until the end of 1974 Uganda had received approximately $20 million in official aid from OPEC sources. Double that amount was promised.

In addition there is a significant area of unofficial aid. This includes aid to Muslim minorities in otherwise non-Muslim countries. The range of such minorities that have received aid include the Muslims of Sierra Leone, Kenya and Ghana (mainly educational aid), the Muslims of Chad and Ethiopia (for partly military and partly welfare purposes) and the Muslims of Dahomey and Upper Volta (mainly educational aid and for missionary work). By its very nature unofficial aid is difficult to compute, but many delegations from Muslim Africa go fund-raising to the Arab world every year, and few come back completely empty-handed. Many African Muslims go to schools and colleges in the Arab world—from Cairo to Kuwait, from Baghdad to Algiers, from Riyadh to Tripoli.

But clearly Afro-Arab relations cannot reduce themselves to inter-Muslim relations. Nor should economic interaction between Africa and the Middle East be limited to bilateral aid. The related questions of multilateral aid, bilateral investment and inter-regional trade need to be explored, strengthened and, whenever possible, institutionalized in the years ahead.

Oil as the new form of black energy has been posing new questions about the future relations between the Arabs, the Africans and the Western world. At least since the Middle East October war of 1973, the Middle East and Africa have edged a little closer towards becoming a single international sub-system. But that is not close enough yet. It remains to be seen whether the Arabs will indeed complete the three stages of their African destiny. To live down their role as accomplices in Africa's enslavement, it was right but not adequate that they should later have become allies in African liberation. For the sake of both their own past and Africa's future, the Arabs must now take the third decisive step, and genuinely become partners in the development of the Third World as a whole.

References and notes

1. Ronald Robinson and John Gallagher with Alice Denny, *Africa and the Victorians* (New York: St Martin's Press, 1961), p. 283.
2. Ibid., p. 320. This point is discussed in related contexts in the following previous papers by the author: inaugural lecture at Makerere University, Uganda, *Ancient Greece in African Political Thought* (Nairobi: East African Publishing House, 1967); and 'Is the Nile Valley emerging as a new political system?', paper presented at the Universities' Social Sciences Council Conference (USSC), held at Makerere University,Kampala,14-17 December 1971.
3. Cited by Colin and Margaret Legum, *South Africa: Crisis for the West* (Pall Mall Press, 1964) pp. 107-8.
4. A. Nasser, *The Philosophy of the Revolution*, Economica English Edition (Buffalo: Smith, Keynes & Marshall Publications, 1959), p. 74.
5. *Sunday Express*, 18 March 1956.
6. *The Arab Observer*, 1 (13 November 1961) 18.
7. Consult *The Guardian*, and *The Times*, 11 September 1972.
8. For one report of Mobutu's break, consult *New York Times*, 5 p. 9 and 6 October 1973.
9. *Christian Science Monitor*, 22 March 1974. See also *N.Y. Amsterdam News*, 9 October 1976, *Washington Post*, 3 May 1975; *Washington Post*, 31 October 1976 and *New York Times*, 3 November 1976.
10. *Christian Science Monitor*, 22 March 1974.
11. N. Azikiwe, *Zik: A Selection from the Speeches of Nnamdi Azikiwe* (Cambridge University Press, 1961), p. 102.
12. *An-Nahar*, a weekly analysis of political and economic development, 4, (5 November 1973).
13. For a succinct digest of the OECD committee's report, see Clyde Farnsworth, 'Oil exporters increasing foreign aid', *New York Times*, 19 April 1975.

CHAPTER 8
Africa & the USA

The year of 1960 saw an independence explosion on the African continent. More than fifteen countries attained sovereign status. It was also the year when the American electorate voted John F. Kennedy into office. The coincidence was perhaps not inappropriate. Kennedy himself was soon proclaiming in his inaugural address: 'Let word go forth from this time and place, to friend and foe alike, that the torch has been passed to a new generation of Americans.' It had now fallen to this new generation of Americans to respond to the emergence of the new Africa.

What is the record of that response so far? On balance the USA has done fewer bad things in Africa than she has done in Asia and Latin America. But she has also done fewer good things in Africa than elsewhere. The anomaly will become clearer in the course of the analysis. We shall address ourselves to the Kennedy years as the beginning of America's involvement in *independent* Africa, but the origins of African-American relations are much older.

One of the earliest links between the USA and African nationalism is the link of American education. As a Nigerian student put it two decades ago, 'The first skirmishes in the struggle for political freedom of the 21 million people of Nigeria are being fought in the colleges of the US.'[1] Almost as if he was making a bid to save this link between Africa and America, one of the first involvements of John F. Kennedy in African affairs on the eve of his election was on the issue of education. Kenya's Tom Mboya saw Kennedy in 1960 in connection with attempts to raise money for the 260 Kenya students who had been offered places in American colleges but lacked the money for fares. Kennedy took up the matter with the Kennedy Foundation, and a $100 000 gift was made.[2]

As soon as he took office Kennedy appealed to that missionary strain in the American temperament. He said to his fellow citizens:

> Since this country was founded, each generation of Americans has been summoned to give testimony to its national loyalty. . . . Now the trumpet summons us again—not as a call to bear arms, though arms we need—not as a call to battle, though embattled we are—but a call to bear the burden of a long twilight struggle, year in year out, 'rejoicing in hope, patient tribulation'—a struggle against

the common enemies of man: tyranny, poverty, disease and war itself.[3]

The missionary factor in the American temperament has its dangers. Sometimes it takes the form of an obstinate plunge into an ideological crusade. American anti-communism is in the tradition of the doctrine of 'manifest destiny'—missionary zeal and patriotism unite to create a militancy that is at once outward-looking and self-centred. But the missionary factor in the American temperament has also less aggressive manifestations. It can take the form of 'boy scout' altruism and go all out to help the needy. Perhaps every president of the United States has had occasion to appeal to the missionary factor in the American temperament for one cause or another. But some presidents succeeded mainly in arousing the aggressive form of this zeal—the ultra-patriotic dedication that seeks to make the world safe for the American way of life.

John F. Kennedy stands out, however, for having put greater emphasis on the boy scout side of that American zeal. On 1 March 1961, less than two months after his inaugural address, he signed the order establishing the Peace Corps. To him the Peace Corps was 'designed to permit our people to exercise more fully their responsibilities in the great common cause of world development'.[4] Though established with caution and misgivings, the Peace Corps has been a modest success. Rupert Emerson once described it as 'the most distinctive contribution which the United States has made to the independent countries of Africa as well as to other parts of the Third World'. He pointed out how, at least for a while, Africa had 'bulked large in Peace Corps operations, coming in a close second after Latin America and far ahead of the two other major categories of the Far East and the Near East and South Asia'.[5]

Kennedy tried to isolate the boy scout from the ideological crusader within the American missionary. In his inaugural address he said:

> To those peoples in the huts and villages of half the globe struggling to break the bonds of mass misery, we pledge our best efforts to help them help themselves, for whatever period is required—not because the Communists may be doing it, not because we seek their votes, but because it is right.[6]

Perhaps unlike many inaugural addresses, Kennedy's was an approximation to real intention. But a complete separation of the boy scout from the ideological crusader was too ambitious an objective. There was in Kennedy a new *emphasis* on the boy scout side, but his Peace Corps and, even more clearly, his Alliance for Progress could not completely tear themselves away from motives of ideological proselytism.

It is the relationship between these two aspects of American missionary zeal which has determined the nature of American policy in Africa. Perhaps more than any other single region, Africa throughout the 1960s appealed to the boy scout side of America. Its disproportionate share of the Peace Corps was a measure of this. But Africa was not a crisis area in American ideological terms. And so the Clay Report on foreign aid which was submitted to Kennedy argued that since immediate security interests were less evident in Africa than in countries adjacent to the Communist bloc, Africa was 'an area where the Western Europe countries should logically bear most of the necessary aid burden'. As Rupert Emerson has again pointed out, this advice was substantially heeded by the United States, in spite of certain important exceptions. In Emerson's words:

> The limitations imposed by the fact that Africa was not a crisis area nor one in which the United States had urgent interests and that it retained special ties to Europe were strikingly reflected in the allocation of only $1 533 100 000 to the entire continent by AID and its predecessor agencies from 1948 to 1964 whereas Korea alone was allotted $2 384 600 000 and Vietnam $1 868 400 000 in the same period, *apart from huge military assistance** to both countries.[7]

These factors produced a situation in which the United States has done less harm in Africa than she has been known to do in Asia and Latin America, but she has also proportionately done less good in Africa than elsewhere. When James Farmer of the Congress for Racial Equality called for a Marshall Plan for Africa, the dominant element in American foreign policy was the ideological crusade, and in general there was no compelling ideological danger in Africa to justify a Marshall Plan.[8]

But it is not merely the issue of aid which is affected by the calculus of American anti-communism. It is also the boundaries of African diplomatic behaviour at large. Here again we might usefully start with Kennedy's declarations of intention as he assumed office. From the point of view of the non-aligned, Kennedy's inaugural address had ominous undertones. He said:

> To those new states whom we welcome to the ranks of the free, we pledge our word that one form of colonial rule shall not have passed away merely to be replaced by a far more iron tyranny. We shall not always expect to find them supporting our view. But we shall always hope to find them strongly supporting their own freedom—and to remember that in the past, those who foolishly sought power by riding the back of the tiger ended up inside.

What was ominous about this passage was that it sounded as if Uncle Sam was once again dispensing advice to the rest of the world about the big, sharp teeth of the Communist beast—warning

*The italics are mine.

solemnly, 'Remember, O children! It was touch-and-go with Little Red Riding Hood.' Was John F. Kennedy merely a new version of John F. Dulles?

Yet that passage from Kennedy's inaugural address did less than justice to the diplomatic horizons of the new administration. Indeed, the Kennedy era had a decisive impact on the nature of non-alignment in both Asia and Africa. The doctrine of non-alignment was not the same again after those three years. The impact of Kennedy took three forms. One was greater American acceptance of neutrality in the cold war as a legitimate stance for the new states. It turned out that Kennedy did mean it after all when, in his inaugural address, he conceded the right of independent thinking to the new arrivals on the world stage. 'We shall not always expect to find them supporting our view', he had affirmed. But at least as important an influence on the nature of non-alignment was the Cuban crisis of October-November 1962 and its effect on Soviet-American relations. The confrontation of the giants over Cuba helped to rescue non-alignment from its own crisis of confidence following China's invasion of India at about the same time. How were these crises interrelated?

According to at least one view at that time, a basic presupposition of non-alignment was the assumption that it was possible for a country to be left alone militarily by *both* blocs without an alliance. In order to invalidate non-alignment all that one therefore needed was an invasion of a non-aligned country by a member of one of the blocs. Mao Tse-tung fulfilled this condition when he attacked neutral India. In other words, Mao succeeded where John Foster Dulles had failed—in murdering non-alignment. Or so concluded a large number of people in the Western world. *The Times* of London had a curt editorial to celebrate the explosion of the myth of neutralism.[9] On 11 November 1962, the *New York Times* even managed to collect quotations from unobtrusive Africans allegedly disillusioned with non-alignment. On the night of 3 December 1962, a professor from the London School of Economics commented on British radio on 'the end of the neutralist myth'. This interpretation of the significance of the Chinese invasion of India was fairly representative of Western opinion.

The *New York Times* might have been right in its reference to a mood of disenchantment in the ranks of the African non-aligned. There might indeed have been a moment of agonizing doubt as to the meaningfulness of the diplomatic stance they had so far fondly cherished. But the implications of the Cuban crisis—when the worst was over and people could reflect afresh—were a *vindication* of non-alignment. The humiliation of Cuba herself in the autumn of 1962 arose out of permitting a foreign nuclear base on Cuban soil—a contravention of one of the basic tenets of Afro-Asian neutralism. In a letter to U Thant on 27 October 1962, Fidel Castro said that his country flatly rejected 'the presumption of the United States to determine what actions we are entitled to take within our country, what kind of arms we consider appropriate for our defence, what relations we are to have with the USSR, and what international policy steps we are entitled to take. . . .'[10] Yet Castro's ally, Nikita Khrushchev, capitulated to Kennedy's demands with little pretence at consultations with Castro. The moral was not lost on the non-aligned in Africa. If an African voice was going to be marginal in influencing big events, it had better be marginal outside blocs altogether. The experience of little Cuba was a warning against allowing oneself to be used in a global nuclear strategy by one of the big powers. The crisis of confidence among the non-aligned which China's behaviour had created was resolved by the new sense of fearful vindication which emerged out of the Cuban confrontation.

Indeed, even while the confrontation was on, African states participated in the search for a solution. Ghana and the United Arab Republic submitted a joint draft resolution to the Security Council on 24 October 1962, urging the parties in the dispute to refrain from further aggravating the situation while the search for a modus vivendi was going on.[11] And the Union of Africa and Malagasy States (the old UAM) submitted a set of proposals on the immediate steps to be taken to reduce the danger of war. It was clear that the survival of humanity was an issue which concerned all states. Africa asserted her right to have a say in a matter so grave,[12] and her freedom from military entanglement with either of the big powers did not appear to be a diplomatic handicap at such a moment.

Yet, much as the Cuban crisis strengthened the case for non-alignment, indirectly it also weakened its impact on world affairs. The Cuban confrontation was the great turning point in Soviet-American relations. The intense ideological competitiveness between the two countries was replaced by a more sober relationship. The Soviet Union was humbled over China. This by itself had a major impact on the Third World. But at least as important was the use to which John F. Kennedy put his triumph. He did not gloat over Khrushchev's capitulation. On the contrary, he congratulated him on his statesmanship.[13] Before long the 'hot line' between Washington and Moscow was established. And Soviet-American détente was born.

This détente helped to reduce what little status Africa had had as a 'crisis area'. From then on the Soviet-American scramble to buy the ideological souls of Africans lost its momentum. Cuba had strengthened the case for non-alignment, but it had also helped to reduce its rewards. The Clay Report on foreign aid was presented to Kennedy soon after the Cuban confrontation. For as long as non-alignment had been regarded as dangerously near to communism, Africa had a chance of being regarded as 'critical'. The year 1962 was, in fact, the peak year of American aid to Africa for that period.[14] But in the fiscal year 1963 the economic assistance programme for Africa began to drop back. From 12.5 per cent of the AID figure, Africa's share dropped to 10.4 per cent in 1963 and then 8.8 per cent in 1964.[15] There are a number of reasons to explain this drop, including the overall global reduction of American foreign aid. But even the global reduction might be somewhat connected with the change in the tempo of the cold war following the Soviet-American détente. With that change Africa shrunk even further in her status as a security risk for the USA.[16]

A third form of influence which the Cuban crisis had on African non-alignment lay in its connection with the Monroe Doctrine. In his ultimatum to the Soviet Union on 22 October 1962, John F. Kennedy described the transformation of Cuba into an important strategic base of that kind as a 'flagrant and deliberate defiance of the Rio Act of 1947' and of 'the traditions of this nation and Hemisphere'. The President went on to say:

> We are calling tonight for an immediate meeting of the Organ of Consultation, under the Organization of American States, to consider this threat to hemispheric security and to invoke articles six and eight of the Rio Treaty in support of all necessary action. The United Nations Charter allows for regional security arrangements—and the nations of this Hemisphere decided long ago against the military presence of outside powers.[17]

This principle of preventing the military presence of external powers from intruding into one's own region is one which was shared by many African nationalists. A major aspect of African non-alignment was to keep military bases of the cold war out of the African continent. The Western Hemisphere had enough power to enforce such hemispheric exclusiveness. The Cuban confrontation with the Soviet Union demonstrated that. Africa aspired to continental exclusiveness without the means to realize it. The difference was a matter of bitter frustration for some African nationalists. As a Minister of State in Uganda, Grace Ibingira, put it some years later:

> In the 19th century President Monroe propounded a doctrine which became acceptable in international law that the American hemispheres [sic] were not opened to any foreign intrusion. More recently still, the late President Kennedy demanded the Soviet withdrawal from Cuba on the grounds that Cuba was in the American sphere of influence. . . .
>
> What is wrong when African States demand to be responsible for the solution of the Congolese problem, since the Congo both geographically and even politically is naturally tied to them?[18]

What Ibingira was here propounding is what might be called the principle of *continental jurisdiction* which has been so much a part of African nationalist thought—the principle that there are certain

African problems which should only be solved by Africans. This is really the African equivalent of the Monroe Doctrine—but using a continent rather than a hemisphere as the unit of exclusiveness.[19] Curiously enough, some of the most bitterly resented violations of African continental jurisdiction have been committed by the USA in relation to what was then called the Congo. Even more curiously, this principle of an African Monroe Doctrine was apparently also violated by Cuban adventurers serving as mercenaries for Tshombe in the Congo (now Zaire). On 16 February 1965, following the bombing of two Uganda villages by Congolese planes of American manufacture, three ministers of the Uganda Government publicly submitted a protest to the American Embassy. The first two demands made in the protest-note were that the USA should stop military aid to the Congo and should 'withdraw the Cuban rebels from the Congo'.[20] The principle of an African continental jurisdiction was being violated both by the USA and by Castro's countrymen in exile. (See Chapter 9.)

In the earlier days of the Kennedy Administration, America's sin in Zaire had been a sin of omission. The USA strongly supported Dag Hammarskjöld, then Secretary-General of the United Nations, in his reluctance to end Katanga's secession. Amidst all the confusion there was a genuine desire on the part of Hammarskjöld to avoid direct political intervention by the United Nations in what he regarded as a fight between Congolese or Zaireans themselves. But the policy was unrealistic from the start. In a situation like that of Zaïre at the time, the UN could not commit itself to the maintenance of law and order and at the same time refuse to maintain the territorial integrity of Zaire. The two things were so closely tied. But it took the shock of Lumumba's death, revealed early in February 1961, to effect a reversal of the policy of the United Nations. On 21 February, the UN Security Council at last conceded the possibility of using force to end Katanga's secession. It is to the credit of the USA that it vigorously supported this change. In fact, by the middle of 1961, Hammarskjöld was almost exclusively relying on the USA for big-power support. The Soviet Union, France and Britain were, for different reasons, all arrayed against him. Nevertheless, many Africans could not forget that it took Lumumba's death to change the policy of the UN, and United Nations policy at the time was identified with the policy of the USA.

We might therefore say that America's first major blunder in Zaire was an excessive attachment to the principle of non-intervention. She refused to support UN action to end Katanga's secession. But by 1964, with Tshombe in the Central Government, American policy in Zaire was considerably interventionist. The difference can be shown by juxtaposing the most emotive event in Zaire during Kennedy's administration with the most emotive during Johnson's. No event while Kennedy was alive aroused greater African passions than the assassination of Patrice Lumumba. And Lumumba's death arose out of a sin of omission by the United Nations and, indirectly, by the USA. The United Nations, which had been called to Zaire by Lumumba, stood by while the man was taken away from Leopoldville (now Kinshasa) and entrusted to the tender mercies of his opponents in Katanga.

But the most emotionally-charged event in Zaire during Johnson's administration was the Stanleyville rescue-operation of November 1964. This was a positive act of *rescue*. Lumumba had not been considered worth rescuing, though UN forces were actually there on the scene. But white hostages in danger of their lives were a different proposition. As Conor Cruise O'Brien pointed out, the humanitarian sensitivity displayed by the West was, at bottom, a case of racial solidarity.[21] O'Brien is often less than fair to Western governments, but in this case it remains suspiciously true that no rescue operation of that scale would have been launched by the USA and Belgium if the hostages had not been white.

On the African side there was a further element in the rescue operation which hurt many of them deeply. The Americans had appealed to Kenyatta, as Chairman of the OAU Conciliation Committee on the Congo, to use his good offices on behalf of the hostages. But it later appeared that the Americans appealed to Kenyatta only as a stalling tactic and a diversion, while behind his back they and the Belgians planned to drop troops on Stanleyville. Comparisons were made between the rescue operation conducted by American aircraft and the treachery of Pearl Harbor. The Rhodes Professor of Race Relations at Oxford has pointed out how bitterly Americans resented such comparisons.[22] American sensitivities were understandable. There were important moral and other differences between Pearl Harbor and the drop of paratroopers in Stanleyville in 1964. But what Pearl Harbor *did* share with the Stanleyville operation was an element of duplicity. In the Stanleyville case, the duplicity took the form of making polite noises and humanitarian appeals to the Chairman of the OAU Committee on the Congo, while Belgian paratroopers were putting on their uniforms and American planes were ready on the runway.

The hostages had been held by the rebels as a method of stopping the flow of American arms to the Tshombe regime. But the fear of American arms bedevilling African politics by no means started with the rescue operation of November 1964 or with the bombing of Uganda villages by American-manufactured planes in February 1965. Julius Nyerere, when he visited the United States in July 1961 as a guest of the Kennedy administration, said he hoped that the USA would not sell arms to African countries. Nyerere asserted: 'If a country has money to spare in helping others it should spend it fighting poverty, illiteracy and disease.[23] Nyerere was concerned lest arms supplied to one African country should end up being used against another country. As he put it the following month after his visit to the USA:

> In the world as it is today nobody could seriously suggest that an African state can arm itself, or be armed, in order to defend itself against attack by one of the Great Powers of the world. If an African state is armed then, realistically, it can only be armed against another African state.[24]

Nyerere was overstating his case. But the troubles between Uganda and Zaire in February 1965 seemed to vindicate some of Nyerere's old foreboding. Prime Minister Obote of Uganda had apparently told the American Embassy in Uganda that there was an urgent need for the USA to revise its agreement with Zaire concluded in July 1963 on the supply of arms. The revisions that Obote had in mind were conditions which would 'ensure that offensive weapons [supplied to Zaire] were not used against Uganda'. The Prime Minister was not prepared to accept the argument apparently advanced by the USA that it had no control over the arms it gave as aid to Zaire. Obote regarded an unconditional and uncontrolled supply of arms to a regime which was unpopular in Africa to be a policy which was 'not only irresponsible but very dangerous to the countries neighbouring the Congo and others who did not agree with Tshombe's objectives.[25] But Zaire at that time was the nearest thing to a genuine security risk that Africa had to offer to American policy-makers. In responding to the problems of Zaire the anti-communist crusader overshadowed the American boy scout. If Ethiopia was excluded, Zaire received 85 per cent of the American military assistance for tropical Africa for the fiscal year 1964. She received about $6.5 million in military aid.[26]

This sort of thing is what makes the American evangelical spirit useful to right-wing regimes in different parts of the world. But it is also what often earns the USA the bitter resentment of nationalists and radicals in the Third World.

The USA and Southern Africa

But is there no service that the American evangelical spirit could render to African radicalism? There is. The passion for ideological proselytism, often so inherent in American politics, could become an ally of radical liberating forces in the African continent.

It might sound like a parody, but supposing we maintained that a basic preoccupation of the American missionary zeal has been to make the world relatively safe for the American way of life. Yet we know that the only quality of the American way of life which the USA had absolutely insisted on in South Vietnam, for example, was the minimal quality of being non-communist. It was a negative quality, but perhaps it was not without some importance.

Yet the American political culture and system of values has more to offer than the mere quality of being non-communist. Among the more distinctive qualities of the American experience is ethnic heterogeneity With that heterogeneity has been the slow but sure progress towards the ideal of racial equality in the USA. There is little doubt that the civil rights revolution has been one of the most inspiring aspects of recent American domestic history, in spite of all the broken promises and unfulfilled hopes which still characterize the mood of the reformers. Could not the same civil rights revolution form the basis of American *foreign policy*, with special reference to decisions concerning Africa? If the American proselytizing spirit is irreplaceable, it should perhaps be more selective in deciding which aspects of the American way of life should be proselytized in which part of the world. There may be some parts of the world to which the best American export might indeed be American anti-communism, in spite of the changing moods in the wake of American détente with the Soviet Union. But for the African continent the best American export might indeed be the civil rights revolution itself, translated into an American commitment towards the liberation especially of Southern Africa.

And yet American performance so far has not been in the direction of adequate commitment to African liberation. On the contrary, the behaviour and policies of the USA, at least until 1974, amounted to significant economic support for South Africa, significant military support for Portugal, and some degree of moral support for Rhodesia. Let us take each of these in turn.

The most important fact is the economic support for the Republic of South Africa. American investment in South Africa has been the largest single American economic commitment within Africa south of the Sahara. By 1970 that investment accounted for $755 million, compared with the investment of $172 million in Liberia and $150 million in Angola, the second and third largest American economic commitments south of the Sahara. Indeed, more than half the American investment in sub-Saharan Africa lay south of the Zambezi. Trade between the USA and South Africa has been commensurate in volume. As the two countries entered the 1970s United States exports to South Africa and Namibia were already worth $563 million (17 per cent of South Africa's total imports); while United States imports from the South African Republic totalled $208 million (over 13 per cent of South Africa's total exports, excluding gold).[27] For black African states eager to see the imposition of economic sanctions on South Africa, and the isolation of the Republic for as long as it maintains the policy of apartheid, the economic contribution of the USA to the prosperity of South Africa is inevitably seen as a disservice to the African cause.

In this connection an important distinction needs to be made between expressive sanctions and instrumental sanctions against South

Africa. Expressive sanctions are those imposed primarily to indicate disapproval. They amount to an expression of moral condemnation, but in themselves are not designed necessarily to change the situation. Instrumental sanctions are those which are imposed in the direct expectation of forcing the guilty party to capitulate and change its conduct.

This distinction also applies to forms of political violence. The assassination of Prime Minister Verwoerd by a fellow white man was at the most an expressive assassination, indicating the individual assassin's desire to express himself in that act of violence. There does not seem to have been a belief on the part of the assassin that the mere killing of Verwoerd would result in dramatic social or political changes in the Republic. The question of whether the assassin's mind was balanced need not change the basically expressive nature of the act. On the other hand, the assassinations of Eduardo Mondlane, the Mozambique liberation fighter, and Amilcar Cabral, the hero of the liberation movement of Guinea-Bissau, seemed to combine expressive and instrumental purposes. The idea behind the two murders was both to express some kind of disapproval of the activities of the victims, and to start a process which might change the course of the two colonial wars in Mozambique and Guinea-Bissau.

When Harold Wilson imposed sanctions on Rhodesia following Ian Smith's unilateral declaration of independence, the sanctions were intended primarily as instrumental, though they also inevitably had an expressive content. Harold Wilson, as Prime Minister of Britain, really believed that the sanctions would bring down the rebel regime in a matter of weeks, and certainly in a matter of months, but in instrumental terms the sanctions proved much weaker than originally hoped.

With regard to South Africa, most African states have imposed a boycott. Some of those who boycott South Africa have had very little economic interaction with the Republic in any case. Indeed, few really believe that their own economic boycotts against the perpetrators of apartheid would by themselves result in any change in the situation. We would therefore say that sanctions imposed by black African states are expressive, indicating moral disapproval rather than directly designed to change the fundamental nature of the South African political system. But when the African states call upon South Africa's main trading partners in the world, especially those of Western Europe and North America, to boycott South Africa, it is assumed that the massive dependence of South Africa on trade with such partners would make a boycott an effective leverage in the direction of systematic change.

Should the USA disengage economically from South Africa? If the disengagement were to be primarily motivated by a desire to express disapproval, the case for it would be strong. American disapproval of apartheid would be expressed more eloquently by such an economic sacrifice than by dozens of speeches delivered by Secretaries of State and White House spokesmen. But would American disengagement also be effective instrumentally in changing the South African situation? The answer to this second question is far less clear. Since the South African situation is unlikely to be resolved without a major internal revolution, the question which arises is whether that revolution would come sooner as a result of South African prosperity or as a result of slow economic growth in the Republic. A case can be made for the proposition that rising prosperity within South Africa would move faster towards creating a revolutionary situation than slow economic growth in the Republic. Two factors are particularly important in this regard. One is the impact of economic prosperity on South Africa's labour requirements. Indications already reveal the potential of greater black penetration into the economy in areas intended to be primarily white in South Africa. The expansion of South Africa's economic base seems for the time being to need ever greater numbers of black people in factories and mines, and should therefore make economic apartheid, in the sense of separating the races in the economic domain, more difficult than ever. Western investment in South Africa, to the extent to which it results in the expansion of the South African economy and its increasing reliance on black labour, is helping to prepare the ground for the funeral of apartheid.

The second factor is the impact of Western investments on black expectations. There is a level of poverty below which the oppressed remain submissive, conformist, ignorant, and bewildered. But above that level of poverty lies the moment of expanding economic horizons, leading in turn to rising political consciousness. The civil rights movement in the USA became more radical precisely as the black population there became better off. The achievements which followed the 1954 decision against school segregation helped to raise the expectations of black people in the USA, and resulted in increasing mobilization and demonstration in favour of further desegregation within the system. Western investment in South Africa could once again be contributing towards the final revolution in South Africa precisely by helping to expand the economic horizons of the black people.

A preliminary step towards that goal might lie in the pressure put on Western companies by their own governments at home to provide higher wages and better working conditions than might otherwise be made available in South Africa. Debates in Britain in 1973 and 1974 concerning minimum wages in South Africa, and resulting in parliamentary moves towards forcing British companies to improve the working conditions of their African workers in South Africa, was certainly a case in point. Some discussion along these lines has also taken place in the USA, and some American companies have already decided 'to adopt more progressive labour practices and to become a more effective force for change'.[28]

What emerges from all this is that while American investment in and trade with South Africa do indeed imply de facto economic support for the status quo, the unintended consequences of American economic engagement could still serve positive functions in the long run.

The Americans and Portuguese Colonialism

If the most dramatic American support for South Africa has been economic in nature, the most dramatic American support for Portugal until 1974 was, either directly or indirectly, military. A major reason for this was Portugal's membership of the North Atlantic Treaty Organization, though there was also the additional point of interaction between American economic investment in Portugal and her colonies, and the impact of that investment on the ability of the Portuguese to maintain their colonial wars for as long as they did.

To those who have argued that arms and equipment for Portugal as a member of NATO was a contribution to Lisbon's capacity to fight her colonial wars, this in turn used to imply that the Atlantic alliance was confined to Europe and the North Atlantic, and was designed for the defence of Europe, having nothing to do with Portugal's colonies. There were indeed arms deals between members of the North Atlantic Treaty Alliance, but there was no such thing as NATO arms. The transfer of equipment and armaments was bilateral between individual allies and was not part of the broader Atlantic alliance. In 1961 it might have been demonstrated that the Portuguese had used American equipment in Africa, equipment allocated to the North Atlantic Treaty Organization for use only in Europe. But since then, so Washington used to argue, the Portuguese had given categorical assurances that no such armaments would be used in the colonial wars.

As William Minter pointed out, Washington's position on this matter rested on the false assumption that Portugal's military role in Europe was deemed by the Portuguese to be distinct from her role in Africa.

> That assumption is false . . . first of all, because the Portuguese make no such clear distinction. The mission of the armed forces is the defence of the national territory. The national territory includes, by definition, the 'overseas provinces'. At present a chief preoccupation of the Portuguese armed forces is, of course, Africa. Portugal is fighting no other wars. The whole character of the defence establishment is moulded by its 'mission' overseas.[29]

Minter went on to point out that Portugal's military budget was constructed in such a manner that Europe and Africa were militarily inseparable. While each territory had its own armed forces budget, that budget included receipts from both local taxes and from the central government. And the central budget in Portugal included an 'extraordinary' defence provision. Both the ordinary and extraordinary provisions included expenditures relevant to the whole of the 'national territory', and for all three forces of the army, navy and air force.

> The deployment of the Portuguese forces also defies a clear cut division between Europe and Africa. Of an estimated 1969 total of some 18 000 troops, only some are assigned to NATO; while 150 000 are in Africa. A given unit in the Army generally serves two years 'overseas', and then is rotated back to Portugal. Although the law provides that the normal term of military service is for two years, the recruit usually spends a time in uniform both before and after his time in Africa. A major function of the Navy, and to some extent of the Air Force, is transport between Europe and Africa. Of the Air Force, only one anti-submarine reconnaissance programme is assigned to NATO. Both Navy and Air Force have regional commands in metropolitan Portugal and overseas.[30]

Equipment and armaments provided by fellow NATO members to Portugal therefore inevitably helped to reinforce and prolong Portugal's capacity to maintain her imperial role in Africa. In response to criticism on the use of Fiat G-91 Jets from West Germany in Africa, a Portuguese Foreign Ministry spokesman retorted:

> The transition was agreed within the spirit of the North Atlantic Pact. It was agreed that the planes would be used only for defensive purposes within Portuguese territory. Portuguese territory extends to Africa—Angola, Mozambique, and Portuguese Guinea.[31]

The bulk of military equipment, aid, and technical assistance in Portugal has in fact come from the USA. To that extent the USA has been the main Atlantic ally indirectly implicated in the long Portuguese military involvement in the colonies.

A major reason behind Portugal's admission to the North Atlantic Treaty Organization originally was the prospect of using the Azores as a critical base. In the Second World War the Azores were used as a stop-over point between Europe and the Middle East. In the early years of the Atlantic alliance much of the American air traffic relied on the Azores in its global movements. By 1968 the percentage of American air traffic had dropped from some 80 to 20 per cent. The American commentator, James Reston, commented in his column in 1969 that the Azores had outlived their original purpose.[32] But another commentator, David Abshire, writing for the Center for Strategic and International Studies at Georgetown University, was more prophetic than Reston. Abshire pointed out that the Azores could prove to be an important shuttle point for air-lifting troops or equipment to the Middle East should Western Europe and North Africa decide to deny refuelling rights to American planes.[33] This important residual role of the Azores was in fact to be invoked in the Middle East war of October 1973. West Germany refused the USA the use of German bases for the transportation of equipment and armaments to Israel in the midst of the war. The Federal Republic regarded itself as being neutral between the Arabs and the Israelis, and felt that the use of German territory for the purpose of militarily reinforcing the Israelis would violate the principle of neutrality in that conflict. The USA was of course indignant. The Germans retorted by reminding Americans that they had ordered a world-wide nuclear alert in the course of the October war without consulting their allies. What remained significant in the heat of these exchanges between Western Europeans and the Americans was the apparently solid reliability of the Portuguese as American allies in any Middle East conflagration. The Americans were thus able to use the Azores as a refuelling point in their airlift of arms and equipment to Israel.

Finally, the American economic role in Portugal has had important military implications. Portugal was a poor country, and would not normally have been able to maintain a sustained military capability without some of the contributions which American investment afforded her. Angola is one of the largest recipients of American investment in Africa. USA exports to Angola by 1970 came to $48 million (10 per cent of the total imports of Angola), and in turn the USA bought up to $68 million worth of products from Angola (16 per cent of Angola's exports). During 1970 the USA also exported goods to Mozambique worth $22 million (9 per cent of the country's imports) and bought from Mozambique goods worth $18 million (10 per cent of the country's exports).[34]

This degree of American involvement in the Portuguese colonies, and the contributions from that involvement to Portugal's resources, inevitably helped to consolidate Portugal's military capability in the face of mounting military expenditure. This is quite apart from some of the covert business deals resulting in militarily relevant equipment being sold to the Portuguese on a private basis. The sale by American and other Western firms of vehicles such as jeeps could so easily be a direct contribution to the mobility of Portuguese armed forces.

In the spring of 1974, General Antonio de Spinola finally overthrew Caetano's government in Lisbon and inaugurated an important new phase in Portugal's relations with those African countries historically associated with her. Discussions were begun with Guinea-Bissau, Mozambique liberation fighters, and later the different movements in Angola. The forces of anti-colonialism in the Portuguese provinces overseas seemed to be on the way towards ultimate triumph. Could that moment have come sooner had Portugal not been a member of NATO? Could the Portuguese capability to maintain colonial wars have been eroded five or ten years earlier had American military and economic participation in Portugal and her colonies not strengthened the arm of Lisbon? Such questions cannot be fully answered, but they raise serious related questions concerning the extent of American complicity in the prolongation of Portugal's role as a colonial power.

America and Rhodesia

In the Rhodesian case the moral support came by a cool calculated decision of the United States Senate to go back on its own treaty obligation concerning sanctions on Rhodesia, and to buy chrome from the rebel British colony. As Donald Rothschild has pointed out, the decision by the American Senate illustrated the intertwining of the economic and political spheres in American behaviour in southern Africa:

> This legislation, enacted in defiance of a United Nations embargo, gave a psychological boost to the Smith regime just at a point when Rhodesian morale was at a low ebb. From an American standpoint, such an initiative was hardly justifiable in economic or strategic terms. The United States had some 5.3 million tons of chrome ore in its stock pile, and additional sources of this precious metal (albeit at higher prices) were available from the Soviet Union. Despite evident reasons for caution, the Senate, on an amendment to the Military Procurement Authorization Bill proposed by Senator Harry Byrd, voted to remove the President's authority to ban the importation of strategic or critical materials from non-communist countries at a time when no prohibitions existed against the importations of such materials from communist lands. The amendment, subsequently signed into law by President Nixon, was quickly put into effect, and in March 1972 some 250 000 tons of Rhodesian ore were unloaded into Louisiana.[35]

Rothschild's reference to 'a psychological boost to the Smith regime just at a point when Rhodesian morale was at a low ebb' captures the moral support which the USA gave to the rebel regime by this clear breach of sanctions. The position of the Nixon administration itself on the Byrd amendment was ambivalent. The American President had not vetoed that amendment from the Senate, though his record of vetoing unwanted pieces of legislation was quite impressive until the Watergate scandal incapacitated him. His decision to sign the Byrd amendment must therefore mean that he was less opposed to such a breach of sanctions against Rhodesia than to a number of other issues on which his veto was more readily forthcoming. By 1973, however, the Nixon administration was moving more decisively towards a campaign to try and get the Senate to rescind the Byrd amendment. Against the background of the administration's policy of detente with the Soviet Union, the fear of buying chrome from communist countries had become less compelling, and the case for closing the ranks with Britain and Africa against Ian Smith's regime was beginning to appear more persuasive. Yet the record of this de facto morale booster to the Smith regime remained a stigma on American performance in the search for a solution to the Rhodesian problem.

Conclusion

In spite of some of the American lapses in southern Africa, and her sins both of commission and omission, it remains true that the USA has done less harm in the African continent than she has done in, say, either Latin America or South East Asia, but she has also done less good in Africa than she has done in some other parts of the world.

The missionary factor in the American temperament has often been behind both American achievements and American excesses in foreign policy. The ideal of revolution and the vision of peace have competed for acceptance in the national imagination of the United States. The ideal of revolution draws from 'the spirit of '76', the memory of American colonies in rebellion against Britain in the eighteenth century, and on the brink of a new experience in political arrangements. The ideal of peace has also found sustenance in the rhetorical Christian religiosity of the USA, and later in America's self-conception as a global policeman. The spirit of '76 has often come into conflict with the ambition of Pax Americana.

In the African continent neither the revolutionary nor the law enforcement traditions of America have so far been especially active, as compared with the tumultuous experiments in Latin America and South-east Asia. Partly because of that fact, the most important sins committed by the USA in Africa have so far been the sins of omission—of indifference and caution, of insensitivity and moral distance.

Yet in situations of acute immorality as racist regimes continue their oppression, and colonialism puts up its last defence, even inaction could amount to hostile activity. Against the background of American economic support for South Africa, military support for Portugal until the coup of 1974, and moral support for the rebel regime in Rhodesia through such cynical moves as the Byrd amendment, American performance in Africa cries out for a re-evaluation.

In its moments of ambition the British Commonwealth of Nations sees itself as an instrument by which the world might be spared a racial war. The ambition is worthy, but the means are weak. If only the USA would take the leadership on a global basis, the horrors of racial war in Africa might at least be mitigated, even if its total prevention is not possible. The USA has the economic means, the diplomatic structure and the national experience of the civil rights revolution at home. She cannot make Africa safe for the American way of life, but she can contribute towards making it safe for the principle on which she herself was born—that all men are created equal. For generations Americans at home did not live up to the ideals of their own revolution. But it still made sense for John F. Kennedy to remind his countrymen: 'We dare not forget that we are the heirs of that first revolution.'

References and notes

1. Prince Okechukwu Ikejiani, 'Nigeria's made-in-America revolution', *Magazine Digest* (January 1946), 57. Cited by James S. Coleman, *Nigeria, Background to Nationalism* (Berkeley and Los Angeles: University of California Press, 1960), p. 244.
2. For Mboya's account, see *Freedom and After* (Boston: Little, Brown & Company, 1963), pp. 145-6.
3. Inaugural Address, 20 January 1961.
4. See *New York Times*, 2 March 1961. See also Executive Order 10924, 26 F.R. 1789.
5. Rupert Emerson, *Africa and United States Policy* (Englewood Cliffs, N.J.: Prentice Hall, 1967). I am grateful to Dr Emerson for letting me see the draft and for the insights that I derived from reading it. See also *Peace Corps in Africa*, Peace Corps brochure (1965), p. 11.
6. Inaugural Address.
7. Emerson, op. cit.
8. Farmer voiced his view on a Marshall Plan for Africa both at home and when visiting African countries. See, for example, *Uganda Argus*, 18 January 1965.
9. Important editorials in *The Times* during this period included 'India's Eddies', 1 November 1962; 'China's Gain and Loss', 22 November 1962; and 'Wooing the Neutrals', 1 December 1962. Refer also to the article by the Delhi Correspondent of *The Times* entitled 'India After the Fighting: Need to Reconsider Nonalignment', 31 December 1962.
10. See UN, *Press Release* SG/1359, 27 October 1962, pp. 2-3.
11. See UN Security Council Document S/5190, 24 October 1962, p. 1.
12. For the UAM proposals, see UN Security Council Document S/5195, 25 October 1962, pp. 1-2.
13. 'I welcome Chairman Khrushchev's statesmanlike decision to stop building bases in Cuba. . . . This is an important and constructive contribution to peace'—Kennedy on receipt of Khrushchev's letter of capitulation on 28 October 1962. See US Department of State, *Bulletin*, **XLVII**, 1220 (12 November 1962), p. 745
14. AID loans and grants $315 000 000; Food for Peace programme $108 400 000; and $67 600 000 Export-Import Bank loans. See *US Overseas Loans and Grants and Assistance from International Organizations, Obligations and Loan Authorizations, July 1, 1945-June 30, 1963,* special report prepared for the House Foreign Affairs Committee, 1964. See also *Proposed Mutual Defence and Development*, Prepared by the Agency for International Development and the Department of Defence (Washington: Government Printing Office, 1965), Table No. 2. See also 'U.S. Economic Aid to Africa, 1950-1964', *Africa Report*, **IX** (December 1964), pp. 8-12. I am grateful to Rupert Emerson for bibliographical guidance.
15. Ibid.
16. See Usha Mahajani, 'Kennedy and the strategy of aid: the Clay Report and after', *Western Political Quarterly,* **XVIII** (September 1965) pp. 656-68. See also Arnold Rivkin, 'Lost Goals in Africa', *Foreign Affairs*, 44 (October 1965), pp. 111-26.
17. See US Department of State, *Bulletin*, **XLVII,** 120 (12 November 1962). The ultimatum was delivered from the White House by television and radio on 22 October 1962.

18. See *Uganda Argus*, 15 January 1965.
19. See Ali A. Mazrui, 'African diplomatic thought and the principle of legitimacy', in *The Congo, Africa and America*, ed. Gary Gappert and Garry Thomas. Occasional Paper No. 15 (Maxwell Graduate School of Citizenship and Public Affairs, Syracuse University, 1965).
20. See *Uganda Argus*, 17 and 19 February 1965.
21. See O'Brien, 'Mercy and mercenaries', *The Observer*, 6 December 1964. Catherine Hoskyns has also pointed out the role of the Western press. She first admits that the Congolese rebels did kill a number of Europeans and Africans. She goes on to add: 'Having said this, however, it is also clear that press and diplomatic reporting did to a considerable degree distort the extent, the circumstances and the political implications of these deaths. . . . The main distortions (included) . . . the suppression of any evidence of violence on the other side; and the much greater coverage given to acts of brutality against Europeans than to those against Africans. The result was to tarnish the genuinely humanitarian reaction. . . .' See Catherine Hoskyns, 'Violence in the Congo', *Transition*, 5 (ii), 21 (1965).
22. Kenneth Kirkwood, *Britain and Africa* (Chatto & Windus, 1965), p. 224.
23. *New York Times*, 15 July 1961.
24. 'The second scramble'—speech delivered on 5 August 1961, to the Seminar of World Assembly of Youth. See 'The Second Scramble' (Dar es Salaam: *Tanganyika Standard*, 1962).
25. See *Uganda Argus*, 16 February 1965.
26. See *The Foreign Assistance Program, Annual Report to the Congress. Fiscal Year, 1964* (Washington: US Government Printing Office, 1965), p. 34. Cited by Emerson, op. cit.
27. For this part of the chapter I have relied heavily both on personal conversations with Professor Donald Rothschild of the University of California, Davis, and on his solid and stimulating essay entitled 'Engagement versus disengagement in Africa; the choices for America', published as a chapter in *US Foreign Policy in a Changing World: the Nixon Administration, 1969-1973*, ed. Alan M. Jones, Jr. (New York: David McKay Company, 1973), pp. 215-40.
28. The formulation of this policy comes from a report of a policy panel of the United Nations Association in 1971, which included among its members a number of figures from the business community. The panel itself was not in favour of increasing American investment in South Africa, but for as long as there was American investment it urged American companies to use their economic presence in South Africa as an opportunity to give leadership in labour practices and create a demonstration effect for other companies. See United Nations Association, *Southern Africa: Proposals for Africans*, report of national policy panel (New York: UNA-USA, 1971), p. 18; *Proposals for Americans*, pp. 48, 49. Cited by Rothschild, op. cit., p. 232.
29. William Minter, *Portuguese Africa and the West*, Penguin African Library (Penguin Books, 1972), p. 101.
30. Ibid.
31. *Flying Review International* (April 1966), p. 459.
32. James Reston's column, *New York Times*, 5 March 1969.
33. Cited by Minter, op. cit., p. 109.
34. See Rothchild, op. cit., pp. 228-9.
35. Rothschild, op. cit., p. 229.

CHAPTER 9
Africa & the Soviet Union

In a curious manner Africa's relations with the Soviet Union have quite often been part of Africa's relations with the Western world. Contacts between African nationalists and Russia have often been in response to disaffection with the Western world. Temporary flirtations with the Communist world have been basically flirtations on the rebound, a response to a fundamental cleavage between the colonized African and the colonizing Westerner. It is in this sense that Afro-Soviet relations until relatively recently have in fact been in part Afro-Western relations.

Taking the last fifty years of Africa's history, it might be said that there has been a transition from the influence of Western ideas to the influence of Russia's example. In the earlier decades of this century Western ideas provided much of the new stimulus for African aspirations and motivations. For a while, the most influential Western ideas were those which promoted conformity with the colonial status and acceptance of the imperial order. Among Africans ruled by France these bonds of empathy included pride in French culture and the French language, a sense of participation in what they regarded as a world civilization, a sense of identification with the basic historical traditions of France. Among Africans ruled by Britain similar tendencies were discernible, with some reduced pride in the British cultural heritage as such, but with an increased identification with Britain through the concept of loyalty to the British monarchy. Just as there were many French-speaking Africans who identified so closely with France that they were capable of saying, 'Our ancestors, the Gauls', so there were many English-speaking Africans who identified so closely with the old imperial order that they talked of 'Our beloved king, His Majesty, King George VI'.

Later it was those Western ideas which legitimized rebellion against the West which captured the imagination of the new African intellectuals and politicians. The revolutionary tradition of France, going back to 1789, was now converted into a basis of legitimacy for anti-colonialism in Africa. The American intellectual tradition of distrust of imperialism also played a part in the general African ferment and the quest for self-determination.

This move from Western ideas favourable to the imperial order to Western concepts of rebellion against that order culminated in a new interest in Western heresies, with special reference to Marxism, an important school of Western dissent. African fascination with revolutionary and liberating ideas in the Western tradition inevitably led to fascination with Marxism as well. As indicated earlier, Marxist ideas became a major source of intellectual stimulation in French-speaking Africa much sooner than they did in English-speaking Africa. The large size of the French Communist Party at home, the philosophical tradition of the French educational system, the policy of cultural assimilation pursued by the imperial power, the policy of political integration which facilitated participation by colonial peoples in national institutions in Paris, and the influence of left-wing French intellectuals in the whole domain of theorizing in politics, all contributed their share to giving Marxism considerable intellectual attractiveness among French-speaking Africans. With this interest in Marxist ideology came inevitably an interest in the Russian example. The connecting link between the power of Western ideas on the African mind, and the power of the Russian example in the Third World generally, was indeed that system of thought which bears the name of a radical Western revolutionary of the nineteenth century, Karl Marx.

Among black people outside Africa there was often a strong link between Marxism and pan-Africanism. Black Americans and West Indians who were pan-African were disproportionately left of centre in their political ideologies, and often explicitly Marxist in commitment. Several of the founding fathers of the pan-African movement, drawn from outside Africa, were either constantly Marxists or at any rate started as Marxists. Such founding fathers include W. E. B. Du Bois, George Padmore, and his fellow West Indian ideological luminary, C. L. R. James. These three people are probably in a class by themselves as founding fathers of pan-Africanism drawn from the Black Diaspora. Du Bois and Padmore became citizens of the first black African country to attain independence, Ghana, and both died there.

Since then there has persisted a correlation between left-wing views among Diaspora blacks and the commitment to pan-Africanism. The correlation is not, of course, neat, since there have been many black pan-Africans who have at the same time denounced Marxism and the whole attempt by white radicals to influence black nationalism. But on the whole it is still true to say that pan-Africanism as a Diaspora movement has had strong links with Marxism as a language of protest. Even the sixth pan-African congress held in Dar es Salaam in June 1974, dominated as it was by representatives of relatively cautious governments in the black world, manifested considerable leaning towards a left-wing language of dissent and protest. There was even a distrust of protest based on colour. The final resolutions of the sixth pan-African congress affirmed the need for liberation, but in a manner which rejected the uniqueness of black experience, and which emphasized instead the shared predicament of exploitation and poverty in the Third World as a whole. Because many at the congress were representatives of governments which at home pursued their own local Marxists and often locked them up, the final resolutions of the sixth pan-African congress were not as explicit in their left-wing commitment as they might have been had more of the private individual, black pan-Africans come from the Black Diaspora. Certainly many black nationalists from the West Indies were either discouraged or prevented from going to the pan-African congress by their more cautious governments. Their presence in Dar es Salaam would have revealed more clearly than ever an enduring link between Diaspora pan-Africanism and Marxist orientation.

George Padmore might well have been merely among the first black nationalists to have at first flirted with communism, and then groped for ways of Africanizing socialism. Padmore was once an active communist, but by the late 1950s he stood for a form of socialism more compatible with the uniqueness of the black experience. His book, *Pan-Africanism or Communism? The Coming Struggle in Africa* (Dobson, 1956), even envisaged a profound tension between a form of international communism with an external leadership in Moscow, on the one hand, and a commitment to the principle of unified African autonomy, on the other. Yet, in a fundamental way, Padmore could at once reduce his love for Marxism and increase his admiration for Russia. This is what constituted the difference between fascination with a particular school of Western revolutionary thought and positive response to Russia's innovative example. To the question whether Africans had a lot to learn from Marxism-Leninism, Padmore argued that the first principle which Africans should learn from Lenin was Lenin's pragmatism. As Padmore put it:

> Lenin, the architect of the first socialist state, and his party, did not blindly follow Marxism in creating the instruments best suited to Russian conditions. Similarly, the African approach to socialism must be based on a policy of adaptation, while keeping constantly in mind our goal—the peaceful advance of African socialism.[1]

Padmore argued that Africans must be free to Africanize Marxism, if they wished, just as Lenin had Russianized it. In fact, Marxism in a particular African country like Ghana should not only be Africanized but should further be adapted to suit the peculiar *Ghanaian* conditions. As Padmore put it:

> It is for us, Africans, to subject Marxism to our own critical examination and see what there is in it which can be usefully applied to the conditions facing us in Africa in general and Ghana

> in particular. The great mistake which so many so-called Marxists have made is to turn their masters teachings into dogma, instead of using it as an intellectual instrument for understanding the evolution of human society and a guide to chart the course of future social development.[2]

But what is the relationship between this approach to Marxism on the one hand and revolution on the other? So far the revolutionary fervour of Africans has been an anti-colonial fervour. According to Padmore, it is precisely this kind of fervour that Marx did *not* allow for. What Padmore describes as the 'orthodox Marxist strategy' was based on the assumption that the proletarian revolution which was to usher in communism would first occur in the highly developed countries of Europe and America, where there existed the economic and social prerequisites as well as an educated and cultured industrial working class who would be the architects of socialism. Padmore asserted that never for one moment 'had Marx conceived that the colonial peoples in the backward countries of Asia and Africa would be more revolutionary than the white workers of Europe. . . .'[3] Padmore and other black radicals who had interacted with the international communist movement in the 1920s and 1930s knew all too well how hard it had been in the days of Stalin to be taken seriously as revolutionaries. The anti-colonial movement was regarded as quite secondary to the struggle of the workers in Europe. Indian radical nationalists encountered similar difficulties in their relationship with communist movements such as the Comintern. M. N. Roy received short shrift in 1920 at the second congress of the Comintern on the subject of the *Report of the Commission on the National and Colonial Question*, when Lenin was still alive. Lenin's successors remained insensitive for a while to the militant potentialities of the colonized peoples in Asia and Africa. The constraints of Marxism, with its emphasis on class rather than on race, and its distrust of 'bourgeois nationalism', had blunted the sensibilities of many otherwise sympathetic Russians to the role of the developing countries in the twentieth century.

But while the ideas and rhetoric emanating from Russia did not always inspire African nationalists, the actual example of Russia's rapid development and emergence as a world power was significantly influential. To some extent it was less the doctrine of international socialism than the practice of socialism in one country which inspired many African observers. The Russian commitment to international socialism did indeed play a part in this whole ferment of defiance and rebellion, but the accomplishment of the Soviet Union in its industrial and structural development was even more compelling. Once again it appeared to be a case of Western ideas and Russia's example jointly exerting an influence on the minds of ambitious Africans.

Non-alignment and Ideological Competition

Although Russian ideas per se, as distinct from Western Marxism, did not have a direct impact to any significant degree in the fortunes of the African continent, the very fact that Russia became the champion of Marxist communism, and sought to spread the ideology to other parts of the world, was an important factor in the history of African liberation. A revolutionary ideology with a powerful advocate became something which the Western powers were increasingly fearful of. A period of ideological crusade between the West and the Communist bloc provided part of the setting for African liberation.

It is arguable that two people, who were either indifferent or hostile to African interests, nevertheless were cast by history in a critical role as inadvertent liberators of the black man. These two people were Hitler and Stalin. Hitler's imperialist ambitions, and his desire to make Germany the centre of the world, precipitated a world war which turned out to have considerable consequences for the future of the British and French empires. The defeat of France reduced part of the mystique of an imperial power and revealed that major European powers were not necessarily invincible. Britain was not defeated, but the great depletion of British resources, and the sheer exhaustion at the end of the Second World War, helped to destroy Britain's will to rule. Even more fundamental, the war had enhanced political consciousness in much of the British empire, and made inevitable increasing anti-colonial militancy. Reluctantly, but with some grace, Britain bowed to historical inevitability. The Asian empire was granted independence, and India, Pakistan, Burma, and Ceylon entered the international community as sovereign states. Adolf Hitler, himself racially arrogant and the embodiment of brutal racial intolerance, had nevertheless initiated a series of events which culminated first in a global conflagration and then in the liberation of Asia.

Africa was served more immediately by Josef Stalin than by Adolf Hitler. Nationalism in Africa gathered momentum after the Second World War, though the roots of that nationalism went back to before Hitler. The liberation of Asia was also a major contributory factor towards the liberation of Africa. India's independence was the grand precedent in decolonization.

Also important in the liberation of British Africa was a more localized war—the Mau Mau insurrection in Kenya. A group of Africans with rudimentary military technology and relatively rudimentary military organization, were nevertheless able to put up a strong fight against the British presence in Kenya. The Mau Mau lost militarily to the British, but they triumphed politically. The scale of killing and resistance made Britain wary about similar outbreaks elsewhere in the African empire, and this helped to undermine the British imperial will to rule.

But behind the triumph of Mau Mau were the ghosts of Hitler and Stalin. Hitler eroded Britain's resources and capabilities and made her more vulnerable to colonial pressures. Hitler's war, by forcing the recruitment of colonial armies, contributed also to the expanding political consciousness of those who travelled far from their villages to fight for the king of England. Both the diminishing capabilities of Britain and expanding political consciousness in the colonies contributed towards the weakening of the British political will. Josef Stalin, especially after Hitler was dead and Germany defeated, provided additional arguments and considerations for cautious Western imperial policies. The ideological and political competition for the control of the world between the Soviet Union and the Western world gathered momentum, and the colonies benefited precisely from the tensions of the competition between the giants.

It was precisely that competition which was in turn responsible for the birth of the non-aligned movement in world politics. As indicated earlier in Chapter 6, India under Nehru was particularly important in the history of non-alignment. Given the competition between the giants, and a reluctance on the part of a newly independent country to be tied to either of the two blocs, a doctrine emerged asserting the right to remain outside military entanglements and the right of diplomatic experimentation for those who are newly initiated into international politics. Non-alignment was an assertion of both rights. A combination of nationalism and pragmatism was at the heart of the new Third World doctrine.

On balance it could be argued that the Soviet Union has so far always been at least a decade ahead of the USA in understanding the forces at work in the Third World. Complete sympathy with Third World nationalism has never been a major feature of Soviet calculations and ideological analysis; nationalism among Third World leaders has always been treated with some degree of reserve by Soviet analysts and policy-makers. Such nationalism was, after all, 'bourgeois nationalism', characteristic of a stage in social evolution well before socialism proper. And yet there has been on the part of Soviet governments greater sensitivity to the aspirations of nationalists than has been the case among policy-makers in Washington. The Western world has prided itself all along on being more pragmatic and less ideological than the Soviet Union. And yet, on the specific issue of the legitimacy of non-alignment, it was the Soviet Union which conceded toleration of the doctrine sooner.

In Africa, the pragmatism and nationalism implicit in non-alignment quite often merged. African nationalism prided itself for a while on readiness to experiment with different ideas and institutions. There was also a readiness to attempt a synthesis of elements borrowed from different sources. Many of the leaders of Africa genuinely believed that it was premature at best to be dogmatic about answers and solutions for their problems. There was, at least for a while, no self-assurance at having arrived at 'the truth'. Preparedness to experiment with institutions, or borrow ideas from diverse sources, was itself an assertion of realism and pragmatic responsiveness. In the words of Léopold Senghor of Senegal:

> To build a nation, to erect a new civilization which can lay claim to existence because it is humane, we shall try to employ not only enlightened reason but also dynamic imagination. . . . In the first, we shall go back to the sources of African-Negro and European civilization in order to grasp what is essential in both—their spirit, their ferment. . . . Thus inspired, we shall seek to create new forms and institutions—cultural, political, social and economic—suited to our present situation.[4]

American distrust of non-alignment in Africa was aggravated for a while precisely by trends within Africa towards a one-party system and the espousal of socialism at least rhetorically. On the socialist rhetoric, we should note that much of the enthusiasm in Africa arose out of a distrust of imperialism. Imperialism had been linked to international capitalism, and for a while after independence there was a feeling in many parts of Africa that only domestic socialism was compatible with international opposition to imperialism. Again the equation of socialism with anti-imperialism was to some extent an outcome of African nationalism. If imperialism was, as Lenin came to affirm, the highest stage of capitalism, the first revolution against Western capitalism was a revolution against its highest stage. What follows from this kind of analysis is that a revolution by Africa and Asia against the imperial manifestation of capitalism might be regarded as a fundamental stage towards socialism. After all, a revolution against the highest form of capitalism should be at least the equivalent of the lowest stage of socialism. For an African to be anti-imperialist is itself a preparation for socialist horizons.

Khrushchev grasped this factor quite early. Scholars in the Soviet Union in the days of Khrushchev could therefore defend these nationalist eruptions. In the words of the late I. I. Potekhin:

> Pan-Africanism as an ideology contains much that is alien to our [Soviet] ideology. But pan-Africanism aims at uniting all the peoples of Africa for the struggle against colonialism and imperialism, and for their national liberation. And from this point of view pan-Africanism deserves the support of all people of goodwill who are striving for the ideals of progress and democracy.[5]

Much of the motivation in pan-Africanism at that stage had a good deal to do with the motivation sustaining the spirit of non-alignment. But whereas the Soviet Union was capable of sympathizing with that spirit, John Foster Dulles and the Eisenhower administration in the USA were still singularly oblivious of the meaning of these forces. For

Dulles the choice between communism and Western capitalism was a choice between the devil and God. In such a choice, according to Dulles, no neutrality could conceivably be legitimate. Those who exhibited the banner of non-alignment were guilty of moral abdication.

It was not until 1960 that the Soviet Union and the USA began to move towards the same level in interpreting Third World intentions. It was in 1960 that John F. Kennedy was elected President of the USA. For less than three years until his assassination he established a relationship with the Third World which narrowed the gap between American and Russian sensibilities. The Soviet Union under Nikita Khrushchev was under the rule of a peasant; the United States under John F. Kennedy was under the rule of a dynastic American millionaire. Khrushchev had already shown sympathy and support for Third World leaders, ranging from Nasser to Nehru, from Sukarno to Nkrumah. John F. Kennedy, considerably more polished and affluent than his Russian political counterpart, showed also a capacity to share the Russian's more developed international sensibility. By that time the Soviet Union was already committed to the building of the Aswan Dam, destined to be Gamal Abdul Nasser's most enduring monument. Kennedy moved in the direction of building the Volta Dam in Ghana, perhaps similarly destined to be Kwame Nkrumah's most lasting monument in his own country. Kennedy ignored the complaints of even the most liberal of his own supporters who had argued against Nkrumah's domestic policies and regarded those as a reason for withholding American participation in the financing of the Volta Dam. Kennedy decided otherwise.

Kennedy was killed in 1963. Khrushchev was replaced in 1964. In many ways the brief period of congruence between Kennedy and Khrushchev in their interpretation of the Third World constituted the heyday of Africa's centrality in world politics. This was not because Khrushchev and Kennedy saw eye to eye on fundamental issues. On the contrary, this was a period of the most acute ideological tension between the two countries, in competitiveness in attempting to control the rest of the world. In the Congo the two giants were immersed in high rivalry, pushing the Congo to the centre of world politics, and threatening to some extent another situation like Korea. Patrice Lumumba lost his life at the hands of his own countrymen, but this was partly because his country had become a competitive arena for the major powers in 1960 and early 1961. In Cuba, too, a confrontation took place, one that was even more perilous for mankind. The missile crisis precipitated a confrontation between Kennedy and Khrushchev capable of pushing the world as a whole down the precipice of nuclear war. The brief period between the election of Kennedy in 1960 and his assassination in 1963 was by no means a period of political cordiality between the Soviet Union and the USA. Nevertheless, from Africa's point of view, it was a period when the two most powerful men in the world agreed for a change that Africa and the Third World mattered.

By contrast, under Nixon and Brezhnev, the total ideological position between the two powers narrowed. There was less ideological tension than there had been in the days of Kennedy. The clarion call from both the White House and the Kremlin was the call of détente. But although the superpowers agreed, it was not an agreement that augured well for Africa. Compared with their predecessors, both invested Africa with less importance than it had enjoyed in the early 1960s. On balance, however, it could still be said that the Soviet Union was a decade ahead of the USA in understanding some of the forces at work. The Soviet Union spent far less money on Africa than the USA did, and there was less Soviet commitment to the alleviation of African problems of poverty and underdevelopment. Yet in spite of this, Russia displayed in the Third World as a whole more awareness of future trends.

In some ways the days of Lyndon B. Johnson were particularly bad for Africa. President Johnson was, in some respects, a great president from the point of view of black Americans, but a poor president from the point of view of the African continent. His administration managed to get through Congress a considerable body of civil rights legislation, and thereby laid the foundations for an amelioration of the black predicament in the United States. Related institutions set up by the Johnson administration in America, ranged from those which promoted minority enterprise and attempted to enhance economic effectiveness among black people to those more narrowly defined in the direction of ending obvious discrimination. But while the Johnson era was one of black achievement domestically, it was certainly one of drastic decline in interest in Africa.

> While Lyndon Baines Johnson was president, the level of the AID programme fell by almost 50 per cent. The burden fell most heavily on Tropical Africa. . . . That this cutback should have occurred in spite of the dire implications of the 1966 'McNamara Poverty Thesis' and the rising incidence of military coups and other forms of political instability in Tropical Africa, provided ample indication that American attention was becoming increasingly inner-directed.[6]

After Johnson, Nixon reduced Washington's commitment to domestic black welfare without increasing the commitment to Africa's economic development. Détente between the Soviet Union and the USA reduced even the competitive motive behind the favours bestowed by the superpowers on the smaller countries of the world. Yet perhaps this is an over-simplification. The legacy of ideological competition had gone too far to be totally reversed either by Lyndon B. Johnson or during the Nixon-Brezhnev flirtation.

The Soviet Union and African Development

Because the first few years of Asian and African independence were characterized by considerable ideological and political rivalry, a new ethos had grown up in the world as a whole. Originally it was no more than a moral rationalization for the competitive ideological crusades. The rationalization hinged on the proposition that the richer and more developed countries of the world had a duty to support the less advantaged nations. In the earlier days of the cold war, such a commitment to international development was legitimized at home in the capitals of the developed world in terms of 'enlightened self-interest', defined in cold-war terms. But what started as little more than a cynical exercise in competitive diplomacy provided a basis for a new economic morality. In reality none of the rich countries has yet shown adequate interest in changing the economic order of the world. Only such a change could fundamentally ameliorate the lot of the underdeveloped. In any case, international charity has its weaknesses, including a propensity to consolidate a dependence complex among those who receive such charity. But when all is said and done, and allowances have been made for the basically inegalitarian relationship which exists between an aid-donor and an aid-recipient, the fact remains that the cold war helped to create the beginnings of a new international economic morality. While this is far from a new economic order and simply indicates a shift in ethical sensibilities on the world stage, that morality might nevertheless be an indispensable precondition for the structural transformation of global arrangements. The world could not conceivably move towards changing the pattern of distribution of the planet's resources without a major change in international ethics.

A distinction has sometimes been made between Soviet and American motives for extending economic aid to the less developed countries. It has been suggested that while Russian assistance programmes were primarily concerned with political considerations, the concerns of the USA were more purely economic. The commitment of the Russians was attributed to a desire to change the ideological orientation of African regimes, while Americans were inspired either by a desire genuinely to ensure economic development in the poorer countries, or to facilitate American economic interests there. At their more altruistic, Americans would thus be champions of realistic programmes for the improvement of the standard of living of the people of these countries. At their less altruistic, Americans would be committed to the preservation of American sources of energy and raw materials, and American markets, as well as the operation of American multinational corporations.

Such a distinction, while explaining certain aspects of the behaviour of the two superpowers, is still inadequate. Much of American commitment to aid in the days of John Foster Dulles, and even in the days of John F. Kennedy, included a high ideological and motivational component. The commitment to promote liberal democratic and capitalist ideas, and keep out the temptations of communism, was often at least as political as anything promoted by the Soviet Union. On the other hand, some of the programmes of aid operated by the Soviet Union in Africa were often geared in part to the economic national interests of the Soviet Union. Considerations of Soviet trade, and acquisition by Russia of foreign reserves, have never been absent in the broad diplomatic interaction between Russia and the African states.

But even if there was a balance in motivation on the American side which made economic considerations more relevant than they were on the part of the Russians, this precise balance of mixed calculations must have now become more blurred. Both Russia and the United States have become more circumspect in their aid commitments on all fronts, and less influenced by a desire merely to win ideological converts in Africa. And just as there are many American voices which say the United States can no longer afford large-scale external charity while domestic problems in the cities are mounting, so there have been Russian voices arguing that the nature of socialism itself in the Soviet Union cannot yield 'surplus capital' to export on a large scale to other countries. As the communist writer, S. I. Tyulpanov, put it:

> The creation of the material and technical base of socialism and communism demands colossal capital investments. . . . Here there is not and cannot be 'surplus capital' by the very economic nature of socialism. The socialist countries have never entered into competition with capitalism in the volume of capital resources they export to the developing countries and in the existing stage of development they cannot do so.[7]

Both the USA and the Soviet Union have been encouraging African countries to be more self-reliant; and both have even invoked the profit motive in some form as a basis for economic reciprocity between the donor country and the receiving country. In the words of one Soviet writer, a socialist country engaged in economic assistance to a developing country should be guaranteed 'not only a recovery of its actual expenditure but also a definite return on the resources invested'.[8]

But while on balance Russian aid to African economic development has been only a fraction of Western aid, Russia's support of African liberation movements has been more substantial than Western aid. Many Western countries, because of their special economic and political relations with the minority regimes of Southern Africa, have all along been reluctant to extend even moral support to liberation movements. For as long as Lisbon was under fascist rule, and was reluctant to liberate Africa, the USA was strongly loyal to Portugal. Even when a hundred other countries were prepared to recognize the independence of Guinea-Bissau in 1973, the USA could still veto the possibility of Guinea-Bissau's admission to the United Nations without permission from Portugal. The Soviet Union and its allies have remained strong champions of African liberation in Southern Africa and have often extended considerable financial and material support to the movements engaged in that liberation.

However, the West has never been monolithic in its approach to African problems. There have been private contributions to liberation movements from Western organizations and Western individuals, including the International Council of Churches. While Western investors have poured money into South Africa in pursuit of profit, Western humanitarians and radicals have been extending support to the freedom fighters and their organizations. Periodically, the black movements in Southern Africa have sent delegations all over the world to raise funds, and these delegations would not only go to Moscow and Peking, but also to Stockholm, Paris, Washington and London. The private sector in Western society was quite capable of supporting liberation movements directly, but Western governments shrank from such activities. It was because of this that Russian and Chinese official material support to liberation movements was so conspicuous, while Western aid was only decentralized and unofficial.

Aid from the communist countries included in some cases offers of training facilities for the liberation soldiers. Sometimes instructors went to Africa from the communist world to impart their skills of guerrilla warfare and jungle strategy. There were also occasions when Africans went to countries ranging from Russia to North Korea as part of the military preparation for the struggle in Southern Africa.[9]

Finally, there is Russia's role in maintaining the territorial integrity of independent African states. The boundaries of all of these states were imposed upon the continent by Western powers, and yet the Soviet Union has been more consistent than any other major power in assuring the security of those boundaries.

Among the major powers, France has the worst record with regard to the issue of the territorial integrity of African states. When both the Congo (now Zaire) and Nigeria were endangered by a strong secessionist movement, French resources were basically employed to support, either by propaganda or in direct material equipment, the side which wanted to break away. Both Moise Tshombe, when he was trying to detach Katanga from Zaire, and Ojuku, when he was trying to create a Biafran state carved out of Nigeria, found a sympathetic ear in France. In the case of the survival of Zaire, the French position was simply that the United Nations had no business trying to save the territorial integrity of the newly independent country. President de Gaulle, by disputing the credentials of the United Nations to intervene, endangered Zaire's territorial integrity at that time. In the case of the Nigerian civil war, the French became increasingly more partisan on the side of Biafra, but fell short of outright recognition of Biafra as an independent state. Instead, the French encouraged at least two of their former colonies—the Ivory Coast and Gabon—to extend recognition to the secessionist state.

Britain's position with regard to the bid by Katanga to secede from Zaire was, curiously enough, substantially similar to France's position. By contrast, Britain became an active supporter of the Federal Government in the Nigerian civil war, maintaining military supplies for Nigeria in spite of heavy political agitation and protest at home in Britain. The British did attempt to influence the Federal Government towards alternative solutions to the crisis, and the British were at times reluctant to give the range of equipment needed by the Federal Government. But, on balance, it was clear that the British Government supported the territorial integrity of Nigeria and continued to strengthen the Federal Government's capacity to thwart the secessionist bid.

With regard to the Russians, they were actively engaged on the side of the territorial integrity of both Zaire and Nigeria. It should be remembered that these two countries constituted potentially the most economically powerful countries in black Africa. But this potential power rested on their remaining intact, as well as independent. The Russians did not support Moise Tshombe or Ojuku. They remained solidly for both Lumumba and Gowon, although in both cases relations between Africans and their Russian supporters were not always smooth. A good deal of irritation was sometimes caused on both sides. But what was clear was that the Russian involvement was on the side of maintaining the territorial integrity of these two potential African giants.

In the Sudanese civil war, again the main changes were in relations between Northern Sudan and Russia from one Sudanese government to another; there were few changes in relations between Russia and Southern Sudan. The Russians remained distrustful of the separatist movement in the south, and the distrust was substantially reciprocated by the southerners. The very fact that the southerners had Western missionaries among their most enthusiastic champions helped to create political distance between the southern insurrectionists and Moscow. This cool or hostile relationship was fairly constant throughout the seventeen years of the Sudanese civil war, and certainly constant in the last ten years of the war.

Relations between Moscow and Khartoum varied substantially according to which regime was in power in Khartoum. At one time relations were quite cold, especially before Aboud's coup in 1958. After Aboud's takeover, Moscow began to take greater interest in Khartoum, on the mistaken belief at the time that the Khartoum coup would turn out to be as progressive as the Egyptian coup of 1952 and the Iraqi coup of 1958. It turned out that Aboud was quite conservative, though not militantly anti-communist. Aboud was overthrown in 1964, and civilian politics resumed in the Sudan. Moscow continued to make the Sudan part of its broad strategy of courtship of the Arab world wherever possible. But it was not until the radical coup in the Sudan in 1969 that relations with Moscow became particularly intimate. Sudanese communists threw in their lot with the Sudanese soldiers, and established a new ideological 'condominium' of the Sudan. This honeymoon between Moscow and Khartoum ended tragically in 1971, when the Sudanese Marxists overthrew Numeiry briefly, were then defeated, and many of their leaders executed. Among those executed was a distinguished black Marxist from Southern Sudan. Like other Sudanese radicals, he had conceded that the south had a grievance, but saw the solution to that grievance in terms of a totally transformed revolutionary Sudan, rather than two separate countries under conservative rulers. Since the end of the civil war in the Sudan in 1972, relations between Khartoum and Moscow, though still not yet restored to their original cordiality before 1971, have begun to take a turn for the better. But the main point to grasp is that in the Sudan, as in the old Congo and in the Nigerian civil war, the Soviet position had remained that of maintaining the territorial boundaries bequeathed to Africa by Western colonial powers. In defence of those boundaries, the Soviet Union has been more consistent than the Western powers themselves.

Angola and Afro-Soviet Relations

More significant than Soviet involvement in the Sudan over the years was the dramatic phase of Soviet participation in the Angolan civil war after the collapse of the Portuguese Empire. Even before the military coup in Lisbon in April 1974, the Russians had been giving support to liberation fighters against Portuguese rule in Angola. By the time of the coup it was already clear that the Russian favourites were the Popular Movement for the Liberation of Angola (MPLA), led by Augustinho Neto. Soviet rivals in global terms were the USA, on one side, and the People's Republic of China, on the other. American support went in the main to the National Front for the Liberation of Angola (FNLA) under Holden Roberto. American aid to Roberto's movement came either directly through the Central Intelligence Agency or indirectly through the government of Zaire. The Chinese, on the other hand, preferred the National Union for the Total Independence of Angola (UNITA) under Jonas Savimbi.

An attempt at forming a government of national unity involving all three movements was made with the assistance of the Portuguese after they had decided to give independence to Angola, and with the mediating efforts of President Jomo Kenyatta of Kenya and his government. This experiment in a tripartite regime for Angola collapsed, and a painful civil war ensued. When the time came for the Portuguese government to hand over power in November 1975 no single faction was as yet in control of Angola. The Portuguese therefore handed over symbolically to the people of Angola, and departed. The MPLA captured Luanda, the capital city, and formed a government of its own, the People's Republic of Angola. The two rival movements, the FNLA and UNITA, entered into a marriage of convenience and formed a government for what they called the Democratic Republic of Angola with a provisional capital at Huando (formerly known as Nova Lisboa).

The civil war escalated, and for a short while it appeared as if the agonies of the former Belgian Congo in the early 1960s would be repeated as superpowers ruthlessly decided to exploit domestic African tensions and drift towards a major international confrontation of their own. But before long a number of decisions made by some of the external participants in the Angolan civil war tilted the balance in favour of MPLA. The Chinese decided that with a major African civil war under way they did not want to be directly involved in militarily supporting one faction. This would be potentially expensive both economically, and also diplomatically in terms of alienating 'progressive' African governments who were leaning towards MPLA. The United States Congress also took steps which, by default, dramatically improved MPLA's chances of victory. Congress explicitly forbade any use of funds by the Ford administration for covert activities in the Angolan crisis. The decision by Congress spelt the end, at least temporarily, of effective American military support to either FNLA or UNITA. South Africa got involved, partly in order to avert the triumph of a left-wing regime in Angola, partly to protect its colonial control of Namibia, and partly to protect the expensive hydro-electric project on the Cunene River in Angola near the Namibian border, which South Africa had financed. But when it became clear that the Western world was not prepared to move decisively in support of FNLA and UNITA, South Africa's own involvement became more visible and conspicuous than ever. That involvement in turn succeeded in swinging a substantial number of African states on to the side of MPLA, not necessarily because they shared MPLA's ideology, but more because their opponents had chosen racists for allies.

It was against this background that Soviet support for MPLA briefly struggled for legitimacy in African eyes. The fact that Americans were not participating in any effective way in the war should normally have made Soviet intervention less justified in African opinion. After all, why should the Soviet Union choose one faction in an African civil war and help towards victory when the other superpower, the USA, was being forced by its Congress to remain neutral? When the Chairman of the Organization of African Unity at the time, President Idi Amin of Uganda, resisted Soviet pressure on him to recognize MPLA, his stand appeared for a while truly nationalist, pan-African, and heroic. Amin's reactions even forced the Soviet Union to interrupt diplomatic relations with Uganda for a while. The entry of South Africa more conspicuously on the side of FNLA and UNITA helped to legitimize further Russia's involvement on the side of MPLA. As one African government after another recognized the government of MPLA, Russia's technical presence in the war seemed to be widely forgiven.

Then there was the involvement of the Cubans. According to calculations, the number of Cuban troops involved in the Angolan war went up to 12 000. By African standards, this constituted the importation of a whole army. With Russia's equipment and Cuban manpower, MPLA became the most externally dependent of all the three movements.

Most liberation movements in the Third World since the Second World War have depended heavily on the outside world for their arms and equipment. But the Vietnamese in their war against first the French and later the Americans used overwhelmingly Vietnamese fighters, even if the weapons came from outside. The Algerians in their war against France needed external funds, equipment and diplomatic support. But the warriors in this struggle were predominantly Algerians. Outsiders, such as the immortal Franz Fanon, who went as a volunteer, were a tiny minority of the fighting force. Perhaps the most self-reliant of all major African guerrilla movements since the Second World War was the Mau Mau in Kenya. The fighters were not in a position to obtain either sophisticated modern weapons from outside sympathizers or even any substantial amounts of external capital. Indeed, the Mau Mau movement had hardly any external diplomatic arm of the kind which enabled people like Ferhat Abbas to speak for the National Liberation Front of Algeria in the capitals of the world. Neto, Roberto and Savimbi of Angola were able to serve both as direct leaders of their movement and international spokesmen in diplomatic circles. They could negotiate for arms, equipment and capital from external sources, while directing operations in the war in Angola. The Mau Mau movement in Kenya in the 1950s had no equivalent diplomatic arm. They were forest fighters with some of the most rudimentary forms of military technology, creating rough-and-ready rifles, and often using only the ordinary rural blade of East Africa, the *panga*. Militarily the Mau Mau movement was defeated, but politically it was triumphant to the extent that it broke Britain's will to continue ruling in Kenya for the interests of a white minority and firmly laid the foundation for African self-rule in the country. The forest fighters were not necessarily the direct beneficiaries of their own war, but without them the era of

Kenya under the domination of white settlers would have been substantially prolonged. What is significant from our point of view is that the Mau Mau had neither Soviet nor Chinese equipment or capital, nor an imported army to wage its battles. The MPLA in Angola can make no such claims. Of all the major liberation forces in Africa's experience since the Second World War, only MPLA went to the extent of importing up to twelve thousand fighters to wage its war against fellow Angolans.

But why did the Cubans do it? Were they simply obeying Russian orders? Was the Cuban factor in Angola simply an extension of the Soviet factor? Such an analysis would grossly oversimplify the issues. Cuba under Castro has aspired to be a major revolutionary force in its own right in the politics of the Third World. The mission to export revolution in Latin America was vigorously attempted by Castro's Cuba in the 1960s, but the commitment to that particular exercise declined partly because the other governments in Latin America were getting more ruthless in dealing with some of their dissidents, partly because Cuba became more interested in improving relations with other Latin American governments, partly because the Soviet Union had entered a period of détente with the USA and did not want to encourage Cuba to upset the Americans too much in Latin America, and perhaps also partly because Cuba was getting more interested in promoting its own détente with the USA if the revolutionary cost was not too high.

Africa provided an alternative venue for a major revolutionary role by Castro's Cuba in other countries. Sometimes the Cuban role has been to maintain a particular regime in power. A Cuban presence in Congo (Brazzaville) and even the Cuban presence in Sierra Leone was supposed to be an element for stability in the country rather than for real social transformation. But Cuba's involvement in other African countries diminishes in importance against the scale of their involvement in Angola. And because of the success of the Angolan involvement, Cuba's sense of vindication in fostering liberation, if not exporting revolution, may well increase its self-confidence as a Third World force.

In addition to fostering its own image as a revolutionary country, Cuba has wanted to demonstrate to the Soviet Union that there were favours that Cuba could render to Russia in international politics in exchange for Russian favours to Cuba over the years. There were roles that the Cubans could play to promote Soviet goals that the Soviet Union could not adequately play in its own right. After all, the Angolan war would have been a dramatically different kind of war if there had been 12 000 Russian troops there, instead of Cuban soldiers. A large-scale importation of Russian manpower would have alarmed the Western world much more, and might well have made an essential difference in Congress about whether or not America should be involved. South Africa's will to fight in Angola might have been strengthened rather than weakened by a direct Russian threat. And the Western world's interest in saving South Africa might well have created a global crisis. Castro was therefore in a position to demonstrate that the relationship between the Soviet Union and Cuba was one of interdependency, rather than mere dependence of Cuba on her senior partner. Russians needed Cubans in some ventures, just as Cubans needed Russians in others.

The immediate consequences of the MPLA victory in Angola, could be ominous for Namibia and Zimbabwe (Rhodesia), but the longer-term implications may be more hopeful. Towards the end of 1974 and early 1975 South Africa was already considering the possibility of Namibia's independence in some form, probably divided into Bantustans and presumably intended to be under puppet African regimes. But whatever the precise intentions of Pretoria, there was a chance that Namibia would enjoy at least the level of autonomy already experienced by Botswana, Lesotho and Swaziland. The victory of MPLA in Angola may well harden South Africa's attitude now towards the question of independence for Namibia. South Africa may feel it needs Namibia as a buffer state more than ever, and cannot gamble on the possibility of a Namibia under an independent African authority in a political alliance with MPLA. The immediate consequences of the MPLA victory may also make South Africa reluctant now to put too much pressure on Ian Smith for concessions to African nationalists. South Africa may well decide that it wants to avert its own isolation, surrounded by African regimes which are either already radical or potentially radicalizable. The previous drive by the Prime Minister to pressurize Ian Smith in the direction of a constitutional settlement with black nationalists had inevitably to come under close reconsideration in the face of the aftermath of the struggle in Angola. But while the immediate consequences for Namibia and Zimbabwe may thus be negative, the longer-term repercussions are more hopeful. With a radical Angola on its border, and potentially with continuing Soviet and Cuban support, the South West African People's Organization (SWAPO) of Namibia could indeed undergo a new lease of life and become a more effective fighting force in the coming years than it has been so far. The liberation of Namibia in a longer-term and more meaningful perspective could thus be more assured as a result of the triumph of MPLA.

Will Zambia in turn become radicalized as it faces Mozambique under Frelimo on its eastern flank and Angola under MPLA on the west? Will Kaunda either have to become radical or leave the seat of power in Lusaka? Are the pressures for the total liberation of Southern Africa gathering momentum as a result of the collapse of the Portuguese empire and the arrival of the Cubans and the Russians?

The answers to these questions are in the womb of history. What is clear is that the Soviet Union's relationship with the African continent, and its influence on the course of African history, may well have entered a new phase in the Angolan civil war and its aftermath.

Conclusion

We indicated at the beginning of this chapter that it has been less Russian ideas than Russian example which has been an inspiration in the developmental history of modern Africa. Many of the ideas associated with Soviet communism were in fact also part of the heritage of the Western world, and were imbibed and assimilated by African nationalists initially through their exposure to Western radical literature rather than to Russian writings. But by being the ultimate protagonists of this particular school of Western dissent, Marxism, the Russians did perhaps blur this distinction between their example and the radical heritage of the West. The whole label of Marxism-Leninism captured the fusion between the practical genius of Soviet Russia and the ideological legacy of Karl Marx.

The Russian example helped also to give greater respectability to the instrument of comprehensive national planning for African countries. The Western countries themselves took a few more decades before experimenting further with that kind of planning, but much of the developing world had been converted to the proposition that national planning made sense. Curiously enough, their conversion to this proposition did not always come out of admiration of the Soviet Union. On the contrary, many of the advisers that these countries had were Western liberal economists, frustrated in their own countries at not having enough power to plan for everything, partly flattered by the Soviet experience of giving economic technocrats so much say in the destiny of the nation, and now seeking to work out in developing countries new models of economic and social engineering.

On balance, almost all development plans in Africa have failed. None of the targets set, none of the presuppositions of the process of change, has ever been adequately realized. But although for the time being there are no impressive achievements of national planning as an instrument of developmental change in Africa, that particular medium continues to enjoy considerable respectability. And ultimately, that respectability could be traced to the achievements of the Russians as the first really large-scale economic engineers in human history. While African plans are demonstrably failing, there is still an illustration of a planned society which has moved quickly to the heights of global power. Once again, the Russian example struggles for recognition and admiration among countries much smaller than Russia, yet capable of seeing a little of themselves in the achievements of the Soviet Union.

But ultimately, there is one theory propounded or refined by a Russian which captured the imagination of large numbers of Africans. This is Lenin's theory of imperialism. All the arguments by old imperialists that they were motivated by considerations of educating the Africans, or spreading civilization, or transmitting the Gospel, were revealed in their nakedness by Lenin's emphasis on economic motivation as the ultimate mainspring of imperial expansion. Out of Lenin's ideas of imperialism emerged concepts like Nkrumah's notion of neo-colonialism, and they gave to African nationalists and radicals a more congenial and convincing perspective on their own predicament as a dominated people.

Many decades ago Africa helped to give Russia one of its greatest poets, Pushkin. Lenin came to reciprocate the debt, and gave to Africans one of the most inspiring explanations of their subjugation as a people. Poetry and power, ideology and war, theory and practice, have all interacted in the stream of African-Russian relations.

References and notes

1. George Padmore, 'A guide to pan-African socialism', written in 1959, just before his death, and published as Appendix 1 in *African Socialism*, eds, William H. Friedland and Carl G. Rosberg Jr. (Stanford: Stanford University Press, 1964), p. 230.
2. Ibid., p. 227.
3. Ibid., p. 225.
4. Léopold Sédar Senghor, 'West Africa in Evolution', *Foreign Affairs* (January 1961), pp. 240-6.
5. Cited by Mary Holdsworth, 'Soviet writings on Africa', *Contact* (summer 1961), 15.
6. Helen Desfosses Cohn, 'Soviet-American relations and the African arena', *Survey*, **19**, (winter 1973), 160. The McNamara Poverty Thesis was: 'There's a direct and constant relationship between the incidence of violence and the economic status of the countries concerned.'
7. S. I. Tyulpanov, *Notes on Political Economy: the Developing Countries* (Russian edn, Moscow: Mysl, 1969), p. 135. Cited in translation by Cohn, op. cit., p. 162.
8. Iu. F. Shamrai, 'Problems of the realization of the economic co-operation between socialist and developing countries', *Narody Azii i Afriki*, No. 4 (1968), 13. Cited by Cohn, op. cit., p. 163. See also 'Tanzania: Soviet views on the Arusha programme', *Mizan*, **9**, (September-October, 1967), 197-202.
9. For a perceptive analysis of the interplay between ideological and strategic factors in this interaction between African liberation movements and the communist world, consult Kenneth W. Grundy, *Guerrilla Struggle in Africa: an Analysis and Preview* (New York: Grossman, 1971). Grundy's analysis is not as deeply rooted in empirical evidence as one might have preferred, but the very nature of guerrilla movements reduces receptivity to direct and comprehensive research for as long as the war continues.

CHAPTER 10
Africa & the United Nations

When the United Nations Organization came into being in San Francisco in 1945, independent Africa consisted of only four countries. One was on the eastern seaboard, Ethiopia, one on the western seaboard, Liberia, the third on the north of the continent, Egypt, and the fourth in the south, the Union of South Africa. Each of the four sides of the campus had a gleam of luminous sovereignty, suggestive of things to come.

And yet the sovereignty of these four at this time was itself ambivalent. Ethiopia had only just emerged from Italian occupation, exhausted and humiliated, but also, in an important sense, proud. Liberia still remained tied to the apron-strings of the USA. Egypt, though technically sovereign, had a British military presence, and was ruled by a monarchical regime characterized by internal deficiencies and external dependence. South Africa had attained autonomous existence within the British Empire, first with a Pact of the Union in 1910 and then with the Statute of Westminster in 1931. But South Africa had attained independence without attaining freedom. It is true that, at that time, Africans, Coloured and Asians had more of a semblance of a say in the affairs of the nation than they now have. African interests had formal representation in parliament, and political participation by the non-white population, though modest, was nevertheless guaranteed by tradition and law. Racialism was already at the base of South Africa's political system, but the highly structured policy of apartheid, with rigid segregation as a major imperative, had yet to come into being. The nationalists, the architects of the most institutionalized form of racism in history, had yet to come into power.

At that momentous meeting in San Francisco to form the United Nations Organization, South Africa was clearly the most influential African state present. It might almost be said that the influence of the African continent at San Francisco was disproportionately exerted by Jan Smuts' Union of South Africa.

Nationalism and Internationalism: the Twins

The curious thing about the Second World War as a global experience was that it reactivated both a spirit of internationalism, as the world searched for means to prevent future wars, and a spirit of nationalism, as the colonized peoples of the world sought to liberate themselves. The participation of India, Ceylon, Burma and the African colonies in the war against Germany, Japan and Italy was an important factor behind the reawakening of Afro-Asian militancy. The question of dismantling the British and French Empires following the war was in the air at the same time as the issue of forming a world organization for peace and security was being debated. On the eve of the formation of the United Nations, a British colonial secretary had things to say which were relevant to those twin processes of nationalism and internationalism in the post-war world. Partly with the impending formation of the world organization in mind, Oliver Stanley, then Secretary of State for the Colonies, said, in March 1945:

> I do not believe that any splinterization of the British Colonial Empire would be in the interest of the world. . . . Would the new machinery for world security, which is to be devised at San Francisco next month, be made any stronger by the substitution of these 40 [new] states for the cohesive Empire able to act as a strategic whole?[1]

In a sense, Oliver Stanley's question has still not been answered. At best, the syllables which will one day form the complete answer are now being assembled, and it will take a while before the effect is adequately intelligible.

But there was one thing which Oliver Stanley did not allow for at the time. One of his fears expressed in the 1945 speech was that a disintegration of the British Empire might, among other things, jeopardize the very existence of the United Nations. In his capacity as Colonial Secretary he should perhaps have been more worried about a reverse possibility—that the existence of the United Nations might itself contribute towards the disintegration of the British Empire. The 'machinery for world security' on whose behalf he seemed concerned was to become a mechanism for the 'splinterization' of empires.

In principle, this reverse occurrence does not necessarily falsify Stanley's prediction. The United Nations' position as an accomplice in the dismemberment of empires might yet turn out to be a case of 'suicidal murder'—that in destroying empires the UN was all along involved in a process of unconscious long-term self-destruction. All this is, in principle, a *prediction* and may or may not be vindicated. We do know that the United Nations has declined in influence in the world in the last ten years. Does this mean that Oliver Stanley's prediction of March 1945 is on its way towards fulfilment? Does it mean that the dramatic increase of membership of the United

Nations, encompassing some weak and poor nations, has infected the organization with a virus imported from the womb of underdevelopment? This is something which only the future can fully reveal in all its implications. What should concern us for the time being is that which has already happened or is continuing to happen—the role of the United Nations in the momentous mid-twentieth century phenomenon of global decolonization.[2]

From the point of view of African nationalism, 1945 was a historic year for two conferences. One was indeed the San Francisco conference, in spite of the fact that Africa was grossly under-represented and her interests hardly recognized. The other historically significant conference took place in England in Manchester. It is sometimes referred to as the Fifth Pan-African Congress, but it is possible to look at it as the fifth pan-black conference but the first pan-African conference.[3]

The distinction between pan-blackism and pan-Africanism can be critical. Pan-blackism was that movement, ideology, or collection of attitudes primarily concerned with the dignity of black people wherever they might be. The banner of pan-blackism brought sub-Saharan Africans and Afro-Americans together. Pan-Africanism, on the other hand, gradually became essentially a continental movement within Africa itself, in which the Arabs of North Africa were more important than black Americans. Indeed, Tom Mboya used to argue that the proof that pan-Africanism was not a *racial* movement lay in the fact that the Organization of African Unity included both Arab and black states. Historically, pan-Africanism was born out of pan-blackism. It cannot be repeated too often that it was black Americans, such as W. E. B. Du Bois, and West Indians, such as George Padmore, who helped to make pan-Africanism globally conspicuous. But while the foundation of pan-blackism remained an affinity of colour, the basis of pan-Africanism became an attachment to a continent.

Until 1945, the leadership of the pan-black movement was clearly in the hands of black Americans and West Indians. Africans themselves were still playing only subsidiary roles. At an earlier conference following the end of the First World War, pan-Africanists such as Du Bois were trying to appeal to the powers at Versailles to let the African colonies be ruled or administered by fellow black people imported from the New World. There was then a definite paternalist streak in black Americans and West Indians in their attitude to their black brothers within the African continent. Africa's children scattered in the Diaspora claimed the right to exercise parental care over the continent of their origin. The black pressure group from the New World at that conference in Versailles even used the rhetoric of the time to legitimate its credentials as a worthy trustee of African interests. Black Americans and West Indians saw themselves as at a higher stage of civilization—and therefore qualified to take charge of their parental continent until the parent was civilized.[3] But although there was this paradoxical filial paternalism in the attitude of black Americans and West Indians towards Africa, there can be no doubt that the greatest of them were passionate lovers of the African continent and deeply concerned about its interests and its future. They saw the liberation of the black peoples in their own part of the globe as inseparable from the liberation of the African continent itself.

Then in 1945 the balance of diplomatic effectiveness among the blacks began to shift. Two participants in the 1945 Pan-African Congress in Manchester came to exercise significant influence over the fortunes of their own countries in Africa, and also over certain aspects of the history of the continent as a whole—Kwame Nkrumah, who later became prime minister of independent Ghana, and Jomo Kenyatta, destined to be the founding father of the Kenya nation.

The Manchester Congress addressed itself to questions of equality and dignity for the black man. Commitment to African liberation in the sense of attainment of sovereignty was still couched in modest terms. The ambition was clearly there, and was beginning to find expression in terms which symbolized the new mood of the awakened black people. But the immediate aims seemed to be more in terms of actual equality in the colonies, greater respect for African dignity, and the elimination of racial segregation, rather than the attainment of independence. Of course, voices were already being heard to the effect that equality and dignity could not be achieved without independence. But this method of reasoning in African nationalism did not fully consolidate itself until much later.

Yet clearly the Manchester Conference was a forum of nationalism, just as the San Francisco Conference was an exercise in internationalism. Indeed, pan-Africanism itself as a movement is at once nationalist and international. It has remained nationalist in its commitment to the dignity of the black man and the well-being of the African continent. But by involving different states and black people from different regions of the world, pan-Africanism has, all along, included a profound international dimension, but of a regional or racial kind. It has been either pan-continental or pan-pigmentational. The internationalism at San Francisco was global. Yet from the African point of view the interaction between nationalism and internationalism, symbolized by the twin conferences of 1945, continued in other forms and other areas in the years which followed.

Peace versus Human Rights

The United Nations Charter, designed to be a foundation for a global restructuring of inter-state relationships, became over the years the ultimate documentary confirmation of the legitimacy of African nationalist aspirations. It is probably still safe to say that very few African nationalists had in fact read the United Nations Charter. And those who had read it were less interested in the specific procedures for assuring world peace than in the reaffirmation of 'faith in fundamental human rights, in the dignity and worth of the human person, in the equal rights of men and women and of nations large and small'.[4] But, in spite of this limited or selected grasp of what the United Nations Charter was all about, it did become a kind of documentary expression of natural law and a global bill of rights in favour of the underprivileged.

By 1955, when Asia had achieved its independence and Africa was at its most militant in the quest for its own, the nationalists of Asia and Africa were still basing their demands soundly on the UN Charter. As the final communiqué of the Bandung Conference put it in that year:

> The Asian-African Conference declared its full support of the fundamental principles of Human Rights as set forth in the Charter of the United Nations and took note of the Universal Declaration of Human Rights as a common standard of achievement for all peoples and all nations.
>
> The Conference declared its full support for the principles of self-determination for people and nations as set forth in the Charter of the United Nations and took note of the United Nations resolutions on the rights of peoples and nations to self-determination, which is a prerequisite of the full enjoyment of all fundamental Human Rights.[5]

The United Nations had, by then, become a liberating factor in practice as well as in principle. It was involved in this process in two paradoxical capacities – in the capacity of the collective 'imperialist' with trusteeship responsibilities of its own, and in the capacity of the grand critic of imperialism at large. Indeed, as early as 1953, exasperated voices were already complaining. A leading analyst of United Nations' affairs, Clyde Eagleton, in an article in the influential American magazine *Foreign Affairs*, wrote that 'perhaps the term "self-determination" should be dropped, now that the United Nations is called upon to do the determining'. He argued that the United Nations now seemed to anticipate the desires of colonized peoples, and to assume that they all wanted to move in the same direction as those which had already found their seats in the UN. Eagleton asserted: 'If the direction on such a claim is made by the United Nations, it is no longer correct to speak of self-determination.' He was sorry to see the United Nations becoming 'the midwife of all groups desiring to be politically born'.[6]

As more and more countries from Africa and Asia became members of the United Nations, the liberating role of the United Nations became even more pronounced. The new members of the world organization were regarding it less as an organization primarily designed to ensure peace and security (as the big powers had intended it to be in San Francisco), and more as an organization which should be primarily concerned with human rights at large. Those who framed the Charter in 1945 first declared their determination to 'save succeeding generations from the scourge of war' and then, only secondarily, to 'reaffirm faith in fundamental human rights, in the dignity and worth of the human person, in the equal rights of men and women and of nations large and small'. But judging by their policies, attitudes and stands, the new states of Africa and Asia would have reversed the order of affirmation.[7]

This has had an important bearing on qualifications for membership in the United Nations as viewed by, on the one hand, countries such as the USA which opposed for many years the admission of Communist China and, on the other hand, countries like Tanzania which have sought South Africa's expulsion from the world organization. Those opposed to Communist China's admission interpreted Article Four of the United Nations' Charter as restricting membership to those countries which are 'peace-loving'. This whole emphasis on peace is more characteristic of the big powers' conception of the United Nations' role than it is of the view held by the new and smaller states.

Towards Applying International Morality

The outcome of the last two decades of the United Nations' history is that the organization has become more a weapon of war against certain forms of international immorality than a mechanism of peace between nations. The United Nations' most important contribution to the world must therefore be seen to be not a contribution to international peace, but a contribution to international morality. The organization has been particularly important in casting a shadow of global disapproval on two phenomena which had been regarded as legitimate for hundreds of years—colonial subjugation and institutionalized racial prejudice.

On colonialism itself, the United Nations' record must already be pronounced successful. The world body became the main forum of censure against colonial policies. The colonial powers first resisted these challenges from world critics. Even those countries being administered on behalf of the world organization as trusteeships had a difficult time persuading the administrative power to speed up the process of liberation. In 1954, a United Nations' visiting mission to Tanganyika (now mainland Tanzania) recommended that a timetable should be drawn up for Tanganyika's independence within twenty to twenty-five years. In other words, the mission was envisaging the liberation of Tanganyika by 1974 and certainly not later than 1979. These suggested dates were rejected by the administering authority, the United Kingdom. It was regarded as unrealistic as well as presumptuous for the world organization to attempt to hurry up an administrating authority in its responsibilities for a trusteeship.

The Tanganyika African National Union (TANU) had just come into being, and was among the organizations which had given evidence to the mission. TANU decided to send its President, Julius Nyerere, to the United Nations to give further evidence when the report was being considered. Members of the party made a collection towards the expenses of sending Nyerere to New York.

Confronting the Fifteenth Session of the Trusteeship Council of the United Nations on 7 March 1955, Nyerere seemed a little overwhelmed by this opportunity. He said:

> It is difficult for me to convey to the Trusteeship Council the depth of my feelings. This is the first time since Tanganyika became a Trust Territory that an African from there has been sent here by a territorial organization to express his people's hopes and fears. I want the Council to know that my people are very grateful for this historic opportunity.

Nyerere then proceeded to make his case for the rapid democratization of the trust territory towards the goal of an African majority on all representative bodies. This, he argued, was in accordance with the terms of the Trusteeship Agreement and Article 76 of the United Nations' Charter.

> When, therefore, the Visiting Mission made the recommendation that Tanganyika should become self-governing in a period of twenty or twenty-five years, we did not expect that either this Council or the Administrating Authority would express violent opposition to that proposal, for although we have never stated a date when we should be self-governing, we had expected that, with your help and with the help of the Administrating Authority, we would be governing ourselves long before twenty or twenty-five years. For how can we be left behind when our neighbours are forging ahead?

It was quite clear that Nyerere's sense of historical timing was much more accurate and realistic than that of those who opposed the deadline of twenty to twenty-five years as being too rapid. Nyerere argued that it was unrealistic to estimate the ability of a community to govern itself by looking at its least progressive members. In every country of the world, there were masses of poor and ignorant people, and yet nobody suggested that those countries should become colonies or trust territories.

> In our view, the best way of estimating our ability to govern ourselves in twenty or twenty-five years is to ask whether, in that period, we can have local men—Africans, Asians, and Europeans—

> sufficiently trained and sufficiently experienced to run the government of the country. . . .[8]

Again Nyerere's insight into the phenomenon of self-government was, in some ways, ahead of that of the Administering Authority. Rapidly the trusteeships of the United Nations were liberated. In their case, the power of the United Nations was especially direct. But one African trusteeship remained in a state of indecisiveness. This was South West Africa or Namibia, originally a mandate of the League of Nations, handed over to South Africa as an administering power. But South Africa refused to recognize the United Nations' capacity as successor to the League of Nations. South Africa was therefore unwilling to become accountable to the new world organization. An attempt to have this issue resolved by the International Court of Justice failed when the Court used a technicality to avert having to make a decision.

But the United Nations' impact on decolonization was also important outside the areas which were trusteeships. Sometimes the United Nations was implicated directly, as in the case of the argument between Indonesia and the Dutch over the control of West Irian. The United Nations interpreted the situation in favour of Indonesia, partly on the assumption that the Dutch were more alien in that area than the Indonesians.

The record of the United Nations as a liberating force became one of the factors which inclined Harold Wilson's government in 1965 to favour the application of sanctions against Rhodesia, however ineffectual they might have turned out to be. There was a genuine fear in the United Kingdom that unless Britain acted firmly against Ian Smith, the initiative for action against Rhodesia would pass to the world body. A bipartisan policy in England in favour of a strong stand against Ian Smith was inspired precisely by this fear of 'a red army in blue berets', implying Russian participation in subduing the Ian Smith regime under the banner of the United Nations.

But the Rhodesian problem illustrates not simply a case of colonial rule, but a case of rule by a white minority. The Unilateral Declaration of Independence was designed by white Rhodesia to end the colonial link with the United Kingdom. In some ways, Rhodesia then became comparable to South Africa rather than to Angola and Mozambique. Rhodesia was under the control of a local white community with no metropolitan source of authority, whereas Angola and Mozambique derived their source of administrative authority from Lisbon.

The distinction between white minority rule and colonial rule is important in assessing the performance of the United Nations. The United Nations has indeed succeeded substantially in facilitating the end of colonial rule; but its success in ending white minority rule in those countries where this still exists has been much more modest. The United Nations' fight against colonialism has had moments of glorious achievement; but the United Nations' fight against racialism has more often been characterized by frustration. The case of Namibia or South-west Africa lies between apartheid and classical colonialism.

Yet the battle continues. When the United Nations Organization was formed in San Francisco in 1945, South Africa was the most influential African state present. But history has indulged her ironic sense of humour once again. South Africa, which had been one of the architects of the world body, has now become the primary target in the Organization's moral war.

Politics and Personal Factors

The ultimate purpose of the African states within the UN has been to try to isolate South Africa diplomatically and, if possible, economically. In the next chapter we shall argue the case for isolation in terms of comparison with an individual criminal in one's own home town. The individual criminal is isolated, first, as retribution for his offence; secondly, in order to deter him from committing it again; and thirdly, in an attempt to reform him.

But although I am in favour of isolating South Africa in many different ways, there is one form of isolation that I hesitate to support. I do not believe that South Africa should be isolated from the free flow of ideas. This would be to isolate her from enlightenment, and in turn could delay the task of reforming her after this solitary confinement. The defenders of apartheid are themselves in favour of South Africa's intellectual isolation. That is why they keep certain books and magazines out of the country. To isolate South Africa from external ideas is to give Vorster a monopoly of propaganda—an undisturbed pulpit for his cult of racism.

When I had occasion to argue the case for isolation in 1964 as a new lecturer at Makerere, and published that case in the journal of the World Peace Council, I had already for many years been exercising my own modest form of boycott. I have a ritual every night when I go to bed. I eat an apple as almost the last event of the day. It started twelve years ago when I was a student in England, and was undernourished and needed extra fruit to survive on the student breadline. But then this habit of eating an apple last thing at night developed into an unfailing ritual. I travel to different parts of the world every year, and wherever I go I attempt to have an apple at night before retiring. As a student in England, wherever I went to buy those apples I first asked where they were from. Sometimes the shop assistant would say they were from South Africa. In that case, I would not buy them, and I would move on to another shop. Occasionally an assistant would say the apples were, in the language of the period, 'Empire made'! I would interpret that ambiguity in a negative sense, since there could be no question of the benefit of the doubt going to the South African regime. All these were very personal gestures, hardly amounting to very much, and hardly calculated to bring the full apparatus of apartheid crashing to the ground. In this case what one is dealing with is a moment of moral expression, a gesture of disapproval, an attempt to concretize the conscience.

But boycotting South African apples or South African wine was, at its most ambitious, in the realm of economic boycott. What entered my life in 1970 in relation to South Africa was a different kind of challenge. What other types of boycott was I prepared to exercise in regard to South Africa?

In May 1970, I received an invitation to give a series of lectures at the University of Cape Town and the University of Witwatersrand the following year. My first reaction as an African and as a black man was that I should not go. I knew there were a lot of good people in South Africa who were unhappy about the situation. But I have shared the view, widely held in Africa, that the international isolation of South Africa, even if it should hurt some of our friends inside, was nevertheless justified if in the end it won for those friends increasing converts within South Africa to the cause of drastic change.

The elections held in 1972 in the Republic seemed encouraging. The Nationalist Party, that architect of apartheid, suffered its first electoral setback since it came into power in 1948. It lost some votes, and these to more liberal candidates. As a friend of mine put it at the time, 'South Africa has taken a modest move to the Left—and this is to be applauded as far as it goes.' Yet it was in the interests of the liberal cause in South Africa that the country should not yet be rewarded by the international community. A reward for a modest change could bring about complacency—whereas there was a lot more to be done in South Africa before the situation could be regarded as having really shifted in a positive direction.

But clearly there were other considerations to be borne in mind in my response to the invitation to lecture in South Africa. As a scholar and a liberal I believe in the free flow of ideas and knowledge at large across national boundaries. I continue to believe that when a source of ideas in one part of the world is suppressed, it becomes a matter of relevance to people in other parts of the world who have an interest in that particular fount of knowledge. South Africa's isolation until now has not been entirely imposed at the initiative of others. There is also the isolation that South Africa imposes upon herself by banning certain books or discouraging certain visitors or suppressing certain ideas.

On the one hand, then, we might want to sentence South Africa to a period of isolation, away from the mainstream of social and sporting events, of political and diplomatic discourse, of academic and intellectual interaction. But, on the other hand, there is also a duty to try to widen the cracks in the regime's walls of self-imposed isolation. The regime's desire to be protected from certain ideas or to keep out certain individuals should not always be facilitated. There may be a case for frustrating the regime's quest for selective intellectual withdrawal. South Africa might then be forced to listen to, or to read, things which the regime would prefer to see well and truly excluded from its borders.

White South Africa is against being isolated economically and politically, but in favour of its own selective isolation from external ideas. My own position is the reverse—I fully support the economic and diplomatic isolation of South Africa, but I am opposed to a policy of making South Africa a soundproof cage, shielded from external voices.

Furthermore, there is my role as a university teacher. The invitation from the University of Cape Town, though it was addressed to me by a distinguished professor at that university, was in fact extended on behalf of the students there. The students at the University of Cape Town had already proved their liberal credentials. Not long before they demonstrated violently when an African lecturer appointed by the university was refused permission by the South African government to take up his post. The lecturer was Dr A. Mafeje, a Cambridge-trained black South African, who later became head of the Department of Sociology at the University of Dar es Salaam. The students were indignant at a policy which denied them the benefit of Dr Mafeje's expertise as a scholar. When the invitation came to me to go there briefly, as a visiting lecturer, one of the questions I asked myself was whether as an African university teacher I should not reward those students for their stand against the ban on Mafeje by simply accepting their invitation to address them.

Again, for a teacher, there is the temptation to try to reach the younger generation. Is there a way of ostracizing the older generation of South Africans which is currently making decisions in support of apartheid, and at the same time reaching the generation which will be making tomorrow's decisions? The problem is difficult. But there is a distinction between cutting off links with those responsible for the present state of affairs in South Africa, and fostering a climate of change among those who will, before long, be assuming the reins of responsibility in multiple roles within the structure of the Republic. In short, while it is true that the grown-ups in South Africa may be too old to change their ways, should an attempt be made to reach the young and convert them into allies of African liberation?

What then is the duty of an African scholar in such a situation? Here a distinction could legitimately be made between importing books into South Africa written by Ali Mazrui and importing Ali Mazrui himself to give a series of lectures in the Republic. The circulation of .books is a straightforward case of disseminating intellectual goods. But giving lectures personally in other countries is both an intellectual activity and a diplomatic activity, a form of academic diplomacy.

Since I am in favour of the diplomatic isolation of South Africa, but against her intellectual isolation, the invitation from the students of the University of Cape Town inevitably left me in a moral dilemma, which I have yet to resolve fully. There is, of course, the further consideration that the South African regime might not be prepared to let me say what I want to say, or address mixed audiences—in which case there would be no point in my going at all.

This personal illustration has been narrated in order to demonstrate, with greater immediacy, some of the dilemmas of the policy of isolating South Africa.

Activating World Opinion

As the United Nations' efforts in trying to globalize the policy of isolating South Africa have not been as successful as her policy on decolonization, the initiative to put pressure on the big powers has been passing directly to regional groupings and individual states. This has been particularly true in regard to the issue of the sale of arms to South Africa. The Lusaka Conference of non-aligned countries in September 1970, and the Organization of African Unity itself, jointly entrusted to President Kaunda of Zambia the responsibility of leading a delegation to the major Western powers to argue the case for a ban on the sale of arms to the Republic. There were some diplomatic mishaps in both the United Kingdom and the USA. In London, Dr Kaunda's encounter with Edward Heath did not have a happy conclusion, partly because Heath regarded the whole Kaunda mission as an instance of external countries trying to dictate to Britain what policies she should pursue. In the USA, President Kaunda never met President Nixon, partly because of a confusion of appointments and a wrong ordering of priorities at the White House. But from the point of view of the role of the United Nations in the fight against racialism, the Kaunda mission illustrated the refinement of a trend which had been continuing for a while—to use the United Nations for passing the necessary resolutions of disapproval, and then attempt to mobilize other diplomatic pressures in order to exact conformity.

But what about reaching the population within South Africa itself? I have already indicated my support for a policy which would facilitate the importation of books and newspapers, and other media of ideas into South Africa. In an interview for the *Uganda Argus*, published on 10 October 1970, I also strongly recommended for consideration in Africa the idea of setting up a special radio station either in Addis Ababa or in Lusaka under the name of 'The Free Voice of Southern Africa'. This radio station would be under the aegis of the Organization of African Unity, and the idea was that it should beam both programmes of rational discussions about the general issues involved in Southern Africa, and also programmes more directly militant and provocatively in support of the rights of black people there.

Free Africa has yet to realize the full potential of counter-propaganda and psychological warfare. There is a case for increasing the use of propaganda as a means of boosting the morale of the oppressed in situations where the local broadcasts are all against them. There may be many black South Africans in Bantustans eager to listen to something like the proposed Free Voice of Southern Africa, if only to remind themselves that they have friends outside the prison walls of their part of the continent. Among the programmes there would also have to be special broadcasts organized by the United Nations to indicate the state of world opinion on issues relevant to the problems of the region.

There is also a case for the systematic smuggling of certain forms of literature into South Africa. Indeed, if it were possible to organize a movement which would smuggle into South Africa all the books which the regime has banned, from the works of Marx and Engels to the writings of Kwame Nkrumah, this might well be the most important single contribution to the principle of the free flow of ideas into the Republic. Among the works to be so imported would be those publications of the United Nations which have not been welcomed by the regime because of their censorious contents.

Finally, there is the role of the United Nations in relation to development. Success here has certainly been much more modest than success in decolonization; and yet the contribution to development which the United Nations has made compares favourably with its work against racialism and apartheid. Specialized agencies on health, agriculture and education have become major factors in the whole arena of developmental diplomacy. The promotion of scientific and educational conferences, the encouragement of certain forms of research and publications, the availability of technical assistance in agriculture, health, industry and education, the initiation of pilot projects in specified areas of developmental endeavour, have all had a modest but significant impact on the ethos of international co-operation for development.

The United Nations' Conference on Trade and Development (UNCTAD) has in part been a failure in practical terms, but important in a pioneering sense. In 1964 at Geneva the poor continents of the world, Latin America, Asia and Africa, confronted the developed countries, and demanded a transformation of the international trade system in the direction of better terms for producers of primary products and more concern for the needs of the underdeveloped world at large. The idea of collective bargaining, which had vastly changed the lives of the poor in the industrialized countries themselves, was now being tried for the first time at the level of inter-state relations. For a brief period in 1964, the poor of the world formed a global trade union, and were bargaining at a conference table. A similar attempt was made at the second conference, in New Delhi in 1968. But, unlike the workers in individual countries, poor nations could not really go on strike and hurt the rich countries. At the level of inter-state relations the poor are more vulnerable than they are in domestic battles of will between employers and workers. The third UNCTAD conference in San Diego provided a basis for a new solidarity of the seventy-one participating states, but the Third World was still profoundly vulnerable.

This is the frustrating aspect of poverty at the international level. Yet, it is precisely this frustration which is slowly beginning to give birth to a new kind of solidarity in world politics, a groping for some kind of collective answer to a shared economic weakness. Afro-Asianism of the old kind was a solidarity of a shared humiliation as *coloured people*. But the new concept of the Third World is an attempt to transcend the bonds of colour and to emphasize instead the bonds of shared poverty. The move here is from what I have called *pan-pigmentationalism* to *pan-proletarianism*. The discovery of Arab power in 1973 and 1974 as a result of the energy crisis opened up new possibilities of Third World challenge. It is to the implications of the rise of Arab power in the United Nations that we must now turn.

Oil Power and the New World Body

For the United Nations the two most important developments of the 1970s were the seating of the People's Republic of China in 1971 and the rise of Arab power from 1973 onwards. Both events signified the erosion of American domination of the world body and the emergence of developing countries as a truly decisive force in the General Assembly.

The architects of the United Nations Organization had thought of it as a body under the guidance of a bi-cameral legislature. The tradition of a bicameral legislature in the history of Western political institutions came to be reflected in the organizational structure of the world body. There was an Upper House with five permanent members; and a Lower House called the General Assembly. In its original conception the Upper House was supposed to be the only decision-making body—the prerogative of the Lower House being at best to 'consult, advise and warn'. The élite of the Upper House, the five permanent members, had the power to veto each other and to defy the wishes of the rest of mankind on certain matters.

This élite of the peace-making body was not chosen from among the most peace-loving countries in the world. On the whole, it was chosen on the basis of military strength, actual or presumptive, rather than by consideration of pacific intentions. The 'House of Lords' was in effect a council of *warlords*. There were perhaps good, solid reasons why a peace-making body should have a military aristocracy. It was arguable that peace could best be assured only by entrusting it to those with the greatest military capacity. For those who saw the United Nations as being primarily concerned with peace and stability—and less with human welfare and social justice—a bi-cameral legislature with an upper house controlled by the war giants was defensible.

In due course the ultimate symbol of military capability became the testing and possession of a nuclear weapon. Here again the original choice of the elite within the Security Council was vindicated. The first five countries to become nuclear powers in this sense were precisely the five original permanent members of the Council—the USA, the Soviet Union, Britain, France and China. But for a while the seat of China, the most populous member of the world body, was ironically occupied by Taiwan, claiming to speak as a warlord when in fact it was a puppet of the USA.

But by the end of the 1960s the balance of influence between the Security Council and the General Assembly was clearly changing. The nature of the change was in keeping with the history of bi-cameral legislatures within individual national traditions within the Western world. The tendency in individual Western nations had been for the Upper House to become progressively less powerful than it was at the time of inception. The ideal type of this tendency is perhaps precisely the British Commons and the Lords. A major reason in the history of Britain behind the rise of the House of Commons at the expense of the House of Lords was the expansion of the franchise. As the vote went to sectors of British society previously neglected, the Commons became both an outcome of this democratization and an instrument of further democratization. Once again the analogy with the United Nations is striking. The equivalent of the extension of the franchise at the global level has been the process of decolonization in Asia and Africa and the extension of the right of participation to Asian and African countries previously excluded from the mainstream of world politics. The franchise by the 1970s was extended to the People's Republic of China, the world's most populous country. The franchise had also been extended to much smaller nations, and their votes helped to increase the influence of those that were previously disfranchised.

When the Organization of Petroleum Exporting Countries quadrupled the price of oil in 1973, and the Arabs used for a while an oil embargo in defence of their interests, an additional factor entered the fortunes of the United Nations. The smaller countries suddenly discovered that from among their own ranks, a new source of power was now visible at the centre of the world stage. Countries like Saudi Arabia, Iran and Venezuela, which had previously been regarded as no more than fellow primary producers or fellow developing countries, were now exercising a new level of influence on world events. This discovery of oil power both enhanced the self-confidence of all developing countries and increased the influence of the Arabs in the politics of the Third World. Within the United Nations Arab leadership was exercised in two major directions—one concerned the situation in the Middle East, and the other concerned the quest for a new international economic order.

The issue of the Middle East in turn was two-pronged. There was the effort towards increasing the diplomatic and political legitimacy of the Palestinian cause under the leadership of the Palestine Liberation Organization; and there were the efforts to isolate Israel. The legitimation of the Palestine Liberation Organization attained its most dramatic moment when the leader of the organization, Yasir Arafat, was not only invited to address the General Assembly but was given the treatment of a head of state. Yasir Arafat's triumph in the General Assembly in 1974, and his organization's participation in the debate in the Security Council on the Middle East in January 1976, were important milestones in the long struggle of the Palestinians to gain international recognition. The admission of the PLO in some of the United Nations Specialized Agencies was also an important aspect of this process of legitimation.

The strategy of the isolation of Israel attained its most dramatic moment with the vote which described Zionism as a form of racism in 1975. On balance this vote was a compromise. The more militant Arab states were unable to get enough support from the Third World either to expel Israel (this would in any case have needed the approval of the Security Council) or to suspend Israel from the General Assembly, as the Assembly had suspended South Africa in 1974. In the face of inadequate support for such measures, the vote denouncing Zionism was regarded as a third option. This was carried, with more votes than many people might have thought feasible just a year previously, and yet still fewer votes than most of the other issues on which the Arabs in the United Nations have sought to exercise leadership. Daniel P. Moynihan, the controversial ambassador of the USA in the United Nations at the time, claimed credit for the reduced vote in support of the anti-Zionism resolution. But whatever the truth about such claims, the denunciation of Israel in terms of an attack on Zionism was the most spectacular of those measures designed to put Israel on the defensive and isolate her diplomatically. There was even a fear that the approval of that resolution would result in an upsurge of anti-Semitism in different parts of the world, drawing justification from no less an authority than the world body itself.

The Arabs have also exercised influence in trying to help create a new international economic order. In this latter venture they have gone beyond their own national or regional interests, and have attempted to serve the Third World as a whole. Especially important in the initial phases of this movement was Algeria, whose president proposed the special General Assembly debate on raw materials and helped to chart a new direction for the world body in economic affairs. The debate in the Assembly in 1974 was passionate and sometimes acrimonious, especially in terms of a basic confrontation between the developing countries and the industrialized states under the leadership of the USA. A second General Assembly session on raw materials took place in 1975, with a moderated stand by the USA as it recognized the depth of the aspirations of many developing countries. Between these two meetings on raw materials was the debate which resulted in the Charter of Economic Rights and Duties of States in December 1974, which in some ways virtually legitimized nationalization by Third World states of important industries without compensation, under certain circumstances.

But clearly no single country, such as the People's Republic of China, or group of states, such as the Arab world, could capture effectively the leadership of the Third World without successfully courting the African states. The strength of the African vote in the General Assembly and in other international organizations is perhaps the only clear diplomatic advantage of Africa's fragmentation into a multiplicity of small countries. The multiplicity is a source of influence, and has contributed to the democratization of the world body.

Conclusion

Has the United Nations much of a future? The mission of the UN in the fight against colonialism has been substantially successful. Decolonization has been the world body's most solid achievement. For a while the UN itself served as a kind of collective imperial power, with the trusteeship territories which it inherited from the League of Nations or acquired after the Second World War. Those who administered the territories on behalf of the United Nations were gradually encouraged to liberate them. Concurrently, the United Nations embarked on a policy of encouraging decolonization elsewhere as well. By 1960 opposition to colonialism had become an essential aspect of the diplomatic ideology of the world body.

The United Nations' struggle to reassert jurisdiction over Namibia (South West Africa), which has been administered by South Africa since Germany lost the First World War, has not as yet been triumphant in practical terms. But at least the United Nations has won its case as legal successor to the League of Nations in terms of jurisdiction over Namibia. The moral opposition to South Africa's continued control over Namibia has been strengthened by legal confirmation. But South Africa has continued to refuse to recognize the United Nations as successor to the League of Nations, and has for the time being maintained its control over that territory. The case of Namibia is perhaps the most important residual colonial problem for the United Nations.

And yet there have been other problems with which it has sought to associate itself, ranging from encouraging sanctions against Rhodesia after Ian Smith's Unilateral Declaration of Independence to a moderating influence over the future of the former Spanish Sahara.

While the United Nations' struggle against colonialism has been quite impressive, its successes with regard to the struggle against racialism have been much more modest. Pressure on South Africa to modify its policy of apartheid is beginning to show some results in the form of attempts to reduce 'petty apartheid' in some sectors of South African life. But the racist regime is still effectively in control and the range of its discriminatory practices remains very wide. Racism as practised by non-white people, such as the action taken by President Idi Amin against Asians in Uganda in 1972, has had less success in the world body. The British Government's attempts in that year to bring the issue of Amin's expulsion of the Asians before the world body, and to get a censure of the Uganda government by the world body, was simply unsuccessful.

Like most major political institutions, both within nations and encompassing many nations, the United Nations has a double standard. It has found it easier in more recent times to denounce Western imperialism than to criticize Russian imperialism. It is more sensitized to racism committed against coloured people than to racism perpetrated by coloured people against others. The General Assembly was aware of the racist aspects of Zionism—including the very idea of creating a Jewish state even if it displaced hundreds of thousands of non-Jews—but the world body has been less sharp in coming to the defence of Jews elsewhere, from the Soviet Union to Iraq. But a dual standard by the world body since it was 'captured' by the Third World may itself be a reaction against the old dual standards when the United Nations was controlled by the Western world. The world body is changing, its morality is still imperfect, but it is much more representative of the human race today than it was before 1960.

As for the United Nations' mission against economic underdevelopment, the struggle has been entering a new phase since the rise of Arab power in world politics. The United Nations' Conference on Trade and Development (UNCTAD) has been one of the mechanisms through which the world body has sought to play a part in creating a new international economic order. Progress has been slow, and the resistance of the industrial nations to a more equitable system of trade and global finance has been a major stumbling block. But the pressure of the oil producers to link a discussion of energy to a discussion of all raw materials has enhanced the leverage of the so-called 'Group of 77', consisting of the developing countries generally. By 1976 it was time for Africa to host the fourth meeting of UNCTAD, and this took place in Nairobi in May. The agonizing debate about a new international economic order entered another phase.

But there is a fourth mission of the United Nations alongside its tripartite struggle against colonialism, racialism and underdevelopment. This fourth mission is the struggle against warfare itself. It is in fact the oldest of the missions of the United Nations, having been made central to the vision of the organization when it was created. Unfortunately the United Nations remains at its most helpless in dealing with problems of war – either war within a member state, such as the Nigerian civil war (1968-70) or the Lebanese civil war (1975-6), or the massive danger of nuclear catastrophe between superpowers. For the time being the United Nations remains unable to save for certain 'succeeding generations from the scourge of war'.

There have been times when the United Nations has played a part in at least reducing the dangers of a major confrontation. From an African perspective a particularly important experiment concerns the United Nations involvement in the Congo after the departure of the Belgians in 1960. The mutiny of the *force publique*, and the general collapse of law and order in large sections of the country, combined with a bid by Katanga under Moise Tshombe to secede from the country, all created a major crisis into which the USA and the Soviet Union might so easily have been drawn militarily. The United Nations voted to move into the Congo mainly in order to avoid the danger of a confrontation between the USA and the Soviet Union comparable in potential to the Korean crisis a decade earlier. On balance the United Nations succeeded in averting that conflict, and played a part in maintaining the territorial integrity of what later became Zaire.

But while there have been occasions when the United Nations has made a contribution towards moderating the danger of war or facilitating the process of peace-making, it has been on the whole more effective in the struggle against colonialism, the campaign against certain forms of racism, and the quest for a more equitable global economic system. The tangible results in this third area are still very modest indeed, but the United Nations has definitely become one of the battlefields for the war against economic injustice and underdevelopment.

However, clouds of uncertainty continue to hang over the destiny of the world body. Its ambition is much greater than its capacity, its potential more impressive than its accomplishments, its ideals more profound than its standards. But it is precisely when man is trying to forge an instrument for the transformation of his own kind that 'a man's reach should exceed his grasp, or what's a heaven for?'

References and notes

1. Speech of the Rt Hon Oliver Stanley to the American Outpost, London, 19 March 1945. See *British Speeches of the Day* (British Information Service, 1945), pp. 318-20.
2. Some of the issues concerning the UN discussed here are analysed more extensively in Ali A. Mazrui, 'The United Nations and some African political attitudes', *International Organization*, **XVIII,** (summer 1964), 499-520, and reprinted as chapter 12 in Mazrui, *On Heroes and Uhuru Worship* (London: Longman, 1968), pp. 183-208.
3. Consult, for example, George Padmore, ed., *History of the Pan-African Congress* (1947; William Morris House, 1963, 2nd edn), pp. 19-20. See also Ali A. Mazrui, *The Anglo-African Commonwealth: Political Friction and Cultural Friction* (Oxford: Pergamon Press, 1967), pp. 53-5.
4. Taken from the opening lines of reaffirmation of the United Nations Charter.
5. Text given in Robert A. Goldwin, Ralph Lerner and Gerald Sourzh, eds, *Readings in World Politics* (New York: Oxford University Press, 1959), p. 539.
6. Clyde Eagleton, 'Excesses of self-determination', *Foreign Affairs,* **XXXI** (July 1953), 592-604.
7. This approach was first worked out in Ali A. Mazrui, 'The United Nations and some African political attitudes', *International Organization,* op. cit.
8. Oral hearing at the Trusteeship Council, Fifteenth Session, Verbatim Record of the 592nd Meeting, 7 March 1955. Extracts from this evidence are reprinted in Julius K. Nyerere, *Freedom and Unity: a Selection from Writings and Speeches, 1952-65* (Dar es Salaam: Oxford University Press, 1966), pp. 35-9.

PART THREE

THE GLOBAL ISSUES

CHAPTER 11

Race & Dignity

In this chapter we are concerned with the field of race relations in Africa and the extent to which domestic initiatives and international action can promote a congruence between protection of rights and harmonious interaction between man and man. A word might therefore first be necessary to define the place of Africa and the African within the whole problem of race relations in modern history.

For one thing it is worth remembering that the black people are perhaps the most aggrieved of all races in moral terms. It was Pandit Nehru of India who once told his countrymen: 'Reading through history, I think the agony of the African Continent . . . has not been equalled anywhere.'[1] This is not necessarily a claim that the black man has been more physically brutalized than other races. There have been cases of genocide in world politics, for example, that have not been directed against black people. The worst case of atempted racial annihilation in this century was directed against Jews and not blacks. There have also been other communities in almost every continent of the world who have suffered brutality and death without hope or justice. Nor is the black man the poorest economically. Black Americans, underprivileged as they are, are easily among the best off of the coloured peoples of the globe. And even Africans are by no means the poorest people in the twentieth century. There is considerably more poverty in India, Bangladesh and Pakistan, for example, than there is in most countries of Africa.

The black man is neither the most brutalized, nor the most deprived of the racial specimens of the world. He has simply been the most humiliated. The black races have historically been looked down upon more universally than almost any other race. And the African continent in historical times has been a vast raiding ground for slaves destined for widely separated parts of the globe. Theories which range from social Darwinism to apartheid in our own day have tended to put the African at the lowest point of human evolution. After all, the black man has been the furthest removed from the white man in colour. The psychological distance sensed by the white man has corresponded with this pigmentational distance. Black humiliation both within Africa itself, and in the Diaspora, has been a major feature of the contemporary world. The humble ranking of blackness even in societies which are otherwise quite tolerant in their racial relations has been a continuing theme of our time.

Another factor which makes Africa distinctive within the whole issue of race relations is the simple fact that the most blatantly racialist regime in the world, that of South Africa, happens to be within Africa. It can sometimes be said that the African members of the United Nations have become among the more racially sensitive of all the membership. They have certainly become more racially sensitive than their Asian counterparts. The very idea of a possible racial confrontation between white and coloured people now sounds more convincing when one is thinking of Africa than of Asia. There is a good deal of 'anti-Americanism' in Asia, and indeed 'anti-Westernism'—but the sentiment of being *anti-white* as such has considerably subsided in the Asian continent in the last decade. Asia is in any case more racially heterogeneous than Africa. And the deep divisions between Asians themselves, either as racial groups or as competitive nation states, have sometimes made anti-white passions almost incidental. The growing hostility in many parts of Asia against Japan's economic pre-eminence in the region is a case in point.

Asia, moreover, does not have the equivalent of a South Africa in its midst. It remains a matter of continuing psychological relevance that the most racist regime in the world is within the African continent, and this has been a major contributory factor to the persistence of racial sensitivity in the rest of the continent. Many African leaders feel that the dignity of the African race is indivisible. As Kenya's Tom Mboya once put it, 'As long as any part of Africa remains under European rule, we do not feel that Africans will be regarded in the right way.'[2]

But given the world as it is today what can be done to help the cause of eliminating racial prejudice and discrimination in human societies everywhere? There are five major fields of possible action. One method is to attempt to change and rearrange the socio-economic structure of the society which has unhealthy race relations. In some ways this is the toughest of the answers to prejudice, as well as being potentially the most effective. The second possible method of mitigating race prejudice is by outlawing certain manifestations of it. In this case the law intervenes to protect the possible victims from overt prejudice and discrimination. The third possible method is by attempted maximization of mutual knowledge between groups. This has its dangers, for familiarity sometimes increases contempt, rather than reducing it. Nevertheless this is an area which needs further exploration. A fourth method is by some kind of international disapproval, as sometimes happens when censorious resolutions are passed by international bodies. But there are other international pressures which could be invoked to help dissuade certain societies from certain courses of action. The fifth method is by confrontation. Conflict between the races is thus allowed to escalate, in the hope that a new beginning could later emerge. Let us explore these five fields of action.

Class-Race Convergence

At the beginning of 1968 there was a dramatic exodus of Asians from Kenya, scrambling to get to the United Kingdom before the door was closed. This was the first Asian exodus from East Africa. The great majority of them were citizens of the United Kingdom and had originally assumed that British citizenship was a greater insurance for their rights than any local East African citizenship. They further assumed that the gates of the United Kingdom would remain open indefinitely for those who held British passports. But then in the wake of the campaign of Duncan Sandys and other leading Britons apprehensive about coloured immigration, rumours started circulating that the British government would before long restrict the entry even of its own citizens if they did not have a 'substantial' connection with the United Kingdom. It was this threat of restricted entry into Britain which greatly accelerated the Asian exodus from East Africa at that time – before Idi Amin captured power in Uganda.

Nevertheless the policy of Africanization of commerce being implemented in both Kenya and Uganda also had a part to play in this movement of populations. For a variety of historical reasons, distributive and commercial activity in much of East Africa had become controlled by non-indigenous people. In the main these were Europeans and Asians (Indians and Pakistanis). Almost from the very day of independence the Kenya government had committed itself to a growing indigenization of the economy. Resettlement schemes on the land were part of the process of de-Europeanizing the richest farming areas of the country, and policies to promote African businessmen were in part designed to reduce the Indo-Pakistan proportion of the commercial activity of the country. Successful businessmen at a level above that of market-hawkers and stallholders were few and far between. The Kenya government and later the Uganda government tried to promote an increasing African share in this sector of national life.

At first the methods used were merely those of appealing to immigrant businessmen to involve more Africans in their activities. One major difficulty was that many Asian businesses were essentially family businesses which did not lend themselves easily to acquiring partners outside the family circle. Since the whole distribution of work and method of involvement had a strong personal element rooted in a family relationship, it was not easy to find a place for a new African partner in the business.

In addition the very idea of creating an African commercial class was inevitably a matter which could seriously undermine the livelihood of some of the poorer shopkeepers among East Africa's immigrant communities. It was at times like inviting certain Asians to commit commercial suicide. There was a third reason why the initial loose appeals to Asians that they should help African businessmen did not yield immediate results. This was the simple fact that Africans were not always effectively competitive in commerce even when given a little push in a situation like that of East Africa.

Partly because of these considerations both the Kenya government and the Uganda government became increasingly militant in their policy of Africanization of the economy. One method used was simply to reduce the opportunities for the non-Africans, in the hope that the gaps left would draw in those Africans who might otherwise have been too timid or too disorganized to be fully competitive with the previous holders of such business opportunities. Out of this grew the idea of the Trade Licensing Acts in Kenya and Uganda in the late 1960s which helped to precipitate Asian fears about their future. After the Act businesses in these countries were licensed more systematically than before, and the duration of licences was limited to one calendar year. The Minister of Commerce had the right to refuse a non-citizen a licence if he was convinced that the business could be done by a citizen.

These policies have certainly been a classic instance of trying to restructure the socio-economic relationships between groups in the country. In a situation where racial and class differences converge, there is a danger not merely of prejudice in a passive form, but of antagonisms which might turn towards violence. The colonial situation, especially in Kenya, had been a pyramid at the top of which was the European elite, holding political power and agricultural pre-eminence. Immediately below were the Indo-Pakistani communities, victimized by the Europeans in some matters, but still enjoying greater economic opportunities than the vast African populations around them. The Asians were excluded from rights on the land, but they made up for it by a vigorous participation in the distributive and commercial sector of the Kenya economy.

On attainment of independence Kenya embarked first on a policy of trying to reduce settler dominance in the fertile areas of the country and introduce instead indigenous farmers. This whole policy has had its ups and downs, but there has been a consistent attempt to de-Europeanize and indigenize the former 'White Highlands' of Kenya. The next target for Africanization in the economic sphere was bound to be the distributive and commercial sector under Asian control, as well as the managerial sector with its Euro-Asian preponderance. It has been these sectors which have been subject to reform under the new Trade Licensing and Immigration Acts.

A major premise of economic policy under both Kenyatta and Obote was the conviction that those Asians who took local citizenship would risk the prejudice of the underprivileged Africans if there continued to be in the country a convergence between class and income differences and racial distinctions. Part of the rationale of Kenyatta's Government, and to some extent Obote's Government, was that in an ethnically pluralist society the first task of those who sought social justice was not to eliminate classes altogether but to avoid this coincidence between class and racial differences. A step towards racial toleration would, it was assumed, be taken if there was an ethnic diversification of the middle and upper classes of the society.

The two most drastic social revolutions that have taken place in Africa since independence have been those of Rwanda and Zanzibar. In neither case was the revolution initially directed against class distinctions as such. The Tutsi were overthrown in Rwanda and the Arab oligarchy was broken in Zanzibar, not as a result of passionate anti-class militancy on the part of the majority of the population but simply because there had been too neat a coincidence between ethnicity and privilege. The elimination of ethnic and racial animosities in such pluralist societies must therefore first seek to create a divergence between these two factors of social characterization.

By 1972 Uganda under Idi Amin was no longer prepared to wait any longer for a fair solution to the inherited problem of racial stratification in Uganda. Amin expelled the non-citizen Asians with three months' notice. But Kenya tried for a little while longer to divorce race from class.

Race and Law

Legal means are not always used in favour of racial tolerance; they are at times invoked to sanctify prejudice and organize discrimination. The whole apparatus of apartheid in South Africa has in part been solidly based on a legal structure. The promotion of racial tolerance is sometimes dependent on the elimination of legal constraints. The law in South Africa, as in some states of the USA, has often been on the side of the bigoted.

But there are times when resort to legal means is an exercise in liberality. In the USA itself there has been an increasing use of federal law to safeguard the rights of minorities. Education, housing, employment and recreation are only a few of the areas of national life which have felt the impact of expanding liberalization under new legislation, in spite of the setbacks to these programmes under the Nixon administration. In Britain too there has been a rising belief in the meaningfulness of legal action to cope with some of the effects of human prejudices. There are still many voices heard in England which express scepticism about the possibility of legislating against human emotions. It is a scepticism which goes far back in British history. But the Labour Government under Harold Wilson finally took the position that although human feelings could not be legislated against, human actions could. To legislate against discrimination in housing and jobs is not to invade the private sanctuary of human prejudice but to cope with concrete manifestations of discriminatory practices. Britain is still careful in the introduction of legislative measures on race relations, but there has been quite a sharp turn towards greater use of legislative measures to cope with problems arising out of race relations in the country.

In Africa outside the white-dominated areas there is as yet inadequate use of the law as a direct answer to aspects of racial prejudice. Bills of rights may often be enacted, but only in Nigeria and Uganda in the first few years of their independence was there a sufficient seriousness invested in bills of rights to lead to a growing body of constitutional law in the countries. In other words, these two were situations where the aggrieved found the courage and the optimism to take their cases against the state to court. And out of this cumulative litigation there began to grow a body of constitutional rights fully tested in the courts. But in Nigeria this whole process was seriously interrupted by the civil war; and in Uganda it was partially interrupted by the violence which broke out in the first half of 1966, culminating in a more centralized political arrangement under Milton Obote's new constitution. The growth of constitutional law in Uganda received a more severe setback after the coup when decrees became the rule of the day.

But on the whole African countries have not really bothered to legislate against racial discrimination. One reason for this in places like Kenya was simply the conviction on attainment of independence that what was needed to reintroduce racial harmony was to repeal the racially restrictive legislation of the colonial period. The law in these colonies had begun to be identified as an instrument of racial regimentation, rather than an instrument which could promote greater tolerance. Sometimes precisely because African countries do have laws against certain forms of prejudice, African governments resort to administrative action which can be more severe than the incident which gave rise to it. Deportation of European residents in African countries on charges of racial prejudice have sometimes been out of proportion with the actual offence. A person who has lived in an African country all his life might suddenly be asked to leave on charges which are not always made explicit.

There are indeed occasions when the charges of racism appear to be serious. For example, there was the notorious Tank Hill party in Uganda in December 1963. It was claimed that on the eve of Kenya's independence a collection of expatriates met in a house on Tank Hill in Kampala and played games designed to parody and ridicule the idea of African readiness for self-rule. It seemed to have been a party farce, with theatrical costume, intended to deride some of the highest ambitions of the new Africa.

No less a person than the then Prime Minister of Uganda himself took the news about the Tank Hill party to Parliament and dramatically related the nature of the ridicule, complete with exhibits of some of the items used in the farce. It was a remarkable occasion. The whole Legislature seemed to be working itself up into a state of political fury over what the Prime Minister reported. 'Hang them!' was among the cries which rang out in the Assembly under the stunning impact of the Prime Minister's report. Several of the Europeans who had participated in the party were expelled from the country soon after.[3]

Was the Prime Minister correctly informed about the party? It is one of the frustrations of a situation where no legal evaluation takes place that the evidence lies hidden in administrative files, instead of being available in judicial records. If the Prime Minister was correctly informed, those particular deportations were perhaps not too severe a punishment for the offence in question, given African conditions. And yet there have been occasions when a different form of punishment, imposed after a judicial process, would have been more consistent with humane principles. It would also have been more consistent with many of Africa's own self-images in this age of ideologies. It is possible to ask the question: what is the place of deportation in African socialism? The egalitarian longing in African socialism is essentially a longing for *racial* equality rather than an equality between classes. The strong commitment to class struggle is a characteristic more of European socialism than of most brands of African socialism which have emerged so far. African socialism might therefore be said to be primarily in a state of war against white racialism and neo-imperial relationships.

But what weapon do African leaders have against manifestations of white arrogance at home in their own African countries? This brings in the difficulty we have alluded to. Unfortunately there are hardly any minor forms of punishment available to African governments in the face of arrogance from European residents. The only obvious method of punishing manifestations of racial aggressiveness is the brutal punishment of deportation. It is this fact which sometimes makes one long for specific laws against certain manifestations of race prejudice in African countries. The penalties inflicted under such laws would not always be as brutal as expulsion from a country in which a person may have lived for ten, twenty, thirty or more years. Moreover, a judicial process would ensure a sifting of the evidence, and reduce the kind of rumours and inconsistent speculations which characterized the atmosphere in Uganda at the time of the Tank Hill party.

Another advantage that a judicial process has over administrative deportation is that a trial in a court of law would enable us to know the specific offence of the expatriate. As matters now stand, people are sometimes deported without even being told precisely what their offence was. And certainly the rest of the public, including other anxious expatriate residents, are only rarely taken into confidence as to the nature of the offence for which the unwanted individuals then in the news are being expelled. If justice is being done in the act of a deportation, it is seldom *seen* to be done.

But it might be argued that on such occasions there is in any case a widespread suspicion that some highly serious breach of racial respect and racial harmony has been caused by the offenders. It might be further suggested that the deportation is intended to deter other expatriates from similar activities or similar attitudes. After all, one of the major philosophies of punishment in relation to justice is that punishment should primarily aspire to deter the commission of offences.

Are deportations really ever intended primarily to deter other expatriates from similar activities? Or are they retribution against the particular expatriates regarded as guilty? If they are intended as a deterrent it becomes more important than ever that the nature of the offence should be explicitly stated. The principle of the deterrent postulates a definition of what we are being deterred from. Such a definition seldom accompanies a deportation from any of the African countries. And yet what alternatives have these African countries? In the absence of laws against manifestations of race prejudice, and considering the complications of any such legislation, what alternative has an African government but to issue deportation orders in the face of racial arrogance against the natives of the country?

One answer would be that it depends upon the degree of arrogance. There must be forms of racial pettiness that should rather go unpunished than be punished too brutally. But there are other forms which could be made subject to greater legal control. It is true that some offences are somewhat elusive manifestations of racial arrogance, rather than specific acts of discrimination in public places. But if, as in the United Kingdom, it is possible to have a law against incitement of racial hatred, it might be possible to have a law against provocative racialist behaviour.

President Nyerere of Tanzania has been known to say: 'Those of us who talk about the African way of life . . . take pride in maintaining the tradition of hospitality which is so great a part of it.'[4] This tradition could now be translated into a more tolerant attitude towards foreign residents in African countries. Kenya's Tom Mboya used to talk of African socialism as being based on a tradition of 'universal hospitality'.[5] How universal is this hospitality? Of course the late Mr Mboya did not intend to be taken too literally. What was being asserted was the tradition of fairly broad acceptance of social obligations, of concern for the hungry, the traveller, and the social guest. Again, in the modern period some attempt might need to be made to give real meaning to the concept of an Africa which really believes in universal hospitality. The African countries cannot afford to leave the doors open to all comers, but at least they could avoid forcing people through the exit door too often. There was a time when independent Africa was in danger of becoming one of the least hospitable areas of the world. People were packed off and deported for what must sometimes have been the flimsiest of reasons. And further, African governments did not always believe in mitigating the effects of their precipitous actions—they were capable of giving a man twenty-four to forty-eight hours during which to pull out the personal roots of a whole lifetime.

But hospitality is always a matter of reciprocal obligations. The guest has certain restraints and sometimes positive duties expected of him; and the host has certain rights against the guest along well-defined lines. Even within the ideological framework of African cultural nationalism, there is this acceptance of reciprocity in the host-guest relationship. It was again Julius Nyerere who said:

> Those of us who talk about the African way of life and, quite rightly, take pride in maintaining the tradition of hospitality which is so great a part of it, might do well to remember the Swahili saying: '*Mgeni siku mbili; siku ya tatu mpe jembe*'—or in English, 'Treat your guest as a guest for two days; on the third day give him a hoe.'[6]

In 1965 a number of European farmers from the Arusha area in Tanzania had to leave the country suddenly. Their lease-rights to their farms were cancelled. The argument which the government put forward was that they had not really attempted to attain maximum productivity in the areas of land put in their hands. There was a time when some of this land was freehold land belonging to the individuals concerned, but on independence Tanganyika decided that freehold land was inconsistent with the collectivist traditions of Africa. Land in private hands was therefore deemed to be leasehold, and the conditions for retaining the right of the lease included the requirement that land be effectively used in terms acceptable to the government from whom it was technically leased. It was therefore asserted that by not developing the Arusha farms fully the Europeans had not fulfilled the conditions of the lease. Relating this phenomenon to the argument about reciprocal hospitality, it might be stated that the European residents of Tanzania were enjoying the hospitality of leasehold land but had not adequately accepted the *jembe* or hoe upon which the hospitality was predicated. To use the words of Ujamaa: 'Each one of those Europeans was perhaps becoming "a modern parasite"—the loiterer, or idler who accepts the hospitality of society as his "right" but gives nothing in return.'[7] And yet being deprived of one's farm was one thing—being deported was another. Tanzania seemed to have opted for a more complete termination of her hospitality, at least in the case of European farmers who were forced to leave the country.[8]

Even the act of depriving the Europeans of their farms itself without due judicial process could be mistaken for administrative or political high-handedness. Some time before independence Julius Nyerere had written a little pamphlet entitled, *Barriers to Democracy*. In it he said:

> In Tanganyika [the European] is in an awkward position. He likes Tanganyika. He does not want to see in Tanganyika what happens or is talked about in other multi-racial countries. Yet he is afraid. . . . I suggest that the European in Tanganyika can serve his fellow Europeans in the rest of Africa by stopping being afraid. . . . Nobody asks him to give up his sisal estate; nobody can deprive him of his tremendous lead in education, in general experience.[9]

The assurance to safeguard Europeans' property rights has not been fulfilled. The assurance to give special recognition to education and general experience has been diluted. To lead in education and general experience is of course now no longer to lead in real promotion or general status in the society of Tanzania. On the contrary, there has even been a growth of some distrust of education as a credential for leadership. This distrust itself arises out of a more general socialist distrust of all forms of special privilege.

On balance, however, we should not deny the existence of a large area of racial toleration in Tanzania and in many other African countries. It might even be said that African countries accept non-Africans and let them enjoy special standards of livelihood to a degree to which Africans do *not* in turn receive from the rest of the world. Certainly Europeans settling in Africa enjoy on the whole a more privileged place in African society than Africans settling in European countries. Nevertheless, the lack of an adequate legal infrastructure for the promotion of greater racial tolerance and discouragement of manifest racial arrogance has reduced Africa's capacity to make a punishment fit a crime, and make the judicial process check some administrative excesses in this field.

Familiarity and Contempt

It is sometimes assumed too readily that people would like each other better if they knew each other better. But in the field of race relations, as indeed in many other fields, this kind of assumption is over-optimistic. Prejudice against a race sometimes increases rather than diminishes with greater knowledge. It partly depends upon the nature of the information that a person had before he became better informed about the people. If my initial information about a distant community was favourable, and even romantic, and I later discovered their faults, this additional information may not be a step in the direction of greater liking. On the other hand, it may be said that my attitude is now based on sounder information than the attitude I had before. If this is the case the elimination of prejudice need not always lead to greater toleration between groups. For prejudice is an attitude of mind that is at once strong and inadequately founded on reliable knowledge and rationality. The distant person who loves the Maoris of New Zealand without knowing a thing about them is operating from greater prejudice than a person more reserved about the Maoris but much better informed. If you gave the first person some information about the faults of the Maoris (all human groups have, of course, their faults) you would be increasing his knowledge of the Maoris and therefore reducing the component of sheer prejudice in his attitude. Yet you are at the same time decreasing his spirit of tolerance and a romantic admiration of this particular human group.

It is also sometimes taken for granted that if Europeans discovered that their differences from, say, West Indians were only skin-deep and accent-wide, they might learn to accept West Indians more readily. The assumption here is that human groups are inclined to have greater affection for those who are more nearly like themselves. This too is over-optimistic. Some of the bloodiest hatreds that have taken place in human history have been between peoples who were alike and knew each other very well. The French in the last world war knew the Germans much better than they knew the Japanese, but they probably hated the Germans much more. Indeed the two major world wars we have had have been basically European 'civil' wars in their origins. Those who precipitated the cataclysm were Europeans who knew each other very well, had felt the force of certain shared cultural characteristics and experienced moments of common civilization.

Precisely because they had mixed so much, and knew each other so well, they had developed passions about each other which were not always conciliatory. Familiarity can at times breed strong discontent. Nor is it entirely without sound psychological reasons that one of the biggest categories of murders in the world is murder within the family.

It is true that there was a time when Europe believed almost anything about the so-called 'dark continent'—from cannibalism to two-headed human monsters. This was the kind of prejudice which rested on the numbing influence of sheer distance. A sense of remoteness sometimes increases credibility, and therefore makes possible prejudices which would not otherwise be tenable. But distance, remoteness, or lack of knowledge are not the only causes of prejudice: sometimes fear and competition are strong factors. There are occasions when the very factor which leads to decreasing ignorance leads also to increased fear and competitive suspicions. The days when the bulk of the British people knew of Indians and Pakistanis only as distant inhabitants of the empire, who were sometimes imitated by actors such as Peter Sellers, are well and truly gone. Now Indians and Pakistanis are next-door neighbours for a number of British families within the United Kingdom. In the old days whatever prejudices these British families might have had against Indians and Pakistanis rested on ignorance and a sense of remoteness. The new prejudices that have been building up rest on a sense of immediacy rather than distance. Immediacy has helped to create certain tendencies of competitive suspicions. These immigrants are deemed to be a danger either to the supply of adequate housing, or good jobs, or in a generalized kind of way, to the standard of living of the British people at large.

But after all these reservations have been made it remains true that there is a degree of knowledge which should reduce hostility and antagonism between groups. As a generalization, the struggle for tolerance might be described as first a process leading to increased tension before it leads to greater amicability. Total ignorance does indeed result in forms of prejudice, either favourable or hostile. A little more information need not result in a lessening of hostility, though it must by definition result in a lessening of the ignorance. But things may get significantly worse in any case before they get better in the whole interplay between tolerance and information. There is always a gap between the dissemination of information and its assimilation into the minds of the people. An English poet, Alexander Pope, once observed:

> A little learning is a dang'rous thing;
> Drink deep, or taste not the Pierian spring:
> There shallow draughts intoxicate the brain,
> And drinking largely sobers us again.[10]

In many fields of experience these observations of Pope's are simply not correct. It is seldom true that one must drink deep of the spring of knowledge or not taste knowledge at all. But in the field of race relations and racial understanding there may be a lot to be said for Pope's admonition. Even if we do not agree that we should not taste the spring of human understanding at all unless we are prepared to taste deep, we should at least agree that it takes more than a small swallow to make sobriety in this sphere. In fact knowing other human groups just a little may be more dangerous than not knowing them at all. But knowing them much more might be the road towards inter-group tolerance.

The Role of International Action

The minimum form which international pressure might take could be simply the expression of disapproval in international bodies, or denunciation by specific influential foreign spokesmen from their own countries. Sometimes there could be strong demonstrations in foreign capitals against the policies of a particular regime.

A maximal form of foreign pressure might be direct intervention in a country to force the state to be more tolerant or prevent it from being too brutal against a particular community. Military intervention is the highest form this could take, but it has seldom happened in modern history except in situations where a big power wants to protect its nationals from the wrath of a local population. There are times when the power need not be big, but it usually has to be strong enough in relation to its 'victim' to embark on an adventure of this kind. In recent days in Africa there was the original Belgian intervention in the Congo soon after independence in 1960 when Belgian troops entered the country ostensibly to protect the lives and wellbeing of Belgian nationals. Then there was the notorious Stanleyville operation of November 1964 when American planes were used to enable Belgian paratroopers to descend on Stanleyville in order to rescue a group of white hostages. These are cases of direct military intervention to prevent what an outside country might regard as a racialist danger to its own citizens in foreign lands.

Another type of international pressure might be that of an economic blockade or some other kind of strong economic sanctions. Some such sanctions were tried against Italy after Mussolini's invasion of Ethiopia, and have been attempted against Ian Smith since Rhodesia's Unilateral Declaration of Independence. In neither case was this international action simply an attempt to eliminate a racial situation; yet in both cases there were important racial principles compromised or endangered. The denial of important economic advantages by concerted international action was being tested as an instrument of safeguarding the interests of weaker racial communities against the power of those with better military capabilities. The case of South Africa itself has sometimes posed the question of whether any concerted international action against such a country could succeed in forcing modifications in the racialist system of the Republic. Some countries have felt that the Republic was too rich and too self-sufficient to be susceptible to this kind of external pressure. Others have pointed out that the only countries that could conceivably have any impact on South Africa – the Western countries, especially the United Kingdom – feel somewhat vulnerable themselves economically to the danger of South Africa's retaliatory measures.

A less ambitious international mode of pressure for the case of South Africa is simply that of increasing diplomatic isolation. The controversy over whether South Africa should or should not participate in the Olympic Games in Mexico in 1968 was only one example of increasing demands by a large number of countries that South Africa should be excluded from more and more activities on the world scene. At the United Nations Conference on Trade and

Development in New Delhi earlier in 1968 there were recurrent interruptions to the proceedings resulting from the presence of South Africa, a presence which led several times to a boycott of the proceedings by a number of Afro-Asian countries.

The fate of 'isolation' as envisaged for South Africa by the new African states rests on philosophical assumptions which have yet to be adequately analysed. The old hazardous tendency to personify countries and then talk about them almost as if they were individual persons sometimes affects people's entire attitude towards South Africa. Although it may be hazardous to treat countries as persons, it is nevertheless an exercise which can afford useful insights into the whole phenomenon of passing a moral judgement on another country's behaviour. Let us take the analogy of someone in a town who commits a crime and gets caught. That person may end up in jail. Now, jail is a form of isolation. The criminal behind bars is thrown back on himself or at best on the company of fellow criminals in a restricted area. Isolation from the rest of society is itself seen as part of the pain which the punishment is supposed to give the criminal.

These same assumptions now appear to be transposed to the international scene. South Africa is viewed as an offender, if not of the law of nations, certainly of the canons of the new international morality. But the international society—unlike the society of, say Great Britain or Tanzania—has no jail to which it can send its worst offenders. South Africa may indeed be placed 'before the bar of world opinion', but can she be put behind the bars of a world prison once judgement has been passed? This is where the penalty of isolation suggests itself in a new form. South Africa is to be sentenced not to the literal isolation of a prison cell but to the limbo of international anomie.

What is the purpose of this isolation? As in the case of the individual criminal in our home town, three lines of reasoning are discernible. First, you isolate the criminal as retribution for his offence. Secondly, you seek to deter him from repeating the offence or to prevent him from continuing it. And, thirdly, implicit in the very idea of deterring him from doing it again, you attempt to reform the criminal to at least this negative extent. In these attempts to isolate South Africa there lies, then, not only the vengeful aim of punishing it for its offences but also the reformative ambition of preparing it for a resumption on some future date of its place in international society. What the African states are involved in is, in other words, a search for a means of getting beyond a mere verdict of 'guilty' pronounced on South Africa. They are seeking ways to make South Africa as a nation serve the nearest thing to a term of imprisonment and become a better member of the international community.

But does imprisonment necessarily succeed in reforming an offender? Here again there is a direct analogy between an offending individual and an offending nation. Some individuals become hardened criminals as a result of imprisonment. Others make up their minds never to see the inside of a prison cell again. How can one be sure of the effect isolation would have on South Africa? After all, many would already argue that America's policy to isolate Communist China has aggravated, rather than mitigated, China's sense of grievance and thereby increased her aggressiveness.

This is where the whole issue of isolation touches that of qualifications for membership in the United Nations. If the United Nations is, as most African states continue to regard it, the very centre of the new international society, then exclusion from it is one of the more obvious methods of trying to isolate a country from that society. In the years when Communist China was outside the United Nations, should she have been in? South Africa is in—should she really be out? These twin issues sometimes invited the charge of a double standard in the policies of some of the new nations. Madame Pandit, leader of India's delegation to the United Nations at the time, was confronted in September 1963 with such a charge in a television interview at the UN. India had suffered direct aggression at the hands of the Chinese and indirect racial humiliation from South Africa. Yet India was in favour of seating Communist China in the United Nations and of unseating South Africa altogether. How could Madame Pandit reconcile the two stands? Her own answer was simply the conviction that South Africa was worse than China.

But on what grounds can this assessment be based? This takes us right back to that Afro-Asian tendency to regard the United Nations not so much as an organization primarily intended to ensure peace and security—as the big powers intended it to be—but as an organization which should be primarily concerned with human rights at large. This has an important bearing on qualifications for membership in the United Nations as viewed by countries, such as the USA, which were opposed to the admission of Communist China, and countries, such as Tanzania, which seek South Africa's expulsion. Article Four of the United Nations Charter was interpreted by those opposed to Communist China's admission as restricting membership to those countries which are 'peace-loving'. This whole emphasis on peace is more characteristic of the big powers' conception of the United Nations' role than it is of the new, smaller powers'. This is not to deny the importance which some of the major powers attach to human rights. Historically, American foreign policy has been known to err on the side of excessive attachment to moral principles of this kind. And even today American pronouncements and rationalizations of political stands are often singularly humanist and moral in tone. On the other hand, it must not be assumed either that the new states are so preoccupied with demands for basic human rights that they have no time to worry about the problem of peace. On the contrary, these states revel in seeing themselves as peacemakers in the disputes of the giants.

Nevertheless, there remains a significant difference in the scale of values between the newer and older states. On India's annexation of Goa, for example, a major power might have argued that the very enjoyment of human rights presupposed a peaceful settlement of disputes. In a sense this line of reasoning made peace more fundamental than those rights—at least to the extent that it made it fundamental *to* those rights. But with that Goan experience in mind the same great power might now have worried lest peace in Western Africa should also be seriously disturbed if human rights were not extended to Angolans. It would at first appear that in this second case the major power was making human rights fundamental to peace instead of the other way round. And yet a good deal would depend upon whether this was an ad hoc calculation by the big power in regard to the particular situation or whether it was a basic general postulate of its diplomatic reasoning at large. If, as is likely in such a case, the calculation was ad hoc, then peace was still being deemed more fundamental than human rights—considering that the granting of human rights by Portugal in Angola was here treated as *instrumental* in the promotion of peace. In general, it was therefore more the new states than the older ones which supported India over Goa. And it tends to be more the new than the old which are concerned about the rights of the Angolans irrespective of the effect of such reforms on peace at large. At times it is almost as if the new arrivals in international politics were reminding the older participants of the simple proposition that the importance of peace is, in the ultimate analysis, *derivative*. Taken to its deepest human roots, peace is important because 'the dignity and worth of the human person' are important. President Carter is adopting this scale of values.

Once humanity is accepted in this way as a more fundamental moral concept than peace, membership in the United Nations might then be based not so much upon a test of being peace-loving as upon a test of being respectful of the dignity and worth of the human person. And in the African estimation—as in the estimation of India's Madame Pandit—apartheid is a more flagrant failure of that test than territorial aggrandisement by the Chinese. This is not necessarily a mitigation of the gravity of territorial aggression; it is just a heightened condemnation of racial arrogance. On this rests the determination of African states to sentence South Africa, if possible, to something approaching solitary confinement.[11]

Internal Confrontation

As for the fifth approach to racial problems, this is quite simply *internal confrontation*. As we indicated earlier, there are no precedents yet of white minorities in power in Africa giving it up without a major domestic upheaval. The precedents we do have are convulsive ones such as Algeria and Kenya. Rhodesia and South Africa are bound to require further convulsions before white control can be broken. Hence the importance of the liberation movements in Southern Africa and the need for more effective support from the Organization of African Unity. The present liberation armies are a mere beginning. They are not yet effective revolutionary instruments. More sustained organization from *within* Rhodesia and South Africa is indispensable before final victory. Meanwhile, the issue of arms remains relevant, as we shall indicate in the next chapter.

Conclusion

We have attempted to demonstrate that the task of eliminating race prejudice and ethnic hostilities in the world needs action in five major areas of policy. The toughest is that of restructuring the socio-economic arrangement in a particular country and attempting to prevent too close a coincidence between class differences and race distinctions. We illustrated this partly with experience from Eastern Africa and the place of the Asians and Europeans in the new economic reorganization being undertaken in this region. The second major area of positive action is that of applying legal solutions to some of the acute racial problems. We argued that the law can be used as easily on the side of prejudice as against it. Perhaps the most legally conscious country in Africa now might still be the Republic of South Africa. There has often been greater respect of legal processes in South Africa than in many other countries on the African continent. And yet the kind of laws passed in South Africa have themselves been morally unjust. The legal apparatus has been used to back and support a system of racial inequity. But the law can be used to break down racial barriers. We have attempted to show that independent African states generally have so far used legal means inadequately as a method of harmonizing relations between groups. There have been occasions when race relations could have been improved by legal sanctions against white racism. Yet very often white racism can only be handled by the brutal reaction of deportation. Alternative methods of punishment might have gone some way towards creating greater social justice in these countries. There are occasions of course when it is black racism that is at play against immigrant communities. Again African countries might have contributed more to the evolution of ethnic amicability if protective legal measures were introduced to safeguard citizens from each other. Tribal injustice too could at times have been averted by legislative means if this had been done early enough. One major magazine in Africa has argued that relations between Ibos and other Nigerians before the civil war might have been prevented from deteriorating too much if the law had been strategically used to prevent intercommunal excesses well in time.[12]

The third area of action we have discussed has been that of increasing and disseminating information in order to promote greater mutual comprehension between groups. But we warned that increased knowledge need not mean increased tolerance, but could in fact mean worsening tensions. Nevertheless, even if the situation in a particular country were inevitably to get worse as groups know each other better and come into competitive confrontations with each other, there might still be a case for a continuing educative campaign. Such a case must rest on the conviction that there is a degree of knowledge, which when finally attained, should drastically reduce the potential for inter-ethnic animosities in the society concerned. Fourthly we discussed the area of international action in race relations, ranging from the simple expression of disapproval by influential spokesmen or by the demonstrations of conspicuous groups in foreign countries, to actual military intervention or economic sanctions to force the hand of a particular racialist regime in the direction of greater liberality. Finally, we examined briefly the fifth option of internal domestic revolution—the mobilization of the victims for a direct and perhaps continuing confrontation with the system oppressing them.

What ought to be borne in mind is that lines of action towards the elimination of racial tensions in the world are more easily defined than implemented. The struggle for racial tolerance in the globe is bound to be hard and drawn out. We may be witnessing in our own day greater racial hatred than most other periods in human history, but at the same time we are witnessing greater racial justice than has ever been possible in human affairs. In other words, part of the explosion of tensions in Africa, the USA, the Middle East and elsewhere is evidence of a growing egalitarian arrangement in the world. When the underprivileged can no longer accept their status, there may develop in their hearts greater feelings of animosity against the 'enemies' than was possible when they were resigned to their fate. To that extent the blacks in the USA may hate white people more today than they have done in past decades. But this is because the gap between them and the white people is narrowing, when all is said and done. Resentment of injustice leads both to hatred of those who practise injustice and to a lessening stability of what they practise. The prospects of improvement become brighter as unjust societies find themselves suddenly unstable. In countries such as the USA there is hope for justice precisely because there is so much hate and unrest. Solutions may be found to reconcile hate with the need for living together. And in Africa the greatest danger to social justice in South Africa would come if African states ceased to disapprove of South Africa. An intense hate of apartheid is itself an important hope for the future.

It is conceivable that some old forms of racism may at long last disappear from human experience in our own lifetime—even if other forms of prejudice persist for future generations to battle with. Given the resilience of human error, that would be no mean achievement for our age.

References and notes

1. See Jawaharlal Nehru, 'Portuguese colonialism: an anachronism', *African Quarterly*, 1, (October-December 1961), 1.
2. Reported in *Mombasa Times* (Kenya) 11 January 1962. This point is discussed in a related context in my book, *The Anglo-African Commonwealth: Political Friction and Cultural Fusion* (Oxford: Pergamon Press, 1967), pp. 36-8.
3. See *Uganda Argus*, 21, 23, 24, 27, and 28 December 1963.
4. Nyerere, *Ujamaa: the Basis of African Socialism* (Dar es Salaam: Tanganyika Standard Press, 1962).
5. Tom Mboya, *Freedom and After* (André Deutsch, 1963), p. 163.
6. Nyerere, op. cit.
7. Ibid.
8. See *East African Standard* (Nairobi), 14 November 1964.
9. See pamphlet by Nyerere, *Barriers to Democracy*, p. 4.
10. *Pastoral Poetry* and *An Essay on Criticism*, Alexander Pope (London: Methuen, 1961).
11. These implications of South Africa's isolation were first discussed in my article 'The United Nations and some African political attitudes', *International Organization*, op. cit. It is reprinted in Ali A. Mazrui, *On Heroes and Uhuru-Worship* (London: Longmans, 1967).
12. Editorial, *Transition*, Kampala, No. 35 (1968).

CHAPTER 12
Arms & Nationhood*

One way of approaching the question of armaments in relation to African development is to examine first the rationale for African military expenditures and their effect on economic and social development. This approach allows the gains from disarmament to become readily apparent. There are three broad arenas from which the urge for African states to seek arms or military establishments might arise: the outside or non-African world, the African world, and the internal domestic world of each African state.

With the exception of the Arab North African countries, independent African states have been fortunate, since attaining independence, in one significant respect: the lack of desire by outside non-African states to infringe on their independence militarily or through physical force. Such cases of military or physical incursion as have taken place to date have emanated from private or non-state elements (private incursions) or, technically speaking, on the invitation of those Africans claiming the legitimate right to rule and hence to invite outside assistance (official intervention). Examples of private incursions include the whole phenomenon of white mercenaries serving in such African internal disturbances as those of the Congo (Zaire), and Nigeria during its civil war. Examples of official interventions, on the other hand, are the UN involvement in the then Congo on Patrice Lumumba's invitation in 1960 and the American-Belgian paratroop drop on Stanleyville in 1965 at the 'invitation' of Moise Tshombe.

On the whole, however, independent Africa has been permitted to enjoy relative security from external military interference. This is particularly fortunate in view of the flimsiness or permeability of African state boundaries, politically and militarily. The power difference between the African states and external powers is so weighted . gainst the African states that any invasion by outside forces, especially from the more developed European states or the USA, would be easy. As a matter of fact, it is doubtful if any black African state south of the Sahara seriously targets its military establishments at

*This chapter is based on a paper by A. G. G. Gingyera-Pincywa and Ali A. Mazrui, 'Regional development and regional disarmament: some African perspectives', given at a seminar on disarmament and development, University of Ghana, June 1970.

the outside world. Helpless as they are in this respect, however, African states have not gone down on their knees before those more powerful than they. If anything, the record of African dealings with such states has ranged from dignified self-assertion in international affairs to intransigence even in the face of external military affront. The latter was expressed by Dr Obote of Uganda, following the violation of Uganda's frontiers by Congolese fighter planes backed by US assistance: 'We blame the government of the United States. . . . We have been attacked without provocation on our part. . . . We must all be prepared to throw sand, and sacks of sand, in the eyes of the mighty.'[1] Dignified self-assertion and dignified death in self-defence then represent the maximum the African states are prepared to do militarily against an outside military threat.

Turning to the situation within the African world itself, there are two reasons that have been recognized by black African states for the maintenance of military establishments: the challenge of racist and colonial Southern Africa; and what might be termed the failure of pan-Africanism.

The Challenge of Southern Africa

There are three basic elements in the attitude of the majority of black African states towards Southern Africa, and all have military implications, which in turn have expenditure implications.[2] The first underlies the OAU support for the liberation movement in Southern Africa.

The most plausible method at the moment to challenge Southern Africa is the guerrilla warfare being carried out by freedom fighters in the affected areas. An OAU committee was set up in 1963 to co-ordinate their efforts and to encourage unity among them. Another of the committee's functions has been to try to give international recognition to the struggle and to generate international diplomatic and material support. Finally, the committee serves as a funnel through which funds from the supporting African states can be transmitted to the freedom fighters.[3]

But Southern Africa is not a dormant target waiting to be attacked and to defend itself against the freedom fighters. It poses challenges of its own beyond its borders—challenges that form another important rationale for military expenditures in the neighbouring independent African states, especially Zambia and Tanzania. The propinquity of the Southern Africa danger must be a strong explanation for the fact that Zambia and three nearby states of East Africa—Tanzania, Kenya, and Uganda—were for a long time the only regular contributors to the budget of the OAU liberation committee. It must also account for the additional military expenditures from these states. As one student of the problem has described it:

> The regional arms race [between Southern Africa and free Africa] is . . . leading to a diversion of Zambia's and Tanzania's resources away from development and towards more sophisticated deterrents. Zambia is buying a £6 million Rapier ground-to-air missile system from Britain, which will be operational in 1970 to deter border incursions by Rhodesian and Portuguese planes; it is the largest ever single military purchase by a black African state.[4]

The need for deterrence against possible attacks from Southern Africa, then, is the second element in the African attitude towards Southern Africa.

The third element, while far less obvious, nevertheless deserves a mention in any examination of the rationale behind military expenditures in Africa: the possibility of a war, not just between Southern Africa and guerrillas, but between Southern Africa and guerrillas joined in field action by the African states. Brigadier A. A. Afrifa, of Ghana, described how close the Ghanaian army came to being sent to fight in Rhodesia towards the final days of Kwame Nkrumah's presidency. Knowing Nkrumah's great passion in pan-African matters, it is easy to give Brigadier Afrifa the benefit of the doubt and accept the veracity of his information.[5]

More recently, and again from as far afield as West Africa, a similar idea indicative of this latent urge to solve the Southern Africa problem through a direct military confrontation was heard—this time from Nigeria. One consequence of the Nigerian civil war was to boost beyond imagination the size of the Nigerian armed forces. From a pre-civil war figure of 10 000, it rocketed to 200 000 by the time the war ended. Such a large contingent of armed men was all right as long as the war continued, but with the termination of the war came the inevitable question of what to do with it. General Yakubu Gowon went on record as saying that these forces would not be used (as rumour then had it) to fight for black Rhodesians, who must exert their own efforts. Nevertheless, it is hardly surprising that the reaction should have come as an answer to the suggestion that the overgrown Nigerian army be made use of in solving the problem of Southern Africa. Whoever first ventured the hint touched on a feeling shared, albeit largely quietly for the moment, by an African leader. Thus it must not be discounted offhand from any catalogue of reasons for military expenditure among countries of black Africa, especially the more radical ones.

The Failure of Pan-Africanism

As to the second reason for the rise in military expenditure—the failure of pan-Africanism—only two aspects of this complex phenomenon are relevant here. Its development will be examined from 1957, the year Ghana gained its independence and proceeded to emphasize one hole in pan-Africanism—African unity. In the forefront of this campaign was Kwame Nkrumah. As is now well known, however, his strategy of a continental union government turned out to be unacceptable to many, in fact to most, of the African states that subsequently achieved their own independence. These considered his strategy to be too fast and impractical and preferred a gradualist or regional approach to African unity.[6] The merit of this debate is far less important to the discussion here than the fact that no continental union government, based on either strategy, has yet been set up. Even leaving aside the goal of union government, there is another sense in which pan-Africanism may be said to have failed. With the egocentric demands of many independent states, the unanimity of purpose characteristic of pre-independence African nationalism is breaking down.

These twin failures of pan-Africanism have, or have had, military implications. The problems of a decentralized state system without an overarching government, of which modern Europe has had so plentiful an experience since the sixteenth century—namely, interstate suspicion, conflict, war, and hence the necessity for military establishments—have as a result begun to appear unavoidable in the similar state system of Africa. It should hardly be surprising, therefore, that Kenya and Somalia should have been involved in a border conflict or Uganda and Zaire in a shooting fray in 1965 toward the end of the Congolese rebellion of 1964-5. The estrangement, accompanied by mutual threats of military measures, between Uganda and Tanzania from 1971 to 1973 was yet another symptom of the conflict potential of Africa's state system in the failure of pan-Africanism to make good its promises.

One of the clearest statements of the importance of this factor as a rationale for military expenditure was once given by a Ugandan foreign minister in a speech, relevantly titled 'Geography as a determinant of Uganda's foreign policy', delivered to students of Makerere University. It was Sam Odaka's contention that Uganda's contiguity with some states that were less than stable made it imperative for that country to develop a large and effective military force. Being landlocked, Uganda sometimes experienced the overflow of violence from Zaire, Rwanda and the Sudan.

What all the above indicates is that, in the absence of overall moderation or of a strong and reliable sense of brotherhood (both of which pan-Africanism had once promised), African states have had to fend for themselves individually for their security and defence in the event of disagreement among themselves.

Internal Disorder

The paramountcy of the civil police in the maintenance of domestic law and order has by now attained worldwide acceptance. But the extent to which they will be permitted to exercise this power may vary from one political system to another, one of the critical determining factors being the political culture of a state. Specifically, a political culture characterized by a high degree of dissension among social groups will tend to resort to the military, rather than to the police, more often than one in which a modicum of basic agreement over important issues exists. The USA, with its recurrent dissension over race, thus tends to make use of its National Guard more often than, say, Britain, which has no similar major cleavage outside Northern Ireland. Following this line of argument, all the African states have the kinds of internal cleavages for which the military, rather than the civil police, are required. The commonest and potentially most explosive of these—what is called the retribalization of politics[7]—concerns the resurgence of ethnic loyalties in situations of rivalry for resource allocation and domestic power.

Since independence, there has definitely been a decline of that phenomenon referred to as 'African nationalism', which had found sustenance in a particular type of colonial situation and was designed primarily to loosen the controls of alien power. The imperial withdrawal meant not an immediate end to those emotions, but rather a gradual decline of their influence on everyday political behaviour. What ought to be noted is that the decline of African nationalism in many of these countries has also meant the decline of national politics. Those parties that rode the wave of nationalist agitation have in many cases now lost their cohesion and sense of purpose and thus their capacity to promote a sense of national involvement. In addition, the decline of political competition and suppression of political rivals has curtailed the openness of debate and public wooing for support, on which politics as an activity must inevitably thrive. In some cases, corruption and electoral malpractices have created widespread political cynicism among the populace, making it harder than ever to achieve a sense of national involvement. In other cases the military has intervened and banned political parties. It is true of many African states that the golden age of modern politics coincided with the golden age of nationalism, and when the latter declined as a major determinant of political behaviour, modern politics declined as a national phenomenon. Be that as it may, it was not merely the boundaries of political activity that were redefined by the rise and then decline of nationalism, but those of political loyalties as well.

The most direct redefinition of loyalties that took place concerned the relative strength of ethnic or tribal loyalties on one side and broader national loyalties on the other. There was often an assumption among analysts of the African colonial scene that nationalism made its recruits from the ranks of the detribalized. From these ranks came the leaders of the anti-colonial agitation. And these agitators were the first distinct and definable class of politicians modern Africa produced. The politicians were, in the majority of cases, Westernized or semi-Westernized; it is partly this factor that tended to distinguish them in the eyes of the spectator as a detribalized group. This language of analysis, however, did not adequately differentiate between tribalism as a way of life and tribalism as loyalty to an ethnic group. There were, in fact, two senses of membership of a tribe: the sense of belonging and the sense of participating. Belonging meant only that one's ethnic affiliation was to that tribe, but participating implied a cultural affiliation as well, a sharing of the particular tribal way of life. When analysts talked about detribalization, they often meant a weakening of cultural affiliation, though not necessarily of ethnic loyalty. A person could adopt an entirely Western way of life but still retain great love and loyalty to the ethnic group from which he sprang.

An alternative formulation of this distinction is to differentiate tribalism from traditionalism. African nationalism gained its leading recruits from the ranks of the *detraditionalized*, rather than the detribalized. The educated and semi-educated Africans who captured leading roles in the anti-colonial movement had indeed lost some aspects of traditional modes of behaviour and adopted others under the influence of Western education and control. But the erosion of tradition did not necessarily mean the diminution of ethnicity. Among the most radically detraditionalized must be included African academics at universities, but even before the Nigerian coup of January 1966, the universities of Ibadan and Lagos were already feeling the internal tensions of conflicting ethnic loyalties.

The University of Nairobi has at times experienced comparable difficulties. The Luos as an ethnic group initially produced more scholars in East Africa than any other single community, and this despite the fact that it was no larger than many other ethnic groups. No sociological or socio-psychological study has yet been undertaken to explain this phenomenon. Perhaps it is too early to see much significance in it, as the sample of East African scholars is still rather limited. But the simple fact that the Luos outnumbered all other ethnic groups at the University of Nairobi was a cause of some tension. The situation now is not as acute as it must have been at the University of Ibadan before the first Nigerian coup, when there was a disproportionate Ibo presence in most categories of staff. But there is no doubt that at Nairobi, as was the case at Ibadan, even the most highly detraditionalized of all Africans, the scholars, have been feeling the commanding pull of ethnic loyalties.

If one insists on looking at the previous colonial phenomenon of agitators as an outgrowth of partial *detribalization*, one must look at some of the events following independence in Africa as illustrations of partial *retribalization*. In Nigeria, the latter phenomenon attained tragic dimensions. The Ibos, for so long part of the vanguard of African nationalism, found themselves retreating into an ideology of the paramountcy of ethnic interests. Their deepest political passions were now retribalized. The painful drama of conflict and civil war in Nigeria began to unfold.

In less stark terms, retribalization is also discernible in other parts of Africa. In Kenya, Luo ethnicity has probably significantly deepened since independence, partly in defensive reaction to some government policies. The political passions of several Luo freedom fighters in the colonial struggle have now become to some extent denationalized. The retreat of African nationalism has helped rekindle some primordial flame. In Uganda, three major attempts to secede have had to be overcome in recent years: first, Buganda's attempt to go it alone in 1960, when it abortively declared its independence from the rest of Uganda; second, Buganda's attempt in 1966 to drive out the central government from Kampala, which is in Buganda; and, third, the Rwenzururu movement of Western Uganda, which sought to detach the Bakongo not only from Toro district, of which they were a part, but also from the whole of Uganda, to form a separate republic with fellow ethnics on the Congolese side. Other instances of separatism in African countries include the civil war in the Sudanese south, which raged from 1955, when southern soldiers mutinied against northern Arab officers until 1972. And in Zaire, there have been repeated eruptions in Katanga (Shaba) from 1960 onwards. There was also the rebellion in Kasai led by J. Mulele and C. Gbenye in 1964-5.

The likelihood of civil disturbances arising from this kind of situation within individual African states is thus a powerful additional reason for military expenditure. In fact, some of the largest military establishments in black Africa are to be found in countries that have experienced this danger of internal fragmentation: Nigeria, with its armed force of 200 000; Zaire, with 300 000; and the Sudan with 200 000. Tanzania and Kenya, though not yet endowed with armies as large as these, have quite well-organized and effective military establishments.[8]

Military Expenditure

But what is the level of expenditure entailed in these military establishments? Unfortunately, this is not an easy matter to tackle with regard to some countries. Sources are either meagre or non-existent, and even where there are annual estimates of expenditure, they are difficult to obtain and often unusable. The UN *Statistical Yearbook*, which provides a wide range of data on diverse countries, was not useful for the purpose, because its entry for military expenditure is amalgamated and entered as a single figure with expenditure on general administration. Another possible source, the *Statesman's Yearbook*, has figures of the sizes of the armed forces and types of weapons, but not the magnitude of expenditure. The International Institute for Strategic Studies in London also has periodic studies. Even so, the data on the armed forces appear out of date, while those on weaponry are inadequate for comparative purposes, as diverse weapons types are catalogued without an effective guide as to how they compare in cost, size, and effectiveness. Tanzania, Uganda, and Kenya each publish statistical abstracts, but the first two countries give no data specifically relevant to military expenditures.

It has thus been necessary to make use of much less direct sources, one method being to estimate the weaponry involved in military establishments south of the Sahara, an aspect on which a detailed study was recently completed. The assumption is that the more sophisticated the weaponry, the higher the level of expenditure involved, and vice versa.

An early study along this line is that by John L. Sutton and Geoffrey Kemp, of the Institute for Strategic Studies in London.[9] Their paper on arms to developing countries analyses the distribution in the developing countries of four major weapons types: aircraft, guided missiles, warships, and tanks. According to their findings, it was only South Africa and Rhodesia that had effective and well-equipped air forces in sub-Saharan Africa. With regard to warships and tanks, the only country that could be said to possess any relevant power was South Africa. Some of the other sub-Saharan countries had armoured cars but, according to the authors, these did not reflect a significant combat capability towards other states, being useful principally for maintaining internal security. The details have changed since then, but the balance of power in the continent has not shifted significantly. Furthermore, Sutton and Kemp discovered that, with the exception of the Caribbean, sub-Saharan Africa had the lowest monetary value in weapons among the zones of the underdeveloped countries studied in the analysis. This meagreness with regard to weaponry is emphasized when a global assessment is made. According to an article by John H. Haagland, which appeared in the Spring 1968 issue of *Orbis*, six countries—the USA, the Soviet Union, the United Kingdom, France, West Germany, and Communist China—account for about 85 per cent of the world's military expenditure; the remaining countries, about 130 in number, account for only about 15 per cent. As has already been seen, Africa, with the exception of South Africa and Rhodesia, comprises very little even of this 15 per cent.

But how does this slight share by Africa in the world's total military expenditure relate to the production of wealth in the sub-Sahara? A suitable index for use in answering this question would be the ratio of military expenditure to gross domestic product. Here again, in the absence of direct primary statistics, one must depend on secondary material. Tim Shaw gives an index of the ratio of military expenditure to gross domestic product (GDP) for four of the selected countries as follows: Tanzania (0.3), Zambia (2.5), Congo (Kinshasa) (1.7), and Nigeria (0.9).[10] The best way to appreciate how high a level of military expenditure these percentages represent is to look at them side by side with those pertaining to some other countries. For this purpose, these countries are divided into two groups: group A, consisting of countries generally known to be militarily active, such as the USA, the United Kingdom, and France; and group B, those military inactive, such as Austria, Denmark and Finland. The figures for group A, compiled by a team of UN economists for the period 1957-9, were 9.8, 6.5, and 6.2, respectively; for group B, they were 1.5, 2.8, and 1.7, respectively.[11] Again the precise amounts have changed in the last decade, but the proportions remain substantially constant.

It becomes clear that percentage-wise the military expenditure of African states is exceptionally moderate.[12] And it is well that it should be, given the miserably low levels of both their absolute and per capita GDP.

Disarmament and Development

Although the level of expenditure is small, it nevertheless represents a diversion of resources from peaceful to military purposes and, as has been shown, these resources originate from a very small base of GDP. Against this meagreness of wealth produced in African countries, there is the staggering array of development problems, all demanding the application of these limited resources for their solution. Without military expenditure, at least two vital savings could be made and used for civilian projects. The first of these savings is in foreign exchange. All African countries have to buy their weapons from outside, using valuable foreign exchange that could be used to import other goods. Although this figure is very low compared with those for the rest of the world, such a foreign-exchange drain from Africa is proportionally serious. A second, more obvious, saving is in manpower. Within military establishments is locked manpower that possesses in some respects technical know-how, discipline, and even the work-oriented ethic necessary for development. With the end of the Second World War, many demobbed soldiers provided economic and sometimes even political leadership among their people. There is certainly room for hope that, once converted to civilian tasks, soldiers could significantly contribute to development in their respective countries. Not all the manpower would be immediately absorbed elsewhere; there would be the tensions of adjustment. But economic expansion is not inconsistent with delayed absorption of available labour.

There is a related respect in which military disbandment would contribute positively to African development. While there are strong reasons for maintaining military establishments, many African countries have not yet solved the problem of what to do with the soldiers during periods of peace. The situation in Nigeria, for example, indicates that, valuable as African soldiers are during crises, they are unproductive and often idle when the threat is over. Tanzania has made a move to involve its soldiers in nation-building; Somalia is now experimenting by engaging soldiers in self-help projects, starting with building their own barracks. Stated simply, disarmament could put to maximum employment people who are now underemployed.

Lincoln S. Bloomfield and Amelia C. Leiss once described sub-Saharan Africa as 'the outer space of regional arms control, for it is not yet militarized'. In an article based on material from a report they prepared under contract with the US Arms Control and Disarmament Agency, the two authors asserted:

> The chances for aborting a regional arms race may be greatest in sub-Saharan Africa, where arms levels are lowest . . . United States policy could well aim at the control or limitation of all arms in both North Africa and sub-Saharan Africa. . . .[13]

To radical African opinion, this kind of recommendation is in an ominous imperial tradition. Lenin once argued that imperialism was 'the monopoly stage of capitalism'. One of the authors of this chapter has had reason to assert elsewhere[14] that it would be truer to say that imperialism was the monopoly stage of violence. Nor was this intended as a mere witticism. Implicit in concepts like that of *Pax Britannica* was the idea that the white races had a duty to disarm the rest of mankind. And so, when the champions of imperial rule were at their most articulate in its defence, one argument they advanced was that imperialism had given the African, for example, a chance to know what life was like without violence. In 1938, Kenyatta could therefore complain bitterly in the following terms:

> The European prides himself on having done a great service to the Africans by stopping the 'tribal warfares', and says that the Africans ought to thank the strong power that has liberated them from their 'constant fear' of being attacked by the neighbouring war-like tribes. But consider the difference between the method and motive employed in the so-called savage tribal warfares and those employed in the modern warfare waged by the 'civilized' tribes of Europe and in which the Africans who have no part in the quarrel are forced to defend so-called democracy.[15]

It is to be remembered that this complaint was made about a year *before* the Second World War. The First World War had been enough to demonstrate the white man's capacity for self-mutilation while still asserting the right to disarm the coloured races, except of course for purposes of fighting the white man's wars.

The Third Pan-African Congress, held in Lisbon in 1923, was already challenging this doctrine of the white man's exclusive right to initiate war. The congress first argued the link between Negro dignity and world peace: 'In fine, we ask in all the world that black folk be treated as men. We can see no other road to peace and progress.' It also asserted a connection between Negro dignity and the right to bear arms, though in a framework that called for general disarmament. Implicit in the demands of the congress was that if the white man was going to insist on disarmament for everyone else, he must also renounce his own weapons. And so the Third Pan-African Congress called for 'world disarmament and the abolition of war; but failing this, and as long as white folk bear arms against black folk, the right of blacks to bear arms in their own defence'.[16]

In each colony the imperial doctrine of monopoly of violence merged with a more familiar doctrine of political analysis—the idea that in a political community only the rulers ever have the right to use violence in dealing with the citizens. Indeed, political analysts since Weber have sometimes *defined* the state in terms of its 'monopoly of the legitimate use of physical force within a given territory.'[17] A variant of this same idea in the West is the ethic that no citizen should take the law into his own hands. This again is an assertion of state monopoly in certain forms of coercion.

When the colonial power became, to all intents and purposes, 'the state' in many parts of Asia and Africa, a doctrinal merger took place between this principle of state monopoly in physical coercion and the imperial claim of monopoly in warfare and violence. In the total ideology of imperialism and racialism, the right to *initiate* violence became a prerogative only civilization and statehood could bestow.[18] Black militancy in both Africa and the United States has since challenged this old Caucasian monopoly of the right to initiate violence.

What emerges from this is that regional disarmament within Africa, though attractive in itself, is politically impossible on its own. Economically, regional disarmament would release resources that could be used in other sectors of national life. There is also the possibility that when law and order are entrusted to a modernized police force in Africa, and armies as such are abolished, African political stability might not be adversely affected.

But African disarmament without world disarmament would *not* be an act of moral leadership. It would not avert world crises. It might enhance Africa's developmental capability, but at the cost of reducing in advance its say in global negotiations about the kind of security system mankind as a whole now needs to devise. An Africa already disarmed would be an Africa without credentials for determining the conditions under which others may also be disarmed. It is the old Bevanite problem of 'going into a conference chamber naked'. In the final analysis, both regional disarmament and regional development require a fundamental reappraisal of the global military and economic systems in their wider ramifications.[19]

References and notes

1. *Uganda Argus*, 15 February 1965.
2. This does not refer to such black or enclave African states as Botswana, Lesotho, Swaziland, and Malawi, whose attitude towards Southern Africa is that of reconciliation or collaboration.
3. Timothy Shaw, 'South Africa's military capability and the future of race relations', revised version of paper presented at the conference on Africa in world affairs, 'The Next 30 Years', at Makerere University in December 1969.
4. Ibid.
5. A. A. Afrifa, *The Ghana Coup* (Frank Cass, 1966).
6. See A. Mohiddin, 'Nyerere and Nkrumah', paper for USSC, Makerere, January 1969; and D. Thiam, *The Foreign Policies of African States* (Phoenix House, 1965), Part II.
7. Ali A. Mazrui, 'Violent contiguity and the politics of re-tribalization in Africa', *Journal of International Affairs*, **XXIII**, 1 (1969).
8. *The Statesman's Yearbook, 1969-70* (Macmillan, 1969).
9. John L. Sutton and Geoffrey Kemp, *Arms to Developing Countries 1945-1965* (Institute for Strategic Studies, 1966).
10. Timothy Shaw, 'South Africa's military capability', op. cit.
11. Seymour Melman, ed., *Disarmament: its Politics and Economics* (Boston: The American Academy of Arts and Sciences, 1962), pp. 383-96.
12. The fact that the indexes of countries in groups A and B, though worked out many years ago, are still higher than the recent ones of the African states adds emphasis to this point.
13. Lincoln S. Bloomfield and Amelia C. Leiss, 'Arms control and the developing countries', *World Politics*, **XVIII** (October 1965), 6 and 7.
14. Ali A. Mazrui, *Towards a Pax Africana: A Study of Ideology and Ambition* (London: Weidenfeld & Nicolson and Chicago: University of Chicago Press, 1967), pp. 195-7.
15. See Jomo Kenyatta, *Facing Mount Kenya* (1938; Secker & Warburg, 1959), p. 212.
16. See George Padmore, ed., *History of the Pan-African Congress* (1947; William Morris House, 1963, 2nd edn, pp. 22-3.
17. See Max Weber, 'Politics as a vocation', in H. H. Gerth and C. Wright Mills, eds, *Max Weber: Essays in Sociology* (New York: Oxford University Press, 1958), pp. 77-8.
18. These ideas are discussed in a wider context in Ali A. Mazrui, *Towards a Pax Africana*, op. cit., chapter 12.
19. See 'Economic and social consequences of disarmament', in Seymour Melman, *Disarmament*, op. cit., p. 332.

CHAPTER 13
Population & Politics

The issue of population control is normally seen either in terms of the survival of the human race or in terms of the economic welfare of a particular family or a particular country. If we were using Africa's three guiding political principles of the optimization of economic welfare, the minimization of violence and the maximization of social justice, we might say that, on the whole, debates about the population explosion have related more to the first two guiding principles than to the last. When we relate the demographic danger to human survival, we are operating in a realm of assessment not far removed from the horrors of violence. The idea of an overcrowded world, not necessarily short of food but conceivably short of conditions for a healthy life and perhaps even of pure clean air to breathe, has the same repellant effect on the imagination as the image of the aftermath of a terrible war. It is true that, in some respects, a good costly war would be an alternative catastrophe to a population tragedy. It has been pointed out often enough that one of the few positive functions mutual human destruction has had for the welfare of humanity has been to keep numbers down. A total abolition of military explosions might well accelerate the approach of a demographic explosion. Nevertheless, in spite of the fact of war and overcrowding being alternative catastrophes, they do remain catastrophes of comparable magnitude. They could, in some sense, both be related to the kind of ambition which made the ideal of minimizing violence a guiding principle.

The relationship between population control and economic welfare is even more direct. It is sometimes attached to calculations about economic growth and per capita measurements of economic improvement. The determination of services—education, hospitals, clinics, sanitation and housing—is affected in situations where the increase in population is more rapid than the country's capacity to cater for it.

On the basis of these remarks, this is the relationship between population growth and Africa's three guiding political principles. An expansion of the population of the world may mean an increase in the incidence of violence, but not necessarily. On the other hand, a very radical decrease in the incidence of violence is bound to result in an expansion of the population should other factors remain constant. Our guiding ambition of the minimization of violence is, therefore, placed in an antithetical relationship to any concurrent ambition to restrict population growth.

As regards the relationship between economic welfare and population growth, it is clear that in the developing countries a rapid expansion of population reduces the economic welfare of the average citizen, in the short run. What is less clear is whether, in the long run, the bigger population might not result in an economically more powerful country, even if the individual citizen is not economically better off. The USA is economically much more powerful than Sweden, but it is not clear that the average American is, as an individual, economically much better off than the average Swede. Will a certain standard of economic welfare result, in any case, in smaller families? Much of the history of the Western world seems to support the prospects of such a trend; although recent American experience has indications in the reverse direction. American population trends continue to fluctuate from year to year, as fashions concerning family sizes vary.

But what is the relationship between population growth and social justice in the world? This is a more difficult issue to tackle, partly because social justice is more culturally relative and more difficult to measure than either economic improvement or any decline in the casualties of violence. What needs to be grasped is the simple fact that numbers have been important for the dignity of coloured people in a sense not often realized by those who are not coloured.

Numericalism and World Order

We have defined 'numericalism' in intergroup relations to be that collection of attitudes or general principles which puts a moral premium on numerical advantage. The range of forms which numericalism takes is from the moral complexities of 'majority rule' to the simple adage that 'there is strength in numbers'. The two ideas do not necessarily amount to the same thing, though they could indeed overlap. The liberal principle of majority rule asserts that those who prevail in numbers ought to prevail in politics. But the adage of inner 'strength in numbers' might be invoked even in situations in which majority rule as an elaborate system of government is not in favour. The strength which is meant here could be physical. Yet even where the power of numbers is thought of in physical terms, numericalism remains, in the ultimate analysis, a belief in the dignity of being numerous.

The ethic of numerical supremacy has played an important part in multiplying the number of sovereign states in the international community since the end of the Second World War. We know that in the history of colonial liberation the principle of 'one man, one vote' was often crucial. And the appeal of this principle for the colonized lay in the assumption that if one man, one vote was conceded, power would inevitably pass to the majority of the people. In practice two concepts of majority rule have tended to operate. One concept postulated that the rulers should be responsive and institutionally answerable to at least a majority of those they ruled. This was the normal, liberal concept. The other concept of majority rule simply required that the rulers should broadly be of the same ethnic or racial stock as the majority of those they ruled. In this latter sense the rulers were still representative, but more in the sense of being ethnically typical than democratically accountable.

In the history of colonial liberation movements in the Third World it was the ethnic conception of majority rule, rather than the orthodox liberal one, which was particularly crucial. And yet for as long as the nationalist movements had the support of the general populace, this distinction was merely academic. The nationalist leaders were representative by the canons of both liberalism and ethnic typicality.[1]

Any discussion of population control in relation to social justice has to take account of this numerical ideological orientation among coloured people. The importance of numbers for the dignity of coloured people is not even limited to situations in which the coloured people are in a majority. The position of the black man in the USA has been as much a part of the total picture of race relations in the world as the liberation movements in Angola. In the latter the Africans are in the majority; in the former the blacks are in a minority. Yet the black American has been no less conscious of the liberating potential of numbers than has the Afro-Asian nationalist in colonial situations. There was a time when the more militant of American blacks saw the significance of their numbers in quasi-military terms. Even as far back as the slave days black numerical superiority in individual situations occasionally turned a black man's thoughts towards a possible rebellion. And where it did not lead to rebellion this was sometimes interpreted by black militants themselves as a sign of their inherent servility. As the defiant black man, David Walker, put it in 1829 in his *Appeal to the Coloured Citizens of the World:*

> Here now, in the Southern and Western Sections of this country [the United States] there are at least three coloured persons for one white, why is it that those few weak, good-for-nothing whites are able to keep so many able men . . . in wretchedness and misery? It shows what the blacks are, we are ignorant, abject, servile and mean — and the whites know it — they know that we are too servile to assert our rights as men — or they would not fool with us as they do.[2]

More recently, the black American has sometimes seen the significance of population figures in electoral terms rather than revolutionary ones. While the Afro-Asian nationalist had previously linked numerical power to the ethic of self-determination, the

American black has linked it with the liberating potential of the franchise. As Herbert Aptheker, a specialist on the history of the black American, once put it:

> It never was right 'for the administration' to 'postpone' effective action on the Negro question because of so-called political expediency; today it is not wrong, it is unwise. This is shown . . . in the fact that President Kennedy would have remained a United States Senator if but 75 per cent of the Negro vote went his way in 1960 rather than the 85 per cent cast for him.[3]

As the black movement has become more revolutionary, the importance of numbers has not diminished. Any speeches to black Americans suggesting they reduce their rate of reproduction are widely interpreted as a device to keep them numerically weak. The battle cry of revolutionary black militancy might almost be paraphrased in the following slogan: 'Burn, baby, burn!—and then breed some more!' It is the dual strategy of engaging both in destructive acts which weaken the power of the white man and in creative acts which strengthen the power of the black man.

Afro-Asianism and pan-blackism were a form of solidarity based on a vague sense of shared humiliation as coloured people. But what defences do the coloured people now have against the technologically more advanced white people? Almost the only measurable military factor in which the coloured races have a superiority over the white ones is that of numbers. It seemed at first that the advent of nuclear weapons had made the numerical factor virtually irrelevant. If war remained conventional, a numerical superiority of soldiers under arms would remain an asset, but in a conflict of massive nuclear destruction the size of a conventional army appeared to be of dubious military significance.

And yet this whole line of reasoning is itself tied to conventional assumptions about 'victory' and 'defeat' at the end of a war. In a nuclear war numbers are indeed irrelevant in determining a conventional victory but that is mainly because a full-scale nuclear holocaust could not have an orthodox victory. As soon as one starts to assess the consequences of a nuclear war less in terms of victories and more in terms of the balance of survival, population figures once again become admissible in the calculations. As Mao Tse-tung is reported to have said to a visiting Yugoslav official in 1957:

> We aren't afraid of atomic bombs. We have a large territory and a big population. Bombs could not kill all of us. What if they killed over even 300 000 000? We would still have plenty more. China would be the last country to die.[4]

It is not certain that Mao ever made such a statement. A specialist on Chinese studies at an American university has even suggested in a conversation that the statement was probably propagated by the Russians in their anti-Chinese strategy for the specific purpose of gaining concessions from the West. But, as the late Edgar Snow put it, 'Even if Mao did not say that, someone would have had to invent it.' The statement was certainly consistent with Mao's general philosophy on the role of population in warfare. Communist China's policy on population control has itself not been consistent. The attraction of an ever-expanding base of humanity has had to be balanced against the fate of policies intended to raise standards of welfare. But there is no doubt whatsoever that China is profoundly conscious of the size of her population and regards it as one of her credentials for leadership in the world.

But, in any case, both India and China, as the two largest nations in the world, can perhaps afford to put the brakes on. There is certainly more consistency in India with regard to the need for some family planning and birth control. When demographic superiority is so far advanced, it is easier to sell the idea of cutting the numbers down.

In Africa the cause of family planning and population control lacks, on the whole, adequate credibility. A few African countries, strongly advised by technical assistance experts, have taken measures to promote some degree of propaganda in favour of population control. Among the East African countries Kenya has gone furthest in this sphere. But the majority of African countries seem to be at best lukewarm in their support, and more often sceptical of population control measures. The continent territorially is large enough to accommodate the whole of India, Europe and the United States. Yet its population is less than half India's five hundred million. The populations of individual African countries range from about 60 million to a mere 250 500.

In situations of confrontation between blacks and whites, either in active combat or in terms of hostile attitudes, the issue of population links our two principles of the maximization of social justice and the minimization of violence. It has been inequalities in other spheres between white and coloured people which has given the status of numerical superiority extra prestige among the more preponderant coloured people. 'We may be unequal to you in technology and education, in physical power and diplomatic sophistication—but when all is said and done there are more of us than of you!'

In 1958 Julius K. Nyerere of Tanzania was quoting from Abraham Lincoln's romanticization of numbers to rebut those who shared Cecil Rhodes' dictum of 'equal rights for all civilized men'. Nyerere quarrelled especially with the 'undignified assertion' of the Colonial Tanganyika Government that in the special circumstances of East and Central Africa universal suffrage would put the common good in jeopardy. He defended the idea of allowing 'the common people' to have their own way—and quoted Lincoln's statement that 'God must love the common people because he made so many of them.'[5]

Sometimes the idea that history is on the side of coloured people derives its credence from the numerical preponderance of those people. An oppressed people that is in a majority often finds a nagging reassurance that the imbalance of power could not possibly last forever. That is certainly the great feeling of the black population of South Africa. For the time being, they are no match for the connivance and technology of the whites, or for their organizational power and industrial sophistication. The blacks might feel that history is on their side not because their cause is just, for the cause of the Jews in Nazi Germany was also just. Yet the condemned Jews did not feel such optimism. The sense of the impending vindication of history in the years ahead for black South Africans arises quite simply out of a refusal to accept that a victimized majority can remain effectively victimized for any length of time.

To ask the black people of South Africa to engage in vigorous family planning and birth control, while the white regime equally vigorously promotes immigration from Europe, is to seek to deny the preponderant blacks even the solace of their preponderance.

Infant Mortality and Parental Immortality

The idea of numbers as an investment for the future goes beyond the security of whole races and social groups. It extends to the psychology of the individual father in situations of underprivilege. It also encompasses cultural factors.

We shall be discussing further in the next chapter population problems in relation to ecological or environmental issues. On the one hand, the high rate of infant mortality in Africa makes parents reluctant to limit the number of children they have. Planning of any kind needs some minimum degree of reliable expectations. Too much uncertainty about the future makes planning impossible. Too much uncertainty about how many of one's children would survive makes family planning hazardous and often meaningless. In rural Africa one out of five babies born does not live to celebrate its first birthday. It is therefore not surprising that less than fifteen out of the forty-eight countries in Africa have any kind of organized family planning activity or voluntary family planning associations. It has been estimated that there may still be parts of tropical Africa 'where not many more than half the children born survive to their fifth birthday'.[6] As for life expectancy in tropical Africa, the figures for the majority of countries indicate life expectancy of less than forty years. This may be compared with over seventy years for Sweden, Norway, the United Kingdom and others.[7]

Furthermore, as we shall elaborate more in the next chapter, there are African societies in which the idea of having many children is connected both to the risks of infant mortality and to the hope of parental immortality. In some African traditional beliefs parents who outlive all their children run into complications in the hereafter, and their own immortality can be seriously compromised. The temptation therefore to have many children is considerable, in order to ensure that at least some outlive the parents. We shall also discuss related issues in African traditional religions in the next chapter, all of which affect the attitudes of African men and women to questions of family size. Some African belief-systems distinguish between two stages of death. One stage permits continuing contact with the living, as one's relatives remember the deceased. The other stage is the stage of final oblivion. Again, a person who is survived by many children is better qualified to delay or even avert oblivion than a person without such offspring to remember him.[8]

Those who wish to change African attitudes to family planning should therefore remember a fundamental law of public relations—in order to change public opinion you have to understand public opinion. The understanding need not be perfect, but it ought to be enough to include some of the aspirations, prejudices, and general emotive predispositions of the particular society with which one is dealing. On an issue as personal as family planning it may even be necessary to understand the world view of the society concerned and how it relates to problems of procreation, and even of life and death.

An initial and even prior question should perhaps have been of the language and vocabulary of discourse. Is it family planning we are worried about? Or is it population control? It may be that for political reasons we do not want to use certain terms. But we should still be aware what it is we want to achieve, even if we have to watch our words in discussing certain issues. Family planning implies a concern merely for the parents and their children. The ultimate unit is merely the family. Population control, on the other hand, implies a concern for the society as a whole, and for its capacity to absorb demographic change without social costs. How fast a rate of increment in population can a particular country sustain without bedevilling the issue of development? Is there a global problem called the 'population explosion', raising issues about human survival and the capacity of this planet as a whole to sustain the numbers which seem to be coming into being? We might therefore say that the slogan 'population control' has society or even humanity as the primary frame of reference; whereas the term 'family planning' has the individual family unit, Mr and Mrs Mukasa and their children, as the focus of concern.

Those who worry about family planning need not necessarily worry about population control or the population explosion in the world. But those who worry about population control in a particular society or the population explosion on a world scale have also to worry about the family unit, and about Mr and Mrs Mukasa as elements in a collective or global problem. Associations of family planning or planned parenthood include both champions of family planning in the limited sense, and champions of population control in the broader social sense. What must not be overlooked is that Mr and Mrs Mukasa are not merely a married couple but also members of a wider society. Their responsiveness to appeals about planned parenthood may depend in part on their own concern for the immediate family welfare, and the future of their children. But it also depends upon their conception of what is proper in their society and what is good for their society. It is considerations such as these which make us believe that an adequate understanding of public opinion in Africa has to include some awareness of the general world view of the African and his conception of his place in the universe.

In Africa we have basically two kinds of religion—traditional indigenous religion and imported universal religions. The traditional indigenous religions are usually limited in their adherence to members of particular tribal communities. The universal religions—Christianity and Islam—are committed to proselytization and general conversion. It is sometimes suggested that it is the traditional religions which are very collectivist, the individual being submerged beneath the concept of tribal identity and tribal ancestors. The imported religions, on the other hand, are deemed to be the ones which emphasize personal accountability and individual conscience. To some extent this is true, but from the point of view of politics an important qualification needs to be made. However personal Christianity and Islam may claim to be as religions, they more easily become political issues than traditional religions. It is the important imported religions that often assume high political sensitivity, and entail the risk of causing political offence.

From the point of view of family planning, the indigenous traditional religions do condition the individual's response to his problem. And if the individual needs to ensure personal immortality when he dies, he may decide to have a lot of children. He will not object to there being special family planning clinics around for those who are foolish enough to want to use them. But he himself will not indulge in such artificial limitations. But universal religions tend to want to reduce things to national policies. It just so happens that on the issue of family planning it is the Catholic Church that has the clearest position on the matter; though on other issues the other religions may be equally insistent on the maintenance of this or that principle. On family planning, then, politics in Africa, as elsewhere, becomes affected by the positions taken by these universal missionary religions. The Catholic Church takes the position that contraception by artificial means is a sin. The issue of family planning becomes therefore a political one in situations where the Catholic Church is politically influential.

Apart from racial and religious considerations appertaining to family planning and population control, there is the additional dimension in Africa of tribal competition. It is to this third area that we must now turn.

Tribal Competition and Population Control

Sometime in 1970 an external observer watched a *baraza* in a small Kikuyu village under the Aberdare Mountains in Kenya. It was a family planning gathering, similar to others that the observer had witnessed before, but there was one important difference in this case. There was an unmistakeable air of hostility pervading the *baraza*. In the middle of the talk on family planning the village chief left rather abruptly. The questions asked were hostile, and inclined towards disruption. And at the clinic there were a number of women, more than usual, wanting their coils removed for a variety of remarkable reasons. The observer later set about making cautious enquiries. He had noticed the presence of the General Service Unit in their purple berets. He had also noticed that the key worker for family planning, a devout Christian, was particularly nervous this time. The explanation began to unfold itself. Oathing had begun once again in the village—'and an essential part of every Kikuyu oath is a vow against any form of family planning or birth control'. Oathing in Kikuyuland often comes with a sense of insecurity. But the insecurity, in this case, did not arise from the very rapid expansion of Kenya's population—a 3.3 per cent increase seems to be the latest calculation, one of the highest rates in the world.

The government as a source of authority is sympathetic to some degree of population control. But there are important explosive issues underlying such a policy, some of them directly connected with the power base on which the government rests. The explosive nature of population control in a situation of high political competitiveness in Africa does not lie in any religious explanation. It is not religious sensibilities that are likely to be offended by the enterprise. It is something much less explicit, and yet sometimes profoundly present. It includes a sense of ethnic insecurity.

This external observer probably exaggerated the dimensions of this factor in Kenya. But he was certainly alluding to something which is all too often overlooked. The writer distinguished between the policy of the government in Kenya and the psychological attitudes of its individual members:

> As a Government it preaches a consistent non-tribalism, but as individuals its members fear for the effect of any birth control policy on the size of their tribe relative to the others. . . . The Kikuyu are still generally believed to be the larger tribe, but reliable census figures are hard to come by, and many think the Luo have already

> attained the numerical majority which, if true, raises again in stronger form the old question as to why they have so small a share of the available power.[9]

In effect the census figures so far still maintain a Kikuyu numerical superiority. But should, in a decade, a census enquiry reveal an altered relationship between the Luo and the Kikuyu, it is almost certain that the revelation would have momentous political implications. A crisis could arise which might again threaten to shake Kenya to its very foundations.

A precedent hovering in the background is Nigeria. The country entered independence with a viable alliance between the Northern People's Congress and the National Congress of Nigerian Citizens. The fact that one was a Northern and the other a Southern organization gave the country the appearance of a broad national government in the critical turbulent early years of independence. The North and East were thus allies once in government; but later the civil war came to appear as if it was indeed primarily between these very same former allies.

The first census in Nigeria after independence was a major precipitating factor behind the initial rupture between the North and the East. A 1962 census was held, and hotly challenged even before it saw the light of day. Another census was taken in 1963, and the rupture began to take shape both between the North and the East and, to some extent, between the North and the South as a whole. The final figures of the 1963 population census published by the Federal Ministry of Information gave the North 29 758 875; the Eastern region 12 394 462; the Western region 10 265 846; and the mid-West 2 535 839. Lagos was deemed to have 665 246. These figures were to form a basis for the Federal Parliamentary Elections later in 1963. The Federal Prime Minister, Sir Abubakar Tafawa Balewa, himself from the North, accepted these figures. The Northern region had accepted them, so had the Western region under the minority government of Chief Akintola. But the National Congress of Nigerian Citizens in the East and the government of the mid-West, also of the NCNC, rejected the census figures. The Federal Coalition between the NCNC and the Northern People's Congress was doomed in the face of this crisis.

A realignment of parties in Nigeria in the course of 1963 was, in an important sense, primarily the outcome of the census, and the kind of insecurity and suspicion generated by the new vindication of Northern numerical superiority over the rest of the country. The Southern part of the country was already more economically and educationally developed than the North. Many Southerners felt that this itself should ensure that Southerners had the pre-eminent say in the destiny of the nation. Yet in Federal politics, the North—after bungling at the beginning—acquired the upper hand in national affairs. There was anxiety following the census that this numerical power which the North had acquired would not only be maintained by unfair means, but might even be expanded. The cleavage between the two parties in alliance, and indeed between the North and the South at large in Nigeria in the course of 1963, had this demographic cloud hanging over it.

The past party alignments culminated, after initial formation of smaller groups, into two broad alliances for the elections of 1965. These were the Nigerian National Alliance consisting of the Northern congress and the party formed by a minority section of the West under Chief Akintola, and the United Progressive Grand Alliance, led by Dr Okpara of the Eastern Region. Further wrangles and distrusts bedevilled the elections, culminating in a wide boycott by supporters of the National Progressive Grand Alliance. But in a sense their boycott itself played into the hands of their enemies, and the Prime Minister refused to call off the elections in spite of pressures from President Azikiwe. Out of an electorate of fifteen million, only four million came to vote. Sir Abubakar Balewa and his allies emerged triumphant, but with an unconvincing democratic base. The President pressed for new elections, resisting first the constitutional presidential function to call on the leader of the party with a majority to form a government. In the end Azikiwe did call upon Balewa to form a government, but only after agreement had been reached to broaden its composition and bring in people from some of the other parties.

The fact nevertheless remained that the new legislature had come into being in the wake of widespread boycott of elections, and against a background of intimidation and suspicion. The cleavage between the North and South was consolidating itself even further. And certainly the division between the North and the East began to blur. The census figures had been a precipitating factor behind the ending of the symbolic alliance—the alliance which had brought the Northern People's Congress in the North and the National Council of Nigerian Citizens of the East into a truly pan-Nigerian exercise for a while. That rupture of alliances also helped to create conditions which finally made the Nigerian army intervene in a coup in January 1966. Problems of ethnic balance were therefore central to the history of Nigeria in its first decade of independence.

Electoral Engineering and Population Control

The issue of political insecurity in relation to the distribution of population has also been present in Uganda's political history, especially since the 1950s. The formation of political parties and the introduction of the whole idea of popular elections suddenly revealed the potential importance of numbers in national affairs. The Baganda had, for quite a while, been among the most nationalist of all Ugandans; but there was a sharp decline in their commitment to the Uganda nation in the face of the rise of political parties and the concept of numerical power. Like the Southerners in Nigeria, the Baganda felt that their part of the country was by economic development and educational success the best fitted to lead in the affairs of the nation. But if the principle of one man one vote was introduced in Uganda, the Baganda would be out-voted by the rest of the country, and a new leadership might arise less 'qualified' for the great trust of the nation's destiny.

Two factors therefore came into play in national politics—anti-partyism and anti-unitarism. The Baganda were opposed both to party politics as a mode of dealing with political affairs and to the concept of a unitary state, which reduced all groups to a collection of potential voters irrespective of the differeing traditions of authority and loyalty. Anti-partyism and anti-unitarism in Buganda created a number of crises in the last few years before independence. And as in Nigeria, the fear of numbers resulted in the boycott of elections in Buganda. The Baganda turned away from the democratic process in 1961, and the Democratic Party came into being in self-governing Uganda. Meanwhile, Buganda had at last decided to have a party of its own, Kabaka Yekka. But it was so conscious of its own anti-partyism that Kabaka Yekka preferred to call itself a 'movement' rather than a party for a while. In any case, the deep distrust of popular democracy, in the sense of one man one vote, and the distrust of unitarism as a principle for the new Uganda, remained very much part of the ideology of Kabaka Yekka.

The 1962 negotiations for a new Independence Constitution granted the Baganda what they wanted. The principle of unitarism for independent Uganda was diluted by the concession given to Buganda as a neo-federal region, enjoying in part its own local autonomy. The other kingdoms were also given concessions of a neo-federal kind, though in effect less elaborate than that which Buganda enjoyed. As for the principle of the popular vote, this too was diluted with a decision to convert the Lukiko into an electoral college for the nomination of Buganda's representatives in the National Assembly. Buganda's twenty-four seats came to be taken by Kabaka Yekka.

On the question of population control, a unitary system of government would have added resistance among the Baganda to any idea of reducing their procreation in the face of competition from other ethnic groups. But the neo-federal system, coupled with the indirect elections by the Lukiko of Buganda's members in the National Assembly, help to reduce the full potential of such a system. It could not completely eliminate the factor of ethnic competition in local attitudes to birth control, partly because Buganda as a region has tended to be attractive to other groups and had absorbed a variety of ethnic elements. The numerical advantage of the Baganda within Buganda could have been seriously threatened if the immigrant population in Buganda rose faster than the Baganda's capacity to keep pace demographically.

Further, the 1962 formula of securing Ganda autonomy against the danger of numerical challenge elsewhere turned out to be less durable than expected. Tensions between the allies—Obote's Uganda People's Congress and Buganda's Kabaka Yekka—began to tell politically. Again, there were elements reminiscent of the Nigerian alliance between the Northern People's Congress and the more progressive NCNC of the Eastern Region. Events first led to the break up of the alliance between Kabaka Yekka and Obote's party in 1964. They later led in 1966 to a confrontation between the central government under Obote and the government of Buganda under Kabaka Mutesa II. Buganda was vanquished, the 1962 Constitution was first suspended and then abolished, and the neo-federal protection for Buganda came to an end. But curiously enough the fear of numbers gradually shifted away from issues of Buganda's autonomy to issues of support for the Uganda People's Congress under Dr Obote. Given that large numbers of people in independent Uganda continued to vote on the basis of ethnic affiliation, it became a matter of significant interest to Dr Obote to devise a mode of election which would diffuse the ethnic factor. The last elections in 1962 had, in effect, indicated an increase in ethnic politics, as compared with the 1961 elections. What sort of scheme was therefore to be devised for 1971?

Obote's Document No. 5 on electoral reform was designed to deal both with ethnicity as a factor influencing voting behaviour and with population distribution. The two issues were of course interrelated, but they were by no means the same. On the issue of ethnicity Obote's whole concept of each parliamentarian standing in four constituencies attempted to make every candidate dependent on more than his own tribe. Northerners might already have had a say in deciding who spoke for Buganda; but Obote's Document No. 5 proposed to give the Baganda also a say in choosing who spoke for the northerners. The Baganda, like other groups, would have had a chance to vote for candidates for areas other than their own. But in addition Document No. 5 grappled with the issue of disproportionate distribution of population. The scheme proposed that votes cast in each constituency were to be computed on the basis of each percentage counting as an electoral vote. All constituencies were to become equal in the electoral power they had regardless of differences in populations within. In the words of Document No. 5, the scheme was designed to ensure that the president was 'elected by the whole country'. It sought to 'remove any possibility that one or two regions with heavy population could dominate the election of the President one way or the other'. The same principle was intended to apply to the election of parliamentarians.

Document No. 5 proceeded to try and illustrate numerically how a simple, straight, popular vote could frustrate the whole idea of making each parliamentarian a representative of four constituencies, and of four regions of the country instead of one. Paragraph 42 attempted to give an illustration of 'how one constituency may frustrate the will of a large part of the country'. It illustrated how one particular candidate could get support from three regions of Uganda—for example, South, East and North—but because he was heavily rejected in the West, some other candidate with massive support from a particular constituency could become the member for all those four constituencies. Document No. 5 therefore proposed that each constituency should have its voting population again computed into one hundred electoral votes, and the question of electoral success by candidates would be on the basis of how many electoral votes from the total four hundred in the four constituencies a candidate had won, rather than on the basis of how many individual votes on a popular franchise he had obtained.

The effect of the implementation of Document No. 5 from the point of view of ethnic competition would have been to depoliticize population spread to some extent. The question as to which region had more people could have become less politically significant in an election. This would have had various implications. With the depoliticization of distribution of population, census figures could continue to be reliable in Uganda, unlike the situation in the old Nigeria where figures began to be 'cooked'. And Ugandans might have learnt to restrict the sizes of their family without worrying whether this was a disservice to their tribes. But Obote's electoral scheme was not destined to be implemented after all. On 25 January 1971, a military coup took place in Uganda and overthrew Milton Obote's government. Among the casualties was an innovative electoral scheme of potential relevance for the task of depoliticizing the issue of population control and family planning in Uganda.

Conclusion

What kind of institutions are required to cope with the whole problem of population expansion on a global scale? Much of the burden has to be in terms of social and cultural reform in individual countries, but there is also room for international action to facilitate this trend with requisite incentives.

Religious inhibitions need not be challenged too blatantly. On questions of parental immortality, for example, no purposeful policy need be undertaken to challenge or support African conceptions of death. If modernization includes a process of secularization, there may be modifications of these conceptions in any case. The notion of having large families in order to ensure parental immortality may fall under revision when the problem of infant mortality itself is tackled. If a smaller number of children live longer, and life expectancy in the society rises significantly, a person may be remembered for many years but by fewer people. Personal parental immortality could still be assured more effectively by three children who live to the ripe old age of sixty-five or seventy than by fifteen children most of whom die before they reach the age of forty-five. What this means, therefore, is that the most critical variable to be tackled is the issue of infant mortality and life expectancy at large. Once these problems are solved it becomes more meaningful to handle population control without violating the legitimate hopes and ambitions of parents.

The world ought to be moving towards a selective international taxation system, tied for purposes of sanctions to an international bank which has the additional function of allocating loans for reconstruction and economic normalization in individual states, for natural calamities, and for other ad hoc issues of economic and social welfare.

Individual countries have had death duties for many years now as a mode of income distribution. The world may be ready shortly for international *birth duties*. The purpose of these birth duties would, in fact, be population control. They would be a tax applied to every member of a nuclear family—parents and children—regardless of age. Under the present taxation system having more children establishes eligibility for tax reductions, at least up to a certain point. But under the proposed restructuring of the tax system, having more children under specified conditions would increase the tax burden. There is an important consideration to be borne in mind about the precise moment of the application of such a tax in a given society. Countries would become subject to population taxation of this kind only after life expectancy in the particular society had reached, say, the fifty years mark. (At the moment life expectancy in much of black Africa is less than forty years.) An alternative measure is to relate the birth duties to infant mortality, asserting that countries become subject to the global population tax as soon as the rate of infant mortality is down to fifty in a thousand. The kind of taxation proposed would, for example, penalize Americans for having four children in a family, but would not penalize Indians or Nigerians for having six children in a family. The tax would be collected by the individual country from its citizens, and the national resources of the country would then add another fifty per cent of the total amount collected before transmission to the global taxation authority. The national supplement provided by the government of the country concerned would be designed to increase the incentives for the paying government to take adequate action in reducing population growth within its own area. The amount collected from these international birth duties would go towards a special fund concerned with problems of infant mortality. These problems in developing countries may include general underdevelopment as such. But there may also be subsidiary matters, ranging from health, education and sanitary arrangements to the availability of powdered milk in remote areas. The fund would be used both for research and for the alleviation of existing hardships. Yet the ultimate strategy must again remain that of reaching the villages with information, convincingly presented, about both the risks and rewards of unplanned procreation. This should be combined with a strategy to influence cultural symbols in the direction of greater responsiveness to discipline and control in this sphere.

The more prosperous nations should aim at zero-growth of their populations, at the same time as the poorer nations grope for ways to reduce their own growth rate. From the point of view of protecting world resources against ever-expanding populations, the heavier duty might well lie on those who already consume a disproportionate share of what this earth yields. And these are not in Africa. It is to this relationship between technology, resource depletion and imperial history that we must now turn.

References and notes

1. These issues are discussed in greater detail in Ali A. Mazrui, 'Numerical strength and nuclear status in the politics of the Third World', *The Journal of Politics*, **XXIX** (November 1967), pp. 791-820. The article is reprinted as chapter 3 in Ali A. Mazrui, *Violence and Thought: Essays on Social Tensions in Africa* (London: Longman, 1969), pp. 50-81.
2. The *Appeal* is an important document in the history of black protest in the USA. It is reproduced in Herbert Aptheker, *'One Continual Cry': David Walker's Appeal to the Coloured Citizens of the World (1929-1830), its Setting and its Meaning* (New York: Humanities Press, 1965). For the above excerpt, see p. 129.
3. Herbert Aptheker, *Soul of the Republic: the Negro Today* (New York: Marzani and Munsell, 1964), p. 109.
4. Cited by, among others, Edgar Snow in his *China, Russia and the USA: Changing Relations in a Changing World* (New York: Marzani and Munsell, 1962), pp. 631-2.
5. Nyerere, 'The entrenchment of privilege', *Africa South*, 2 (January/March 1958), 86-9.
6. Consult Fred T. Sai (International Planned Parenthood Federation), 'Can family planning succeed in Africa?', *Third World* (London) 3 (November 1973); J. C. Caldwell and C. Okonjo, eds, *The Population of Tropical Africa* (London: Longman, 1969); J. C. Caldwell, 'The control of family size in tropical Africa', *Demography*, **5**, 2 (1968), pp. 598-619; William Brass, et. al., *Demography of Tropical Africa* (Princeton, N.J.: Princeton University Press, 1967); and S. K. Gaisie, 'Demographic prospects for tropical Africa for the next thirty years', in Ali A. Mazrui and Hasu Patel, eds, *Africa in World Affairs: the Next Thirty Years* (New York: Third Press, 1973).
7. Gaisie, ibid., pp. 137-8. See also G. A. Saxton, Jr, 'The price of death control without birth control in Africa over the next thirty years', in Mazrui and Patel, eds, *Africa in World Affairs*, ibid., pp. 157-72.
8. John S. Mbiti, *African Religions and Philosophy* (London: Heinemann, 1969), pp. 25-6.
9. Yorick Wilks, 'Family planning or tribal planning', *Cambridge Review* (England) **92** (23 October 1970).

CHAPTER 14
Ecology & Culture

In an important sense, the ecological debate for Africa started with the European explorers in the eighteenth and nineteenth centuries. Hardy and enterprising individuals or groups from Europe descended upon the African continent, propelled by a fascination for sources of rivers, location of lakes, heights of mountains, and boundaries of the wilderness.

But here one must distinguish between ecological curiosity and ecological concern. Ecological curiosity is that framework of intellectual agitation which seeks to explore and discover new factors about nature. The impulse behind ecological curiosity is, quite simply, the excitement of thirst for knowledge. Certain forms of ecological curiosity are very selective, as individuals sit for hours studying birds and their habits just for the sheer enjoyment of observation. Other individuals develop appetites for underwater exploration, studying shells, fish, and geological formations beneath the seas.

Such extra-curricular interests are more prevalent in Europe than in Africa, and what they represent has been of considerable political importance in Europe's relations with the rest of the world. The rise of European exploration is an aspect directly descended from cultural orientations which included ecological curiosity. Human motives are never completely pure. The explorers were more often inspired by ambition than by mere curiosity. But the support which they received at home, and the enthusiasm which greeted some of their discoveries, were conditioned by a civilization which was becoming impressively curious about its wider environment.

Ecological concern goes beyond mere fascination. It implies commitment to conserve and enrich. Ecological concern also often requires a capacity in man to empathize with nature. It requires a readiness on the part of man to see a little of himself, and a little of his God, in his surroundings. Ecological concern requires a totemic frame of reference. To that extent it is much more deeply interlinked with fundamental aspects of African belief-systems than it is to European ones.

Ecological curiosity is an aspect of science in its quest for explanation and comprehension. Ecological concern is an aspect of morality in its quest for empathy. Africa's record in the field of ecological concern is more impressive than that of Europe; Europe's record in ecological curiosity is more dazzling than that of Africa. Behind both curiosity and concern are issues of survival, livelihood and aesthetics. We shall return to these in due course. Meanwhile, let us look more closely at the dialectic between curiosity and concern, between science and morality, and relate the dialectic to Europe's relations with Africa as a fundamental background factor to the contemporary global debate on ecology.

On Science and Commerce

Historically, Europe's ecological curiosity was linked to both science and commerce. The sources of funds for explorations, both seafaring and overland, were varied. Bodies like the Royal Geographical Society important in the exploration of, say, Africa, were primarily motivated by scientific considerations. On the other hand, much of the vigorous exploration to find sea routes to the Orient was inspired by considerations of trade and diplomatic rivalry between European countries. But even in the latter instances the romance of curiosity was hardly ever absent. Great explorers were not only benefactors to their rich patrons, they were also quite often popular heroes. The range of such figures is from Christopher Columbus to David Livingstone, from Prince Henry the Navigator to Captain J. H. Speke.

As Europe discovered for herself the wider world, she also prepared for herself the role of conqueror. European exploration and European imperialism became intricately intertwined. But there was also a European restlessness, culminating in huge movements of populations. Some of the areas which the explorers 'discovered' were merely put under European rule but not necessarily European settlement; others were made subject to both forms of colonization. A whole new hemisphere, the Americas, was inhabited in the wake of this new restlessness, ambition, and adventure. Later the explorers touched base in Australia, New Zealand, and neighbouring islands. New white nations came into being in those parts.

But European ecological curiosity did not limit itself to parts of the world which were habitable or commercially exploitable. The same spirit which made many a European adventurer seek to conquer Mount Everest simply because it was there made him also explore other unknown areas of the human environment, often at considerable physical peril to himself. There is little doubt that Europe's record in ecological curiosity is second to none in human history.

With that curiosity Europe's technological and scientific edge over the rest of the world began to be consolidated. As older scientific civilizations, such as those of China and Islam, subsided into intellectual stagnation, the European mind attempted to scale new intellectual Everests. The restlessness which had made Europe produce physical explorers, travelling on the high seas, also made Europe produce scientific investigators. The consequences for the rest of the world included the momentous experience of European imperialism. Europe's technological superiority increased her capacity for physical mobility and geographical penetration. The technology of travel, combined with the technology of war, sealed the fate of many a helpless society in Asia and Africa. In addition Europe acquired new extensions in the achievements of the Americas.

But the curiosity went further than technological and economic needs dictated. The Newtons looked into the skies, standing on the shoulders of giants, and speculated about the proverbial apples and the stars. The laws of gravity were discovered under the impact of this curiosity. On the ground itself the Darwins sailed on their HMS Beagles, studying exotic plants and mossy formations on rocks, from one port of call to another. Curiosity about the firmament fused astronomy with physics and produced first Newton and then Einstein. Curiosity about this planet linked botany and zoology, and provided the explanatory power of Darwin's theory of evolution.

Europe's insatiable curiosity continued to widen man's comprehension of his environment, and at the same time enhance man's capability to control and exploit that environment. This latter factor is what later came to create an ecological crisis for mankind. As commerce exploited the insights of science, the erosion of nature's resources got under way. First an agrarian revolution hit Europe's countryside, followed shortly by an industrial revolution. The first victims were not the rivers and the seas but the peasants of Europe and those under European rule. In the words of a nostalgic poet writing at the time of the painful depopulation of the English countryside:

Ill fares the land, to hastening ills a prey,
Where wealth accumulates, and men decay;
Princes and lords may flourish, or may fade;
A breath can make them, as a breath has made;
But a bold peasantry, their country's pride,
When once destroyed, can never be supplied.
A time there was, ere England's griefs began,
When every rood of ground maintained each man;
For him light labour spread her wholesome store,
Just gave what life required, but gave no more;
His best companions, innocence and health,
And his best riches, ignorance of wealth.[1]

The poet, Oliver Goldsmith, saw an important link between the accumulation of wealth and the decay of men, but he had yet to grasp fully the link between accumulation of wealth and the decay of the environment. Goldsmith saw the impact of England's agrarian revolution on the peasantry, but at that time it was nevertheless possible to say that the countryside was still abloom with a new fertility. The paradox of elegance and death had a new meaning at the time. In the poet's words, 'The country blooms — a garden and a grave'. It was not until the industrial revolution got fully under way that questions arose about the survival of the garden. The ugliness of the new industrial cities, the rise of ghettos and pollution, the new forms of cruelty to man in his physical and aesthetic needs, heralded an impending ecological crisis.

The industrialization of Europe needed new natural resources and raw materials, as well as new markets. Since the days of Marco Polo, Asia has been an attractive market for certain sectors of European trade. European explorations to find new routes to the Orient included the failure to find a north-east passage, the potentially creative 'discoveries' of the Americas, and the successful journeys around the Cape of Good Hope. Africa was circumnavigated less for its own sake than as a continent inconveniently obstructing Europe's access to Asia.

Finding markets for Europe's industrial products was to plan for the tail-end of production. Finding resources and raw materials was part of the initial moment of production. Asia's attractiveness was initially as a market; Africa's attractiveness when it came was initially as a source of natural and human resources. The products needed from Africa over the centuries ranged from slaves to uranium, from peanuts to diamonds.

Explorers and exploiters were in alliance. Science had enabled Europe to understand the boundaries of her environment. Technology has enabled Europe and Europe's extensions in the Americas to exploit that environment more effectively. Between the science of curiosity and the technology of exploitation were the motives of commerce and gain. Nature had been desacralized, and the stage was set for a new conflict between man and the planet he inhabits.

On Morality and Concern

Africa never attained the scale of ecological curiosity which Europe exhibited at her most adventurous. In relative terms, much of Africa was left behind in those activities which took men beyond the horizons to populate new lands, or inspired individuals to study the behaviour of animals for the sheer joy of observation. The idea of trying out one's wits against the elements, confronting miles of ice and snow or miles of desert sand, simply because they were there, was pre-eminently an aspect of European rather than African culture. Ecological curiosity could lead to either invention or discovery. The black poet, Aimé Césaire, in his poem, *Return to My Native Land* (1939), quoted earlier, captured the dichotomy between the culture of towers and the culture of tillage, between the culture of construction and the culture of cultivation.

My Negritude is no tower and no cathedral
It delves into the red flesh of the soil.

The culture of construction is nearer to ecological abuse than the culture of cultivation. The culture of the tower is widening the distance between man and nature; the culture of tillage maintains a primordial nearness between the two.

In Europe defenders of ecology were for a long time disproportionately poets. They could see more clearly than 'practical men' the hazards of endless construction. When technology is mobilized behind the task of endless construction, depletion of resources is an inescapable outcome. But when technology is rallied behind boundless cultivation, what emerges is abundance rather than depletion. For so long only poets could talk in those terms in Europe without attracting ridicule. It was also a few select poets in Europe who saw a deep link between nature and man, and sometimes discerned divinity itself in nature. Poets of nature like William Wordsworth were precursors of some modern conservationists. Other poets at least discerned that in cultures of the pre-industrial man an important link between man, nature and divinity existed.

But outside the circles of poets and romantics in Europe, ecology had few friends, not even religion. Christianity limited the possession of the soul to homo sapiens. In that very factor lay the hazards of inadequate ecological concern. Since only man as a species possessed a soul, the rest of creation could be taken to be available for the pleasure of man, almost without restraint. Egocentrism of this kind carried the seeds of peril for other animals, and perils for the rest of the environment. The actuation for such dangers is what has more recently been called 'ecocide'—the murder of ecology. In his passionate plea at the Stockholm conference on the environment in 1972, Richard Falk asked for special penalties against those who perpetrated the sin of ecocide. And yet Falk's position sometimes still continued to link the value of nature to the value of man. If nature is important only if man is important egocentrism is still with us. If ecocide is wrong only because it endangers this planet, creating doubts about *man's survival*, the environment is still denied a soul of its own. Ecophiles of this persuasion have made a good deal of progress since the days when the world itself was regarded as the centre of the universe, but there may still be one more step to take.

As I have argued elsewhere, the step implies going back to totemism, and investing the environment with a value independent of man.[2] Driberg defines the Nilotic concept of 'Jok' in terms which see it once again as the force which unifies the whole of nature.

> Jok, like the wind or air, is omnipresent, and like the wind, though its presence may be heard and appreciated, Jok has never been seen by anyone. . . . His dwelling is everywhere: in trees it may be, or in rocks and hills, in some springs and pools . . . or vaguely in the air.[3]

It was a Kenyan Nilote, B. A. Ogot, who helped to confirm this interpretation of a force permeating all things.

> The spiritual part of man, the only part which survives death, is *Jok*, and it is the same power which is responsible for conception as well as for fortunes and misfortunes. Hence to the Nilote Jok is not an impartial universal power; it is the essence of every being, the force which makes everything what it is, and God himself, 'the greatest Jok' is life force in itself.[4]

Totemism in Africa led to groups identifying themselves with objects or other animals. Clans among communities like the Baganda adopted totemic symbols which established a sense of continuity between nature and man. Indeed, many African belief-systems still include animistic tendencies, which blur the distinction between man and nature, the living and the dead, the divine and the human. The belief systems of indigenous Africa did not assert a monopoly of the soul for the human species alone. Could a tree have a soul? Could a mountain have a soul? Could a river, in spite of its flow, retain a soul? Again it took poets in Europe to appreciate the belief-systems of societies such as those of Africa and the Americas before the ecological curiosity of Europe hit them hard. Alexander Pope, in spite of himself and his desire to be proper in Christian terms, nevertheless felt his muse drawn to the world-view of the so called 'savage'.

> . . . whose untutored mind
> Sees God in clouds, or hears him in the wind;
> His soul proud Science never taught to stray
> Far as the solar walk or Milky Way;
> Yet simple nature to his hope has given,
> Behind the cloud-topt hill, and humbler Heaven. . . .

Pope himself moves then to a pantheistic interpretation of the relationship between man, nature, and divinity reminiscent of precisely those societies which believed in such concepts as *Jok*. Carried away beyond his orthodox Christianity the poet asserted:

> All are but parts of one stupendous whole,
> Whose body Nature is, and God the soul;
> That changed through all, and yet in all the same,
> Great in the earth as in the ethereal frame,
> Warms in the sun, refreshes in the breeze,
> Glows in the stars, and blossoms in the trees;
> Lives through all life, extends through all extent,
> Spreads undivided, operates unspent;
> Breathes in our soul, informs our mortal part,
> As full, as perfect, in a hair as heart;
> As full, as perfect, in vile man that mourns,
> As the rapt Seraph that adores and burns.
> To him no high, no low, no great, no small;
> He fills, he bounds, connects, and equals all![5]

But unlike the totemic assumptions of some African traditional religions, Pope's pantheism in his essay on man could as easily be reconciled to the destruction of nature as to its conservation. The philosophy underlying this version of pantheism gave legitimacy to 'whatever is'. Though nature was indeed art, the destruction of nature could also be presumed to be divinely inspired.

All Nature is but Art unknown to thee;
All Chance, Direction, which thou canst see;
All Discord, Harmony not understood;
All partial Evil, universal Good;
And spite of Pride, in erring Reason's spite,
One truth is clear, *Whatever is, is right*.[6]

Pope's position on this point is not uncommon among pantheists generally. Indeed, European pantheism has often been accused of recognizing no distinction between good and evil, of being too deterministic, of deciding to be neutral as between destruction and preservation.

But to tame science in our day requires a commitment to *preserve*. African totemism, in spite of its selectivity, provides this massive commitment to preserve. There are communities along the coast of East Africa who would not kill a snake because of a bond of brotherhood between the snake and members of that community. The lion clan of the Baganda has the eagle as a secondary totem. Kintu, the royal ancestor of the clan and indeed of the nation, killed a lion and an eagle, and turned their skins into royal rugs. The lion and the eagle thenceforth became sacralized. Members of the leopard clan may not eat meat which has been torn or scratched by an animal. A sense of identification so deep that one shrinks from abusing the totem is what is probably needed as a foundation of the new ecophilia. We define ecophilia as an affectionate concern for nature and the environment, tending towards their preservation. Because of the massive dangers of pollution and dissipation of natural resources in recent times, ecophilia has entered a new level of militancy.

Of all the continents of the world, Africa has per capita the largest number of people who still refrain from drawing any sharp distinction between nature and man. Animism and totemism are still numerically stronger in terms of the following they command than either orthodox Islam or orthodox Christianity. And even among Christians and Muslims in Africa one finds strong continuing traditions of either animism or more selective totemism as a specialized form of naturalism. It is therefore fitting that the first United Nations agency ever to be placed in Africa should in fact be one concerned with ecology and environmental problems. The decision by the United Nations in 1972 to make Nairobi the headquarters of the specialized agency on the environment was, in philosophical terms, a fitting recognition to a continent whose population has departed least from a doctrine linking man with nature.

African Culture and Population Growth

Traditional African belief-systems also link the past with the present so intimately that life and death themselves become points on a continuum rather than opposing sides of a sharp dichotomy. The living and the dead move on a plane of continuity.

While African beliefs linking man to nature are potentially valuable for ecological preservation, African beliefs linking the past with the present carry the hazards of unplanned population growth. In many African traditional societies the idea of having many children, as explained in the previous chapter, is connected not only with the risk of infant mortality but also with the hope of parental immortality. The hazards of infant mortality in African conditions are quite familiar. Parents who limit themselves to two or three children only, while living in conditions of poverty and low life expectancy, are taking a serious risk. By the time they themselves are so old as to need the assistance of their children, they may have lost one, two, or all of them. Families who have lost several children are quite common in low-income countries. Having a large family then becomes an insurance policy for old age: an attempt to ensure that there is a son at the end of the road to help in feeding the family, or a daughter to help in tending the sick.

Modernization can be defined, in part, as an expanding capacity to look to the future rather than the past. The argument framed in this way is open to attack from a number of viewpoints, but it does have some profound suggestiveness. Ideas of saving, of long-term investment, of planning for the future, all have important modernizing implications. Of course, all societies have some kind of planning, and some concept of the future. But the variety of uncertainties in underdeveloped countries tends to restrict planning to shorter periods. It does not always make sense in economic terms to plan beyond the next harvest or two. The hazards of the weather (too much rain or too little, or an army of ominous parasites afflicting the cultivated land), and the uncertainty of disease as it takes its toll in a family, are factors which make it difficult to plunge into calculations too far ahead. Yet, in their very desire to have many children, traditional families often manifest a consciousness of the future. Children are a primordial form of insurance. Yet the very idea of insurance is connected to some of the defining characteristics of modernity.

But, as we have indicated, the idea of having many children in Africa is connected with the hope of parental immortality, as well as with the risk of infant mortality. The period after death in some

African traditional belief-systems is often divided between an earlier period of 'death within living memory' and a later period concerning 'death beyond living recollection'. Professor John S. Mbiti has called the first period *Sasa* (the now or the recent) and the second period *Zamani* (the long ago). Mbiti recounts that death is a process by which a person moves gradually from the *Sasa* phase to the *Zamani*. For as long as the individual is remembered by relatives and friends who knew him in his life, and who have survived him, he remains in the Sasa period. For as long as the deceased is remembered by name, he is not completely dead: in fact he combines death with life. He is a member of what Mbiti calls 'the living-dead':

> The living-dead is a person who is physically dead but alive in the memory of those who knew him in his life as well as being alive in the world of the spirits. So long as the living-dead is thus remembered, he is in the state of *personal immortality*.[7]

Mbiti is not specifically concerned with the issues of family planning and population control in Africa in his book, but what he has to say about dominant themes in African traditional religions is relevant for an understanding of African traditionalist attitudes towards these matters.

> So long as the living-dead is thus remembered, he is in the state of personal immortality. This personal immortality is externalized in the physical continuation of the individual through procreation, so that the children bear the traits of their parents or progenitors. . . . This concept of personal immortality should help us to understand the religious significance of marriage in African societies. Unless a person has close relatives to remember him when he has physically died, then he is nobody and simply vanishes out of human existence like a flame when it is extinguished.[8]

Mbiti goes on to tell us that it is these considerations which make it a duty, religious and ontological, for everyone to get married. If a man has no children or only daughters, he finds another wife so that through her, children (or sons), may be born who will survive him and keep him with the other living-dead of the family in personal immortality. 'Procreation is the absolute way of ensuring that a person is not cut off from personal immortality.'[9]

Some traditional African societies use the principal of the levirate as an additional means of ensuring the personal immortality of a deceased husband. A man dies, and his wife becomes the wife of his surviving brother. The offspring born after the brother has taken over could be regarded either as a child of the original deceased brother or as a child jointly of the dead man and the living brother. This whole complex of values and ideas is clearly an important point of contact between African culture and the whole problem of population growth in so far as this might be related to issues of ecological *balance*.

The idea of insuring for the future is, as we have indicated, modern. The idea of the future consisting of what happens to the dead after death is primordial. Large families in Africa become therefore symbols both of a forward-looking orientation and a backward-looking tradition. And the two issues of fear of infant mortality and hope for parental immortality jointly contribute towards a reluctance to engage in devices which circumscribe the creative potential of procreation.[10]

Such aspects of African culture are directly relevant to the problem of ecological balance if we agree with those writers who see the environmental crisis in the following terms:

> The world's population is continuing to grow at an alarming pace; finite resources are being utilized at exponential rates; and technological advances are contributing to negative ecological outcomes. . . . Thus, it is imperative that population, resources, technology, and environmental effects be considered jointly.[11]

One major cause of the technological advances was that original ecological curiosity in Western culture; two major consequences of those advances in technology have been depletion of resources and the decline of the death rate. Nazli Choucri might have been overstating her case when she saw a resource cost on every technological innovation.

> One key to defining the energy vector of the environmental crisis lies in the consideration that every advance in technology—every application, every invention, and every discovery—requires resources from the environment. Historically, technological developments have given rise to new energy and resource requirements without marked advances in energy-saving and energy-producing technologies, and there is every reason to believe that future developments in technology will occasion more extensive resource requirements.[12]

In reality certain innovations, by being more efficient, have used resources less wastefully than others. But technological improvements have often been part of the process of rising *consumption* patterns. A car built today may consume less fuel per mile, than a car built in the 1930s provided both are driven at the same speed. But due to improved road conditions, and to the escalating population of those who can afford cars, the technological advancement which resulted in lesser fuel per mile at the same speed has been totally negated by other factors. A combination of ecological curiosity and human ambition has resulted in both impressive technological performance and alarming resource depletion.

Technological advances have also resulted in staggering population growth in the nineteenth and twentieth centuries. The growth was dramatic in Europe in the nineteenth century, in the wake of the industrial revolution. Technological and medical advancement drastically curtailed the death rate in Europe and set the stage for a demographic revolution. The twentieth century has seen a similar revolution in much of Asia and Africa, and has therefore created concern about the capacity of this planet to meet the needs of its inhabitants. It has been estimated that the food supply on the planet could be increased ninefold if new technological breakthroughs were sought and all possible land used. If food resources were thus multiplied nine times, the earth could sustain a population of thirty billion.[13]

This kind of estimate gives mankind some time. At present growth levels, a thirty billion population for the world will take another seventy to one hundred years. There have been estimates of the carrying capacity of this planet in terms of roughly forty billion human beings. But these estimates might be over-estimating the time that mankind has to control population before it reaches tragic consequences. In any case, this has to be related to a number of other factors concerning resources other than food, and the hazards of new forms of imperialism and human aggression as societies compete to control mineral and energy resources. The Middle East and Africa might conceivably become vulnerable afresh as the desperate developing states seek to ensure their standards of affluence by renewed annexation of areas of raw materials and fuel.

But is this really an argument for reducing the population growth in Africa and the Middle East? Could it not even more convincingly be used to defend that population growth as a way of increasing the capacity of these areas to resist the ambitions of the more powerful states? There is indeed considerable logic in this latter position. The Malthusian view could, and has been, reversed in examining new relationships between standards of wealth and levels of population. Instead of getting the poor to reduce the rates of their population growth, why not get the rich to stop growing altogether?

Western Culture and African Resources

It is clear that the greatest consumers of resources on our planet are in fact the more developed and more affluent societies. It has been estimated that about six per cent of the population of the world consumes nearly forty per cent of the processed resources of the world from year to year. Thirty per cent of the world's population living in industrialized areas appropriate to themselves about ninety per cent of the total world production of mineral resources and energy. It is clear that the affluent do make greater demands on the ecology, inflict greater levels of pollution, and indulge in greater waste, than the less privileged sectors of the human race.[14]

If the citizens of the developed countries consume so much, their numbers ought to be completely stabilized, and even reduced, before pressures are put on African countries for greater restraint. That side of African culture which has been concerned for both infant mortality and parental immortality need not be too circumscribed while the populations of Western Europe, the USA, and the Soviet Union continue to rise, however modestly. And yet some degree of planning in Africa is not uncalled for. Population planning is not the same thing as a drastic reduction in population growth. From Africa's own point of view some degree of planning may be needed to reduce the social costs involved in any alternative strategy. Greater dissemination of information about birth control, combined with a new and more sophisticated response to the needs of ecological balance, should serve Africa well for the time being. The population of Africa needs to expand considerably from where it is now, but some calculations should be undertaken to determine what populations the continent can sustain in which parts, and at what rates of economic expansion, in the rest of this century.

European exploration resulted in part in disseminating the benefits of medical science, and these in turn led to impressive population growth in Africa. But that growth has now to be married to Africa's traditional ecological concern, and made more responsive to precise calculations about what the continent can bear. The African people themselves are a resource for the continent but they should also become increasingly the ultimate beneficiaries of what the continent has to offer. Europe's ecological curiosity resulted in 'opening up Africa'. Europe's new ecological concern is now inclined to encourage a latter-day African retreat from the mainstream of technological change. Europe's ecological curiosity in the old days of the explorers had prepared the way for the exploitation of African resources. Europe's new ecological concern is now advocating a conservation of African resources. Europe's old ecological curiosity had helped to establish systems of communication and patterns of exploitation with clear developmental consequences for Africa. Is Europe's new ecological concern designed to slow down Africa's newly acquired developmental impetus?[15]

Yet even the developmental role while it lasted was, by a curious destiny, often oriented towards precisely those pursuits which were least likely to result in the depletion of resources by the Africans themselves. The whole imperial tradition of giving a special premium to literary (rather than technical and engineering) skills was a tradition which was inadvertently but definitely kind to the African ecology in the short run. Certainly both France and Britain inaugurated in their colonies systems of education which were *not* inspired by ecological curiosity. British and French systems of education, if anything, diverted the attention of Africans away from their immediate surroundings towards romantic images of the metropolitan countries. Linguistic and literary skills achieved considerable emphasis. Proficiency in metropolitan languages was accorded the status of high prestige and often became a key to considerable social mobility. Shakespeare was more important than the steam engine; theatre art more fundamental than spadework. The Europe which had tamed nature through its ecological curiosity was at the time a Europe incapable of arousing similar levels of ecological curiosity among the colonized peoples under its subjugation.

The educational institutions in much of Africa were disproportionately academic rather than technical. A schoolboy with a Cambridge School Certificate in English Literature and the British Constitution was often more highly regarded than a motor mechanic or electrical technician. The nature of colonial education imparted the sort of skills which could indeed leave the ecology safe and unchallenged, simply because they were the skills of elegance rather than exertion, poetic inspiration rather than physical engineering, clerical work rather than technical labour. Partly because of this important distortion in colonial education, industrialization in Africa has been slowed down, and with that retardation has come the accidental benefit of delayed pollution.

Japan today has more serious problems of pollution than almost any other country in the world. A major background factor to Japanese pollution was precisely the rapid expansion of Japanese technical education, resulting in an effective dissemination of technical skills and the rapid expansion of industrialization. There are of course other major differences between Africa and Japan pertinent to problems of technological growth and ecological pollution. What needs to be grasped here is simply the different approaches to Westernization which Japan and Africa have experienced. Japanese selectivity, in their process of learning from the West, put a special premium on the technological skills of the West, rather than on Western literary and linguistic bequests. Westernization in Africa took a reverse direction of priority.

This did not mean that African resources were not exploited. On the contrary, the copper and gold, the diamonds and the agricultural products, served the appetites of others abroad. Africa might indeed have been impoverished by much of the resource exploitation which went on, but the bulk of the resultant pollution took place in the lands to which African goods were exported. There was a resource depletion in Africa, and ecological pollution in the West. Africa's relative backwardness in technological capabilities made her vulnerable to the risk of having her resources depleted by others, but at the same time that relative backwardness spared her the kind of technological infrastructure among her own people which might have put a strain on the ecology. Africa borrowed that part of Western culture which was not energy consuming, and thereby delayed her own ecological crisis.

Non-alignment and Ecological Concern

As independence approached, Africa had to seek new values to accompany her entry into the mainstream of international politics. There was indeed a decline in the emphasis on literary and linguistic skills as a basis of African education, but this decline was only modest. Basically, the educational institutions of Africa continued to be disproportionately academic and non-technical, thereby continuing to retard both industrialization and pollution. But independence carried additional normative imperatives. Among these were guidelines to international diplomacy. Will Africa evolve in her diplomatic reorientation a world view relevant to ecological balance?

Non-alignment emerged quite early as a strategy of diplomacy with an important ecological theme. In the 1950s and the early 1960s India under Jawaharlal Nehru was clearly the leader of the non-aligned states. Many Africans regarded Nehru as the founder of non-alignment, and for a while responded impressively to Nehru's leadership in some international issues. Nehru was convinced quite early about the dangers of atomic radiation for the quality of life on this planet. On 2 April 1954, Prime Minister Nehru urged the world to ensure that full publicity was given to the probable consequences of atomic radiation. On 8 April 1954, the Indian government communicated to the Secretary-general of the United Nations concern about atomic tests, and submitted proposals to the United Nations Disarmament Commission. In July of that year India raised the issue in the Trusteeship Council of the United Nations, thus implying an important link between the politics of nuclear power and the fate of the colonized territories.

In April 1955 the Bandung Conference took place in Indonesia. At that time Africa had only a few independent states. Although the Bandung Conference of 1955 was regarded as 'Afro-Asian' it was much more Asian than African. Nevertheless, India's leadership in matters connected with sensitivity to nuclear radiation was striking a responsive cord even among African observers at Bandung. At the conference India suggested a chain of stations to maintain continuous vigilance and calculation on the impact of radioactivity. The communiqué of the Bandung Conference included the proposition:

> Pending the total prohibition of the manufacture of nuclear and thermonuclear weapons, this conference appeals to all the powers concerned to reach agreement to suspend experiments with such weapons.[16]

In 1960 Africa asserted her presence in international affairs more decisively. Seventeen African countries attained independence and became members of the United Nations. Ghana had led the way in 1957. Before long it was clear that African states wanted to have their say in sparing this planet the hazards of nuclear pollution. Ghana, Ethiopia, India, the United Arab Republic, Yugoslavia, and Nepal, introduced a six-power resolution at the United Nations expressing a 'deep concern and profound regret' that tests were continuing, urging nuclear powers to refrain from further explosions pending the conclusion of a treaty, and asking those powers to conclude an agreement as soon as possible.[17]

In December 1961 a formula was found for the composition of the eighteen-nation committee on disarmament. This convened in Geneva on 14 March 1962.

> For the first time, this post-war disarmament conference contained independent or non-aligned states as full participants. Eight such states were named as members: Mexico, Brazil, Ethiopia, Nigeria, United Arab Republic, Sweden, India and Burma. . . . Some powers, including initially the United States, did not look approvingly at the inclusion of non-aligned states in disarmament negotiations, fearing that they had much to learn about disarmament and that, in any case, they might automatically tend to side with the Communist bloc.[18]

In fact African and other non-aligned countries had already demonstrated that on this issue of the nuclear pollution of the planet they were concerned regardless of who was exploding the devices. On 1 September 1961, the Soviet Union resumed nuclear tests at a time which coincided with the Belgrade Conference of the twenty-five non-aligned states. Russia's fifty-megaton explosion was described by Kwame Nkrumah at Belgrade as 'a shock to me'. Nehru asserted, 'I regret it deeply'. And Nasser of Egypt called the Russian tests 'another cause for deep regret'. The communiqué of the Belgrade Conference said:

> The participants in the Conference consider it essential that an agreement on the prohibition of all nuclear and thermonuclear tests should be urgently concluded. With this aim in view, it is necessary that negotiations be immediately resumed, separately or as part of the negotiations on general disarmament. Meanwhile, the moratorium on the testing of all nuclear weapons should be resumed and observed by all countries.[19]

Kwame Nkrumah organized a ban-the-bomb conference in Accra, rallying international opinion behind a commitment to control this particular way of polluting the world's atmosphere. Nigeria under Prime Minister Tafawa Balewa broke off diplomatic relations with France for a number of years following France's nuclear tests in the Sahara.

These were indeed the days of high African sensitivity to issues concerned with nuclear ecological abuse. Since then, Africa, because of her internal problems, and because of a certain sense of frustration on the global plane, has left the task of protesting about these matters to other countries abroad. Even those who were previously aligned to the West—such as Australia, New Zealand and, in a different sense, Chile and Peru—have now become vocal in their complaints against those who subject the planet to further dangers of nuclear pollution. The French tests in the Pacific in July 1973 aroused these and other countries, and featured in solemn deliberations at the Montreal Conference of the Commonwealth Heads of Government in August 1973.

Europe's ecological curiosity had indeed resulted in major technological discoveries in the nuclear field. But these discoveries had not been accompanied by ecological concern. The hazards of this kind of ambition had also been ignored by Communist China, as she responded to the demonstration effect of the Euro-American experience.

Africa watches helplessly. And the voices of those non-aligned giants—the late Nehru, the late Nkrumah, and the late Nasser—come echoing with the words 'this is yet another cause for deep regret'.

Conclusion

The dialectic between ecological curiosity and ecological concern has provided a framework for our analysis in this chapter. Five hundred years ago European culture began to develop a profound new inquisitiveness about man's environment. Out of this cultural component arose a new scientific civilization, which gradually gave Europe the technological capability to expand her influence and subject much of the human race to varying degrees of European control.

Africa experienced some of the first manifestations of Europe's ecological curiosity through the activities of the explorers and adventurers from the Northern Hemisphere. These in turn prepared the way ultimately for the trader, the miner, and the administrator. Africa's experience of colonialism was intimately connected with the consequences of Europe's ecological curiosity.

Culturally Africa's own orientation was in the direction of ecological concern. There were levels of identification between man and nature in Africa which were distant from at least the new wave of Europe's cultural militancy. Ecological curiosity as a base for science has to be put alongside ecological concern as a foundation for environmental morality.

What should be noted now is the impact of Europe's own scale of preference on those Westernized Africans in charge of affairs in the continent. The totemism so characteristic of some indigenous African cultures is not always appreciated by the Westernized decision-makers in African capitals. A retreat from some fundamental African values and norms has been discernible among the African intelligentsia. And yet it is precisely those values of ecological concern that might in time constitute Africa's most important contribution to the safety of this planet.

On the issue of population in relation to ecological balance, the plea for the time being is merely for more systematic planning in Africa, rather than for a drastic reduction in the rate of growth. Again the African intelligentsia in charge of policy-making might more purposefully respond to this potential demographic challenge, just as they once responded to the arrogance of nuclear pollution as perpetrated by others.

As for the new military regimes where the intelligentsia has declined in influence, these would need to relate their military ambitions to environmental safeguards in their own continent. In time Africa might learn to make her ecological concern more scientific, combining cultures for the greater protection of man, and of the planet of which man is the ultimate trustee.

References and notes

1. Oliver Goldsmith, 'The Deserted Village' (1770).
2. This new totemism is discussed in a wider context in Ali A. Mazrui, *A World Federation of Cultures: an African Perspective* (New York: Free Press, 1976).
3. J. H. Driberg, *The Lango*, cited by Okot p'Bitek in *Religion of the Central Luo* (Nairobi: East African Literature Bureau, 1971), p. 50.
4. B. A. Ogot, 'Concept of Jok', *African Studies* **20** (1961).
5. Alexander Pope, *An Essay on Man*, op. cit.
6. Ibid.
7. John S. Mbiti, *African Religions and Philosophy*, op. cit., pp. 25-6.
8. Ibid.
9. Ibid.
10. These issues are also discussed in a wider context in Ali A. Mazrui, *A World Federation of Cultures*, op. cit. Consult also Ali A. Mazrui, 'Public opinion and the politics of family planning', *Rural Africana* (Michigan) (Spring 1971), 38-44.
11. Nazli Choucri, assisted by James P. Bennett, 'Population, resources and technology: political implications of the environmental crisis', *International Organization* **26** (Spring 1972), 176, 182. Consult also United Nations, Population Division, *World Population Prospects, 1965-1985 as Assessed in 1968* (Working Paper No. 30) New York, 1969. See also United States House of Representatives, Sub-committee of the Committee on Government Operations, *The Effects of Population Growth on Natural Resources and the Environment, Hearings,* 91st Congress, First Session, 15-16 September 1969; Philip M. Hauser and Otis Dudley Duncan, *The Study of Population: an Inventory and Appraisal* (Chicago: University of Chicago Press, 1959); and Myron Weiner, 'Political demography: an enquiry into the political consequences of population change', in National Academy of Sciences of the USA, *Rapid Population Growth: Consequences and Policy Implications* (Baltimore: John Hopkins Press, 1971), pp. 567-617.
12. Choucri, ibid., p. 188.

13. See United States House of Representatives, Sub-committee of the Committee on Government Operations, *The Effects of Population Growth on Natural Resources and the Environment*, op. cit., p. 5.
14. Consult M. Tim Hubbert, 'Mineral resources and rates of consumption', *Proceedings of the World Population Conference, 1965* Vol. 3, p. 318. See also Emilio Q. Daddario, 'Technology and the democratic process', *Technology Review*, 73 (July-August 1971), 20. Consult also *Man's Impact on the Global Environment: Assessment and Recommendations for Action*, Report of the Study of Critical Environmental Problems (MIT Press, 1970); Richard A. Falk, *This Endangered Planet: Prospects and Proposals for Human Survival* (New York: Random House, 1971); and Meadows, Meadows, et. al., *The Limits to Growth* (Club of Rome, 1972).
15. For an alternative interpretation of the impact of imperial Europe on Africa consult Walter Rodney, *How Europe Underdeveloped Africa* (Dar es Salaam: Tanzania Publishing House, 1972).
16. Consult Homer A. Jack, 'Nonalignment and a testban agreement: the role of the nonaligned states', *Journal of Arms Control* 1 (October 1963), 636-46.
17. This resolution (1648) was approved by the plenary session, 71 to 20, with 8 abstentions. The NATO and Warsaw Pact countries voted against the resolution, while the non-aligned were preponderantly in favour of it.
18. Homer A. Jack, op. cit., p. 640.
19. Ibid., p. 639.

CHAPTER 15
Towards the Year 2000: A Conclusion

We started this book with a future-oriented chapter, and then went back into the historical background of the different aspects of Africa's international relations. In this concluding chapter we shall be concerned with both the past and the future, and with how each is related to the present in all its immediacy.

The first half of the twentieth century for Africa was dominated by the central experience of colonization and foreign rule. Under such conditions the distinction between domestic affairs and foreign relations for most of Africa was virtually non-existent. After all, foreign powers were 'domestically' entrenched in African capitals.

Outside such countries as Ethiopia and Liberia, formal African diplomacy in the twentieth century was not resumed until the third quarter, in the wake of decolonization. The new African states confronted a bipolar world with two superpowers, two major economic systems in competition with each other, two ideologies struggling for converts among the newly liberated countries. The cold war, while it lasted, helped to give birth to *non-alignment* as a principle of African diplomacy. The implications of the bipolar world in the third quarter of the twentieth century were wide ranging. Let us first re-examine these implications before we turn to the most likely trends in the final quarter of the century.

The Cold War as a Creative Confrontation

There is a Swahili saying along the coast of Kenya which philosophizes in this vein: '*Ndovu wawili wakipigana ziumiazo ni nyasi*' (When two elephants fight it is the grass which suffers). This old saying was sometimes invoked in conversations among East Africans in the early 1960s to denote the predicament of small powers in the shadow of conflict between superpowers. But in a literal sense the Swahili saying is discussing the consequences of an actual fight between two elephants. It is discussing not a cold war, but a hot conflict between these two super-animals. But what if the elephants are not actually engaged, tusk to tusk, in a live fight? What if the situation is one in which one elephant is facing another in a stalemate, each afraid to approach any nearer to the other, keeping a substantial patch of grass between them, afraid to tread on that piece of grass lest this neutral territory should be converted into a battleground? In this case the elephants are facing each other in a mood of hostile stillness, in a state almost of petrified confrontation. We can thus modify the Swahili saying to the effect that 'When two elephants are confronting each other in petrified stillness, each afraid to move any nearer to the other, it is the neutral grass in between which *benefits*.'

The cold war between communist states and the West was a creative confrontation partly because of its impact on the relations between big powers and smaller ones. In their first years of independence Afro-Asian neutrals sometimes spoke as if they had to be non-aligned in order to prevent the big powers from going to war. What was nearer to the truth was that the small powers could afford to be non-aligned precisely because the big powers were already afraid of going to war. It was not a case of non-alignment making peace possible – it was more a case of a fear of war making non-alignment possible. The voices of the weak became relatively strong because the strong were already afraid of one another. At any rate this is how it started. But although indulgence towards the weak may be the child of a mutual fear between the strong, that indulgence may already be changing into the beginnings of genuine respect. This respect would in turn make non-alignment more effective as a moderating influence on the big powers. The whole process has aspects of sheer circularity: fear of war among the big powers leads to toleration of presumptious small powers; that toleraton makes non-alignment possible; habit turns that toleration into the beginnings of genuine respect; and such fragile respect makes the powers more responsive to the opinion of the non-aligned, on at least some marginal issues; and non-alignment does at last vindicate the peace-seeking side of its existence.

But was the cold war simply the product of confrontation between capitalism and communism? In reality the cold war was an outcome of interaction between two important phenomena – ideology and nuclear power. What made the superpowers afraid of each other was not simply the ideological division; it was also the simple fact that they were engaged in such a confrontation at a period of history fraught with the danger of a nuclear holocaust.

However, it must not be assumed that the cold war was simply a case of a nuclear stalemate. Revolution as a phenomenon was internationalized in the eighteenth century. The impact of the French Revolution on neighbouring European countries was itself profound. In addition there was a mutual influence between events in the American colonies and events in France. The American War of Independence preceded the French Revolution; and yet the full maturation of ideas in the American revolution bore the impact of the French experience.

If France and America between them succeeded in internationalizing the phenomena of revolution, Marx and his successors came in turn to globalize that revolution. The explosive Marxist idea that the entire human race was engaged in successive revolutionary eruptions, and was heading, in any case, towards an ultimate socialist revolution, came to affect profoundly the nature of human expectations in the decades which followed.

In 1917 the Russian communists overthrew the Czars, and the first Marxist state came into being in the world. For a short while Stalin retreated into a doctrine of 'socialism in one country', in order to consolidate the socialist achievement within the Soviet Union. But Russia's commitment to playing a role in the globalization of socialism was not completely discarded. It kept on rearing its head, sometimes momentarily retreating in the face of changing world circumstances. The Russians joined hands with the capitalists in order to fight Fascism during the Second World War. But in the aftermath of the war itself Russian occupation of 'enemy territory' became a method of extending the frontiers of Marxism.

Considering that the Americans had adopted an ideology which sought to internationalize certain revolutionary ideas derived from liberalism, and considering further that the Soviet Union in its Marxist transformation was similarly committed to expanding the area of socialist revolution, the stage was set for an important ideological confrontation. Both the Soviet Union and the USA had become missionary powers in an ideological sense. The Soviet Union saw its revolution as the first of a series in the world as a whole. On the other hand, Chester Bowles in an article in the *New York Times Magazine* made a claim that the American revolution of the eighteenth century was 'a revolution intended for all mankind'.[1]

Given the missionary orientations of both the Soviet Union and the USA, their scramble for influence in the newly liberated areas of the world was bound to have a strong ideological component. But the nuclear stalemate and the ideological competition between the superpowers was soon accompanied by the phenomenon of global decolonization. The cold war became a major challenge to the newly independent states. Should they take sides in this confrontation? If so, should they side with the powers with whom they were familiar as a result of past experience? And yet those very powers were the ones which had once colonized them. Was it a case of the devil you know being better than the devil you do not know?

The answer to the agonies of these dilemmas came from India. As indicated in a previous chapter, India contributed to the diplomatic nationalism of the new states the concept of non-alignment, which served as the basis of their foreign policies on attainment of independence. It is worth repeating Milton Obote's tribute to Pandit Nehru on his death: 'Nehru will be remembered as the founder of non-alignment. . . . The new nations of the world owe him a debt of gratitude in this respect.'[2]

Independence is a time when a newly created state has to seek direction for its diplomacy. The experience of conducting international relations as a sovereign state is entirely new. The idea of a foreign policy is also relatively new. The concept of non-alignment was therefore a useful guideline for the newly decolonized states of Africa. Non-alignment was essentially a policy of pragmatic non-committal. By eschewing commitment to alliances in the early post-independence period, and by rejecting the notion of automatic alignment in the cold war, the non-aligned countries gave themselves time to think. Non-alignment as a policy was well-suited to a period of experimentation. It enabled the new states to try out relations with countries in both the Western and the Easten bloc, to seek direct knowledge and contact with various other countries, and to find out for themselves what the rest of the world was like. The opening of embassies is expensive, and if the policy of non-alignment had not required contact with both sides it might have seemed wasteful for an African country to establish embassies among eastern European countries.

Non-alignment and the pattern formulated by Nehru set the stage for a period of diplomatic maturation. It allowed new states a period of trial and error in a variety of relationships. Of course, there was always the risk of having one's fingers burnt. It has even been suggested that India's faith in Chinese good intentions, stemming in part from the policy of non-alignment, resulted in India's unreadiness to meet the Chinese invasion of 1962. If this interpretation were true, it could still be argued that burning one's fingers as a result of direct trial and error was part of the process of growing up in a world of diplomacy.

The Rise of Arab Power

Nehru died in 1964. India by that time was already in diplomatic decline. One big question which arose was who was going to lead the Third World next?

The People's Republic of China — though on its way towards becoming a superpower — is still widely accepted as a partner in Third World struggles. Was China going to capture the leadership of the developing world as a whole? Her credentials were strong. She was still excluded from the United Nations, but she was already active in global politics. For a while it seemed almost logical that the mantle of Third World leadership should pass from India to China. After all, those two were the largest countries on earth, and they were both committed to the anti-imperialist struggle.

Until 1970 the Arabs had Nasser—but he had been defeated even more decisively by Israel in 1967 than India was defeated by China in 1962. The credentials of the Arabs for Third World leadership seemed rather modest by comparison with China's credentials.

Suddenly, from 1973, things began to change. If China thought that power resided in the *barrel of a gun*, the Arabs discovered that power could also reside in a *barrel of oil*. The application of the Arab oil boycott against the USA in the course of the Middle East October War revealed new potentialities of political leverage.

Since 1973 there has been emerging an Arab leadership within the Third World. Major diplomatic initiatives since that year on a wide range of issues relevant to the Third World have originated from the Arabs. Countries of the Third World are producers of raw materials and other primary commodities. The whole struggle for a new international economic order has to some extent been led by the Arabs. Third World causes are being championed by some Arab countries, and are being pushed by them into the main arenas of international discourse. Algeria virtually initiated the raw materials debate at the United Nations in 1974. This was followed by the special session of the General Assembly in 1975. We are witnessing the beginning of serious consideration of the issue of restructuring the world economy. The diplomatic triumph of the Palestinian cause, as symbolized by the arrival of Yasir Arafat (leader of the Palestine Liberation Organization) in the UN General Assembly in 1974, was again the result of substantial effort by the Arab world to give this particular movement the kind of global legitimacy which had eluded it since the 1940s. The chairmanship of Algeria in the General Assembly in 1974 was a factor behind that particular triumph for the Palestinian cause.

Within the same session of the General Assembly there was, to the fury of much of the Western world, the suspension of South Africa from that particular session. With the USA reacting with cries of 'the tyranny of the majority' in the General Assembly, there was in this very complaint the beginning of the genuine independence of the United Nations. For much of its life the world body had been substantially dominated by the USA and was often an extension of United States' diplomatic leverage.

After 1973 evidence of increasing autonomy of the General Assembly under Afro-Asian initiative, instigated usually by Arab states, created a picture of the beginning of genuine independence for the world body. Then there was a debate in December 1974 about a charter of economic rights and obligations. The charter was discussed in the General Assembly and adopted. Certain aspects of the charter virtually asserted that nationalization without compensation was legitimate in certain circumstances. Again the Western world was horrified by this assertion and by this whole militant trend within the United Nations.

There has also been the controversy about linking energy to raw materials in a conference on the world economy. The USA wanted the conference to be between the oil producers and oil consumers only. It was substantially at Arab initiative that the idea of linking energy to other products of the Third World became a major stumbling block at the first preparatory meeting early in 1975 in Paris. At that time it was impossible to arrive at an acceptable agenda for the international meeting because the Western powers remained adamant in refusing to link energy to raw materials, while the Arab world, especially Algeria, remained adamant in wanting international discussion to take into account other Third World needs. What we were witnessing were sensitized Arab states newly concerned about major issues of relevance to the Third World as a whole. The Conference on Economic Co-operation between developing and developed states has now established working commissions.

It is unlikely that Arab leadership of the Third World will remain permanently, but for the time being it is there, and that might itself be one of the most significant events of the century.

The Palestine question has had a lot to do with the Arab desire to identify with the rest of the Third World. It is possible that this Arab concern for political allies on the specific dispute over Israel had the effect of substantially broadening the political horizons of the Arab world. Once a people need political allies they gradually begin to identify with areas that might otherwise have been regarded as irrelevant to them. The Palestine question as a background factor in the history of the Middle East has been part of the process of radicalizing even the conservative regimes in the Arab world; and part of the process of internationalizing the horizons of Arab leaders as they have sought to mobilize international and global support on the Middle East issue.

OPEC as a Muslim Organization

Connected with these developments is the link between the political resurrection of Islam and the rise of the Arab world. Underlying the rise of the Arab world is the Organization of Petroleum Exporting Countries (OPEC) and its entry into the mainstream of economic diplomacy.

OPEC in composition is an overwhelming Muslim institution. The largest oil-exporting country, as we know, is Saudi Arabia, the custodian of the holy cities of Mecca and Medina, and one of the most fundamentalist of the Muslim countries on the world scene today. The second largest oil-exporting country is Iran, another major Muslim country, perhaps with potentialities for considerable expansion as an influential power in world politics. If you regard Indonesia as the most populous Muslim country after the collapse of old Pakistan, then Indonesia as a member of OPEC is also part of the Islamic composition of OPEC.

The Gulf States are mostly very small, but precisely because they are small and with enormous financial resources, they have surpluses capable of being mobilized for political and economic projects in different parts of the world.

Black African members of OPEC at present are Nigeria and Gabon. In the case of Gabon we have a convert to Islam (President Omar Bongo). In the case of Nigeria we have an African country which best encompasses within itself the three parts of the soul of Africa—the indigenous, the Euro-Christian and the Islamic. All three forces are strong in Nigeria. What is more, the Islamic factor has been growing in national influence since independence.

If you look at OPEC as a whole you can say that it is virtually two-thirds 'Islamic' in oil production and over two-thirds in number of states. Thus the emergence of OPEC and petroleum on the world scene signify the beginning of the political resurrection of Islam.

A related issue is the nature of the regimes that are in power in those resource-rich Muslim countries. It just so happens that Iran still has a monarchical system in a conservative Irano-Islamic context. On the Arabian (Persian) Gulf there are also traditional rulers. There is a tendency to regard this as a cost in the equation. But it is possible to examine it as a benefit in global terms. The influence within OPEC does not lie merely in Westernized or relatively secular Muslim countries such as Algeria. It lies even more among countries whose Islam has been less diluted by Westernism.

From the point of view of the Muslim world as a whole there is now a dialectic between underpopulated but very rich and religiously traditional countries on one side, and more populous, more secular and less endowed Muslim countries on the other. A dialectic between resource-poor populations on one side and resource-rich traditionalists on the other could provide the kind of transformation in the Muslim world which could change the balance between the forces of secularism and the forces of traditionalism in the years ahead.

The Palestinian question in this domain again has been a catalyst of radicalization. The idea of Saudi Arabia applying the oil weapon against the USA would have been inconceivable without an issue like Palestine and Jerusalem. So again a traditionalist country, very highly pro-Western, could under the stress of war and of anxiety over the future of the Palestinian question be prepared to invoke a political weapon which would not have been readily invoked by such a regime in other circumstances. In looking at the political resurrection of Islam one must once again add the Palestinian factor as part of the total picture.

We may therefore infer that there are positive elements in the problem of Palestine from a Third World perspective. The problem has indeed helped to create greater internationalism among the Arabs. One question which now arises is whether, if the Palestine problem were solved tomorrow, the Arabs would become more isolationist. Would there be an Arab retreat, a lack of interest in what happens in Africa or what happens in Bangladesh, Pakistan and Latin America. One scenario before us is therefore the self-isolation of the Arab world if the Palestine question is solved and peace is restored in the Middle East. Another scenario is the 'northernization' of the Arab world; that is to say the Arab world increasingly regarding itself as part of the developed Northern Hemisphere of the world and not as part of the underdeveloped Southern Hemisphere of the world. Would the solution of the Middle East problem lead in either of these two directions? We do not know yet. What we do know for the time being is that the fate of Palestine is a factor behind Arab interest in, say, Africa. It is conceivable that without the Middle Eastern crises many Arab countries, not all of them by any means, would have no interest at all in Africa south of the Sahara. Once again the issue of needing allies on major issues of this type leads to Third World solidarity.

We have indicated in earlier chapters that Africa's most natural allies consist of the Black Diaspora and the Arab world. The Arabs are within Africa. So is the bulk of Arab land. Black and African states share the Organization of African Unity. This organization and the Arab League have overlapping membership. There are possibilities of exploiting this relationship to the mutual advantage of both peoples. Before the end of this century, African Muslims will probably outnumber the Arabs and will be making a strong bid for shared leadership of Islam. It would not be surprising if, within the next decade, black Muslims direct from Africa are seen establishing schools and hospitals in Harlem and preaching Islam to black Americans. The funding for this Islamic counter-penetration will probably come from the oil-producers of the Arab world. But since African Islam is distinct from Arab Islam, and carries considerable indigenous culture within it, Islamic counter-penetration into the USA would also be in part a process of transmitting African indigenous perspectives as well. Islam, Africanity and Western civilization may thus find new areas of interaction.

But at least as important as Arab money for African cultural entry into the West is the sheer potential of the black American population. It is the second largest black nation in the world (second only to Nigeria) and it is situated in the middle of the richest and mightiest country in the twentieth century. At the moment black American influence on America's cultural and intellectual life is much more modest than, say, the influence of Jewish Americans. But as the poverty of black Americans lessens, its social and political horizons widen and its intellectual and creative core expands, black American influence on American culture is bound to increase. And the links between Africa, the Arab world and the Black Diaspora may in turn find new areas of creative convergence.

The Future of Southern Africa

Other major developments in Africa in the coming years will concern southern Africa. Let us speculate about the immediate future on the basis of what is now happening.

The timetable for liberation in southern Africa has been compressed since the April 1974 coup in Portugal. It will probably still take fifteen to twenty years for the process to be completed. Some degree of violence will be necessary in each remaining case – Zimbabwe (Rhodesia), Namibia and South Africa.

The most difficult problem will be South Africa. Black liberation fighters will be driven to use tactics of terror, harassment and attempts to embarrass the enemy. Within the next few years black liberation fighters will start a serious study of the tactics of urban guerrillas in Latin America and the Palestinian commandos. Air traffic, especially within Africa and between Africa and Europe, will become more vulnerable to skyjacking by African liberation fighters. The purpose will be partly harassment of the South African regime and partly an attempt to punish those Western countries that have intimate economic relations with South Africa. As in Latin America, political abduction will also be used in Africa in order to demand ransom and raise funds for African liberation movements. These movements may come to depend less on such sympathetic governments as Russia and China for financial support, and more on raising money by abduction and 'whitemail'. The governments of independent black Africa may at times get embarrassed by the tactics of black liberation fighters – just as Arab governments are at times embarrassed by the Palestinians.

There is also a serious risk that South Africa will one day resort to reprisal raids against African countries which harbour the so-called 'terrorists'. When South Africa in the 1980s begins to feel as insecure as Israel now feels, neighbouring African governments might have to put up with reprisal air-raids from time to time.

What is certain is that many Africans will die for each white man killed. This is also what has already happened in Angola, Mozambique, Rhodesia and Guinea-Bissau. It is also what happened in Kenya under the 'Mau Mau' emergency. It is also what happened in Algeria in the fight against the French. And of course many more Vietnamese communists than American soldiers died in Vietnam.

For many countries dominated by others, the price of liberty is not only eternal vigilance but also inevitable violence. Certainly none of the remaining southern African countries could approach majority rule without going through the fire of political terror. The white regimes may give a lot of concessions to blacks under peaceful pressure, but the regimes will always fall short of conceding majority rule—for that would be the end of their own power! Only further violence can ultimately break the white stranglehold on the remainder of southern Africa. Once violence breaks out on a sufficient scale, it begins to put strains on the cohesion of the dominant group within itself. An internal black military challenge in South Africa and Rhodesia will first bring whites closer together, but will later begin to turn white man against white man. A lot depends on how sustained is the black challenge.

A phenomenon which needs to be examined in the wake of the military coup in Portugal and its aftermath is, quite simply, the impact of European military coups upon African liberation. We may be witnessing a pattern concerning the significance of such metropolitan coups—a pattern which might have relevance for the liberation not only of Portuguese colonies, but even conceivably of Rhodesia and South Africa. Will the first signs of a crack in the political system of Rhodesia or South Africa be a military challenge by the white Rhodesian military forces themselves against civilian authority in Salisbury or white South African soldiers against the Prime Minister in Pretoria? It is now conceivable that the trend of events in southern Africa will be in the direction first of increasing pressure from black liberation fighters; secondly, frustrations among the so-called security forces fighting on behalf of the regimes; and thirdly, new strains on civil-military relations within the white regimes themselves.

In recent African history the first major case of a metropolitan coup leading to colonial liberation was the military situation between Algeria and France, which culminated in the assumption of power by General Charles de Gaulle in 1958. After the First World War the French army had become increasingly frustrated as a result of major setbacks, first in Indo-China and later in Algeria. In the earlier insurrection the French army had had to face the humiliation of Dien Bien Phu in Vietnam. The ultimate capitulation of the French attempt to retain Indo-China, and French withdrawal from that region, stiffened for a while French determination to resist all claims for independence in Algeria. In other words, the very success of the Vietnamese against the French was for a while an obstacle in the way of the National Liberation Front in Algeria. A level of stubbornness and obstinacy in the ranks of French soldiers, and within successive French governments, prolonged the Algerian war of independence.

By 1958 France herself was weary of the war, and the politicians had not moved much further towards finding an adequate solution. The soldiers in the field in Algeria were growing increasingly frustrated. Finally a revolt by the French, challenging the very existence of the French Fourth Republic, created a national crisis of considerable proportions. There seemed to be only one man high enough in stature in France, and acceptable enough to large numbers on both sides of the confrontation, to be capable of averting a civil war in France. Charles de Gaulle had his second moment in history. He emerged from the self-imposed oblivion which had lasted since his resignation as head of government in 1946, and assumed once again supreme authority in France. The military challenge within the colonial power which had resulted in the collapse of the Fourth Republic had immense consequences for the French colonies at large, and not merely for Algeria.

Just as the Algerian war of independence had been a fundamental precipitating factor behind the rise of Charles de Gaulle in Paris in 1958, so the Portuguese colonial wars in Angola, Mozambique, and Guinea-Bissau were a fundamental precipitating factor behind the rise of Antonio de Spinola in Lisbon in 1974. France before de Gaulle had insisted with obstinacy that Algeria was not a colony but was part of France; Portugal before Spinola had insisted that Angola, Mozambique, and Guinea-Bissau were not colonies but were integral provinces of metropolitan Portugal. But just as de Gaulle said after his assumption of power that Algeria was Algerian after all, Antonio de Spinola had argued even before he assumed power in the following terms:

> . . . it is not national unity that is at stake but imperial unity, and today's conscience does not accept empires. . . . The future of Portugal depends on an adequate solution to the war in which we are involved.[3]

In fact Spinola – like de Gaulle before him – flirted with alternative solutions of integration between the overseas provinces and the metropolitan country in Europe. The idea of a federal relationship did intrigue Charles de Gaulle at some stage. A similar idea of federation between Portugal and her colonies was central to Antonio de Spinola's book *Portugal and the Future*. In both cases it was the continuing determination of the freedom fighters in Africa that gradually tilted the balance of opinion in the imperial capitals.

Problems of Cultural Dependency

On the cultural front we are, at the moment, still moving towards a Euro-centric world culture. We have arrived closer to having a world culture than to having a world government. As we indicated, languages from Western Europe are spoken by populations far distant from their origin in both geography and culture. International law as a body of norms to govern relations between states was born out of the European states. Each one of us probably has two forms of dress—his national dress and European dress. Each one of us probably has two dominant cuisines—his national cuisine and European cuisine. An Indian, if he is not wearing Indian dress, will wear Western dress. It is inconceivable that he will wear Chinese, Yoruba or Arab dress. An Arab, if he is not wearing Arab regalia, will be wearing a European suit. He is unlikely to be geared in Indian or Chinese fashion. Basically, the major impact on our cultural life has come from Western Europe, in domains as varied as international law and food culture, in areas as diverse as dress, the languages we use, and the school systems that we employ.

As we indicated in an earlier chapter, we even choose our leaders partly on the basis of credentials in the skills of Europe. I was in Uganda on the day of Amin's military coup. The voice on the radio was ill at ease with the English language. The voice gave eighteen brilliant reasons why Milton Obote had to be overthrown. The reasons were written in English, but the significant thing is that the man who was reading the statement was not at home with that language. My students at Makerere laughed at the idea of having a president who spoke broken English. Many would listen to Idi Amin with bemused negativeness. Their negative attitude was not because he had overthrown a duly constituted government; nor was it because he was capable of using rather harsh methods against his opponents. They despised him instead because he was not Westernized. 'Listen to his English! And this man is President of Uganda!'

In short, we evaluate our leaders in external terms, and find a sense of incongruity in having major political figures who cannot express themselves adequately in the English language. This is a situation of linguistic and cultural dependency. Before the Amin coup took place, it was impossible for someone to become the President of Uganda with Amin's linguistic qualifications. In the old days a Ugandan who did not speak English would not get into parliament even if he spoke twelve Ugandan languages fluently. Parliamentarians were chosen partly on the basis of their competence in the English language. Nor was that unique to Uganda. One African country after another had electoral laws which did not require competence in any African language as a condition for a parliamentary career. It was even possible to have a Hastings Banda as President of Malawi although he had lost direct linguistic touch with his people. Competence in multiple African languages has not been permitted to outweigh the handicap of not speaking the imperial language. We even categorize ourselves in terms of being 'French-speaking Africans' or 'English-speaking Africans'. Asia has less of an intellectual and cultural dependency than Africa has. Asians do not speak of themselves as French-speaking Asians or English-speaking Asians just because they were once ruled by nations of those languages. In contrast, Africans are in a state of heavy cultural dependency; and because of that they are more infiltrated in this fundamental sense. However, there are likely to be changes in the two decades before us. A good deal will depend upon whether there is a growing awareness among Africans of the degree to which they are an external appendage to an alien civilization.

Part of this growing awareness will in turn depend upon the military. 'Is the military a modernizing force?' That debate has been going on; there is another debate which has not even started—'Is the military a traditionalizing force? Are the soldiers likely to be a force that will reduce the cultural component of our dependency, and revive to some extent certain trends towards indigenous ways of handling things?' The question arises because the soldiers in African countries are often among the least Westernized of those who wield power. In some societies, they are, if you like, raw peasants drawn from the womb of our countryside. They are what I have had occasion to call the 'lumpen militariat', really drawn from sectors of the society which would be relatively underprivileged but for the use of the gun to improve their effectiveness in society. If these rural sectors from which the soldiers are recruited are less Westernized, are they not likely to emphasize things indigenous in the years ahead? It is a meaningful question. The experience in Zaire and Uganda seems to indicate that there are possibilities of the military playing a traditionalizing role, sometimes in very simple and naïve ways, but nevertheless raising fairly fundamental issues. Take the question of whether Christians must be called John, Peter or Joseph—Christian names in modern Africa. President Mobutu Sese Seko of Zaire suddenly decided in 1971 that, if Christianity is a universal religion, why could not African names be counted as Christian names? Why should African Christians have to adopt Euro-Hebraic names? A simple point! All of a sudden, one citizen of Zaire after another was called upon to surrender his passport and substitute a Zairean name for his 'Christian' name. Each citizen was thus called upon to make clear in his passport that he is indigenous in identity. The policy caused considerable personal anguish. People can get possessive about their names. If one has spent twenty or forty years being called Peter or Joseph, it is tough to be suddenly called upon to change to Kabongo. In spite of the pain of this experience, it did imply a revivalist tendency which then moved on to a campaign of authenticity in Zaire. A demand for a re-examination of the educational system, discouragement of Western suits for Zairean men, discouragement of Western-style cosmetic improvement for Zairean women—all these are reforms which are both tough and naïve. But they capture a mood that is important.

Another naïve type of reformer in many ways is in North Africa—the President of Libya. Again, Gaddafy captures important themes.

'Why must passports always carry the details in a western language? Why can't we give a non-western language international currency, and make it more of an instrument in mobility?' The Libyan government ends up saying that no one can come into Libya without some Arabic on his passport. Again this is naïve as an idea; but it captures an important factor in our predicament. One possible conclusion to be drawn from this is that it is possible for the soldiers in the Third World, and certainly in Africa, to play a role that reduces our heavy dependency on the cultural symbols of others. Mobutu's idea of beating the drums instead of firing a twenty-one-gun salute to receive state guests is certainly in a similar mood.

Towards Transcending Economic Dependency

In the next few years, African countries will encounter severe economic difficulties. Some countries may have a hard time maintaining themselves at all; but there will be some significant breakthroughs in a number of others. The acquisition of economic expertise and the transformation of economic culture in African countries is a serious question. The degree to which Africans become economically effective and internationally competitive might in part depend on changing the international stratification system, but it also depends on important modifications in the culture of the African people themselves with regard to certain forms of economic behaviour. The interaction between the economic domain and the political domain is a major factor to bear in mind. African soldiers will probably get more commercialized for at least part of this period. The commercialization of the military, though carrying certain hazards with regard to the social system as a whole, could conceivably also increase their readiness to engage in cost-benefit analysis, their concern for stability, and bring a reduction in their readiness to invoke violence as a solution to problems. In Uganda, in the wake of the Asian expulsion, the question arose whether the commercialization of the soldiers would indeed have this effect. If it were to happen like this, the commercialization of soldiers, while implying a lack of professionalism in the military, would also have enhanced the chances for some degree of stability in the economic and political systems at home.

Meanwhile the international economic system will remain rigid, but not unchallenged. Indeed the challenges have started. While the international hierarchy of rich versus poor, developed versus underdeveloped, will remain obstinate, some erosion is already underway. The energy crisis has been specially important from this point of view. Until the Arabs applied their boycott, it was widely believed that a country had to be economically developed in order to be economically powerful. But the oil crisis revealed that Saudi Arabia, much less economically developed than Holland, was globally much more economically powerful. Economic power itself could derive, not necessarily from technological and industrial achievement, but from the possession of certain resources critical for the achievements of others. This new equation is a fundamental change in the world balance, and could be a change that would give the Third World leverage in the struggle to change the economic order of the globe. I define the Third World once again as the world of the underprivileged. It is also tri-continental in that it encompasses Africa, Asia, and Latin America, along with related islands. It is this Third World which has been in danger of being perpetually underprivileged for the foreseeable future.

Moreover, the oil resources may play a part in sharpening the strategy of *counter-penetration*. Until now, the Third World has been penetrated by the developed world, culturally, economically, and politically. The question which now arises is whether it is possible for some of the new resources of Third World countries to be used for counter-penetration into the major citadels of the economic powers in Western Europe and North America. Such counter-penetration into Western economies should to some extent make them as vulnerable to pressure from the Third World. Some Third World intellectuals say the answer is *disengagement*. They urge: 'Let us move in the direction of disengagement, let us cut loose from the international capitalist system, let us assert our own autonomy.' Disengagement as a strategy would probably be less effective than the strategy of counter-penetration. Imagine Saudi Arabia disengaged from the international capitalist system! Where would Saudi Arabia's economic power be in such a move? The whole effectiveness of its role in the global system presupposes its involvement in the international economic system. To sell oil, to get people to need its oil, to get the mighty to be dependent on it—that is an act of counter-penetration. To move towards mere autonomy would deprive the Third World of a say in changing the total international system in the direction of greater equity.

The oil-rich Third World countries should indeed use some of their dollar reserves to buy shares in major multi-national companies in the West. They should invest in new industrial ventures, buy out the major powers themselves in their own companies, give loans to major industrial countries, and increase the vulnerability of the Northern Hemisphere to effective economic lobbying by the underprivileged Southern Hemisphere. The ultimate purpose should be the quest for a new economic order in the world, fairer to the poor and the less developed.

Class, Ethnicity and History

Finally, there is the issue of relations among Africans themselves within the continent. Especially relevant in this regard are two forms of intra-African conflict – the tensions which are caused by economic factors and those which spring from ethnic loyalties. The two forms of conflict are often profoundly interrelated, as Africa's domestic wars have often illustrated.

Civil war in Africa as a form of instability will continue to be a threat for the rest of this century. What may become less likely are *secessionist* civil wars. The failure of the Biafran bid to secede from Nigeria, and the lessons of the Sudanese civil war add up to a major disincentive for would-be secessionists in the future. We may have civil wars that seek to control the centre, but not to break up a country. We may have civil wars that seek to overthrow a government but not to carve out a new state. Civil wars that seek to redefine the frontiers of the political community and create additional entities are likely to recede in the period under discussion. We shall still have bids of a secessionist and separatist kind, like the one in Eritrea. But, in general, we will be moving in the direction of conflicts within the prescribed inherited boundaries rather than conflicts generated by a desire to redefine the frontiers of our nations.

The actual experience of a civil war itself could have consequences domestically in the future. In Nigeria, one question which arises from the agony of the civil war is the question of the need for Nigeria to re-civilianize itself, for the soldiers to get back to the barracks. Certainly, if we look at the English Civil War, and its aftermath, we see the agony of the civil war combining with the experience of Cromwellian militarism, and resulting in a new national desire to return to civilian rule. The Restoration of 1660 was significant not just in terms of the return of the monarchy but, much more fundamentally, the return of civilian supremacy in British politics which has lasted for a long time. The question which arises is whether the experience of civil war, because of the levels of agony involved, leads to disenchantment with militarism and facilitates an early return of soldiers to the barracks. This is a question to which Nigeria and the Sudan may conceivably provide an answer in the years ahead.

What the experience of both countries reveals once again is that Africa is caught between the birth of her modern nationalism and the quest for nationhood. Her nationalism is a reality which played a part in ending territorial colonialism but nationhood itself is an ambition rather than a reality. The agonies of Africa in the second half of the twentieth century have been ultimately derived from the pains of intermediacy between nationalism and nationhood.

A basic dialectic to understand in Africa is that while the greatest friend of African nationalism is race-consciousness, the greatest enemy of African nationhood is ethnic-consciousness. Ethnicity and stratification are fundamental aspects of the social structure in African conditions. Which of the two forces – kinship or class – will be primary in Africa? What is involved is a distinction between the *forces of biological reproduction* and their impact on kinship, and the *forces of economic production* and their impact on social classes. The reproductive forces emanate from concepts of family and the obligations which are presumed to exist from both marriage and consanguinity. Filial and parental love, matrimonial loyalties, fraternity, and the wider circles of kinship are all part of the social implications of human reproduction, and among the major forces behind human behaviour.

The forces of reproduction lie behind social and political phenomena which range from ethnic consciousness to race prejudice, from nationalist assertiveness to ancestor worship. When a black man was lynched in the USA for taking a sexual interest in a white woman, when General Idi Amin expelled the Asians partly because he thought they were socially and sexually exclusive, when Hitler asserted a doctrine of Aryan purity, when the Jews created the State of Israel, when the British started passing Commonwealth Immigration Acts and later invented a grandfather clause as a basis for entry into Britain, when the French looked up to Charles de Gaulle and thought of him as a father figure symbolizing the nation—in all these instances primordial forces of reproduction and their consequences were at play in varying degrees. Even pride in the history of one's nation is a form of ancestor worship, a modernized version of political lineage.

Certainly the temptation in political behaviour to use the symbols of kinship, ranging from concepts of fatherland and mother tongue to phenomena like cultural nationalism, are all partly derived from the universe of familial emotions and loyalties. Certainly patriotism is itself one of the great political consequences of the forces of reproductive symbolism. These are aspects of human culture which have developed from particular aspects of human biology.

Alongside the socialization of biological reproductive forces is the other familial factor behind human behaviour—economic production. Both biology and economics are in part concerned with human survival. As Marx and Engels reminded humanity, man had first to eat before he could build a civilization. The processes by which man was enabled to eat became the genesis of economics. But man had also to reproduce himself in order to survive beyond a single generation. Marxist analysts, in describing social and political behaviour, have correctly pointed to the economic factor as part of the primary background to that behaviour. What Marxist analysts have not always adequately recognized is the equally powerful force of reproductive symbolism. Out of the economic domain social classes and class conflict did indeed grow; but equally true is that out of the reproductive symbolism other loyalties and antagonisms emerged, at times much more powerful than economic considerations.

Two factors help to determine which of the two forces, kinship or class, are more politicized in a given society. These factors are the scale of the economy and the extent of ethnic pluralism. In a society which is ethnically homogeneous, operating on the basis of a small economy with simple technology, ethnicity tends to swing between being politically neutral and politically reinforcing. It becomes politically reinforcing when the group as a whole senses a need for reaffirming a shared ethnic identity. It becomes politically neutral when members dispute on the basis of other loyalties and interests, including the class dimension and the narrower unit of the family in competition with another family within the same broad ethnic category. Kinship factors are indeed still at play even in situations where the broader ethnic category is politically neutralized, but these kinship factors would tend to focus on sub-units.

If the society is not only ethnically homogeneous, but also produces its means of livelihood on the basis of a small economy and rudimentary modes of production, the class factor would again be relatively weak. Even the stratification system is more likely to be based on symbols of reproduction, namely heredity and ascription, than on rational economic factors. The local notables might indeed be relatively affluent economically, but the chances are that they add economic affluence to a prior quality of being relatively well descended.

In many African societies before independence stratification was either very rudimentary or elaborately based on ethnicity and lineage. People were high or low in the social structure either directly because they came from a particular clan or family, or indirectly because they had been given honorary kinship status by such a clan or family. All social analysis at a broad interpretative level is bound to distort and oversimplify. This is also true of these generalizations about pre-colonial African societies. The main point to be grasped is the primacy of biological reproductive symbolism in situations of a small-scale economy, rudimentary technology and relative ethnic homogeneity.

What happened with colonization and later independence was both the enlargement of the economic base of African societies and the pluralization of their ethnic base. Under the impact of Europe's economic technology, new trends got under way in African countries in the direction of greater economic complexity and scale. And under the impact of the imposed colonial boundaries, multiple ethnic communities were forced to share a new national collective identity. With the enlargement of the economies and the pluralization of the ethnic composition of the new African societies, are the symbols of reproduction to decline in the future and give way to the economic forces of the social classes? So far, the forces of reproductive symbolism have not declined in post-colonial Africa, and have quite often become more politicized. Yet at the same time new forces of economic competition and class conflict have also arisen. While pre-colonial

African societies were generally characterized by high reproductive symbolism and low class conflict, post-colonial African societies are characterized simultaneously by both high reproductive symbolism and a rising class conflict.

The pluralization of the ethnic base of the new African society was certainly bound to lead in the direction of politicizing reproductive symbolism as kinship groups competed with each other for scarce resources. The enlargement and modernization of African economies have in turn resulted in the rise of class antagonism. On the other hand, that very modernization of African economies and their enlargement should have initiated a partial erosion of kinship and reproductive loyalties in favour of more purely economic rivalry. But so far this has not happened. The modernization of African economies has not as yet served to neutralize the heightened sense of ethnic affinity which has come with ethnic pluralism in the new African nation-states.

In such a situation even the class factor is often defined in ethnic terms. Members of certain ethnic communities have easier access to certain opportunities than members of other ethnic communities. While in large-scale developed economies in the Northern Hemisphere individuals, or at most families, become members of particular social classes, in Africa there are times when entire clans, tribes, or sub-nationalities, enter particular class levels in their societies. The Kikuyu in Kenya in part of the colonial period were virtually among the 'untouchables' of the colonial society. The people who emptied latrine buckets and cleaned lavatories in parts of Kenya were disproportionately Kikuyu. By the time of independence this whole ethnic category was reclassified by political history and political realities. Instead of being among the untouchables, the Kikuyu moved up to become relative brahmins.

In reality, just as there are different classes within each caste in India, so there are different levels of advantage and prosperity within each ethnic community in Africa. The Kikuyu as a total group have easier access to certain opportunities, especially in the main cities and in government, than most other ethnic communities. But there are of course poor Kikuyu as well as rich ones, indigent Kikuyu as well as powerful ones. The foreign company in Nairobi or Mombasa which employs a Kikuyu clerk as an exercise in public relations is, on the one hand, merely absorbing one more indigent proletarian into an alien economy, but is also, on the other hand, paying tribute to the special status of the whole Kikuyu community. The Baganda during the colonial period in Uganda were also a privileged group, although within the Buganda kingdom itself there were peasants as well as aristocrats. The Amhara in Ethiopia have even more clearly been an ethnic caste, dominating the country. There were millions of poor and indigent Amhara, as well as immensely powerful and affluent

Amhara, but the community as a whole was in a fundamental sense classified as a privileged group within the national hierarchy. In such a situation one makes comparisons along occupational lines. If an Amhara houseboy, even after the deposition of Haile Selassie I, has a better chance of improving his status, or obtaining other fringe benefits, than a Gala houseboy, then clearly in this horizontal comparison, status derived from being descended from an Amhara creates inequalities within the same level of economic arrangements.

Some of these prior advantages for particular ethnic groups will have future consequences. The distribution of the occupations in the past on the basis of reproductive symbolism could prolong the advantage enjoyed by that group for at least another generation. In proportion to population, there will probably be many more Amhara doctors and lawyers than Gala doctors and lawyers in the 1990s, many more prosperous Amhara landowners and businessmen than Gala landowners and businessmen, many more Amhara bishops than Gala clerics, and by definition many more Amhara aristocrats than Gala pretenders to such a status. Millennia of Amhara privileges will prolong the existence of an Amhara social aristocracy in some fields at least until the end of the century, in spite of the Ethiopian military coup.

In countries such as Nigeria and Zaire such allocations of economic opportunities on the basis of reproductive symbolism could be a little more complicated, but by no means fundamentally different. Ethnicity played a decisive role in the events which led to the Nigerian civil war; and ethnicity has been part of the tumultuous life of Zaire since it exploded into independence in 1960. These clusters of reproductive symbolism will influence the destinies of those countries for at least another few decades.

The process of national integration in such countries requires a partial decline in the power of kinship symbolism and ethnic confrontation, but this decline in itself might first require the modernization of social conflicts in the direction of new economic classes. For a while class antagonism and ethnic antagonism will simply reinforce each other, but as the economy becomes more complex and its productive capacity becomes enlarged, kinship competition should begin to subside significantly by the year 2000, especially as the ethnic pluralism itself becomes less distinct in the wake of cultural integration and geographical and biological intermingling among the groups.

In terms of loyalties, a Kikuyu labourer in Nairobi is probably a Kikuyu first and a labourer second 'when the chips are down' for the time being. In identifying his ultimate interests, a Kikuyu businessman sees his future in the survival of Kikuyu pre-eminence in Kenya much more than he sees his future in terms of a shared destiny with a Luo businessman. Although both the forces of production and the symbols of reproduction are exerting a powerful joint influence on the political and economic behaviour of most African societies, the kinship factor in its broad meaning continues to have the upper hand. Only an adequate modernization of the economy could one day restore balance, reducing the power of ethnicity without necessarily emasculating it. And that process will be only half-way at the most by the year 2000.

Meanwhile soldiers and civilians will continue to compete for political power, and for a role in determining both the economic and the ethnic future of their countries. By the nature of their profession, soldiers will aspire to introduce the principle of discipline as a mechanism for national integration. Civilian politicians will attempt one day to realize the principle of dialogue as a mechanism for national integration. In reality, neither the soldiers nor the civilians are likely to live up to their professional aspirations. Discipline under military regimes will for a while continue to be a principle honoured more in the breach than in the observance; dialogue under civilian regimes will for a while be a victim of repressive and intolerant authoritarianism. But those very failures themselves, as well as some of the emerging successes, will be the resilient manifestations of a continuing struggle between the symbols of kinship and the interests of class.

Conclusion

We have attempted to demonstrate in this book both the anguish and the ambitions of an Africa in the process of moving from modern nationalism to modern nationhood. New loyalties have emerged and new horizons have been revealed as a result of the colonial impact. A new consciousness of being black, a new awareness of belonging to a continent, a rebellion against subjugation by others, have all played a part in the rise of pan-Africanism and the consolidation of political consciousness.

Both nationalism and nationhood have strong reproductive origins. The idea of belonging to the same race, or sharing a fatherland is part of the heritage of the concept of family in human affairs. The transition from nationalism to nationhood must therefore be regarded as in part a transition from kinship sentiment to kinship fulfilment, from a desire to see all Nigerians or all Ugandans as one people to the actual realization of such a familial concept. But the reproductive symbolism has also its disruptive consequences, as communities which believe themselves to be descended from the same ancestors compete with communities alleging descent from other ancestors.

While African solidarity was helped by race consciousness among black people as an affirmation of familial solidarity, nation-building in individual African countries has been disrupted by narrower ethnic consciousness and politicized lineage. Political parties have risen and fallen, governments have been established and collapsed, soldiers have commuted between the barracks and state house—and Africa has struggled each year to narrow the gap between the depths of its longings and the fragility of its achievements.

But Africa is not a continent in either splendid or squalid isolation. It is a region operating in a global context. We have attempted to outline both the internationality of Africa's past and the globalism of Africa's future. We have seen ancestral African contacts with regions which range from India to the Iberian peninsula, from China to the Middle East. The issues at stake have in turn ranged from technology to religion, from problems of population to the tensions of cultural dependency. At the centre of it all is a race of people which was once relegated to the outer periphery of world events, and condemned to the menial roles in diplomatic history. These people are now reaching out for a new definition of their place in the global scheme of things. That is what black diplomacy is all about—a new resolve by black nations to help decide the destiny of the human race and the fate of the planet they share.

References and notes

1. Chester Bowles, 'A revolution intended for all mankind', *New York Times*, 10 December 1961.
2. *Uganda Argus* (Kampala), 29 May 1964.
3. Antonio de Spinola, *Portugal and the Future* (Lisbon, 1947). The English translation is borrowed from the cover story of *Time* magazine entitled 'A book, a song and then a revolution', *Time*, 6 May 1974.

INDEX

Countries are indexed under their modern names, using acronyms for USA and RSA (Republic of South Africa). Other acronyms are frequently used, such as EEC and OPEC. The letter-by-letter system of alphabetization has been followed.